Women, Work, and Coping

Women, Work, and Coping

A Multidisciplinary Approach to Workplace Stress

EDITED BY
BONITA C. LONG AND
SHARON E. KAHN

The University of British Columbia
Academic Women's Association

Canadian Centre for Policy Alternatives, Ottawa
Centre canadien de recherche en politiques de rechange

McGill-Queen's University Press
Montreal & Kingston • London • Buffalo

© McGill-Queen's University Press 1993
ISBN 0-7735-1128-8 (cloth)
ISBN 0-7735-1129-6 (paper)

Legal deposit fourth quarter 1993
Bibliothèque nationale du Québec

Printed in Canada on acid-free paper

Canadian Cataloguing in Publication Data

Main entry under title:
    Women, work, and coping : a multidisciplinary
    approach to workplace stress
    (Critical perspectives on public affairs)
    Co-published by: University of British Columbia
    Academic Women's Association.
    Includes bibliographical references and index.
    ISBN 0-7735-1128-8 (bound) –
    ISBN 0-7735-1129-6 (pbk.)
    1. Women—Job stress.   2. Women—Employment—
    Psychological aspects.   3. Psychology, Industrial.
    I. Long, Bonita Clarice, 1945–   .   II. Kahn,
    Sharon E., 1946–   .   III. UBC Academic Women's
    Association.   IV. Series.

    RC963.6.w65w65 1993   158.7'082   c93-090409-5

Published in co-operation with the University of
British Columbia Academic Women's Assocation

Consulting Editor
Dianne Newell

Editorial Board, UBC Academic Women's Association:
Dianne Newell, Department of History and General
Editor
Alison Buchan, Department of Physiology
Margaret E. Prang, Professor Emerita, Department of
History

Contents

Foreword

One discovers upon reading this book that its theme – women, work, and coping with workplace stress – is deceptively straightforward. Deceptive, I suggest, because only recently have studies of workplace stress and coping begun to focus on women's experience. Women face quantitatively more and qualitatively different sources of work-related stress than do men. So, research on this topic, the editors argue, is essential if we are to understand the effect of employment on women's well-being.

In all societies, past and present, sex is fundamental to the way work is organized, and work is central to the social construction of gender. And beyond that, as Ava Baron reminds us, in *Work Engendered: Toward a New History of American Labor* (Ithaca: Cornell University Press 1991), we need to think of gender not only as a noun but also as a verb. It is commonly understood that women in contemporary North American society face glass *ceilings* at work and school; that is, invisible obstacles that delay, obstruct, or limit advancement. New research shows that these are not the only symbolic barriers for women outside the home. Women also run into glass *walls*, obstacles that deny women the freedom of lateral movement and thus deprive them of the experience that they need to advance vertically. Women may rise to the ranks of management, for example, only to discover that their opportunities are limited to institutionally marginal spheres, such as public relations and caregiving, rather than core areas, such as marketing, finance, and engineering.

The glass *boxes* that entrap women are not merely symbolic. We know that occupational segregation by sex usually means physical separation, which may further reinforce women's inequality. Multidisciplinary, historical research, such as Daphne Spain's *Gendered Spaces* (Chapel Hill: University of North Carolina Press 1992), shows that when combined, the physical and symbolic barriers that separate women and men ultimately block women's access to the socially valued knowledge and networks that enhance status. The prejudices and privileges of ethnicity and class further shape the situation. What are women's coping resources and coping strategies? What are the appropriate methods for identifying and evaluating them?

The Academic Women's Association at the University of British Columbia wants to promote this young field of scholarly inquiry. It recently sponsored two separate workshops on women, stress, and coping, and it is now pleased to publish *Women, Work, and Coping: A Multidisciplinary Approach to Workplace Stress*, a collection of scholarly essays commissioned and edited by Bonita Long and Sharon Kahn. Drs Long and Kahn, who are members of the Department of Counselling Psychology at the University of British Columbia, have been researching and writing on the subject since the early 1980s. They are innovators in the field.

Women, Work, and Coping is the second in the AWA's book series on the subject "Women and Universities." The series is intended to promote women's connections with university communities, both past and present. The first volume is a work of history by Lee Stewart, *"It's Up to You": Women at UBC in the Early Years* (Vancouver: UBC Press 1990). Stewart argues that the notion of university education as a cultural birthright, inherent in the literal translation of UBC's motto *Tuum Est* as "it is yours," was always more applicable to university men than university women before the revolutionary decade of the 1960s. She examines the experience and strategies of female advocates, educators, and students against the background of the social and cultural conditions that enveloped them and, of course, changed over time. *Women, Work, and Coping* is a quite different book. It is an explicitly multidisciplinary collection of contemporary studies, quantitative analyses, and theoretical discussions. This university-based research takes as its focus employed women and investigates the special issue of coping with workplace stress today.

On behalf of the AWA I wish to thank the other members of the editorial board, Alison Buchan and Margaret Prang, and the AWA Chair, Brenda Peterson. Philip Cercone, Director and Executive Editor of McGill-Queen's University Press, and Peter Milroy, Director of UBC Press, offered much-needed advice and support at critical stages of the project. I wish also to acknowledge the backing of the President of UBC, David Strangway, who authorized a generous grant from the University Development Fund to support the AWA book series.

Dianne Newell
General Editor
AWA Series

Acknowledgments

We are grateful to the University of British Columbia Academic Women's Association (AWA), which co-sponsored the research workshop, "Women and Work: An Integrated Approach to Stress and Coping," and to Dianne Newell, general editor of the AWA book series, "Women and Universities," for her sage and sensitive guidance. We also thank the Social Sciences and Humanities Research Council of Canada, and the National Centre for Management Research and Development, for providing grants to the research workshop. As well, we thank Employment and Immigration Canada, and the President's Office at the University of British Columbia, for their support of both the workshop and this book.

In addition, we owe a great intellectual debt to the chapter authors, each of whom engaged in productive discussions with us, discussions that began at the research workshop and continued throughout the process of reviewing and revising chapters. We extend special appreciation to Anita DeLongis for her general counsel during the development phase of the book. As well, we are indebted to Sara Comish and Margalo Whyte for their many hours of editorial assistance during the preparation of this book. Finally, we acknowledge the helpful comments of the unnamed readers for the press.

About the Contributors

NINA L. COLWILL has recently left her position as professor, Faculty of Management, University of Manitoba, to begin her own management consulting practice, but retains affiliation with both University of Manitoba and University of Western Ontario. Her primary research for the past fifteen years has been in the area of gender issues in the workplace, and she has written numerous articles in the area. Dr Colwill is the author of two books: *The Psychology of Sex Differences*, with Dr Hilary Lips, and, more recently, *The New Partnership: Women and Men in Organizations*. She is a member of the advisory board for the Women in Management Program, National Centre for Management, Research and Development, University of Western Ontario.

BRUCE E. COMPAS is associate professor of psychology at the University of Vermont. He received his PHD in clinical psychology from the University of California, Los Angeles in 1980. His current research interests include stress and coping in families exposed to the acute stress of parental cancer and the chronic stress of parental alcohol abuse; and prevention of stress-related disorders, specifically depression and conduct disorder in children and adolescents.

ESTHER R. GREENGLASS, PHD, is professor of psychology in the Department of Psychology at York University. Her main areas of research and writing/publication/speaking have been in job stress, women, gender differences, burnout, and coping. She has written two books and several invited book chapters, as well as numerous journal articles. She is currently collaborating on research with colleagues in Finland and Germany, where the focus of her studies includes social support and Type A behaviour. Her research examines the individual within the social context and incorporates the interaction between them.

BARBARA A. GUTEK is professor of management and policy at the University of Arizona. Topics of her research include gender issues in organizations, use of computers in work groups, interaction in groups, and job satisfaction. She is an editor for the "Women and Work" series published by Sage Publishers. Among her publications are several books, including *Women and Work* with Veronica Nieva and *Sex and the Workplace*, and numerous journal articles. Professor Gutek is a Fellow in the American Psychological Association and served as chair of the Women in Management Division of the Academy of Management in 1990–1.

CATHERINE A. HEANEY is assistant professor of preventive medicine in the College of Medicine at the Ohio State University. She earned her PH D and her MPH in health behaviour and health education from the University of Michigan School of Public Health. Her main area of research is the development and evaluation of theory-based worksite stress reduction programs. Her research projects address both white-collar and blue-collar occupational stress, and focus on changing the psychosocial work environment in order to facilitate employee well-being.

SHARON E. KAHN, associate professor of counselling psychology at the University of British Columbia, currently directs the University's employment equity program. She earned her PHD in counselling psychology from Arizona State University in 1975. Her publications explore gender-role issues in counselling, women's career development, and stress processes and coping strategies, as well as organizational equity in hiring and promotion.

RONALD C. KESSLER is professor in the Department of Sociology and a program director in the Institute for Social Research, University of Michigan. He has been involved in studies of job loss, widowhood, caregiving for mentally ill relatives, and exposure to the AIDS virus. His current activities include directing the United States National Study of Comorbidity, a study of dyadic adjustment to stress among married couples, and (with Kenneth Kendler) a study of gene-environment interactions in a large-scale study of twins.

KAREN KORABIK is associate professor of psychology at the University of Guelph. She earned her PHD from St Louis University in 1975. Her current research examines several aspects of women in management, including androgyny, leadership and conflict resolution styles, turnover, and work stress, social support, and coping.

BONITA C. LONG, PHD, is associate professor of counselling psychology at the University of British Columbia, where she earned her PHD in interdisciplinary studies in 1982. Her research interests include the stress-coping process of managerial men and women, clerical workers, and individuals with chronic illnesses. In addition, she is interested in stress-management interventions, particularly cognitive-behavioural and exercise programs.

JUDI MARSHALL, PHD, is reader in organizational behaviour in the School of Management, University of Bath, United Kingdom. Her main areas of research and publication have been managerial job stress (the topic of her thesis), women in management, organizational cultures and change, and post-positivist approaches to inquiry. Her publications include *Understanding Executive Stress* (with Cary Cooper) and *Women Managers: Travellers in a Male World*. Current projects include a study of why some senior women managers decide to leave their jobs.

DIANA L. MAWSON, MA, is senior consultant for worker-client employment services at Employment and Immigration Canada, British Columbia/Yukon Region. She has also worked as a women's counsellor and as coordinator of the Women's Employment Counselling Unit. Her research interests include the career psychology of women, group process in women's groups, women's developmental issues, and women and work.

LISA M. McDONALD received her MA in applied social psychology from the University of Guelph in 1987. The topic of her master's thesis was work stress, coping, and social support among managers. She is currently employed as mental health coordinator for a social planning council where her interests are in the area of community-based planning and development of mental health services.

PAMELA G. OROSAN is a doctoral student in clinical psychology at the University of Vermont. She received her BA in psychology at Miami University in Ohio. Her current research and clinical interests include the role of gender in psychopathology and mental health, and the treatment and prevention of eating disorders.

HAZEL M. ROSIN is associate professor of organizational behaviour in the Faculty of Administrative Studies at York University. She received her PHD in organizational behaviour from Yale in 1986. Her research interests include the relationship between work and nonwork, the effects on men of women's changing roles, professional women's experience of organizational life, and cross-cultural differences in attitudes toward work and the management of work and personal life.

CRAIG A. SMITH received his PHD from Stanford University in 1986. Since 1988 he has been assistant professor in the Department of Psychology and Human Development at Vanderbilt University. His research efforts are directed toward the development and testing of a comprehensive theory of human emotions. His current projects examine the dispositional antecedents of appraisal and the interaction of these antecedents with situational factors in producing appraisal and emotion, and the role of emotion in adaptation to stress.

ANNE STATHAM is professor of sociology and women's studies at the University of Wisconsin-Parkside. She has published numerous articles on women and work and has coauthored *The Worth of Women's Work: A Qualitative Synthesis* and *Gender and University Teaching: A Negotiated Difference*, both published by SUNY Press. She has just completed a third book manuscript, *The Decline of Patriarchy: Women Managing Work*. She has been heavily involved in community action projects, including a longitudinal study of displaced auto workers and the organization of community women with common problems. She is beginning a sabbatical project on eco-feminism that will draw together concerns about gender, race, class, and environmental degradation.

ALLISON TOM is assistant professor in the Department of Administrative, Adult, and Higher Education at the University of British Columbia. She teaches classes in feminist studies and research methodology. She earned her PHD in anthropology and education from Stanford University in 1986. Her current research is in the feminist study of child care and in adult literacy and ethnographic evaluation methods.

LOIS M. VERBRUGGE is research scientist at the Institute of Gerontology, University of Michigan. Her current research interests as a social demographer are osteoarthritis and its impact on musculoskeletal, physical, and social functioning; patterns of change in disability over time for older persons; and theoretical and survey research issues in disability. Underlying these special topics is a long-standing interest in women's health and a commitment to understanding how, and why, chronic health, disability, and mortality outcomes differ for women and men. Verbrugge has held a Research Career Development Award (NICHD, 1982–7) on sex differentials in morbidity and mortality and a Special Emphasis Research Career Award (NIA, 1987–92) on arthritis and daily life.

ELAINE WETHINGTON is assistant professor of human development and family studies in the College of Human Ecology, Cornell University. She earned her PHD in sociology at the University of Michigan in 1987. Her current research focuses on gender differences in psychological distress, social role transitions and health, processes of social support, and dyadic responses to stress.

Women, Work, and Coping

Introduction

North American women have joined the paid work force in record numbers, and much-needed attention is now focused on the effect employment has on women's well-being. Until recently, theories and research about job stress and ways of coping have been directed primarily at men's experience, and as a result, women's experience of stress and coping remained relatively unexplored. A perusal of the stress literature suggests that women, compared to men, are confronted with more and different work-related stressors arising from a multitude of sources. Taking care of children and aging parents continues to be a source of stress for women who work outside the home. Two other major sources of workplace stress are sex segregation and sex discrimination. Recently, sexual harassment, a particular form of discrimination, has received considerable media attention.

Sex segregation of work roles creates unique stressors for women. Despite the growing number of women in the work force, most women in paid employment continue to perform different types of jobs from men. For example, in 1988, 58 per cent of Canadian women worked in clerical, sales, or service occupations, while men were employed in a wider range of jobs, and more frequently in those offering higher pay (Statistics Canada 1990). In traditionally female jobs – as secretaries, waitresses, and nurses – women experience high demands, but receive limited autonomy and low pay. In addition, women in jobs that remain male-dominated often suffer social isolation. And for both groups of employed women, whether in traditional or nontraditional jobs, gender-role stereotypes may not only be a cause of stress, but also affect a woman's ability to cope with stress. Moreover, sex discrimination places limits on the opportunities that women have in the workplace.

An intriguing paradox is revealed by these data. Even though women in the paid work force face numerous stressors, conventional wisdom that work is necessarily harmful to women has not been borne out. Women can derive greater satisfaction from some employment roles than from traditional roles as wife, mother, and community volunteer. If employed women are confronted with work-related stress, yet appear to be better off than women who are not employed, the implication is that employed women have developed effective resources and coping strategies to deal with these additional stressors. This book is an attempt to examine this paradox by focusing on the ways women cope with work stress and the social-cultural context that surrounds employed women.

In our own research on working women, we have found it necessary to sort through a rich and sometimes confusing array of findings in social sciences that study work (anthropology, economics, sociology, counselling psychology, organizational behaviour), stress (social and clinical psychology, health psychology), and gender issues (anthropology, sociology, psychology, history, education, family studies). Although these distinct approaches have individual value, each one may come up short because of the complexities of the systems involved and the subtleties of their interactions. For example, to focus on specific coping efforts may ignore the influences of social and cultural expectations that limit women's options. An examination of workplace stress may ignore women's coping resources or stressors that stem from other spheres of their lives (e.g., parental roles). However, most researchers readily acknowledge the complexity of the processes involved in women's experience of workplace stress and the decisions and choices these women make to cope with it. This book brings together these diverse perspectives with chapters that focus on the individual, the work environment, and social and cultural systems, as well as providing a theoretical framework with which to integrate the multiple influences on women's ways of coping.

We have also found that our work is enhanced by drawing on psychology's traditional statistical approach as well as the qualitative approaches taken by the other social sciences. Although these different approaches may represent opposing philosophies of science and therefore create particular tensions, we rely on both approaches to provide a fuller picture of women's experiences. We have also drawn on feminist theoretical perspectives because they provide a critical context for our understanding of women's lives. Thus, in this book we bring together authors from a variety of academic backgrounds and methodological traditions. Their chapters inform us of their various research programs and collectively contribute to stress and coping theory and methodology. This book reveals the emerging dynamics of the stress and coping processes for employed women.

Our project began in January 1991 with an invited workshop to develop the book. Twenty social scientists from eight different disciplines and three countries took part in a research workshop at the University of British Columbia. The purpose of the workshop was to provide a forum whereby our assumptions could be challenged and thus our understanding of the ways women cope with work stress enhanced. Not all those invited to participate had studied women, job stress, and coping in combination, though all had produced research or theoretical conceptualizations in one or more of these broad areas. We asked these scholars to apply their research and ideas to the topic of the ways women cope with employment stress. Although they did not entirely agree with one another, the contributors all accepted stress and coping as processes that are relational or transactional, rather than states or outcomes, and they acknowledged the need for multidisciplinary and interdisciplinary approaches to its study.

Workshop participants agreed on two assumptions. First, they acknowledged that women's work in the home may include both caring and nurturing activities as well as paid work, but they agreed to focus on women who work for pay outside the home and to use only paid work outside the home in defining women's jobs, occupations, careers, or employment. Second, workshop participants acknowledged that much of women's work (e.g., blue-collar, clerical) is still ignored by researchers and that future research must consider individual differences among women, including ethnic background, sexuality, age, and life-stage.

This book is a direct outcome of papers and discussions at the workshop. The fourteen chapters range widely among issues concerning the individual, the workplace context, theoretical frameworks, policy and interventions, and research methods, as well as views and research that represent different disciplines, and both quantitative and qualitative methodologies. The contributors examine the sources of stress for employed women, the structural and psychosocial moderators of workplace stress, and the appraisals and coping strategies that mediate the stress outcome relationship.

We begin with an overview of the tremendous social and cultural changes that are affecting women's roles in both the family and the workplace, changes that compel women to develop new coping strategies. Barbara Gutek cogently describes how women's training for and participation in the labour market has changed, with women moving into what were once nontraditional occupations. At the same time, men have not moved into traditionally female occupations or taken responsibility for unpaid family work. The result is the continuation of sex segregation in the workplace. Moreover, the increasing demands on employed women lead Gutek to predict that women will be forced to divest themselves of work outside the home, unless the demands on them are buffered by changes in the workplace as well as by men's participation in unpaid family work. Allison Tom, an anthropologist, presents a compelling argument that traditional dichotomies (e.g., paid vs nonpaid work) do not accurately reflect women's experiences across cultures. She describes the benefits to women of all types of work and urges researchers to take a holistic and cross-cultural view of women's roles. Tom also presents a brief summary of several qualitative methodologies that enable the researcher to avoid dichotomization. In the last chapter in this section, Diana Mawson summarizes the literature on the typical and not so typical stress-management approaches available to female employees, approaches that are both structural and individual in nature (e.g., job redesign, equity programs, child care, coping-skills training). She reviews the limitations to each of these approaches and recommends a reframing of social policy on women and paid work.

The social and cultural context that surrounds and impacts working women is examined from a feminist theoretical perspective. Several authors describe women's experiences in different occupational contexts including both organizational structures that are hostile to women and those that are hospitable. Although one of the most rapidly growing careers for women is in management, Nina Colwill argues that, despite many supports in place for women, women fail to move up in management positions because they fail to access power. She explores the unique forms of power men and women experience in the workplace and relates power to women's coping resources. In the next chapter, Judi Marshall poses the intriguing question: Are women in management thriving or surviving? She explains that women must deal with change-resistant, male patterns of value and behaviour in the workplace, that is, a patriarchal organizational culture. After detailing the different experiences of the men and women who inhabit this culture, she presents us with a unique four-stage model of how women cope with male-dominated workplaces. This model promises a new perspective on coping that relates to a growing feminist consciousness. Next, Anne Statham discusses the impact of two employment contexts on women – technological change and the relationship between managers and their secretaries. Her research is illustrative of the contextualizing nature of qualitative research and it provides a contrast with a more traditional quantitative study.

Although a structural perspective suggests several means of intervening, an individual's perspective is also critical in understanding stress and coping. The personal resources an individual has to draw on when confronted with workplace stressors may moderate (e.g., buffer) the impact of stress on the woman's well-being. Several authors describe psychosocial factors that have been found to moderate the stress and coping process. Karen Korabik and her colleagues first focus their review on sex differences in managerial work stress. They identify and examine an apparent paradox – despite women's exposure to more and qualitatively different job stressors, managerial women do not seem to suffer greater stress consequences than their male counterparts. These authors offer coping abilities and the utilization of social support as explanations for this paradox. Esther Greenglass explores sex differences in social support as well as the function of social support for a range of work groups (e.g., teachers, managers). She provides a compelling argument that interpersonal competency is a critical coping resource for women. Then Lois Verbrugge, a social demographer, determines the benefits of certain marital and parental role combinations for young women through a series of comprehensive regression analyses. Her provocative conclusion suggests that women's marital status is critical for their well-being, particularly for handling employment and parental roles. And finally, Catherine Heaney focuses on perceptions of control, an important variable that has a long history in organizational health research. She demonstrates that individuals' perceptions of control over workplace stress either buffer or aggravate stress, and these perceptions of control result in complex relations with stress outcomes.

An examination of what leads to effective coping provides us with an even more fine-grained analysis of the coping process. The researchers working at this level are studying the mediating effects of appraisals and coping on the stress-outcome relation. Bruce Compas and Pamela Orosan provide an overview of one of the most cited stress theories: Richard Lazarus's cognitive-relational theory of stress, appraisal, and coping (Lazarus & Folkman 1984). They direct researchers to pursue the meaning of a stressful event, to determine what values, ideals, or goals are at risk, in order to understand what coping responses might be effective. Based on the same presumed "gender-free" cognitive theory of stress and coping, Craig Smith extends our theoretical understanding of appraisals and coping by integrating emotions and attributions into the appraisal coping process. Empirical support for this exciting work remains the next frontier for researchers.

Because of the complexity of the coping process, it is a challenge for researchers to identify adequate research methods. Elaine Wethington and Ronald Kessler critique several research methods commonly used to study work-related stress and coping; as well, they suggest some new and innovative methods. These authors note the special problems inherent in studying job stressors and coping strategies that are chronic and self-selected. Finally, to provide an integration of this material, as editors we return to Richard Lazarus's theory of stress and coping (Lazarus & Folkman 1984). In our concluding chapter, we link this theory to earlier chapters in the book and briefly describe how our own research provided an integrative test of Lazarus's theory. In this way, we organize the multitude of factors and relationships of importance to women's ways of coping with employment stress.

Our book has a unique focus – women's experience of workplace stress, their coping resources and coping strategies. The chapters consider perspectives drawn from psychology, sociology, anthropology, and management sciences about women's ways of coping with work stress and the social and cultural context of women's work lives. The integration of these multidisciplinary views represents a new and exciting contribution to our understanding of the ways women cope with work stress.

Bonita C. Long
Sharon E. Kahn

REFERENCES

Lazarus, R.S., & S. Folkman. 1984. *Stress, appraisal and coping*. New York: Springer.
Statistics Canada 1990. *Women in Canada: A statistical report*. 2nd ed. Ottawa: Ministry of Supply and Services.

PART ONE

Overview of Women and Work

1 Asymmetric Changes in Men's and Women's Roles

BARBARA A. GUTEK

In the 1970s and early 1980s, Jessie Bernard wrote a series of books and articles focusing on men's and women's worlds or spheres of activities (e.g., Bernard 1971, 1972, 1978, 1981a, 1981b). A major emphasis of these works was the psychological and often physical separation of men and women, who, according to Bernard, live out their lives in different worlds. Men and women experience the world differently because they have very different experiences, starting from birth. Another way of stating the same point is that the sum of experiences of the average adult man is likely to differ substantially from that of the average adult woman.

In this chapter, I would like to use Bernard's notion of men's and women's worlds as a way of analysing and organizing some of what we know about women's changing roles throughout the last several decades, especially as these changes affect stress and coping processes in women. In addition, I would like to use the notion of spheres of activity to speculate on the direction and magnitude of change in the future. Will the influx of women into the paid labour force in general and into traditionally male fields in particular continue? Have we reached the limit of the change, or will we see a reversal in the future, with women retreating to the family sphere and men reclaiming paid work as their domain? I am going to argue that the last suggestion is a definite possibility, largely because change in gender roles has been asymmetric. Gender-role change has, in general, left the average woman in a significantly more stressful position than the average man, and, perhaps, in a more stressful position than the average woman of the 1950s.

This chapter is divided into three sections. The first section briefly reviews the spheres of activity of men and women and then focuses on changes in those spheres. The second section lists some of the factors that relate to stress and coping in working women. In the third section, I raise some questions about the viability and permanence of the current status of women relative to that of men.

CHANGES IN MEN'S AND WOMEN'S WORLDS

Numerous social scientists (e.g., O'Neill 1985; Parsons & Bales 1955) have argued that men and women can or should have specialized activities in society, with men focusing on instrumental (paid work) activities and women focusing on expressive (family) activities. Whether these different worlds of men and women are viewed as having a biological origin (see Bardwick & Douvan 1971), or simply as making economic sense for the family unit (O'Neill 1985), the assignment of men and women to these different worlds has a long history (Bernard 1981b) and it is widely discussed in many books and articles on male and female roles. Thus, the fact that the world has been divided into male and female spheres in which women focus on the private sphere of the family and men focus on the wider public world including work is nothing new.

Nor is it news to anyone that these separate spheres have been eroding for the past several decades. This erosion has taken a very specific form, namely the movement of women into the public sphere, including the paid work force. At this point, I would like to review some of the "facts" of this change. First is the sheer magnitude of the movement of women into the North American labour market. After the war, the proportion of women in the United States in the labour force increased from 34 per cent to 55 per cent between 1950 and 1985 (U.S. Department of Labor 1985, cited in England & Swoboda 1988). As late as 1970, only 38.3 per cent of Canadian women were in the paid labour force, but by 1988, 57.4 per cent of the Canadian female civilian population (Statistics Canada 1990) and 56.4 per cent of the U.S. female civilian population were in the labour force. The rate of labour force participation in the United States is expected to reach 61.9 per cent by 2000 (Statistical Abstract of the United States 1990).

Second is the influx into the labour force of women who had been especially underrepresented in the past, namely women of child-bearing age. In the past, women's labour force participation formed a u-shaped distribution by age: women in prime child-bearing years were much less likely to be in the labour force than their younger and older counterparts. By the mid-1970s, the distribution by age had flattened out considerably (Klein 1975) and the u-shape disappeared in the early 1980s (England & Farkas 1986, 151, figure 7.1). By 1988, women of prime child-bearing years actually were more likely to be employed than older women (Statistical Abstract of the United States 1990). For example, 76.5 per cent of Canadian women aged 20 to 24, 74.9 per cent aged 25 to 34, and 72.7 per cent of u.s. women aged 20 to 34 were in the paid labour force, as were 74.9 per cent of Canadian and 75.2 per cent of u.s. women aged 35 to 44. In comparison, 66 per cent of Canadian women and 69 per cent of u.s. women 45 to 54 years of age, and 35.5 per cent of Canadian women and 43 per cent of u.s. women aged 55 to 64 were employed (Statistical Abstract of the United States 1990; Statistics Canada 1990). In 1988, 51 per cent of u.s. mothers of children under one year of age were employed, as were 58.3 per cent of Canadian mothers whose youngest child was under age three.

Third is the movement of women into previously male occupations that require specific educational credentials. Women make up a larger share of the college population now and they receive a larger share of degrees in traditionally male areas. In Canada in 1971, women received 38 per cent of bachelor's degrees, but by 1987, they received 53 per cent of them (Statistics Canada 1990). In the u.s., women received 33.5 per cent of the bachelor's degrees in 1952, but by 1984, they received 50.5 per cent of them (Jacobs 1989, 114, table 6.1). The increase in the percentage of women in many traditionally male fields is particularly impressive. In North America, women have made the greatest inroads in the professions that do not depend on an extensive science or math background. For example, in 1968, women were 5.9 per cent of pre-law bachelor's degrees in the u.s., but by 1984, they made up 58.1 per cent of the pre-law degrees. In 1968, women received 6.8 per cent of the business bachelor's degrees, but 43.5 per cent in 1984 (Jacobs 1989, table 6.1). In Canada the percentage of law degrees awarded to women increased from 9.4 per cent in 1971 to 46.7 per cent in 1987. Undergraduate degrees in commerce showed a similar increase, from 6.2 per cent in 1971 to 43.8 per cent in 1987 (Statistics Canada 1990).

Women have also increased their representation in the most male-dominated professional areas. In 1984, for example, they received 12.8 per cent of the undergraduate engineering degrees in the u.s., up from 0.6 per cent in 1968. In 1984, women received 8.2 per cent of the military science degrees in the u.s., up from 0.5 per cent in 1968 (Jacobs 1989, table 6.1). In Canada, women represented 12.2 per cent of the undergraduate engineering and applied science degrees in 1987, up from 1.2 per cent in 1971 (Statistics Canada 1990).

The increase in percentage of college degrees as well as increase in percentage of degrees in nontraditional areas has, to some extent, carried over to the workplace. For example, women now make up 39 per cent of the people classified as managers by the u.s. Census Bureau (Jacobs 1992) and 34.5 per cent of Canadian managers (Berthoin Antal & Izraeli 1993), although the percentage is lower in many Western European countries (e.g., 20 per cent in the Federal Republic of Germany, 22 per cent in the United Kingdom, and 9 per cent in France and Ireland; Berthoin Antal & Izraeli 1993, table 1). Women have made substantial inroads into law, medicine, and psychology in North America, as well as a variety of fields that are less clearly related to educational background, such as real estate, insurance, and public relations. And women went from being a minority to being a majority (55 per cent) of bartenders during the decade of the 1970s (Reskin & Roos 1990). After an in-depth analysis of sex segregation and women's careers, Jacobs (1989, 187) concluded that "The evidence suggests that women are highly responsive to the opportunities provided by the weakening of discriminatory barriers."

Finally, a smaller proportion of men are employed now than in the past. Although the percentage of women who are in the paid labour force has been steadily rising, the percentage of men has shown a slight gradual decrease (England & Farkas 1986, 151, figure 7.1). In 1988, 76.6 per cent of Canadian and 76 per cent of u.s. adult men were employed, down from 78 per cent and 80 per cent, respectively, in 1970 (Statistics Canada 1990).

This picture of steady growth in female participation in the North American paid labour force is marred by several features suggesting that the change is not uniform and has been met with a certain amount of resistance. First, sex segregation has not decreased much. The index of dissimilarity (D), which indicates the percentage of women who would have to change jobs to be distributed in the same manner as men, was 74 in 1910 in the u.s., 67 in 1970 (Jacobs 1989, 25, table 2.4), and about 57 in 1986 (Jacobs 1989, 29, table 2.5). This relatively small change in the amount of sex segregation is due to two factors. First, despite the movement of women into nontraditional jobs and the attention that movement has generated, the majority of women take jobs that are in traditionally female fields. In the u.s. in 1985, over two-thirds of women worked in occupations that were more than 70 per cent female. Furthermore, many of the women who work in a traditionally male field tend to leave for a traditionally female field. Jacobs (1989) characterizes this phenomenon as a revolving door, but one that results in a steady increase in the percentage of women in male-dominated jobs. Specifically, for every eleven women who enter a male-dominated field, ten leave, resulting in a net gain (Jacobs 1989, 4). Second, very few men have moved into traditionally female jobs, and those who do tend to leave "women's work" for traditionally male fields (Jacobs 1989).

A second unsettling feature of women's increased participation in the labour force is the existence of sex segregation in new fields. For example, newly formed areas such as computer science and systems analysis tend to be as sex-segregated as many established fields. In computer-related fields, women predominate in only the lower-paying and lower-status positions such as data entry (Strober & Arnold 1987).

Third, in some areas desegregation appears to be accompanied by resegregation at a lower level (Reskin & Roos 1990). For example, women "desegregated" management, but they did not infiltrate all areas of management uniformly. Instead, they tend to select or be selected into a subset of areas that become female ghettos: personnel, finance, and corporate giving, for example, in the case of management. To cite another example, in psychology, women have become the majority of counselling and school psychologists and about half of clinical psychologists, but they are still a small minority of industrial psychologists or cognitive psychologists (Cohen & Gutek 1991).

Fourth, although women have moved into previously male-dominated jobs, their wages are still low relative to men's. In the United States in 1988, the median weekly earnings for a full-time male worker were $449 and for a full-time female worker $315, 70 per cent of the median male wage (Statistical Abstract of the United States 1990). The same proportion holds true in fields that women have recently entered; for example, in managerial and professional occupations, the median income of full-time female wage earners is 70 per cent of that of men, $465 versus $666. In a careful analysis of the income of male and female managers, Jacobs (1992) found that the gap between the pay of men and women managers is somewhat larger than the gap in pay between men and women in general. Although the gap in wages represents an improvement over the past thirty years, it is still considerable and generally still exists when other confounding factors are considered (England & Farkas 1986;

Nieva & Gutek 1981; Olson & Frieze 1987; O'Neill 1985). Thus, one might question whether women are being compensated at the same rate as men for their participation in the labour force.

In sum, there is no question but that women are moving into the world of paid work and that they are moving into men's occupations. But men are not moving into women's jobs. Thus, in the world of paid work (and education as a preparation for paid work), women are the ones doing the changing. This point has not been emphasized sufficiently in the literature, as England and Swoboda (1988, 157) noted: "few observers emphasize the profound asymmetry characterizing this change."

Now it is time to turn to changes in the private sphere of the family, traditionally women's world. It is important to note that there has been relatively little change in family roles. This finding was not particularly expected. Early studies of husbands and wives presumed that, as wives entered the paid labour force, husbands would respond by increasing their amount of family work (Blood & Wolfe 1960). Empirical results, have, however, not supported this presumption. In a secondary analysis of national data sets, Pleck (1985), for example, found that husbands of employed wives did a higher proportion of family work than husbands of housewives, but they did not necessarily spend more hours in family work than husbands of housewives. This apparent paradox can be explained by the fact that employed wives spend substantially less time in housework than housewives (see also Crosby 1982). Thus, the reason why employed wives' husbands do a larger proportion of housework than other husbands is because their wives do relatively little. In two-income families, there is less housework being done than in families composed of an employed husband and a homemaker wife.

It is important to note the differences in responsibilities associated with family roles for the two sexes, i.e., gender asymmetries in expectations about the parent and spouse roles. The fact that men spend relatively little time in housework does not mean they are neglecting their families, according to traditional notions of male and female worlds. Men do have family roles. The father and husband roles, however, do not take up the time (or perhaps make the emotional demands) that the mother and wife roles entail. In addition, as Bernard (1981b) so beautifully described, one of the main obligations of the husband and father has been to be a good provider. Thus, a man can partially fulfil his husband and father role through his participation in the labour force. Not so a woman. The woman who spends sixty or seventy hours per week pursuing a partnership in a law firm, or who travels two weeks out of every month because her job "demands it," may well be viewed as neglecting her family, not providing for them. (See also Gutek, Searle, & Klepa 1991 for a discussion of this point.)

The larger issue is whether or not family roles will eventually change. Will men enlarge their world to include a significant involvement with the nitty gritty of housework and child care? Is family just lagging behind paid work? The answer to this question is not obvious. There is, for example, considerable evidence that, although many women would like their husbands to do more in the way of housework and child care, neither men nor women expect men to do half of the family work (Gutek et al. 1991; Piotrkowski, Rapoport, & Rapoport 1987; Pleck 1985), despite the fact that increased involvement of the husband/father in family affairs is associated with psychological health for parents of both sexes (Piotrkowski et al. 1987; Pleck 1985).

A comparison of North America with the experiences of countries in which a majority of women have been active in the labour force for a while also gives little cause for optimism about the prospects of desegregating family work. In the Soviet Union, for example, the Communist government expected women to be full participants in the labour force, but women were also given full responsibility for the family domain (Lapidus 1988). In order to give women opportunity in the labour force, the State provided women with child care. Husbands/fathers were not, and are not, expected to be responsible for housework, shopping, or child care.

In sum, an examination of women and work shows that women have moved into paid employment in massive numbers. Surely this is an important social change. But not much else has changed. Men have changed neither their college majors nor their job aspirations (Jacobs 1989). Neither have men substantially increased their participation in the family domain. Women have been responsible for most of the change.[1] They have had to cope with a major new role without abdicating any of the responsibilities of the "old" ones. Can women continue to do this? Can we expect all women to be superwomen, putting in fifty or more hours of paid work while raising children

---

[1] England and Swoboda (1988) argued that gender asymmetry in the form of women "doing all the changing" is not limited to family and work roles. They provide evidence that women have taken on men's roles and behaviour in a variety of areas, including sex-typed play and toys in childhood, clothing, and criminal behaviour, all with no evidence of reciprocation on men's part. They also point out that these asymmetric changes have alarmed some scholars, who view the general trend as a devaluation and negation of "feminine" values and virtues such as nurturance and caring, without which society will surely fare badly.

and supporting their husbands? Women have been expected to cope with a lot.

SOURCES OF STRESS FOR WORKING WOMEN IN THE 1990S

I would like to emphasize the importance for research of the two major domains of life as sources of stress and means of coping. Gender-asymmetric change is an important factor to consider in assessing stressors faced by employed women. One source of stress comes from women's moving into the workplace, a movement that has not been smooth or without resistance. The second source of stress is the lack of change in family role responsibilities, which leaves many women with a "second shift" (Hochschild 1989). Women would be under less stress if either they were accepted as equals in the workplace *or* they could abdicate some family responsibilities. Both aspects – that women face unique stressors in the workplace *and* assume more responsibilities in the family – must be considered in studying stress in working women in the 1990s.

Perhaps ironically, work and family may also provide coping mechanisms for working women. For example, a woman who finds solace and meaning in her work right after her husband's death is using her work as a coping mechanism, if a coping mechanism is defined as "efforts to reduce negative impacts of stress" (Edwards 1988, 243). Similarly, as Crosby (1982) noted, the trials and tribulations of work may be washed away by the joys of family life. One of the ways of coping with work-related stress is to have an active, supportive family life. Each of the following sections considers work and family not only as sources of stress but also as opportunities for coping with that stress.

Paid Work as a Source of Stress for Women

Under the limited options available to women in the 1950s, many women may have felt isolated from the real world, left at home to worry about clean ovens and shirts. Many women in the 1990s who have been able to capitalize on the opportunities available to them in the labour force no doubt feel liberated and relish their new larger world, a world that often overlaps with that of the men in their lives. But for many women whose participation in the labour force consists of boring, routine, and poorly paying jobs with little opportunity for advancement, the enlarged world may feel demanding, not liberating. Both where paid work is stimulating and liberating and where it is routine and boring, the addition of a paid work role that takes up considerable time is potentially an additional source of stress for women, a source of stress not faced by most men.

Whereas much of the early research on work and family focused on the effects of a wife/mother's employment (Nye & Hoffman 1963), a dichotomy of being employed or not is no longer adequate for studying stress and coping because so many women are now employed in a diversity of jobs. It is not simply the condition of being employed but the conditions of employment that are important for understanding stress and coping.

Women have sought entry into many male-dominated fields because those fields offered a variety of intrinsic and extrinsic rewards such as money, challenge, job security, opportunity for advancement, the opportunity to have an impact, and the like, which few female-dominated jobs are able to offer at the same level.[2] Although there are female-dominated jobs that offer challenge, the opportunity to help others, and other intrinsic rewards, there are no high-paying female-dominated jobs, and there are no female-dominated jobs that offer generous fringe benefits (i.e., generous pensions, ample paid vacation, company-sponsored advanced education).

Both directly and indirectly, differential treatment of the sexes at work is a major source of stress for women, especially those employed in nontraditional jobs. Although many women believe that women in general are victims of discriminatory behaviour at work (Crosby 1984) and some believe that their organization favours men over women (Gutek 1988), relatively few believe that they personally are victims of discrimination, even when there is some evidence that they are (Crosby 1984). Thus, in considering sources of stress in the workplace, it is necessary to go beyond what is reported to be a stressor and examine aspects of the work situation that are associated with stress, although they may not be perceived as such.

One of the subtle sources of stress is stereotyping, which portrays women as less qualified than men for many professional and managerial jobs. The fact that competence seems to be defined as a male trait (Deaux 1976) may be responsible for a variety of unsettling findings. For example, in the mid-1970s Schein and her colleagues found that both sexes associated successful managers with traits they also associated with men. Relatively little had changed by the late 1980s, except that women managers in the 1980s associated successful male managers with both male and female traits (Brenner, Tomkiewicz, & Schein 1989; Schein 1973, 1975). Men had not changed.

---

[2] Apparently, traditionally women's jobs do not offer comparable opportunities to men: as described above, few men have entered traditionally female jobs and, of those who do, most leave (Jacobs 1989).

In a recent meta-analytic review of the research on the evaluation of people in positions of leadership, Eagly, Makhijani, and Klonsky (1992) found that, although the effect was small, women leaders were evaluated less favourably than men, especially under the following conditions: when they used stereotypically male styles (i.e., directive or autocratic), when the leaders occupied male-dominated roles, and when the evaluators were men.

In addition, there is the widely cited set of findings showing that when women perform well it is more often attributed to effort and less often attributed to ability than it is when men succeed (Deaux 1976). These subtle biases affect all working women, although, in many cases, the effect is stronger when the work is male-dominated or when the task is considered male (Deaux 1976; Eagly et al. 1992; Nieva & Gutek 1981).

Another source of stress is being a woman in a group in which men predominate. Kanter's (1977) original formulation that token dynamics applied equally to any group has been revised. Being the sole man in a group of women is not the same as being the sole woman in a group of men (Fairhurst & Snavely 1983; Izraeli 1983; Konrad, Winter, & Gutek 1992; Spangler, Gordon, & Pipkin 1978). Women do seem to experience some social isolation (Konrad 1986; Spangler et al. 1978), and performance pressures are heightened by the visibility that comes with being relatively rare (O'Farrell & Harlan 1982). Men do not appear to be devalued, isolated, or subject to female hostility (Schreiber 1979), although the situation of being numerically rare may not be all that comfortable for them (Etzkowitz 1971). The ultimate benefit for a woman of being in the majority (in a group of mostly women) versus in the minority (in a group of mostly men) is not entirely clear. Konrad and Gutek (1987) reviewed the effects of being in the numerical minority for women and ethnic minorities and suggested that a woman might well receive more benefits in a high-status male field, even if she is evaluated less favourably than a man, than in a female-dominated field, where she may be highly valued within the group but the group itself is devalued.

The concept of sex-role spillover, i.e., the carryover of expectations about gender-based roles into the workplace, developed by Gutek and colleagues (Gutek 1985; Gutek & Morasch 1982; Nieva & Gutek 1981) is useful in differentiating how stereotypes affect women in male- versus female-dominated jobs. When women are in the numerical minority, individual women may be expected to exhibit appropriate gender roles that may swamp expectations about work roles, but when women are in the numerical majority, the job itself takes on aspects of the female gender role. Thus, the stereotypes described above also affect women in traditionally female jobs; however, not only the women in the job but also the job itself may be affected. Thus, secretaries, elementary school teachers, and nurses are all expected to be nurturant and caring, whereas managers, school principals, and physicians, as a group, are not.

This emphasis on the expressive function of female-dominated jobs may blind people to other requirements of female-dominated jobs such as competence, management skill, special expertise, logic, and analytic ability. The assumption that jobs in which women predominate have a primarily expressive function may be a significant source of frustration for women in these jobs. It may also serve to devalue the jobs, because, although nurturance and caring are valued traits in North American society, they are less valued than traits that are associated with men, such as competence and activity (Deaux 1976).

It is relatively easy to build an argument that jobs in which women predominate are undervalued in North America. To the extent that pay is an indicator of the value of the occupation, female-dominated jobs are of low value because it is well documented that female-dominated jobs, professional and otherwise, tend to pay less than male-dominated ones (Gutek 1988; Stromberg 1988) and have low pay relative to the amount of education held by their occupants (Oppenheimer 1968).

Jobs that are undervalued may be especially subject to social control, whether through bureaucratic policies and regulations or close supervision. In our studies of white-collar, computer-using work groups, the work in groups in which women predominate tends to be more routinized than the work in groups in which men are in the majority (Gutek & Winter, in press). They also tend to have older, less complex computer systems that are used for relatively few, often routine, tasks (Gutek & Winter, in press). It is not surprising that women in traditional jobs often cite co-workers as a prime source of satisfaction at work (Nieva & Gutek 1981). In many cases, neither the jobs nor the opportunities for advancement and prestige are likely to be sources of satisfaction (Kanter 1977).

In summary, for women in both nontraditional and traditional jobs, the effects of subtle gender-role stereotypes may be a significant source of frustration and stress. Although I have focused on the effects of stereotyping on perceptions of competence in women vis-à-vis men, stereotyping also has other effects (e.g., the sex-object aspect of the female stereotype may contribute to unwanted sexual overtures, including sexual harassment [Gutek 1985]). For women in nontraditional jobs, there are a variety of effects of token dynamics that also can be stressful, whereas for women in traditional jobs two prime, subtle sources of stress are the low value ascribed to the job itself and the routine, bureaucratized work.

Having pointed out some of the potential stressors faced by women working in traditional and nontraditional jobs, I would like to note some of the ways in which work can mitigate stressors associated with work and with family life. All of the reasons why women have entered nontraditional jobs (e.g., much of the work is intrinsically interesting, it may pay well, it provides adequate fringe benefits and opportunities for advancement) can be sources of comfort and well-being for women in those jobs. Having an interesting or well-paying job can also provide material goods for one's family and can be a source of pride that may be some solace when one faces a ruined meal or a crying baby. If the dinner is ruined, for example, one can afford to have dinner delivered.

For the women in traditional jobs, there may be fewer resources for coping, but the sense of satisfaction that comes with helping others, for example, or the good companionship of "the girls on the line," is a resource for coping with the frustrations of other aspects of the work and may be a welcome alternative to spending every day alone or with several preschoolers.

It should be noted that if a woman does not want to be employed, if she would prefer to be a full-time homemaker, and/or if she feels guilty for leaving her children, then even the positive aspects of her job may fail to provide her with means of coping. For most women, however, being employed is associated with a number of positive benefits, from a greater sense of general well-being (Barnett & Baruch 1979) to more power within one's marriage (Nieva & Gutek 1981).

Family-related Sources of Stress

The fact that her role in the family has not shrunk to offset the increase in the average woman's role in the labour force means that balancing work and family looms as a large source of stress for women. The following discussion of family factors that one might consider in studying women's stress and coping borrows heavily, in abbreviated form, from Gutek, Repetti, and Silver (1988). Most of the factors are not solely sources of stress. They may also be sources of satisfaction and happiness and/or means of coping with stress. Because women feel responsible for and enjoy many family duties, they do not necessarily *report* that these responsibilities are stressful. In fact, in our research (Gutek, Searle, & Klepa 1991) and in the research of others, women do not generally report their families as a source of stress, although factors such as the number and ages of children, support-iveness of husband, amount of discretionary income to buy support services, and the like may well have an effect (Gutek et al. 1988). Thus, as in the case of employment, it is important to study both those factors that women report to be stressful and those that are as-sociated with stress although they might not be perceived as such.[3]

First are the roles of wife and mother. Although it appears that marriage limits the occupational achievement of women, in that a higher proportion of high-achieving women than men are unmar-ried (Cohen & Gutek 1991; Herman & Gyllstrom 1977; House-knecht, Vaughan, & Statham 1987), married women consistently re-port higher levels of job satisfaction than single women (Crosby 1984; Valdez & Gutek 1987).

Children, like husbands, appear to be a mixed blessing for em-ployed women. Because the number and timing of children can be controlled to some extent today, women are able to consider the po-tential impact of children on their work and adjust either accord-ingly. The stories of women who are not able to produce a child at exactly the planned time have received a lot of media attention. Al-though many of the stories are sympathetic to the plight of such women, others seem to suggest that the inability to have a child at the desired time is just comeuppance of some sort.

The fact that many career women have relatively few children, if any (Gutek et al. 1991; Herman & Gyllstrom 1977), suggests that children can be a source of job-related stress. Although the findings are not consistent, some studies suggest that the presence of children affects a woman's career advancement (Gwartney-Gibbs 1988; Olson & Frieze 1987); nevertheless, children, like husbands, appear to have a positive effect on job satisfaction (Crosby 1984). Finally, although children themselves are often sources of satisfaction for women, *child care* is a source of stress for a large percentage of working mothers. Social policy experts agree that there is a child-care problem in North America, but the failure of governments or employers to re-spond to this problem is at least partly influenced by the traditional assumption that women are responsible for raising their children (Kammerman, Kahn, & Kingston 1983). The child-care problem can be viewed as a direct outgrowth of the asymmetry in changes in social roles.

Not only can the acquisition of the role of wife or mother affect

[3] For example, cigarette-smoking might be reported to be an enjoyable, relaxing activity, but that does not negate the fact that it is a health hazard. It is important to explore both those factors that are reported as stressful and those that are not but can be shown to affect stress level.

women's level of stress, but so can the characteristics of other family members, husband, and children. A husband's career, for example, may place constraints on a wife's career that she finds stressful. Nieva and Gutek (1981) suggested that a husband's career may limit a woman's ability to relocate for her own, her career may be interrupted if they relocate so that he can advance in his field, and, more generally, she may limit her aspirations or hours at work to accommodate his career. In a sample of members of two divisions of the American Psychological Association, Gutek and Burley (1988) found that the most common response given by women to a question asking why they had moved was: to accompany husband/significant other when he accepted a position requiring relocation.

A husband's attitude toward a wife's employment or career also affects her level of stress. Sekaran (1986) and others (Hiller & Philliber 1982) explored the sensitive topic of who earns more. Although a wife who earns a substantial income greatly increases the total family income and enables the family to purchase a variety of products and services that reduce the work load, a higher family income may also lead to marital conflict. Sekaran (1986) reported that the most common response of women was to reject promotions and try not to be too successful if they felt their husbands were competing with them. In general, the research suggests that the important factor is whether the husband and wife have similar attitudes about wives' employment (Beutell & Greenhaus 1982; Ross, Mirowsky, & Huber 1983).

Both the husband-wife relationship and the mother-child relationship affect a woman's level of stress. Husbands and children who are supportive of a woman's career and contribute to household labour appear to be sources of satisfaction and appreciation for employed women (Piotrkowski et al. 1987; Repetti 1987).

A final family factor to consider is the relationship between number of roles occupied and stress. Although having multiple roles might well lead to role conflict, under the assumption that people have limited energy, time, and other resources, the accumulation of roles has also been touted as having positive effects (Sieber 1974). So far, most studies of multiple roles have tended to favour the role-accumulation hypothesis. Women who have multiple roles appear to be more satisfied than those who have fewer (Crosby 1982; Pietromonaco, Manis, & Frohardt-Lane 1986; Valdez & Gutek 1987). A somewhat more complex look at roles – for example, the time and energy expended or expectations about them – may lead to additional insights about the circumstances under which several roles are perceived as stressful or beneficial. For example, if the tasks associated

with two or three roles overlap or are complementary, will the accumulation of those roles be less stressful than where the roles call for
very different traits, behaviours, or skills?

In their review of the literature, Nieva and Gutek (1981, 44) concluded that the impact of family roles for women is to "reduce a
woman's involvement in the labor force, lower her career commitment, steer her into a traditional career, and reduce her career attainment." Similarly, Lewis and Cooper (1988) concluded that dual-
career couples reduce overload along traditional lines, e.g., women
reduce their involvement with paid work and increase domestic involvement. Although this may be true, family roles appear to have a
variety of salutary effects as well. Understanding when and under
what circumstances the family, the source of the most personal of relationships, is a source of stress rather than a source of satisfaction
must surely be a key to understanding stress and coping in women.

SUMMARY

Overall, this chapter considered the effect of gender-asymmetric
changes in men's and women's worlds as they may affect stress in
working women. Researchers interested in stress and coping might
consider examining sex-role stereotypes that affect women in both
traditional and nontraditional jobs, assorted outcomes of being the
only woman or one of a few women in a male-dominated field, and
routinized, bureaucratized work, which is especially common in female-dominated jobs such as clerical work. Among the family factors
that should be considered in the study of stress and coping are the
number and nature of family roles a woman occupies, the characteristics of other family members, and the relationships among family
members.

The various factors considered in this chapter raise three important comparisons. First is whether women are faced with more or
fewer stressors than men. Second is whether or not the current situation is better or worse for women than the 1950s. Third is whether
the current situation of significantly more change in women's worlds
than men's has resulted in a more equal situation for men and
women than that of the 1950s, say, when men and women occupied
separate worlds.

Based on the issues discussed in this chapter, it certainly appears
that women are faced with more stressors, on average, than men.
These are due to gender-asymmetric change in work and family
roles. Employed women today face a variety of stressors because of
major commitments of energy and time in all three adult life roles of

spouse, parent, and worker. The second and third comparisons are not easily assessed. In part, they depend on whether the current situation represents an end point in change in male and female roles, or whether it is an intermediate point in an ongoing change.

Have the hard-won gains in the workplace been offset by the lack of changes in the family domain for many women and the lack of change in men in either their career aspirations or their family activities? Is the average woman in North America today better off than the average woman in 1950? Certainly the situation is very different and there is more variety in women's circumstances today than in the 1950s, but it is not clear whether the situation of women vis-à-vis men has improved over the past thirty-five years. Right now many women are having to rely on themselves to cope with the overload required of fulfilling the roles of wife, mother, and employee. Whether women employ cognitive coping mechanisms such as prioritizing, rely on co-workers or family members for social support and child care, use some of the financial resources their work has garnered to relieve their family responsibilities (e.g., to provide child care, meals, housecleaning), or try to limit their career involvement to provide time and energy for family is not the only issue. More important is the fact that *they* must generate coping skills; there is very little support from men in general or from various social institutions to help women in what is potentially a much more stressful world than that of the average adult woman in the 1950s.

I believe that the current situation is not a stable one. It is unrealistic to expect 70 to 80 per cent of adult women to contribute fully in the paid labour force, especially if their labour yields fewer and lesser rewards than men's, *and* retain most of the responsibility for the private sphere. The current situation requires considerable coping skills on the part of almost all women who have taken on the roles of wife, mother, and worker. Some percentage of women will be able to marshal sufficient skills to handle all three roles with aplomb. In the past, we have referred to such women as "superwomen." But for the majority, the cost of "having it all" is much greater than it is for men. Considerable additional change in the distribution of activities in both the work and family domains is necessary to even out the workloads and responsibilities of men and women. In the absence of any support for a more equitable distribution of the job-and-family workload, I would not be surprised to see a considerable number of young women retreat from the workplace because the cost is too great.

This is, of course, just one opinion. Many of the other chapters in this volume also have something to say about these very thorny issues.

REFERENCES

Bardwick, J., & E. Douvan. 1971. Ambivalence: The socialization of women. In V. Gornick & B. Moran, eds., *Women in sexist society* (pp. 225–41). New York: Mentor.

Barnett, R.C., & G. Baruch. 1979. Career competence and well-being of adult women. In B. Gutek, ed., *New directions for education, work and careers: Enhancing women's career development* (pp. 95–101). San Francisco: Jossey-Bass.

Bernard, J. 1971. *Women and the public interest*. Chicago: Aldine.

– 1972. *The future of marriage*. New York: Bantam Books.

– 1978. Models for the relationship between the world of women and the world of men. In L. Kriesberg, ed., *Research in social movements, conflicts, and change* (pp. 291–340). Greenwich, CT: JAI Press.

– 1981a. *The female world*. New York: Free Press.

– 1981b. The good provider role, its rise and fall. *American Psychologist 36*, 1–12.

Berthoin Antal, A. & D.N. Izraeli. 1993. A global comparison of women in management: Women managers in their homelands and as expatriates. In E.A. Fagenson, ed., *Women in management: Challenges in managerial diversity* (pp. 52–96). Newbury Park, CA: Sage.

Beutell, N.J., & J.H. Greenhaus. 1982. Interrole conflict among married women: The influence of husband and wife characteristics on conflict and coping behavior. *Journal of Applied Psychology 21*, 99–110.

Blood, R.O., & D.M. Wolfe. 1960. *Husbands and wives: The dynamics of married living*. Glencoe, IL: Free Press.

Brenner, O.C., J. Tomkiewicz, & V.E. Schein. 1989. The relationship between sex role stereotypes and requisite management characteristics revisited. *Academy of Management Journal 32*, 662–9.

Cohen, A.G., & B.A. Gutek. 1991. Sex differences in the career experiences of members of two divisions of APA. *American Psychologist 42*, 1292–8.

Crosby, F. 1982. *Relative deprivation and working women*. New York: Oxford University Press.

– 1984. The denial of personal discrimination. *American Behavioral Scientist 27*, 371–86.

Deaux, K. 1976. Sex: A perspective on the attribution process. In J.H. Harvey, W.J. Ickes, & R.E. Kidd, eds., *New directions in attribution research* (1:336–52). Hillsdale, NJ: Erlbaum.

Eagly, A.H., M.G. Makhijani, & B. Klonsky. 1992. Gender and the evaluation of leaders: A meta-analysis. *Psychological Bulletin 111*, 3–22.

Edwards, J.R. 1988. The determinants and consequences of coping with stress. In C.L. Cooper & R. Payne, eds., *Causes, coping and consequences of stress at work* (pp. 233–63). Chichester, UK: John Wiley.

England, P., & G. Farkas. 1986. *Households, employment, and gender: A social, economic, and demographic view.* New York: Aldine.

England, P., & D. Swoboda. 1988. The asymmetry of contemporary gender role change. *Free inquiry in creative sociology 61*, 157–61.

Etzkowitz, H. 1971. The male sister: Sexual separation of labor in society. *Journal of Marriage and the Family 34*, 431–4.

Fairhurst, G.T., & B.K. Snavely. 1983. A test of the social isolation of male tokens. *Academy of Management Journal 26*, 353–434.

Gutek, B.A. 1985. *Sex and the workplace: Impact of sexual behavior and harassment on women, men, and organizations.* San Francisco: Jossey-Bass.

– 1988. Women in clerical work. In A.H. Stromberg & S. Harkess, eds., *Women working* (2nd ed., pp. 225–40). Mountain View, CA: Mayfield.

Gutek, B.A., & K. Burley. 1988, August. Relocation, family, and the bottom line: Results from the Division 35 survey. In V. O'Leary, chair, *Women and men in psychology: Career similarities and differences*, Symposium conducted at the meeting of the American Psychological Association, Atlanta, GA.

Gutek, B.A., & B. Morasch. 1982. Sex ratios, sex-role spillover, and sexual harassment of women at work. *Journal of Social Issues 38*, 55–74.

Gutek, B.A., R. Repetti, & D. Silver. 1988. Nonwork roles and stress at work. In C.L. Cooper & R. Payne, eds., *Causes, coping and consequences of stress at work* (pp. 141–74). Chichester, UK: Wiley.

Gutek, B.A., S. Searle, & L. Klepa. 1991. Rational versus gender role explanations for work-family conflict. *Journal of Applied Psychology 76*, 560–8.

Gutek, B.A., & S. Winter. In press. *Women workers, women managers and computers.* Chapter prepared for R. Burke & C. McKeen, eds., a volume on women in management.

Gwartney-Gibbs, P. 1988. Women's work experience and the "rusty skills" hypothesis: A reconceptualization and reevaluation of the evidence. In B.A. Gutek, A.H. Stromberg, & L. Larwood, eds., *Women and Work* (3:169–88). Newbury Park, CA: Sage.

Herman, J.B., & K.K. Gyllstrom. 1977. Working men and women: Inter- and intra-role conflict. *Psychology of Women Quarterly 1*, 319–33.

Hiller, D.V., & W.W. Philliber. 1982. Predicting marital and career success among dual-worker couples. *Journal of Marriage and the Family 44*, 53–62.

Hochschild, A. 1989. *Second shift: Inside the two-job marriage.* New York: Penguin.

Houseknecht, S.K., S. Vaughan, & A. Statham. 1987. The impact of singlehood on the career patterns of professional women. *Journal of Marriage and the Family 49*, 353–66.

Izraeli, D.N. 1983. Sex effects or structural effects? An empirical test of Kanter's theory of proportions. *Social Forces 62*, 153–65.

Jacobs, J. 1989. *Revolving doors: Sex-segregation and women's careers*. Palo Alto, CA: Stanford University Press.

– 1992. Women's entry into management: Trends in earnings, authority, values and attitudes among salaried managers. *Administrative Science Quarterly 37*, 282–301.

Kammerman, S.B., A.J. Kahn, & P. Kingston. 1983. *Maternity policies and working women*. Irvington, NY: Columbia University Press.

Kanter, R.M. 1977. *Men and women of the corporation*. New York: Basic Books.

Klein, D.P. 1975. Women in the labor force: The middle years. *Monthly Labor Review 98*, 10–16.

Konrad, A.M. 1986. The impact of work group composition on social integration and evaluation. Unpublished doctoral dissertation, Claremont Graduate School, Claremont, CA.

Konrad, A.M., & B.A. Gutek. 1987. Theory and research on group composition: Applications to the status of women and ethnic minorities. In S. Oskamp & S. Spacapan, eds., *Interpersonal processes: The Claremont symposium on applied social psychology* (pp. 85–121). Newbury Park, CA: Sage.

Konrad, A.M., S. Winter, & B.A. Gutek. 1992. Diversity in work group sex composition: Implications for majority and minority members. In P. Tolbert & S. Bacharach, eds., *Research in the sociology of organizations* (10:115–39). Greenwich, CT: JAI Press.

Lapidus, G.W. 1988. The interaction of women's work and family roles in the U.S.S.R. In B. Gutek, A. Stromberg, & L. Larwood, eds., *Women and work: An annual review* (3:87–121). Newbury Park, CA: Sage.

Lewis, S.N.C., & C.L. Cooper. 1988. Stress in dual-earner families. In B.A. Gutek, A.H. Stromberg, & L. Larwood, eds., *Women and work: An annual review* (3:139–68). Newbury Park, CA: Sage.

Nieva, V.F., & B.A. Gutek. 1981. *Women and work: A psychological perspective*. New York: Praeger.

Nye, F.I., & L. Hoffman. 1963. *The employed mother in America*. Chicago: Rand-McNally.

O'Farrell, B., & S. Harlan. 1982. Craftworkers and clerks: The effect of male co-worker hostility on women's satisfaction with non-traditional jobs. *Social Problems 29*, 252–65.

Olson, J., & I. Frieze. 1987. Income determinants for women in business. In A.H. Stromberg, L. Larwood, & B.A. Gutek, eds., *Women and work: An annual review* (2: 85–121). Newbury Park, CA: Sage.

O'Neill, J. 1985. Role differentiation and the gender gap in wage rates. In L. Larwood, A.H. Stromberg, & B.A. Gutek, eds., *Women and work: An annual review* (1:50–75). Newbury Park, CA: Sage.

Oppenheimer, V. 1968. The sex-labeling of jobs. *Industrial Relations 7*, 219–34.

Parsons, T., & R.F. Bales, eds., 1955. *Family socialization and interaction process*. Glencoe, IL: Free Press.

Pietromonaco, P.R., J. Manis, & K. Frohardt-Lane. 1986. Psychological consequences of multiple social roles. *Psychology of Women Quarterly, 10*, 373–82.

Piotrkowski, C.S., R.N. Rapoport, & R. Rapoport. 1987. Families and work. In M.B. Sussman & S.K. Steinmetz, eds., *Handbook of marriage and the family* (pp. 251–83). New York: Plenum Press.

Pleck, J. 1985. *Working wives/working husbands*. Beverly Hills, CA: Sage.

Repetti, R.L. 1987. Linkages between work and family roles. In S. Oskamp, ed., *Applied social psychology annual*, vol. 7, *Family processes and problems* (pp. 98–127). Newbury Park, CA: Sage.

Reskin, B.F., & P. Roos, eds. 1990. *Job queues, gender queues: Explaining women's inroads into male occupations*. Philadelphia: Temple University Press.

Ross, C.E., J. Mirowsky, & J. Huber. 1983. Dividing work, sharing work, and in-between: Marriage patterns and depression. *American Sociological Review 48*, 809–23.

Schein, V.E. 1973. The relationship between sex role stereotypes and requisite management characteristics. *Journal of Applied Psychology 57*, 95–100.

– 1975. The relationship between sex role stereotypes and requisite management characteristics among female managers. *Journal of Applied Psychology 60*, 340–44.

Schreiber, C. 1979. *Changing places*. Cambridge, MA: MIT Press.

Sekaran, U. 1986. *Dual-career families*. San Francisco: Jossey-Bass.

Sieber, S. 1974. Toward a theory of role accumulation. *American Sociological Review 39*, 567–78.

Spangler, E., M.A. Gordon, & R.M. Pipkin. 1978. Token women: An empirical test of Kanter's hypothesis. *American Journal of Sociology 84*, 160–70.

Statistical Abstract of the United States. 1990. *The national data book*. Washington, DC: Bureau of the Census.

Statistics Canada. 1990. *Women in Canada: A statistical report* (2nd ed.). Ottawa: Ministry of Supply and Services, Canada.

Strober, M.H., & C.L. Arnold. 1987. Integrated circuits/segregated labor: Women in computer-related occupations and high-tech industries. In H. Hartmann & R. Kraut, eds., *Computer chips and paper clips: Technology and women's employment* (pp. 136–82). Washington, DC: National Academy Press.

Stromberg, A.H. 1988. Women in female-dominated professions. In A.H. Stromberg & S. Harkess, eds., *Women working: Theories and facts in perspective* (2nd ed., pp. 206–25). Mountain View, CA: Mayfield.

Valdez, R., & B.A. Gutek. 1987. Family roles: A help or a hindrance for working women? In B.A. Gutek & L. Larwood, eds., *Women's career development* (pp. 157–70). Newbury Park, CA: Sage.

2 Women's Lives Complete: Methodological Concerns

ALLISON TOM

I have six kids and I'm thirty-six years old. I'm a mom. I'm a housekeeper ...
I'm everything. I just do the things that's natural for my children. And working is one of them ... working is a part of my job.   (Sacks 1989, 89)

As an anthropologist, I am fascinated by people's work lives. I am
also puzzled and frustrated that the study of work is often carried
out in oppositional and dichotomized frames of reference: men's
work and women's work; paid work and unpaid work; work and family. An assumed opposition between masculine and feminine domains underlies many of these dichotomies. The uncritical use of
such frames distorts rather than facilitates understanding of what
work is and of the meaning of work for different people of different
gender, class background, racial background, and stage of life. This
chapter outlines and challenges researchers' dichotomization of public and domestic realms in the study of women's lives and discusses
the methodological implications.

Sandra Harding's (1987) recent discussions of the power of feminist research have focused on three new ways of understanding social
life. She argues that feminist research is distinguished not by "a"
feminist methodology but rather by certain significant features.
First, exemplary feminist research uses women's experiences as theoretical and empirical resources; second, it addresses goals that are

I have benefited immensely from Jane Gaskell's extensive comments on an earlier
draft of this paper. I am also grateful to Carol Barnhardt, Jane Collier, Bonita
Long, and Wendy Wickwire for their helpful insights.

significant to women, that is, it is research for women; and third, it overtly places the biases, perspective, and position of the researcher "in the same critical plane as the overt subject matter" (Harding 1987, 8). The purpose of this chapter is to explore one of these attributes of feminist scholarship – the use of women's experiences – in terms of feminist anthropology's struggles with the problematic constructs of oppositional domains such as "male" and "female," "public" and "domestic," "culture" and "nature," and "work" and "family."

In *Feminism and Anthropology*, Henrietta Moore (1989) demonstrates how feminist anthropologists have continued to refine and challenge these dichotomizations and to question their universal applicability in explaining women's subordination. Moore's book sharpens our understanding of how women's kin and family relations shape their access to economic and social power cross-culturally. Women's lives are influenced by their kin roles and obligations, but, as she demonstrates, we must not take this to mean that women's lives are everywhere shaped in the same way (Moore 1989, 72). In particular, we must not take this to mean that women's lives are always patterned by an opposition of public to domestic or by their biological roles as mothers – as they seem to be in our own culture. Although dichotomizations may be found cross-culturally, there is danger in assuming that our interpretation of dichotomy is universal.[1]

The study of women's work and lives in nonmarket societies has been influenced by the challenge to the dichotomy of the public and the domestic to a greater extent than similar research in highly industrialized, market-dominated capitalist societies (Moore 1989). The uncritical application of these dichotomies to other cultures has long been seen as potentially ethnocentric and inaccurate (e.g., Rosaldo 1980), but the realization that these dichotomies may not always fit well in the societies that generated them has been less quick to come. Such sensitivity to the full meaning and range of women's productive activities is as necessary in highly industrialized, market-dominated settings as it is in industrializing and nonmarket settings.

In terms of Harding's criteria for feminist research, overcoming dichotomization is necessary if women's lives and experiences are to be genuine theoretical and empirical resources. As long as the study of work is dominated by the tendency to posit women's relations to their work in oppositional terms, more complex realities will be misunderstood and overlooked. In this chapter, I discuss briefly ways

---

[1] I am not arguing in this chapter that dichotomization and dichotomized thinking *per se* cannot be found cross-culturally. I am arguing that researchers must not assume that their dichotomized frameworks are the same as others'. I am grateful to Jane Collier for pointing out the need to clarify this point.

the application of dichotomized schemas has distorted understanding of women's work and limited the research questions asked in the study of women's coping with employment demands. I also present alternate research which, in challenging or surmounting oppositional schemas for understanding women's work, best illustrates Harding's vision of the heart of feminist social science.

In the first section of this chapter I review the concept of the male/female dichotomy as it has been used by feminist anthropologists and current critiques of that conceptualization. In the second section I discuss studies of women's work in North America that demonstrate the rewards of challenging these boundaries. In the final section I discuss the methodological implications of these studies.[2]

THE MALE/FEMALE DICHOTOMY

A primary focus for feminist anthropologists in the 1970s was explaining the apparently universal subordination of women. In the introduction to their 1974 edited volume, Rosaldo and Lamphere articulated some of those concerns:

Are there societies that, unlike our own, make women the equals or superiors of men? If not, are women "naturally" men's inferiors? Why do women, in our own society and elsewhere, accept a subordinate standing? How, and in what kinds of situations, do women exercise power? How do women help to shape, create, and change the private and public worlds in which they live? New questions demand new kinds of answers. (1974, 2)

One kind of answer proposed to this question was that women's apparently universal association with child-rearing rose out of their biological functions in child-bearing and lactation and that the association with child care seemed necessarily to confine women to the domestic sphere and household responsibilities. This was contrasted to men's extradomestic, or public, roles and responsibilities (Chodorow 1974; Ortner 1974; Rosaldo 1974). Feminist anthropology has thus been built upon the concept of the male/female, public/domestic dichotomy.

The notion that the social world divides up into opposing halves of "male" (public) and "female" (domestic) domains is a powerful and attractive one, appealing to the way many in the West – anthropolo-

---

[2] This paper makes use of Harding's (1987) distinction between methodology and method and is addressed primarily to the issue of methodology – a theory of how research ought to be done and what its proper concerns are – rather than to method – the techniques for carrying out research.

gists and others – understand their own lives. In adopting this notion of the bifurcation of social life, feminist anthropologists were following a pattern that was familiar and made sense to them and that carried the weight of historic precedent. Many earlier scholars accepted as unproblematic the notion of the two spheres; some posited them as opposing and others as complementary. The notion of opposed male and female spheres did not originate in Victorian England, but Rosaldo maintains that that era's interpretation of the distinction was particularly important in developing our own conception of male and female worlds. In Victorian theory the sexes were seen as dichotomous and in contrast, and the ideology of the Victorians "opposed natural, moral, and essentially unchanging private realms to the vagaries of a progressive masculine society" (Rosaldo 1980, 404). Rosaldo goes on to assert that many modern ideas – such as maternity as a biological role in contrast to paternity as a social role – are the heirs of Victorian ideology (Rosaldo 1980, 404).

As Rosaldo (1980) points out, these distinctions are social and mutable rather than rigidly tied to biology. And yet they come to be taken for granted and to frame popular and policy statements about women and their lives. For example, discussions of the rapid entry of young women into teaching in Victorian America were carried out in terms of men's and women's proper spheres. The notion of these separate spheres was not challenged even by the massive movement of young women into paid labour. There are characteristics of teaching school that could easily have led policy-makers and the public to interpret the job as women's entry into a male domain – the women who taught school were paid, they left the household to teach, and they taught under the public supervision of (usually male) school boards, trustees, parents, and principals.

Those in favour of the feminization of teaching did not emphasize the symbolic distances between domestic woman and the public school. Rather, they portrayed the school itself as a domestic domain. "The very characteristics that made women good mothers – their nurturance, patience, and understanding of children – made them better teachers than men, they argued" (Strober & Tyack 1980, 496). Gendered characteristics are mediated through social interpretation, and interpretations change as the social situation changes. The dichotomy, however, remains.

Contributions of Recent Feminist Anthropology

The argument put forward by the contributors to the 1974 Rosaldo and Lamphere edition (especially Rosaldo, Chodorow, and Ortner) that women's association with children confines them to a devalued domestic realm has been criticized recently by Moore and others (Lamphere 1990; Moore 1989; Rapp 1991). New scholarship has refined the theory that women's subordination is created through a universal association with the domestic realm, but it has not discarded the idea that women's lives are structured in important ways by their daily responsibilities and by the structural significance and power associated with those responsibilities. It is this idea that made early feminist anthropology so powerful and exciting.

Moore demonstrates that we ought to think of women's lives as being structured by kin and family structures and meanings and that the identity of adult women is not everywhere constructed in terms of maternity as it is in North America and Western Europe. In other cultures, "the processes of life-giving ... are social concerns ... and not confined to women or the 'domestic' domain alone. ... In a wide range of different societies the concept of 'woman' is not elaborated through ideas about motherhood, fertility, nurturance and reproduction" (Moore 1989, 28).

This is a subtle but significant revision of the argument that women's association with child-rearing and other household functions always structures their subordination. It is dependent on the work inspired by the original conceptualization of the universal categories of public and domestic, culture and nature, male and female, even as it challenges that work.

These lessons and refinements of the original theory of the cross-cultural significance of separate male and female domains can be applied back to an analysis of the society that gave rise to them. In the next section of this chapter I demonstrate ways in which the study of women's work in industrialized settings has wittingly and unwittingly been dominated by the same set of dichotomized conceptions of women's relation to labour. These theories can consistently be linked to the central idea that men and women inhabit different worlds, and that the difference between these worlds lies in women's relation to child-bearing and -rearing. Even where the link to specifically male and female realms is not made explicit, the continuing compulsion to divide motivations, attitudes, and lives into two distinct and opposing categories dominates and distorts much of the scholarship on women's work.

WOMEN'S WORK IN WESTERN INDUSTRIALIZED SOCIETIES

Many studies of women's work replicate the Victorian notion of a private, affective realm sealed off from the public, instrumental realm.

A primary way in which this division is perpetuated is in the common use of the word "work" to mean "paid work." Feminism has made many researchers aware that this equation is problematic, but most often scholars accommodate this by adding a footnote that reassures readers that no slight is intended to women's unpaid work in the home by the exclusive application of the term "work" to paid work. The central notion that work that earns a paycheque and work that does not earn a paycheque are fundamentally and obviously different remains unchallenged by such reassuring footnotes. Such addenda furthermore reinforce rather than challenge parallel assumptions about women's attitudes to employment, and about the source and nature of rewards to women's work of all kinds.

Similarly, women's motivation for paid work is examined through a dualistic model: some women have jobs because they and their families need their earnings and other women have jobs to feel fulfilled. It seems that women are not permitted to enjoy their paycheques and their jobs at the same time. Women's work and lives are likewise oversimplified and misunderstood when researchers assume that having a job and having a family always put a woman in a position of conflict and that the conflict that can result is always the same. There is an implication that women must choose to live in either a "public" or a "domestic" world and that it is not possible to live a life that includes elements of both. The study of women's work has been dominated in large part by these and other such oppositional models.

In contrast, holistic studies of women's work overcome these dualisms and focus on the reality of women's work experiences regardless of where that work is carried out. They explore women's work across their lives rather than in isolated sectors of their lives. These studies of women's work seek the many strands that compose women's work experience and acknowledge that the strands are woven together such that the individual strands are sometimes distinct and sometimes merged into the whole. The strands are also seen as being in a relationship to each other that is not necessarily oppositional. These studies acknowledge that women's lives are made of elements that can be complementary and additive as well as contradictory and fractured. A few such studies are discussed below.

Why Women Have Jobs

The majority of studies of women at work have looked either at women as workers in need – working-class women, for the most part – or at women as workers for personal fulfilment – professional women. These divisions, like most divisions, have some relation to the situation they depict, but they oppose and exaggerate the differences. Many researchers have found that women working in factory situations often do consider income the primary reason for having a job, and that some of these women would quit their jobs if they were financially able to (Cavendish 1982; Howe 1977; Porter 1982; Wajcman 1983). In contrast, much of the research looking at professional women has concentrated on their desire for personal fulfilment (e.g., Baruch, Barnett, & Rivers 1983; Coser & Rokoff 1982; Hunt & Hunt 1982; Osako 1982; E. Pleck 1976; J. Pleck 1982). But women's employment is not uniform in its demands and experiences, and the differences between the jobs, motivations, and satisfactions of professional women and those of the majority of women in clerical, sales, and factory jobs should be neither ignored nor exaggerated.

The fact that many women have paid jobs because they and their families need their income should not be taken to mean that money is all that women get from their jobs. Myra Ferree (1976) has looked in depth at working-class women's relationship to their paid labour. She points out that the women she interviewed need both the money and the non-economic rewards their jobs give them; neither motivation was presented as primary. The need for money does not imply total lack of interest in the other rewards of work, and "the fact that paid employment may be better able than housework to meet the non-financial needs of working-class women should not be taken to imply that these women are working 'just for the fun of it' " (Ferree 1976, 433). Ferree demonstrated that the women's economic need did not eliminate their equally strong need for social relationships and extradomestic sources of self-esteem (Ferree 1976). Ferree's work is a major criticism of the assumption that women's responsibilities in the domestic realm and in the public employment realm are clearly separate from and in opposition to each other.

This research brings to light for our inspection the assumption that women always put their roles as wives and mothers ahead of other roles and needs. A more accurate picture of women's lives, built from their perspective rather than from the perspective of male-stream theory, demonstrates the ways in which women weave their lives into a pattern more complex than a dualistic model can capture. This pattern includes their many roles and needs without necessarily placing any one ahead of others. Ferree summarizes eloquently the difficulties inherent in asking whether any person has a job primarily for the pay or primarily for non-economic rewards. "An unqualified preference for either paid work or housework requires the individual to deny the real problems or ignore the real rewards that exist in both forms of work, as well as in the combination of the two" (Ferree 1985, 531). The model of women having jobs either because of money or because of personal rewards distorts understanding of women's work lives. The idea of personal fulfilment is applied almost exclusively to women who have professional jobs (or to women who are married to men with professional jobs and high incomes). This splits women into class divisions and portrays only part of the lives of each group. What is needed is research that creates rich descriptions of women's lives and the differences between them without casting any in rigid stereotypes.

Researchers also need to be aware of the damage that is done to understanding when a model developed to understand one kind of situation is applied unmodified to a very different one. The "dual-career model" of families where two adults have highly paid jobs has limited relevance for the experiences and lives of most employed women and their families. Benenson (1984) argues that the dual-career model assumes that women are gaining increased access to elite jobs, that families with two working adults have the financial resources to purchase expensive services and time-saving goods, that the salaries of elite husbands and wives are of equal significance to family income, and that elite wives have jobs primarily for "cultural" rather than economic reasons. By focusing on elite couples and their work patterns, he argues, researchers are ignoring the critical problems facing middle- and low-income families and women supporting families alone.

The "Problem" of Women's Families

Another assumption distorting the study of women's work is that women who are both paid employees and mothers (and, to a lesser extent, wives and/or daughters) are necessarily experiencing conflict. This assumption is based both in the conceptual opposition of the two realms – that is, in a notion that women who try to live in both the public and the private realm are courting conflict – and in the reality that our society currently does not accommodate women's movement between the realms. Of course, the assumption that women who have responsibilities in both arenas are somehow unnatural and unusual continues to perpetuate a social lack of support for women who are trying to live lives that extend across these boundaries.

It is important to be careful when arguing against the idea that women's family lives necessarily create conflict for them in pursuing paid employment. Given women's current primary responsibility for caring for children, employment that cannot be carried out simultaneously with child care does present conflicts for mothers of small children (and, similarly, for others with heavy caregiving responsibilities, e.g., daughters of aging parents). What must be kept in focus is that much, if not all, of this conflict is created by social structures rather than by the natural demands and needs of children. Our ways of caring for children and others are bound up in cultural and social structures and values. It is necessary that children be well cared for; it is not necessary that their mothers provide all of that care (Ruddick 1989; Scarr 1984).

The literature which assumes that women are put in positions of conflict by the combination of paid and unpaid work neglects another important issue; that is, that family can be a help as well as a hindrance to women pursuing paid jobs. In their families of procreation, women find that responsibility for children can be an incentive to find good jobs and to do well at their jobs even though that responsibility complicates having those jobs. Furthermore, the notion of family must be extended beyond the notion of family of procreation. In their natal and extended families, women can find networks of support that help them find and do their jobs.

My own research (Tom 1986) on the lives of sole-support mothers provides evidence of the ways in which women are motivated to find employment because of their children and their hopes for their children. Having a paid job may not make an enormous financial difference to their families in the short term. The difference between a woman's income on state assistance and her income from a minimum- or low-wage job may not be much, once child care and other expenses have been paid (in many cases women bring home less by having a job). All the same, these women felt that for them to have a job was essential to their children's welfare. They looked for jobs because they wanted their children to be proud of them and because they wanted to set an example for their children. It was important to them to give their children the assurance of having a self-supporting and self-respecting mother. As one woman said of her motivation for training for a job,

I think I wanna work because I feel independent. And like I'm working to look after myself and nobody's gonna look after me but me ... And I have my kids and I feel they're my kids and I wanna support them. Cause they're my kids.

Another woman commented,

and then, my kids are old enough that, like they were proud of what I was doing, you know ... My kids go to school with the some, with the little richer kids, you know. And like, they were proud to say, like my mom, she works too, she works in a bank, and ... they had categorized themselves as in another kind of a group.

These women's children often got very involved in their mothers' employment lives, listening to their mothers' stories, helping to choose their mothers' clothes on important days, and visiting their mothers' workplaces. The women found that although their children complicated their pursuit of employment, they also enriched that pursuit and gave it meaning, even if only the meaning of escaping the stigma of welfare dependence.

Just what people, you know, think that you're like. It's the quote old welfare mother syndrome, you know, people think that people that are on welfare have to be sloppily dressed or overweight and don't give a damn about their kids, you know.

These women also got enormous support from their parents, siblings, and friends in carrying the load of employment and parenting. Some parents provided assistance with child care, car repairs, and other practical matters; others provided moral support and encouragement to their daughters (Tom 1986).

Karen Sacks (1989) also provides detailed information about how women's family and extended kin networks can strengthen rather than weaken their employment involvement and power. Her research on union organizing at Duke Medical Center focuses on the ways in which "family life ... facilitated women's militance and participation in protest movements" (Sacks 1989, 85). She criticizes Marxist conceptions of women's "political conservatism, short-sighted vision, and retrograde sentiments" that were "continually recreated in their narrow and oppressed sphere of family experience" (Sacks 1989, 87). In doing life histories of a number of different women, she discovered that the women's ideas about work conflicted with management's ideas and job descriptions. The job descriptions emphasized a division between mental and manual labour, but the women emphasized "the unity of the two and the continuity of waged and unwaged work" (Sacks 1989, 89).

Sacks's determination to view women's lives as wholes rather than as fragmented pieces also helped her find ways in which these women's family lives and values actively supported their union activism. When she put the life histories and the stories of union militants together, she identified a number of "centerwomen" whose family values were connected to their workplace organizing (Sacks 1989, 91).

Centerwomen took the consensus values of their colleagues and translated them into union terms such as "decent pay, nondiscriminatory promotion ladders, freedom from supervisory harassment, impartial grievance procedures, and so forth" (Sacks 1989, 92). These women's sense of justice was based, not in lessons about fairness learned in the public realm, but about lessons about adulthood and responsibility learned in the private realm of the family. Similarly, their willingness to fight together was shaped not in the public realm of official relationships but in the private realm of social events and relationships. This web supporting women's union activism could easily have been missed by a methodology that assumed a separation between personal and employment lives.

Sacks's work provides one demonstration of how the dynamics of women's lives are distorted when they are studied in oppositional frameworks. She demonstrates how women's employment activities may derive meaning and impetus from family values and personal relationships. She is, in essence, demonstrating how women carry elements of each realm across conceptual boundaries and into other parts of their lives. Another approach to the study of women's work can emphasize the many kinds of work that women do which defy or confound oppositional classifications.

Child Care

Caring for children is work women do in a variety of circumstances: they can do it in a mode that seems entirely private, such as caring for their own children in their own homes; or in modes that combine the private and the public, such as caring for others' children for pay in their own homes. Even caring for other people's children in an entirely public space such as a child-care centre constitutes a mixing of public and private domains. There, the conflict is most commonly acted out in child-care workers' struggles to defend the legitimacy of their skills and expertise, because caring for children is, in and of itself, seen as a domestic task regardless of where it takes place.

Margaret Nelson (1988, 1989, 1990) has documented many of the struggles and conflicts confronting women who care for other people's children in their own homes. Significantly, this drama is played out primarily as a struggle between *mothers* – the family-care providers and the mothers of the children being cared for. Two kinds of conflicts occurring in this situation are especially salient: the actors' alternation between seeing the relationship as a market exchange and as a personal exchange, and conflicts between the two sets of mothers over what good mothering is.

Nelson demonstrates that at one level both parents and providers have strong motivations to define the relationship "in terms of the norms of a market exchange" (Nelson 1989, 7). In a market-exchange relationship, the obligations between the parties are limited to contractual responsibilities such as paying bills, attending to time schedules, and the like. This relationship is unsatisfactory to both groups of women, but, Nelson emphasizes, at different times and for different reasons. Mothers may be dissatisfied with the market exchange as a way to perceive and discuss the care of their children; they may also resist this norm when they need accommodations from the providers that are not included in the market exchange (such as allowing late payments or caring for children out of "normal working hours"). Providers may be dissatisfied with the market norm because their need to have the value of their work recognized is limited to the payment they receive (Nelson 1989, 8).

Conflict over what constitutes good mothering arises because of the essential contradiction underlying the motivations of most care providers. "Because many of the providers felt it is wrong for mothers to leave their children, they were in the curious position of offering a service in which they had no faith" (Nelson 1989, 12). That is, providers were offering care in their homes because, though they wanted to earn money, they felt that it was wrong to leave their children in the care of others. The research of Innes and Innes (1984) supports these interpretations. In their study, caregivers who identified themselves primarily as mothers chose to provide care because they could simultaneously care for their own children. "Virtually all of the family day home caregivers had intact families and did not believe women with young children should work" (Innes & Innes 1984, 145).

Chiara Saraceno (1984) also argues that the feminist study of child-care work reveals the ways in which the boundaries between the public and the private are constantly shifting and being challenged by the provision of child care for pay in extra-family settings. In looking at child-care providers in centre settings in Italy, she noticed a division between the providers; some viewed their work in terms of service to the mother, whereas others viewed their work in terms of the education and welfare of the child. Saraceno also points out another split that occurs in the discussion of child care and women's lives: "it seems that women as mothers cannot avoid speaking of [their] children, but women as feminists are not capable of thinking about them theoretically, even when speaking of motherhood" (Saraceno 1984, 25).

Child care thus can be a particularly rewarding area for feminists interested in the impact of the public/domestic dichotomy. The opposing worlds are here brought into close contact and sharp relief. Caring for children belongs in the symbolic domain of the domestic; when this work is moved into the domain of the public – when it is located in centres rather than homes and is carried out for pay rather than "love" – then the interactions of the individuals acting in these realms both demonstrate and challenge the veracity of the symbolic dichotomization of women's lives.

Kin Work

Another domain of women's work and experience that is neglected and distorted by the opposition of the realm of paid employment and the realm of responsibility for their household and family of procreation is what has come to be called kin work. There is a growing body of scholarship on the experiences of women struggling with responsibilities to employment, to families of procreation, and to their aging parents. Like many others, Micaela di Leonardo (1987) argues that we need to "fuse, rather than to oppose, the domestic network and labor perspectives" (442). She conceives of kin work as a third kind of work that women undertake and defines it as "the conception, maintenance, and ritual celebration of cross-household kin ties" (di Leonardo 1987, 442–3). This work includes the labour necessary to maintain these ties and the thought that goes into deciding which ties to strengthen and which to abandon. This work is carried out through often disregarded activities such as making telephone calls, writing letters, arranging and making visits, buying gifts, and organizing holiday and other celebrations. Kin work is heavily dependent on women; often this work is left undone when there is no adult woman in a household.

Di Leonardo (1987) maintains that understanding the significance of the work of kinship helps to challenge the opposition between self-interest and altruism that often typifies studies of women's work. "Revealing the actual labor embodied in what we culturally conceive as love and considering the political uses of this labor helps to deconstruct the self-interest/altruism dichotomy and to connect more closely women's domestic and labor-force lives" (di Leonardo 1987, 452). As we continue to study women's lives in ways that allow the complexity of those lives to speak to us, the damage done by preconceived oppositional frameworks will become increasingly clear.

Employment: Breaking Free of Family?

In studying women's lives we must be willing to pursue finely distinguished threads of meaning and then to weave those threads back into the whole fabric. The task of distinguishing any number of kinds of work, for example, should not keep us from also seeing that these different ways of working are woven together in patterns that demonstrate the ways that individual women, as well as groups of women, make sense of their lives and work to establish control over their social and economic environments.

Employment helps women break free of domestic dependency in some situations; in other situations, women perceive their employment through their awareness of their domestic responsibilities and possible dependency. The extent to which employment actually does work to counter women's economic dependency is very much reliant on the context. For example, if the income a woman can earn through employment is not sufficient to support her (or her and her dependents) then employment does not provide independence. Similarly, a woman's employment is often framed within obligations to the family and domestic unit; rather than marking her independence from the household, it can be part of her intense relationship with it (e.g., Salaff 1981).

Jane Gaskell's (1983) research on the course choices and employment expectations of high school girls illustrates how their knowledge about the distribution of domestic labour and the varying economic rewards to men's and women's paid labour interact. She studied working-class girls' course choices and found that these girls chose courses leading to clerical work for very practical reasons. They felt that after marriage they would be responsible for the majority of the work of caring for children and maintaining a household and they formed their employment plans in response to this expectation. "The prospect of domestic responsibilities diminished the attraction of more demanding and responsible jobs" (Gaskell 1984, 95). These young women constructed an approach to paid work that incorporates both their desire for the rewards of employment and their understanding of the reality of the distribution of domestic and paid labour and the relative rewards of each.

STUDYING WOMEN'S LIVES

Women's lives can and must be studied in ways that respect the significance of individual meanings, broad patterns, and whole pictures. The study of women's lives should meet Harding's criteria for taking women's lives as a source of both theory and empirical knowledge by honouring what women say and do and how they live and think, even when this honouring confounds established frameworks. Our study of women's lives is distorted by assumptions about work and family that do not match the way women themselves see their work. We must be open to understanding women's work from their point of view before we worry about which kind of work it is or before we attempt to place it in categories when the appropriateness of the categories for the task at hand has not been established. When used carefully and analytically, the notion of work can be a creative and productive concept; when used without careful consideration, the notion of work can distort and disguise significant elements of women's lives. The preceding pages have outlined arguments relating to a methodology for studying women's work; the remainder address some research design issues that are consistent with the goal of studying women's work as part of the overall pattern of their lives.

Defining Work

A primary concern to be addressed is the way in which the term *work* itself is defined and used. The anthropology of work has struggled long with the definition of just what the activity "work" really is. June Nash (1981) defines it as "purposive activity directed toward meeting physical and social needs satisfying to those who either produce or consume goods and services" (3). Much earlier, Raymond Firth (1965) described the Tikopians' definition of work. The Tikopia have one term that covers activities that are not rest or recreation, including participation in ritual acts as well as daily production. By adopting such complex definitions of work, the mandate for the study of work is broadened and deepened.

A definition such as Firth's clearly includes work such as household work and kin work, and, because it is not dependent on payment as a defining element, encourages – indeed forces – us to look at women's work in a different light. We are compelled to ask not, "How does a woman's 'work' life conflict with her 'home' life?" or "How does a woman cope with her conflicting lives?" but questions such as "What difference does it make when the work a woman does is paid?" "How do women cope with the challenges of their lives?" and "What is the relation between women's unpaid work and the amount they are paid when they do work for pay?" These questions are the type of questions that have been asked in holistic studies; answering such questions will continue to reveal the ways in which women's lives are cohesive wholes and the ways in which inappropriate theoretical categories can chop those entities into smaller meaningless bits.

Dichotomy as a Research Problem

Resistance to and avoidance of dichotomous frames is one approach to the problem of dichotomization; another more aggressive approach is to investigate the concept of dichotomy itself. Important research has been done and remains to be done in investigating the way in which concepts and domains are constructed in opposition to each other. Why are people seen in either/or frames when those frames do so much violence to the fine detail of their lives? What is the significance and impact of seeing in this way? When are issues framed in oppositional terms and when are they seen as more multidimensional? These kinds of questions can be addressed when the notion of the separation of spheres and their opposition into contradictory stances is examined critically.

Rethinking dichotomies is aided by the deliberate choice of sites that bring supposedly oppositional categories into contact and interaction with each other. The case of paid child care is an example of such research, but many other sites can be selected or framed in such a way as to make possible the examination of dichotomization of spheres, as Strober and Tyack's (1980) discussion of women's mass movement into public school teaching has demonstrated. Research on occupations traditionally filled by women can also focus on the significance of domestic and public meanings and symbolism, as Kanter (1977) did in her classic *Men and Women of the Corporation*. She found, for example, that the meaning of secretarial jobs was heavily influenced by the domestic and helping symbolism associated with these jobs.

Research Methods

It will not do to replicate the qualitative/quantitative dichotomy in a paper whose fundamental purpose is to challenge dichotomization. Neither "quantitative" nor "qualitative" methods in and of themselves guarantee a certain approach to studying women's lives, as Statham's essay in this volume would confirm. Benenson's (1984) work on the class bias of the dual-career family model was achieved with quantitative methods and many qualitative studies have "discovered" frameworks that belong more to the researcher than to the subjects of the research. Women's own frameworks will be understood and honoured more often when research brings women's own pictures of their individual circumstances together in analytic combination with an understanding of the social, cultural, and economic setting of those circumstances.

Methods such as life history, diary collection and analysis, in-depth interviewing, and participant observation present some ways of getting at women's own individual stories and of approaching women's lives on their terms. These, in combination with methods that illuminate the "context" of women's lives, form a repertoire that may be used to answer the challenge of overcoming dichotomized frameworks. Methods such as these can be seen as extensions of each other, or as methods that naturally blend together in a research approach that respects women's lives and experiences as the source of both data and theory.

CONCLUSION

In this chapter I have argued that the study of women's work has been dominated by oppositional models of data collection and interpretation. Theories and research questions have been shaped by this dichotomy. In order to overcome dichotomization of our research results, we must consider our research questions and design our studies in the way that best suits the research problem at hand. Attention to methodological issues can overcome the dismemberment of women's lives and experiences by researchers and their theories. Broad pictures of women's work lives may still be created by methods that fit women's lives to a pre-set pattern, but pictures of the meaning attributed to those working lives must be created with methods that capture and honour individuals' words and nuances.

The dichotomization of women's lives into public and private realms presents those lives without their essential cohesiveness and can produce tales that make the women seem like willing participants in the creation of their own powerlessness rather than intelligent actors dealing as competently as they can. When dichotomy is challenged, data can be collected in analytic frameworks that both honour and add to the sense that women make of their own lives.

REFERENCES

Baruch, G., R. Barnett, & C. Rivers. 1983. *Lifeprints: New patterns of love and work for today's woman.* New York: Plume.
Benenson, H. 1984. Women's occupational and family achievement in the US class system: A critique of the dual-career family hypothesis. *British Journal of Sociology 35*, 19–41.
Cavendish, R. 1982. *Women on the line.* London: Routledge and Kegan Paul.
Chodorow, N. 1974. Family structure and feminine personality. In M.Z. Rosaldo & L. Lamphere, eds., *Woman, culture, and society* (pp. 43–66). Stanford: Stanford University Press.
Coser, R.L., & G. Rokoff. 1982. Women in the occupational world: Social

disruption and conflict. In R. Kahn-Hut, A.K. Daniels, & R. Colvard, eds., *Women and work: Problems and perspectives* (pp. 39–53). New York: Oxford University Press.

di Leonardo, M. 1987. The female world of cards and holidays: Women, families and the work of kinship. *Signs 12*, 440–53.

Ferree, M. 1976. Working-class jobs: Housework and paid work as sources of satisfaction. *Social Problems 23*, 431–41.

– 1985. Between two worlds: German feminist approaches to working-class women and work. *Signs 10*, 517–36.

Firth, R. 1965. *Primitive Polynesian economy*. New York: W.W. Norton.

Gaskell, J. 1983. The reproduction of family life: Perspectives of male and female adolescents. *British Journal of Sociology of Education 4*, 19–38.

– 1984. Gender and course choice: The orientation of male and female students. *Journal of Education 166*, 89–102.

Harding, S. 1987. Introduction: Is there a feminist method? In S. Harding, ed., *Feminism and methodology* (pp. 1–14). Bloomington, IN: Indiana University Press.

Howe, L.K. 1977. *Pink collar workers: Inside the world of women's work*. New York: G.P. Putnam's Sons.

Hunt, J.G., & L.L. Hunt. 1982. Dilemmas and contradictions of status: The case of the dual-career family. In R. Kahn-Hut, A. Kaplan Daniels, & R. Colvard, eds., *Women and work: Problems and perspectives* (pp. 181–92). New York: Oxford University Press.

Innes, R., & S. Innes. 1984. A qualitative study of caregivers' attitudes about child care. *Early Child Development and Care 15*, 133–48.

Kanter, R.M. 1977. *Men and women of the corporation*. New York: Basic Books.

Lamphere, L. 1990. Feminism and anthropology: Book review. *American Anthropologist 92*, 815.

Moore, H.L. 1989. *Feminism and anthropology*. Minneapolis: University of Minnesota Press.

Nash, J. 1981. The anthropology of work. *Anthropology of Work Review 2*, 3–7.

Nelson, M.K. 1988. Providing family day care: An analysis of home-based work. *Social Problems 35*, 78–94.

– 1989. Negotiating care: Relationships between family daycare providers and mothers. *Feminist Studies 15*, 7–33.

– 1990. Mothering others' children: The experiences of family day-care providers. *Signs 15*, 586–605.

Ortner, S. 1974. Is female to male as nature is to culture? In M.Z. Rosaldo & L. Lamphere, eds., *Woman, culture, and society* (pp. 67–88). Stanford: Stanford University Press.

Osako, M.M. 1982. Dilemmas of Japanese professional women. In R.

Kahn-Hut, A.K. Daniels, & R. Colvard, eds., *Women and work: Problems and perspectives* (pp. 123–35). New York: Oxford University Press.

Pleck, E.H. 1976. Two worlds in one: Work and family. *Journal of Social History 10*, 178–95.

Pleck, J.H. 1982. The Work-family role system. In R. Kahn-Hut, A.K. Daniels, & R. Colvard, eds., *Women and work: Problems and perspectives* (pp. 101–10). New York: Oxford University Press.

Porter, M. 1982. Standing on the edge: Working class housewives and the world of work. In J. West, ed., *Work, women and the labour market* (pp. 117–34). London: Routledge and Kegan Paul.

Rapp, R. 1991. Feminism and anthropology: Book review. *Gender and Society 5*, 122–3.

Rosaldo, M.Z. 1974. Woman, culture and society: A theoretical overview. In M.Z. Rosaldo & L. Lamphere, eds., *Woman, culture, and society* (pp. 17–42). Stanford: Stanford University Press.

– 1980. The use and abuse of anthropology: Reflections on feminism and cross-cultural understanding. *Signs 5*, 389–417.

Rosaldo, M.Z., & L. Lamphere. 1974. Introduction. In M.Z. Rosaldo & L. Lamphere, eds., *Woman, culture, and society* (pp. 1–16). Stanford: Stanford University Press.

Ruddick, S. 1989. *Maternal thinking: Toward a politics of peace.* New York: Ballantine Books.

Sacks, K.B. 1989. What's a life story got to do with it? In Personal Narratives Group, ed., *Interpreting women's lives: Feminist theory and personal narratives* (pp. 85–95). Bloomington: Indiana University Press.

Salaff, J.W. 1981. *Working daughters of Hong Kong: Filial piety or power in the family.* Cambridge: Cambridge University Press.

Saraceno, C. 1984. Shifts in public and private boundaries: Women as mothers and service workers in Italian daycare. *Feminist Studies 10*, 20–1.

Scarr, S. 1984. *Mother care, other care.* New York: Warner Books.

Strober, M.H., & D. Tyack. 1980. Why do women teach and men manage? A report on research in schools. *Signs 5*, 494–503.

Tom, A.R. 1986. To make a life for myself: An ethnography of a job training program. Unpublished doctoral dissertation, Stanford University, Stanford.

Wajcman, J. 1983. *Women in control: Dilemmas of a workers' cooperative.* New York: St Martin's Press.

3 Implications for Employment Intervention and Policy

DIANA L. MAWSON

The theory and research presented in this volume reflect the complexity of women's experience of paid work, stress, and the myriad factors affecting women's coping. The purpose of this chapter is to translate theories of employed women's stress and coping into interventions that facilitate women's effective coping with employment-related stress.

I define intervention as any measure that helps employed women cope with stress. Interventions may be designed and implemented at personal, organizational, and/or socioeconomic levels. Both women and men might have access to or be affected by such interventions. I include policy because it can serve employed people's interests by articulating mandates and objectives that focus on employment-related stressors. Policy provides the foundation from which practical intervention measures can evolve to specifically address working women's needs.

This chapter explores the development of women's stress interventions by asking three key questions: What is currently available as intervention, including policy, to address employed women's stress? Why is there a gap between existing interventions and women's apparent needs? And finally, what type of framework and process can we use to develop and implement interventions that help employed women cope with stress?

The following discussion of these three questions is based on Marshall's (1986) exploration of an ecological understanding of occupational stress. According to Marshall, "an ecological appreciation requires suspending bounded notions of cause and effect, and moving towards a more systemic way of thinking" (273). This systemic or ecological approach to understanding women's stress directs us to acknowledge those variables occuring at the micro (individual) and macro (organizational and societal) levels that account for women's experiences of inequity. Furthermore, an ecological perspective of women's workplace stress helps researchers and practitioners identify barriers to interventions that can effectively help women cope with employment stress.

INTERVENTIONS FOR WOMEN'S WORKPLACE STRESS

What interventions currently exist to help women cope with employment-related stress? The literature is replete with descriptions of approaches/philosophies, programs, and services that are geared to meet all employees' needs regardless of sex, and most interventions addressing workplace stress use one of two common approaches (see Ivancevich, Matteson, Freedman, & Phillips 1990).

Micro-level Interventions

The first approach focuses on the individual worker's experience of stress. Interventions using this approach teach individuals how to appraise, react, and cope with stress in ways to help them better manage stressful working situations. The strength of this approach is that it empowers individual workers and teaches them coping skills that can generalize across all life roles. The major weakness of this approach, however, is that it permits the status quo of the work environment and job-specific stressors to remain unchanged. Carried to an extreme, this can lead to a "blame the victim" attitude in which individuals are assumed not to have worked hard enough to adapt successfully to work stress. For example, working women may be seen as victims of their choice to work outside the home. Organizations, therefore, are not held accountable for adapting structure or policy to focus on women's stressors.

Macro-level Interventions

The second common approach to reducing workplace stress is through structural or institutional changes. The focus is shifted from the individual worker to job design and content, organizational structure, and working conditions. Interventions attempt to reduce the stress potential in work situations by reducing the number of stressors affecting workers. Management may address workplace stress by instilling more decision-making responsibility and control in specific jobs, by improving the structure of opportunities for employees, and by changing environmental conditions. To ensure comprehensive and successful intervention, the structural approach requires consideration of individual, job, and environmental factors to ensure comprehensive and successful intervention.

There are far fewer stress-related interventions at this macro-organizational level than those directed to the micro or individual level (Murphy 1988; Shipley & Orlans 1988). Employee-based interventions are easier to implement, require less involvement by management, are relatively inexpensive, and do not mandate large-scale structural changes. Moreover, individual-level interventions pose little threat to managers who resist change in their management style or in the corporate power structure. A major challenge facing intervention designers, then, is to ensure that diagnoses of workers' stress and implementation of subsequent interventions are made at the appropriate levels (Shipley & Orlans 1988). Placing the burden of coping on individual workers is likely to be ineffective at producing change when the stressor occurs at the organizational level.

Similar to the case for stress-related programs and services, there is a surprising paucity of reports on policies created specifically to address issues of employed women's stress. Policy regarding women and paid work has emerged in the areas of family care, sexual harassment, employment equity, pensions, and occupational health and safety. These policies function primarily to establish guidelines for gender equality in the work force and function only indirectly to reduce women's employment-related stress.

Employment-equity (Canada) or affirmative-action (United States) policies are examples of broad-based policy development aimed at improving women's status in the labour force. Specifically, equity policies represent governments' initial response to societal biases against women in the labour force. Equity policies have succeeded in drawing attention to the proportions, positions, and patterns of women's employment. However, equity and affirmative-action policies defined and enforced by government legislation have only begun to have an impact on issues of gender inequality and discrimination in the workplace. The organizations in which women will benefit most from equity policies are those that not only develop in-house equity policies but also make structural changes to facilitate women's entry and movement through the work force (e.g., Hall 1990; Harkess 1988).

Only one policy area more directly addresses women's employ-ment-related stress than do equity policies. This policy area focuses primarily on easing the strain between employment and family roles (Matthews & Rodin 1989; Schroeder 1989; Solomon 1991). More or-ganizations are recognizing that employees' family lives influence employees' productivity and effectiveness at work. The work and family domains can no longer be considered mutually exclusive, par-ticularly since employed women are still considered the primary caretakers in society. Policies that ease women's responsibilities in the caretaker role thus directly address family care as a major stressor among working women. According to Scarr, Phillips, and McCartney (1989), "working parents, especially mothers on whom most of the household and child care burdens fall, are constantly threatened psychologically by makeshift child care arrangements that fail unex-pectedly and by the high cost of quality child care" (1407). Working mothers of all social classes and cultural groups need access to child care (Schroeder 1989). To support women who are attempting to bal-ance work and family roles, different levels of government and many organizations in North America have instituted policies concerning leave time, child and elder care, and flexible working hours (Mat-thews & Rodin 1989; Solomon 1991).

Recommendations

Despite the paucity of existing interventions and related policies fo-cusing on employed women's stress, researchers provide numerous recommendations for designing and implementing approaches to support working women. Two themes characterize these recommen-dations: (a) systemic approach to change, and (b) management com-mitment to change.

Systems approach. Perhaps the most apparent theme is that workplace stress must be addressed using a systems approach (Akabas 1988; Il-gen 1990; Needleman & Nelson 1988). In a review of the World Health Organization's Health for All strategy, Levi (1990) describes work-related stress as an outcome of interactive processes in the "psychosocial occupational environment-stress-health system" (1143). To reduce the frequency and intensity of stressors emanating from this system, problem-solving must be primarily systems-ori-ented and interdisciplinary. Stress-management interventions or policies can target stress at several levels: (a) individual, (b) work-group unit, (c) organizational (system/structural), and (d) the interface between organization and individual (e.g., Hart 1987; Ivancevich et al. 1990).

In a discussion of the challenges and stresses experienced by professional employed women, Bhatnagar (1988) recommends a systems perspective for integrating women's problems into the larger organizational framework. Issues facing professional women are not solely concerns of women; rather, they should be seen as issues of a subsystem that have consequences for other subsystems and the organization as a whole. Systemic identification and analysis of *all* working women's problems (professional and nonprofessional) as organizational problems can therefore lay the foundation for corporate-level problem-solving.

Management commitment. The second key theme emerging from recommendations for addressing women's workplace stress is that management needs to make a significant and overt commitment to addressing the problem. This commitment will be most strongly conveyed when management agrees to the importance of making structural and cultural changes, and to policy implementation and enforcement. Together management and employees can review the organization to identify options for reducing workplace stress potential (Hall 1990). A review of organizational culture should be included to determine the extent to which broad socio-organizational norms and values are represented in the corporate culture (Bhatnagar 1988; Chusmir & Durand 1987; Hall 1990; Shipley & Orlans 1988; Solomon 1991).

Management's commitment to reducing work-related stress can be demonstrated by cooperating with labour. Together management and labour can actively introduce stress interventions to workers for whom the interventions are relevant. Unions can also be invaluable for soliciting women employees' participation in interventions. Management can simultaneously assure women employees that the organization is making concomitant changes in its structure to support individual-level changes, that use of interventions is valued by management and not stigmatized, and that the intervention is geared to meeting women's immediate needs. In addition, management can extend its concern for women employees beyond the organization by supporting community organizations and influencing public policy for women's issues (Hierich 1989). Employers are in a unique position to observe how public policy influences change in the workplace, and organizations can provide feedback to government about equity issues, gaps in policy coverage, and conflicting objectives of policies

(Nollen 1989). Employers can also effect significant change in social policy by influencing government to participate in solving women's work-home conflicts.

Finally, in order for organizations to operationalize their commitment to reduce workplace stress, it is necessary for management to be *motivated* to pursue change. Specifically, management will need to communicate its desire to create change and invite employees to share the initiative in achieving successful outcomes from stress-reduction strategies (Shipley & Orlans 1988). However, motivation to pursue change can only be derived from *awareness* of the need for change among *all* concerned parties: management, women and men employees, work units, and persons and organizations outside the workplace (Harkess 1988; Shipley & Orlans 1988). For women employees, being unaware of the chronicity of work stress may be the primary barrier preventing them from requesting change or help from management. According to Shipley and Orlans, "we can get locked into a behavioural chain under stress which is so automatic and habitual that we do not stop to think about it. Implicit here is a recognition of the sub-conscious as a potent force ... To bring such processes into awareness is to render them potentially amenable to change" (113).

Similarly, many organizations are unaware of the pervasiveness of gender inequality and its relationship to women's experience of employment stress. One possibility is for management to collect employees' reports of workplace stress in order to become fully aware of the specific manifestations of women's stress.

INTERVENTIONS AND WOMEN'S NEEDS: WHY THE DISPARITY?

It is apparent that governments and organizations have not fully addressed issues of employed women's stress by developing relevant policies and interventions based on published recommendations. Why is there a significant gap between existing interventions and women's apparent needs?

Denial of Personal Disadvantage

An explanation for why employed women have not received adequate organizational, community, or government support in dealing with employment-related stress may be provided by the theory of denial of personal disadvantage (Crosby, Pufall, Snyder, O'Connell, & Whalen 1989). Crosby and colleagues have examined the general failure to correct social and structural problems that maintain inequality in favour of the dominant culture. These researchers suggest that in the workplace women deny experiences of personal disadvantage and thus fail to acknowledge that they are affected by systemic problems of inequity. Working women therefore may not ask their employers to implement interventions and policy that could better support women employees.

Denial of personal disadvantage may occur for two reasons. First, women may compare their circumstances to those of selected individual women or subgroups of women, and not to the entire female work force within an organization (Crosby et al. 1989). Without aggregate data, individual women may not detect patterns of disadvantage that affect all women in an organization. Instead, individuals may mistakenly judge themselves more fortunate or less disadvantaged than other known women. Individual women may also validate and reinforce their coping skills by viewing their situations and opportunities as superior to those of similar other women. Second, if women deny experiences of disadvantage, they can avoid seeing themselves as victims of undesirable and uncontrollable circumstances.

The principles of Crosby et al.'s (1989) theory of denial of personal disadvantage may apply equally well to studying women's employment-related stress. In discussing stress interventions, I presume that employed women's stress is an outcome of social inequity and disadvantage. Hence if women use denial to cope with disadvantage, they may also use denial to cope with experiences of work-related stress. As with Crosby's hypotheses of women and disadvantage, unless individual women have information about all their workplace peers, they may not see common manifestations of stress and women employees' struggles to cope. Failing to gain the "bigger picture" of women and stress throughout the workplace, and failing to acknowledge the impact of stress on themselves as individuals, women do not ask employers for support and change.

Crosby et al. (1989) also challenge assumptions that employers knowingly deny, ignore, or otherwise fail to identify inequity and disadvantages experienced by women employees. Instead, employers may not respond to women employees' disadvantages because they do not correctly collect and use human resources data. Employers may review occupational group or individual-specific data for evidence of discrimination against women. However, only analysis of aggregate employee data can ensure identification of patterns in women's placement or movement in the work force. Without appropriate data to indicate inequities in opportunity and status and without women employees' requests for change, employers may fail to make improvements in the workplace.

A FRAMEWORK FOR WOMEN'S STRESS INTERVENTIONS

Ambiguous results of research on women's stress, combined with women's denial of personal disadvantage and related stress, may in part explain why women and organizations have failed to table work-stress as an issue for joint action. How then can governments, organizations, and women employees ensure development of relevant and effective interventions to help women cope?

Stress researchers have presented a variety of suggestions and recommendations for addressing women's employment-related stress (e.g., Akabas 1988; Bruening 1989; Chusmir & Durand 1987; Lowe 1989; Scarr et al. 1989). What is needed now is a comprehensive and cohesive approach to employed women's stress that can be designed, implemented, and evaluated from an identified theoretical position. Such a theoretical and practical framework would allow an integration of the numerous strategies proposed in the literature and allow for forging the link between research and intervention. The framework will necessarily be founded on a clear definition of stress relevant to working women. Furthermore, this framework will conceptualize women's workplace stress in systemic terms with accountability for change shared across individual, familial, organizational, and societal levels.

The definition of stress underlying my proposed framework presumes that women's work-related stress is a result of social inequality in work across all women's roles – work, family, and community (e.g., Akabas 1988; Lowe 1989). Inequities of power, reward, opportunity, status, and responsibility are examples of stressors familiar to women of all age, race, and occupational groups. Women's experiences of group and personal disadvantage follow from such conditions of inequity and may account for much of women's work-related stress.

The framework for addressing women's employment-related stress builds on the four models presented by Nieva and Gutek (1981) to explain women's status in the labour force. Each model presents a perspective for diagnosing the causes of inequity experienced by women. The perspective chosen for diagnosis also determines the approach(es) chosen to initiate change. These four causal models lend themselves particularly well to explaining and addressing women's workplace stress because of the presumed relationship between women's experiences of inequity, personal disadvantage, and stress. The following is a brief explanation of each model, including examples of interventions that reflect the underlying principles of each model.

Individual-deficit Model

The individual-deficit model assumes that women's problems are a result of their own weaknesses and character. These deficits may be due to socialization, but women are still blamed for their plight of low social and occupational status relative to men. The focus for change in this model is on women's self-improvement. An infrequent variation would suggest that male co-workers and managers confront their respective "deficits" of stereotyped thinking and insecurity about women in the workplace and at home (Tougas & Veilleux 1990).

Any interventions based on this model will require individuals or groups of women to learn about employment stress and coping, either through self-help materials or through training, counselling (including Employee Assistance Programs), workshops, or support groups. Topics might include time management, appraisal of stressors and resources, or barriers to career development. If organizations view individual-level workplace interventions as the only viable option for supporting their women employees, then management could also teach women about the use of power, politics, and resources in the organization (Chusmir & Franks 1988). When there are few women role models available in-house for women protégés, some authors suggest that organizations should enlist help from women outside the organization (e.g., Chusmir & Durand 1987). However, the onus remains on the woman employee to make use of such role models, whereas the organization frees itself of the responsibility to promote women internally to role-model status.

Structural/institutional Model

The structural/institutional model focuses on the impact that the organization's hierarchy, work-force composition, and career tracking has on individuals, and how individual employees' behaviour is determined by the work environment. Hence women's aspirations and personalities are considered products of their workplace. In terms of this model, problem-solving requires change in established formal and informal organizational systems. Solutions using this model may meet with resistance from organizations that do not perceive the need for change, or whose management or male work force is threatened by change.

Unfortunately, many organizational structures create and maintain sex-role stereotypes and power differences between the sexes. Women experience frustration and stress when an organization's structure and culture fail to acknowledge their talents, skills, and experience to the same extent as those of men. Management can help by increasing investment in women's career development, especially in nontraditional areas (Akabas 1988; Chusmir & Durand 1987; Needleman & Nelson 1988). In addition, when women are given token promotions or placements in male-defined and male-dominated structures, management can be sensitive to women's stress by downplaying differences between token women and the dominant male culture (Bhatnagar 1988; Chusmir & Franks 1988). Increasing the numbers of women throughout the structure can complement reductions in tokenism.

With regard to the interface between work and family, there are several places where institutional changes can assist. When promoting and transferring workers, organizations could also be aware of women's stress in the face of conflicting spousal career paths (Stoner & Hartman 1990). To better support women's continuous career development and ease the work/family strain of two-career families, organizations might consider eliminating hiring practices that disallow nepotism (Hall 1990). Consequently, organizations would lose neither husbands nor wives because of spousal promotions and transfers. Women's career development would be accommodated through promotions, lateral moves, or transfers. Organizations can also offer workshops for dual-career couples to help them cope with the stressors of career planning and spousal/family relocation (McCook, Folzer, Charlesworth, & Scholl 1991). Such workshops can teach dual-career couples how to balance career and family life effectively. Organizations benefit from such interventions with increased work performance, improved employee relations, and more successful human resource planning.

As part of an organization's efforts for change at the structural/ institutional level, management can also review and adjust salary policies (Akabas 1988; Needleman & Nelson 1988; Nieva & Gutek 1981). Equal pay for work of equal value will begin to address the stress associated with working women's experiences of poverty (Needleman & Nelson 1988; Scarr et al. 1989). Organizations can also help women employees by facilitating training for women in nontraditional work (Needleman & Nelson 1988).

Sex-role Model

The sex-role model considers how social norms determine the behaviours and attitudes appropriate to sex roles in and outside the
workplace. Sex-role prescriptions direct women to assume jobs that
have women performing the same functions at work as in other
roles. Organizational structures and cultures too often incorporate
societal sex-role prescriptions and therefore maintain in the workplace the inequity inherent in those prescriptions. Changes in sex-
role prescriptions are almost preconditions to successful structural
and cultural changes. Resocialization of men in the workplace and at
home is part of the solution based in this model. The goal is to loosen
sex-role constraints for both sexes.

The sex-role model accounts for the stress women experience as
they attempt to balance work and family roles (e.g., Nollen 1989;
Stoner & Hartman 1990). Sex-role prescriptions continue to feature
women as primary caretakers of home and family, in addition to
work-role responsibilities. Sex-role spillover from home to work has
created women's occupational ghettoization in the high-stress jobs of
the service, health-care, and clerical occupational groups (Lowe
1989).

Organizations have two major tasks to assume in order to help
women cope with sex-role conflicts: (a) support women's and men's
family roles, and (b) change sex-role perceptions in the workplace.
Regarding the work-family role conflict, organizations can help
women employees by not forcing women to choose between career-
only or career-and-family tracks (Hall 1990). Instead, child- and el-
der-care policies can be implemented to include flexible rules concerning work hours, work location, and leave options (Davidson &
Cooper 1986; Nollen 1989). Corporations might also consider spon-
sorship or development of care facilities to meet employees' family-
related needs (Needleman & Nelson 1988).

Breaking away from sex-role perceptions of women's work and career potential requires both short- and long-term strategies. Sex
roles have evolved in the workplace in response to those in society at
large and hence are extremely resistant to change and redefinition.
Improper sex-role socialization at work remains a primary cause of
women's stress (Chusmir & Durand 1987), and should be addressed
by management despite the slowness of society's shift away from sex-
role stereotypes. Organizational strategies include self-examination
by management of stereotyped values, expectations, and biases that
contribute to women's work stress (Bhatnagar 1988; Hall 1990; Nollen 1989). Sexual harassment of women employees is an example of

a stressor resulting from sex-role stereotyping. Sexual harassment policies can be created to protect and support women employees and to educate the workforce on inappropriate behaviours and related disciplinary actions (Rubenstein 1991).

Management can also address sex-role biases in the workplace by actively promoting acceptance and encouragement of women in equal roles (Chusmir & Durand 1987). Hiring, promotion, and evaluation of women ought to rely on nonsexist job descriptions and on performance measurement that does not devalue jobs prescribed as "female" or overvalue those prescribed as "male" (Needleman & Nelson 1988).

Finally, the social limitations experienced by women in male-dominated occupations or work-groups are an ongoing stressor resulting from sex-role stereotypes (Chusmir & Franks 1988). Management can help to reduce the isolation of women employees by promoting treatment of women as colleagues and by including them in formal and informal social circles at work.

Intergroup Model

The intergroup model focuses on the relationships between men and women as groups. The model suggests that stereotypes and rigid organizational structures emerge from exaggeration of between-group differences and within-group similarities. Interaction between groups is a major source of workplace stress, as are the hierarchical and power differences that emerge from polarization of sex-group differences.

Nieva and Gutek (1981) suggest that dispensing with group differences to produce a homogenized work force is not the ideal, nor is it a likely outcome of efforts for change. Instead, one means of reducing polarization of group differences is to shift organizational power structures. For example, organizations can provide women employees with more autonomy in determining their career paths and more management support in pursuing them (Akabas 1988). In addition, organizations can also rearrange the gender composition of the hierarchy by exposing men to the *advantages* of less powerful and less responsible positions (e.g., increased time with family, reduced stress). Women employees can also increase their power within the organizational structure if management invests more in women employees' career development at the top levels of the corporate hierarchy.

Reducing structural segregation that results from perceived sex differences can also help women employees cope. This can be partly accomplished by circulating among men accurate information on women's work performance. For example, Tougas and Veilleux (1990) demonstrated that when men are informed of unjust sex inequalities in the work force and of women's work performance, and if they are dissatisfied with these differences, they are more likely to initiate affirmative action strategies. Moreover, women can ensure that accurate information about their performance is available to work performance evaluators. Isolation and competition are both significant work stressors for women that are caused by the polarization of intergroup differences. To help reduce the impact of these stressors on women, management can create policies to help minimize or eliminate men-only networks. Management could also support the formation of mixed-group networks based on work skills or occupational groupings (Chusmir & Durand 1987; Chusmir & Franks 1988). Finally, male mentors can be assigned to women, and where possible female mentors to men (Bhatnagar 1988; Chusmir & Franks 1988).

The four models may provide the theoretical bases for proposing organizational change, thereby making interventions more effective in helping women cope with different aspects of employment stress. However, it is also apparent that no single model is sufficient to completely explain all types of women's workplace stress and to prescribe all possible solutions. Stress attributed to one factor or cause of inequity will always be linked to experiences of stress associated with another. Practitioners, program designers, and organizations are thus challenged to choose a model or set of strategies to work with as they seek ways to help women cope with employment stress.

A PROCESS FOR IMPLEMENTING WOMEN'S
STRESS INTERVENTIONS

Organizational Change

In their discussion of strategies to address work-force inequity, Nieva and Gutek (1981) suggest that the four causal models of inequity should be priorized to ensure effective implementation of strategies for change. The effectiveness of these strategies to address women's employment-related stress might be further enhanced if they could be implemented in a structured and ordered manner. Hall (1990) suggests such a process for the implementation of change, with a focus on the strain associated with work/family conflicts. However, Hall maintains that the proposed process can be applied to a broad range of employment-related stressors. The value of Hall's three-step process is its potential to help management organize an approach to women's workplace stress. Furthermore, employment-related stress can be analysed and addressed using any one or more of the four models (Nieva & Gutek 1981).

The first step of Hall's (1990) process requires senior management to set policy and values. Management is required to subject its members and the corporate culture to thorough examination. Hall argues that if traditional corporate values remain unchallenged, top management will fail to eliminate barriers to women's equality. As part of this exercise in the exploration of values, top management would identify what definitions of "good" executive, "good" parent, and "good" career are upheld by the existing structure. Career tracks for women could also be examined. This phase of self-reflection and participation by management can provide significant leverage for shifting the power structure in an organization. Rather than focusing on confrontation and criticism of existing structures or values, this step provides insights for valuing differences and respecting employed women's unique needs.

In step two, management creates dialogue about work-related stress experienced by employees at all levels of the organization. Women and men employees, management, and labour can report experiences and implications of work-stress in discussion or written form. Hall (1990) suggests that reflections on work-family stressors can be the basis of further dialogue about other work-related stress. At this stage it might be helpful to establish task groups to research and address particular stressors and coping mechanisms used by women employees.

The final step of Hall's (1990) proposed process for change focuses on creating and implementing strategies. Goals may include easing women's experience of the strain associated with home/work conflicts, discrimination in the workplace, and lack of supporting policies and interventions. Using results from research conducted in step two, strategies for change can be derived from one or more of the four causal models. This multifaceted approach to helping women cope with stress also allows management to mount a two-pronged action plan to affect change. Some efforts can be directed to reducing resistance to positive change, whereas others can focus on generating conditions conducive to it.

Potential Barriers

The drawbacks of Hall's (1990) model are common to other models that prescribe organizational change processes to address employment stress (e.g., Arroba & James 1990). These weaknesses reflect the challenges of overcoming specific barriers encountered during

design and implementation of interventions. In keeping with an ecological perspective of women's workplace stress, these barriers can be
of individual or systemic nature and can interact to confound change
processes.

Possibly the most significant barrier to initiatives for change like
those of Hall (1990) is the existing organizational structure and culture. Processes for change that propose top-down initiatives following an organization's hierarchical structure tend to protect and maintain existing structures and cultural norms of power. In most, if not
all, organizations, the power to generate or to deny change rests with
the majority male management complement. In models like Hall's,
the management faction defines, prescribes, and directs change. Ex-
pecting the male management cadre to publicly challenge and de-
nounce its own and therefore the organization's values and norms
may not produce notable changes in favour of women employees.
Changes relevant to working women's needs cannot be realized until
women are represented in numbers and status equal to men during
exercises of management and corporate self-analysis.

A second potential weakness in Hall's (1990) work is the linear process of problem analysis and action used to address work stress. Lin-
earity of process is assured when change is managed according to the
hierarchical structure of an organization. It is further enforced when
management has a pre-set agenda of steps for data collection, problem analysis, decision-making, and intervention implementation.
This sequenced approach to change effectively limits opportunities
for women employees to participate spontaneously and fully in identifying work stressors and appropriate coping interventions.

A third challenge to successful implementation of women's work-
stress interventions is striking a balance between attention to individual women's experiences of stress and the common needs of women
workers as a group. Two complementary tasks must be pursued to
achieve this balance. First, employers and men and women employees are required to move away from the dominant ideology of individual-deficit causes and solutions to women's work stress (e.g., Nelson & Quick 1985). By focusing on individual women or specific
occupational groups, organizations risk deflecting or even contra-
dicting the common needs of women workers. Instead, male and female workers and management need to facilitate development of a
collective identity of women workers. Within this collective, individual women can safely seek help to cope with workplace stress. The
collective with its consolidation of women's power can also provide a
voice for advocacy of individual members' needs.

The second task in establishing a balance between individual and group priorities for intervention is for organizations and all employees to respect the heterogeneity of women's needs and interests (Whitting & Quinn 1989). In order to develop relevant stress interventions and policy, management, employees, and labour must define and work from a theory of women workers' differences. Such a theory will acknowledge that women in any workplace are constituted not only of gender but of characteristics like race, class, and sexual orientation.

CONCLUSION

Although women compose a significant and growing portion of the paid work force, we see that they are mostly left to their own resources to cope with work stress. It is imperative that employers and government begin to realize that the difficulties experienced by employed women are in fact issues of organizational and social concern. Hence, the interests of women, labour, employers, and government must converge in looking for solutions to women's problems related to work stress. Solutions must be developed at both the macro level of policy, structural, and cultural changes, and the micro level of formal and informal interventions for individual employed women.

If work is to continue on developing strategies for addressing women's employment-related stress, research must continue to explore its variety and dynamics. Specifically, information is needed regarding women's perceptions of work-related stressors and their resources for coping. With this information, researchers and program designers can formulate an accurate and comprehensive definition of working women's stress on which to base development of relevant interventions.

Research on the relationship between women's experience of disadvantage and stress will contribute significantly to a more refined definition of employed women's stress. Specifically, it is important to establish if and to what extent working women experience personal and member-group disadvantage as a stressor. Moreover, women's use of denial as a coping strategy in relation to work stress requires further clarification. For example, is denial used more often in response to some disadvantages than others? And what other forms of coping are women using in response to stress associated with different types of disadvantage?

Evaluation of efforts for organizational change and stress interventions is essential to determine their appropriateness and effectiveness in helping women cope with workplace stress (Hierich 1989; Murphy 1988, 1989). When conducting evaluations, organizations and governments need to work with aggregate data (Bhatnagar

1988; Crosby et al. 1989; Sauter, Murphy, & Hurrell 1990). Only ag-gregate data will reveal patterns of intervention usage and outcomes, and women's perceptions of the relative merits of stress interven-tions. In keeping with a systems-oriented approach to problem solu-tion, feedback on interventions should be sought not only from women who have access to or who are exposed to interventions, but also from women who decline services, men employees, manage-ment, and labour.

REFERENCES

Akabas, S. 1988. Women, work and mental health: Room for improvement. *Journal of Primary Prevention 9*, 130–40.
Arroba, T., & K. James. 1990. Reducing the cost of stress: An organizational model. *Personnel Review 19*, 21–7.
Bhatnagar, D. 1988. Professional women in organizations: New paradigms for research and action. *Sex Roles 18*, 343–55.
Bruening, J. 1989. Women's stress quotient is climbing. *Occupational Hazards 50*, 45–7.
Chusmir, L., & D. Durand. 1987. Stress and the working woman. *Personnel 64*, 38–43.
Chusmir, L., & V. Franks. 1988. Stress and the woman manager. *Training and Development Journal 42*, 66–70.
Crosby, F., A. Pufall, R. Snyder, M. O'Connell, & P. Whalen. 1989. The denial of personal disadvantage among you, me, and all the other ostriches. In M. Crawford & M. Gentry, eds., *Gender and thought: Psychological perspectives* (pp. 79–99). New York: Verlag.
Davidson, M., & C. Cooper. 1986. Executive women under pressure. *International Review of Applied Psychology 35*, 301–26.
Hall, D. 1990. Promoting work/family balance: An organization-change approach. *Organizational Dynamics 18*, 5–17.
Harkess, S. 1988. Directions for the future. In A. Stromberg & S. Harkess, eds., *Women working: Theories and facts in perspective* (2nd ed., pp. 348–60). Mountain View, CA: Mayfield.
Hart, K. 1987. Managing stress in occupational settings: A selective review of current research and theory. *Journal of Managerial Psychology 2*, 11–17.
Hierich, M. 1989. Making stress management relevant to worksite wellness. *Advances 6*, 55–60.
Ilgen, D. 1990. Health issues at work: Opportunities for industrial/ organizational psychology. *American Psychologist 45*, 273–83.
Ivancevich, J., M. Matteson, S. Freedman, & J. Phillips. 1990. Worksite stress management interventions. *American Psychologist 45*, 252–61.

Levi, L. 1990. Occupational stress: Spice of life or kiss of death? *American Psychologist 45*, 1142–5.

Lowe, G. 1989. *Women, paid/unpaid work, and stress: New directions for research*. Ottawa: Canadian Advisory Council on the Status of Women.

McCook, L., S. Folzer, D. Charlesworth, & J. Scholl. 1991. Duelling careers. *Training and Development 45*, 40–4.

Marshall, J. 1986. Towards ecological understanding of occupational stress. *International Review of Applied Psychology 35*, 271–86.

Matthews, K., & J. Rodin. 1989. Women's changing work-roles: Impact on health, family, and public policy. *American Psychologist 44*, 1389–93.

Murphy, L. 1988. Workplace interventions for stress reduction and prevention. In C.L. Cooper & R. Payne, eds., *Causes, coping and consequences of stress at work* (pp. 301–39). Chichester, UK: Wiley.

– 1989. Overcoming industry's reluctance to use mind-body techniques. *Advances 6*, 49–52.

Needleman, R., & A. Nelson. 1988. Policy implications: The worth of women's work. In A. Statham, E. Miller, & H. Mauksch, eds., *The worth of women's work: A qualitative synthesis* (pp. 293–307). New York: State University of New York Press.

Nelson, D., & J. Quick. 1985. Professional women: Are distress and disease inevitable? *Academy of Management Review 10*, 206–18.

Nieva, V.F., & B.A. Gutek. 1981. *Women and work: A psychological perspective*. New York: Praeger.

Nollen, S. 1989. The work-family dilemma: How H.R. managers can help. *Personnel 66*, 25–30.

Rubenstein, M. 1991. Devising a sexual harassment policy. *Personnel Management 23*, 34–7.

Sauter, S., L. Murphy, & J. Hurrell. 1990. Prevention of work-related psychological disorders: A national strategy proposed by the National Institute for Occupational Safety and Health (NIOSH). *American Psychologist 45*, 1146–58.

Scarr, S., D. Phillips, & K. McCartney. 1989. Working mothers and their families. *American Psychologist 44*, 1402–9.

Schroeder, P. 1989. Toward a national family policy. *American Psychologist 44*, 1410–13.

Shipley, P., & V. Orlans. 1988. Stress research: An interventionist perspective. In J. Hurrel Jr, L. Murphy, S. Sauter, & C. Cooper, eds., *Occupational stress: Issues and developments in research* (pp. 110–22). New York: Taylor and Francis.

Solomon, C. 1991. Twenty-four hour employees. *Personnel Journal 70*, 56–63.

Stoner, C., & R. Hartman. 1990. Family responsibilities and career progress: The good, the bad, and the ugly. *Business Horizons 33*, 7–14.

Tougas, F., & F. Veilleux. 1990. The response of men to affirmative action strategies for women: The study of a predictive model. *Canadian Journal of Behavioural Science* 22, 424–32.

Whitting, G., & J. Quinn. 1989. Women and work: Preparing for an independent future. *Policy and Politics* 17, 337–45.

PART TWO

Employed Women in Context

4 Women in Management: Power and Powerlessness

NINA L. COLWILL

Women form about one-third of the management work force in Canada and the United States, depending on the source of information that one cites and the definition of "manager" that one is willing to accept. One cannot accurately assume that a manager is a manager is a manager, however. The large majority of women who are classified as managers make little money and exert little authority (Hymowitz & Schellhardt 1986). At the board level, only 44 per cent of the Fortune 1000 companies have even one female director (Friedman 1988). Among the Fortune 500, only 3.6 per cent of directors and 1.7 per cent of corporate officers are women (Von Glinow & Krzyczkowska-Mercer 1988).

I cannot remember a time when I was not bothered by the obvious paucity of women in management. In my twenties, I believed that education was all that was needed to rectify the situation – more university education and technical training for women and more formal and informal strategies for change in attitude aimed at men. It was all a matter, I believed, of educating women to fill the managerial positions and educating men to accept women as their managers. Men did not believe that women could manage organizations. Women only had to demonstrate their competence. Life was simple then. The task was clear.

Today, I am less naïve. Women are not finding it difficult to work their way into management because they have spent too few years in universities and community colleges. Women are not dead-ended in lower positions because there are too few books to guide them or because there has been too little research to document their dilemma. Women have not failed to educate themselves and they have not failed to explain their situation to others articulately and eloquently. If women have failed at anything, they have failed merely to understand power.

During the fifteen years that I have been working in the area of power, at least one fact has become clear: there is no one way to define it. Thus, in this chapter, I examine power from three different perspectives: (a) personal power – feeling in control of one's environment, feeling good about oneself; (b) interpersonal power – the ability to influence another; and (c) organizational power – the ability to mobilize resources, the ability to get things done.

Personal power is a belief – the belief that one is or is not in control of one's own environment – and it is virtually synonymous with Rotter's (1966) notion of Internal-External Locus of Control. Personal power is, therefore, the belief that one is powerful. Interpersonal power is power viewed at a more macro, dyadic level. It is the ability to influence another. Whether that influence stems from a property of the individual, a property of the interpersonal relationship, or a property of the organization (Ragins & Sundstrom 1989), it is the ability to influence rather than the antecedents of influence that forms the definition of interpersonal power. Organizational power is viewed as occupying the most macro position in this analysis. It is, in Kanter's (1977) words, "the ability to mobilize resources." Again, that ability can stem from many sources, including personal power, interpersonal power, or any of their antecedents. But organizational power, as discussed here, simply refers to one's ability to accomplish things, to "get things done" as Kanter (1977) says, to conduct the business of the organization effectively. Thus, personal power is a belief, interpersonal power is an ability (the ability to influence another), and organizational power is another ability (the ability to mobilize organizational resources).

In this chapter I examine these three perspectives on power as they apply to women in management and conclude that male and female managers face a power differential. As managers, women and men do not appear to differ in personal power; they are equally likely to feel in control of their own environment. In the realm of interpersonal power, the research suggests that women are less effective than men – that they are less able than men to influence others. In the area of organizational power, the latest research indicates that women are more effective than men at doing the business of these organizations (Tsui & Gutek 1984). Having thus argued that women and men face a complex power imbalance in their organizations, I then examine the strategies that female managers employ for coping with this imbalance.

In writing this chapter I explore, not the vast literature on gender differences that has been generated in the past thirty years, but merely the organizational literature since 1980. Thus, I have attempted to combat the accusation that "things" have changed too dramatically in the past few decades for us to consider the literature of the 1960s and the 1970s in the analysis of the problems facing today's managerial women. Fortunately for my argument and unfortunately for women in management, the literature of the 1980s and 1990s appears to reinforce the literature of the past. The story of women in and out of management is not merely a story of increased education, demonstrated competence, and logical progression. The story of women in management is a story of pain and frustration, a story of trust and mistrust, a story of power and powerlessness.

PERSONAL POWER

Personal power is a belief – the belief that one is in control of one's own environment. To have personal power is to feel good about oneself, to feel comfortable in one's own skin. The concept of Internal-External Locus of Control (I-E) probably comes closest to the notion of personal power. Internality, according to Rotter (1966), who brought us the concept and the measure twenty-five years ago, is the belief that one's destiny is determined by one's own efforts and endeavours; externality is the belief that one's fate is in the hands of luck or chance or powerful others. Although Rotter and his followers have conceptualized I-E as a personality characteristic (see, e.g., Lefcourt 1991), I see personal power merely as a belief that is as subject to change as are the circumstances or the insights that created that belief in the first place. When one views I-E in this way, it comes as no surprise to learn that women tend to be less internal than men, a finding that has been replicated in many cultures (Lefcourt 1982). The reality of women's lives in most countries is that the situations in which they often find themselves are situations that foster a feeling of "learned helplessness" (Lips 1981; Seligman 1975) – situations in which their actions do not produce the expected outcomes (Lefcourt 1991). Neither should it come as a surprise that women and men who find themselves in similar circumstances exhibit no such gender differences in locus of control. Over the past ten years, I have measured the I-E of hundreds of Bachelor of Commerce students, MBA students, and managers in Canada and abroad, and have never found consistent gender differences among these groups.

Nor have consistent gender differences in other personality traits been found among managers or would-be managers, and the similarities between men and women increase as their tenure in the managerial role increases (Gomez-Mejia 1983; Harlan & Weiss 1982; Miner & Smith 1982). The similarity between male and female managers is usually attributed to the fact that female managers, female entrepreneurs, and female management students all demonstrate more masculine personality characteristics than do women in less male-dominated fields (Brenner 1982; Miner & Smith 1982; Steinberg & Shapiro 1982; Sztaba & Colwill 1988). Even among female managers, those in the higher-echelon, male-dominated positions tend to demonstrate more masculine characteristics than do their sisters in less prestigious managerial positions (Moore & Rickel 1980). The jury is still out on this topic, however; there is a need for more systematic and controlled research comparing men and women in male-dominated and female-dominated occupations, before one can conclude that female managers are more like men than male managers are like women.

There are many specific sex differences in the general population that have not been found among managers, because people differ by circumstance as surely as they differ by sex. People with similar characteristics seek similar education and similar occupations, and these self-chosen circumstances render them even more similar (Colwill 1990). Whether men become more like their female colleagues or women merely become more like men has yet to be examined thoroughly. The attitudes, values, beliefs, and personalities of male and female managers are more similar than different, however, and there appear to be no consistent and significant differences in personal power between these two groups. The fact that female managers are no more external than are their male counterparts has positive implications for the coping strategies of women in management. The literature on self-efficacy, which is a cognate of I-E (Lefcourt 1991), suggests that people who consider themselves able to affect their environment are those most likely to persist with whatever coping strategies they employ (Bandura 1977). In the following section, I examine some of the many issues with which managerial women must cope daily – the myriad issues surrounding interpersonal power.

INTERPERSONAL POWER

Paula Johnson provides a good definition of interpersonal power through her definition of power: "the ability to get another person to do or to believe something he or she would not necessarily have done or believed spontaneously" (Johnson 1976, 100) – in short, "the ability to influence another person." At this more macro level, the dyadic level, power becomes more visible, and other people are more clearly able to detect and articulate its presence.

People exert interpersonal power through communication – through their verbal, nonverbal, and paraverbal communications. They convey their relative status through the words they speak (verbal), the way they speak these words (paraverbal), and the ways in which they communicate without words (nonverbal). Thus, interpersonal power goes beyond mere persuasion, which psychologists usually consider to be the ability to influence verbally (Stang & Wrightsman 1981). Neither the influenced nor the influencer need be aware of the process in order for influence to be exerted, in order for interpersonal power to be demonstrated. Whether communicated verbally, nonverbally, or paraverbally, the communication of status can define, maintain, or even change the balance of interpersonal power in a relationship (Spinner & Colwill 1982).

Do men and women differ in their interpersonal power – in their ability to influence others? And, more important for the purposes of this chapter, do male and female managers differ in this ability? There is some evidence among Israeli union leaders that women perceive themselves to be less influential than men (Izraeli 1985) – to have, in the language of this chapter, less interpersonal power than men. If organizational recognition, compensation, and perquisites are considered to be a measure of a person's ability to influence others, then women in organizations clearly have less interpersonal power than men do. They are paid less than men, even in female-dominated occupations (Abella 1984), a fact that women tend not to recognize (Major & Konar 1984). Women are, in fact, more than twice as likely as men to earn less than $15,000 a year for full-time work (Abella 1984). Even as managers, women are paid significantly less than men are, regardless of their educational backgrounds (Larwood, Szwajkowski, & Rose 1988), and, all things being equal, women move up the organizational ladder more slowly than do men (Stewart & Gudykunst 1982). Women are offered fewer training opportunities in their organizations and are less likely to be granted time off for educational purposes (Cahoon & Rowney 1984; Colwill & Josephson 1983).

At the presidential and vice-presidential level, where one would assume that interpersonal power is at its highest, women's salaries are 42 percent of the salaries of their male counterparts (Nelson & Berney 1987). Furthermore, women at the top are significantly less likely than men to receive other organizational perks such as stock options and bonuses. In one study (Kosinar 1981), male senior corporate officers received an average of six such perks, whereas no female senior corporate office received more than two.

But these data are drawn primarily from corporate North America. Surely one would expect that there are pockets of our working society in which women and men experience interpersonal power equally – in unions, for example, or in their own small businesses. But even in these areas, a gap exists. North American women are grossly underrepresented among union executives, and are, in fact, rarely found in those positions unless the union represents a female-dominated occupation (Chaison & Andrappan 1982). As for entrepreneurs, women tend to receive less favourable treatment from their banks than do men (Hinrick & O'Brien 1982). Although there is one study showing that men and women are equally likely to be offered funding by their lending institutions (Butner & Rosen 1989), women are more likely to be required to provide collateral for their loans (Swift & Riding 1988).

Moreover, the working lives of women extend beyond the realm of what we traditionally call "the workplace," and into the home. If interpersonal power is measured by the extent to which people can influence others to do work for them, then the family situation of most men renders them interpersonally powerful. The female sex role in at least thirty countries holds women responsible for work in the home, and this is true in our society even in families in which men's "help" is substantial (Bem 1987; Williams & Best 1982). The Basset Report (Basset 1985), an in-depth study of Canadian dual-career families, showed that substantial housework among husbands is anything but the norm, however; in only half of Basset's households did men *ever* do cleaning and grocery shopping; in only one-third did they share cooking and laundry.

One might assume that the frustration of such inequitable treatment would prove to be extremely stressful for any woman, yet only 56 per cent of Basset's dual-career women reported that responsibility for housework caused stress in their families. It is difficult to imagine why this might be the case. Perhaps there are many women who do not consider the unequal distribution of household labour to be inequitable, so the situation is not a source of frustration to them. In Yogev's (1981) study of married female professors, for instance, many of these women acknowledged that they spent less time on their careers and more time on child care and housework than did their husbands; yet they did not consider the division of labour in their homes to be inequitable.

Women's and men's relative positions of interpersonal power are reinforced at home by women's and men's relative positions of interpersonal power in the workplace, and are reinforced in the workplace by their relative power positions at home. It is known, for example, that many family decisions are made on the basis of financial contribution – that the spouse who earns the lowest salary, for instance, is the spouse who stays home with sick children (Friedman 1988). Since women are more likely to earn less than their husbands, their bargaining power is lower, and they are usually left with the lion's share of family responsibilities. By assuming greater home responsibilities, a woman can place herself in a precarious organizational position, allowing her energy to be sapped and reinforcing the sex-role stereotype of the poorly committed female worker (Blau 1984).

Prejudice and discrimination against women clearly pervade today's organizations, but the situation is more complicated than psychologists and sociologists had previously supposed. It is known, for instance, that gender is most likely to be used as a basis for discrimination in hiring and promotion situations in which insufficient information about the competence of the applicant has been provided (Hodgins & Kalin 1985). Even in such male-dominated fields as engineering, women are more likely to be treated objectively when information about their competence is provided (Gerdes & Garber 1983). As Drazin and Auster (1987) point out, however, it is not always the people who have objective information about the competence of a female manager who are making decisions about her promotional opportunities and financial remuneration; such decisions are often made above the head of the direct supervisor, by people who have little daily contact with the incumbent. As long as a general bias against women prevails in our organizations, individual decisions will continue to be biased toward men (Nieva & Gutek 1981), and men will continue to gain interpersonal power at the expense of women.

There is some evidence that prejudice against women, per se, may not be as strong as a prejudice against the things that women do – that it is doing womanly things rather than being a woman that renders one relatively powerless. In a series of in-basket studies conducted at the University of Manitoba, both women and men elicited greater compliance when they used traditionally masculine language, or traditional male power strategies, or when they were employed in a male-dominated occupation (Colwill, Perlman, & Spinner 1982, 1983; Colwill, Pollock, & Sztaba 1986; Sztaba & Colwill 1986). The latter study is particularly telling; subjects (home economics students) did not rate home economists as less powerful than engineers, but regardless of the sex of the would-be influencer, engineers elicited greater compliance with their requests than did home economists. This finding suggests that the factors determining interpersonal power may operate below the awareness of the people interpreting that power. Taken together, the University of Manitoba studies suggest that there is a perceptual differentiation between the stereotypes of and attitudes toward "women" and "the things that women do."

Although the distinction between "women" and "the things that women do" may appear initially to be trivial, it is, in fact, an extremely important distinction. As sex roles begin to change, or as people perceive that they change, "the things that women do" will not be as easily distinguished from "the things that men do" as they were three, two, or even one decade ago. The distinction between "men" and "women" is an obvious one – an obvious basis for allocating interpersonal power – but the distinction between the male and female sex role has the potential to disappear over time. If "the things that women do" and "the things that men do" begin to blend, then the entire gender-determined basis for allocating interpersonal power also has the potential to disappear. As a society, however, we do not seem to be ready to allow ourselves to be influenced by others on the basis of their competence and their arguments rather than their sex or their sex role. On the dyadic level, on the level at which managers must interact hundreds of times daily, men have a clear edge, an edge that is reinforced in their roles of husband and father as surely as it is reinforced in the workplace. Little is known about the ways in which female managers cope with this inequity through explicit attempts to exert interpersonal power. Persuasion, or interpersonal power gained through verbal appeal (Stang & Wrightsman 1981), is an obvious coping strategy for study, being one of the most easily measured routes to interpersonal power. The collection of such data is a complex matter, however, because of the difficulty in separating gender and organizational status. In Mainiero's (1986) study of organizational empowerment strategies, for instance, women were found to be more acquiescent than were men; yet Mainiero's reanalysis of her data showed job dependency to be a better predictor of acquiescence than was gender. Ironically, the greatest hope for gender equality in the interpersonal power of managers may lie in the area of organizational power.

ORGANIZATIONAL POWER

Rosabeth Moss Kanter (1977) has defined power as "the ability to get things done, to mobilize resources, to get and use whatever it is that a person needs for the goals he or she is attempting to meet" (166). It is this definition that I have adopted, not to define "power" as Kanter has done, but to define the third, most macro level of power in this analysis, organizational power. It is to this level of power – the level of mobilizing resources of "getting things done" – that most management texts are addressed, with personal power and interpersonal power being discussed only as they have bearing upon organizational power (see, e.g., Mintzberg 1983).

Dipboye's (1987) review of the area of managerial effectiveness is the literature most closely related to organizational power, for it examines the extent to which male and female managers are able to and are perceived to "get things done" in their organizations. This literature on managerial effectiveness shows a definite edge for women. Female and male managers are evaluated by their subordinates as being equally effective (Terborg & Shingledecker 1983), but female managers are viewed by their immediate supervisors, and by their peers as being more effective than their male counterparts (Tsui & Gutek 1984). This positive evaluation of women as managers is particularly strong among women – among female MBA students (Mickalachki & Mickalachki 1984) and among female managers (Jabes 1980). In Jabes's study, in fact, female managers rated their managerial sisters as more intelligent, more likeable, more successful, and more able than their male counterparts.

The discrepancy is an obvious one: when organizational power is defined as the ability to mobilize resources, women have greater organizational power than do men, in a world in which their access to organizational resources (Stewart & Gudykunst 1982) and interpersonal power is more limited than that of their male counterparts. In the fairest and most rational of systems, today's top executives would recognize this discrepancy and women would be skyrocketed into upper management with the tools to affect even greater change. While awaiting this event, it might be interesting to examine the coping strategies of today's managerial women.

WOMEN IN MANAGEMENT

The thesis of this chapter is a simple one that will provide no startling revelation for even the most naïve. The lack of women in management is an issue, not of education and training, but of power. Time, patience, and women's self-improvement do not appear to be the solution. The solution, in fact, is similar to the problem: power.

Now, to review the power scores of male and female managers. In personal power, in beliefs about one's own control of one's environment, there are no consistent sex differences among managers. In interpersonal power, the ability to influence others, there are large and many sex differences, with men enjoying greater influence than women at home and in their organizations. And finally, in the area of organizational power, in the ability to mobilize resources, it is beginning to appear that managerial women are perceived by more people as being more effective than their male counterparts.

This beginning research raises as many questions as it answers. Foremost among them is the obvious question: "If women are less interpersonally powerful than men – if they are less able to influence others – how are they better able than men to mobilize resources?" or more simply, "How can women be more effective than men, while being less influential?" Although I know of no clear answer to this question, I find myself returning, when I consider it, to the concept of personal power – feeling in control of one's environment. Personal power or internal locus of control is an important organizational concept, because it is strongly related to organizational power. It is known, for instance, that internals are better than externals at negotiation and at solving difficult job-related problems, and that their workers tend to be more satisfied than are the subordinates of externals (Brousseau 1984; Johnson, Lathans, & Hennesey 1984; Stolte 1983). Furthermore, within supportive organizational environments, internals take more active roles in their career management than do externals and are more likely than externals to be promoted (Hammer & Vardi 1981). Although there are no consistent sex differences in locus of control among managers and managerial students, it is possible that locus of control and gender interact in some way, so that for women even moderate levels of internal locus of control may result in high levels of managerial effectiveness.

In any case, women's organizational effectiveness will, in the long run, undoubtedly increase their status, which will, in turn, increase their interpersonal power. As their interpersonal power increases, women cannot fail to become even more organizationally effective, for the ability to mobilize resources is often dependent upon the ability to influence others. In the short run (and the short run, Morrison, White, & Van Velsor [1987] predict, will span several decades), there are day-to-day inequities in interpersonal power to address. It is to these inequities that people usually refer when speaking of sex discrimination in the workplace. And it is women's techniques for coping with these inequities that are of interest here.

Women learn to cope with discrimination in a variety of ways. One of these methods, which researchers are only beginning to address,

has come to be known as "the denial of personal discrimination."
There is strong evidence that women, while clearly recognizing the
fact of sex discrimination in the workplace, fail to see how they, personally, have experienced discrimination (Crosby 1984). Against all
evidence to the contrary, individual women tend to see themselves as
being justly treated (Abbondanza 1982; Guimond, Dubé, & Abbondanza 1984). How is this possible? Abbondanza's (1982, 1983; Abbondanza & Dubé-Simard 1982) research indicates that women,
striving to perceive their world as a just and fair place, compare their
situation, not to the situation of men in comparable positions, but to
the condition of other, less fortunate women.

Although denial is usually considered to be an ineffective coping
strategy, it may have some advantages. Denial of personal discrimination may prevent individual women from solving their unseen
problems, but it has not prevented women in large numbers from
fighting for the rights of women in general. Denial of personal discrimination may make it possible for women to get on with the day-
to-day business of effective and competent work behaviour. Perhaps,
by refusing to accept the possibility that they are the objects of discrimination, individual women are creating a new reality for themselves, and, by association, for women in general.

Another way in which women cope with an inordinately difficult
climb up the organizational ladder and an inability to strike a fair
bargain at home is to eschew marriage and family. In Canada, 91 per
cent of male managers but only 62 per cent of female managers are
married. Of these married managers, 73 per cent of the men have
children living at home, but only 41 per cent of the women do (Nakamura & Nakamura 1989). In the United States, women without
children tend to experience slight upward mobility by the age of
thirty-two, whereas women with children experience slight down-
ward mobility by that age (Sewell, Hauser, & Wolf 1980). Even for
childless women, however, upward mobility is slower than for men,
whether those men have children or not.

One rational way in which women could cope with their family and
managerial lives would be to leave their organizations. Whether or
not they are really making this choice in large numbers, however, is
open to debate. Taylor's (1986) study of 1,039 female MBAs from sev-
enteen American business schools shows that 30 per cent of these
fast-trackers left their jobs ten years after their graduation for self-
employment or unemployment, and Fraker (1984) argues that female managers are quitting at a faster rate than are men. However,
Karen Korabik's (personal communication) more recent research
suggests that these preliminary data were not representative, and

that the picture is more complex than it appeared initially. Whether or not women are leaving their corporations at a faster rate than men, as recent magazine articles (DeGeorge 1987) and books (Bools & Swan 1989) suggest, they are certainly starting their own businesses at an unprecedented rate – at five times the rate of men (Statistics Canada 1988).

Whatever the organizational problems facing them, women, like men, learn to cope with the stress of their working lives through the support of other people. However, there is increasing evidence that the nature of this support differs for males and females. Women, in general, are known to have emotionally richer relationships than men, characterized by greater emotional sharing and intimacy, and less activity-orientation, task-orientation, and interest-orientation, than are the relationships of men (Aries & Johnson 1983; Caldwell & Peplau 1982). Although women tend to value their co-worker relationships more highly than men do and tend to form same-sex networks, they often find themselves excluded from the informal, male-dominated networks of their organizations, a process that bans them from the power strongholds of the organization, even to the extent of lowering their probability of promotion (Brass 1985; Forisha & Goldman 1981). Instead, women are more likely than men to rely on sources of support that are external to the organization – family and non-co-working friends (Etzion 1984; Schilling & Fuehrer 1987).

Research and writing in the area of women in management has been classified as being of two types – person-centred and organization-centred (Fagenson 1988; Gregory 1988). In this chapter, as in most of the literature in this area, I have taken a person-centred approach, addressing those things that women can do and have done in order to cope with the situation they face as managers. Clearly, the organization-centred approach has received less attention than it deserves, perhaps because it is less gratifying and more difficult for researchers to address these macro issues of organizational restructuring and massive economic social change than it is for them to study the behaviours of women and men as they play their managerial roles with other women and men. Few organizations but many individual women have contributed greatly to change; few organizations but many individual women seek information to affect change. Yet, however new and underdeveloped the field of women and management (Sekaran 1988), it is beginning to tackle the big issue – "the 'genderedness' of organizational management practices and conditions" (Calas & Smirchich 1989, 3) – the issue of power.

REFERENCES

Abbondanza, M. 1982, July. *Categorization, identification and feelings of deprivation: A multidimensional study of the homemaker and employed mothers' social perceptions.* Paper presented at the Twentieth International Congress of Applied Psychology, Edinburgh.

– 1983, June. *Cognitive barriers to intergroup equality between the sexes.* Paper presented at the meeting of the Canadian Psychological Association, Winnipeg.

Abbondanza, M., & L. Dubé-Simard. 1982. La mère au travail et la mère au foyer: deux réalités cognitives et évaluatives. *Revue québecoise de psychologie 3*(3), 3–16.

Abella, Judge R.S. 1984. *Equality in employment: A Royal Commission Report.* Ottawa: Supply and Services Canada.

Aries, E.J., & F.L. Johnson. 1983. Close friendship in adulthood: Conversation content between same-sex friends. *Sex Roles 9*, 1183–96.

Bandura, A. 1977. Self-efficacy: Toward a unifying theory of behavioral change. *Psychological Review 84*, 191–215.

Basset, I. 1985. *The Basset Report: Career success and Canadian Women.* Toronto: Collins.

Bem, D. 1987. A consumer's guide to dual-career marriages. *ILR Report 25*(1), 10–12.

Billings, A.G., & R.H. Moos. 1982. Stressful life events and symptoms: A longitudinal model. *Health Psychology 1*, 99–117.

Blau, F.D. 1984. Occupational segregation and labor market discrimination. In B.F. Reskin, ed., *Sex segregation in the workplace: Trends, explanations, remedies* (pp. 117–43). Washington: DC: National Academy Press.

Bools, B., & L. Swan. 1989. *Power failure.* New York: St Martin's Press.

Brass, D.J. 1985. Men's and women's network: A study of interaction patterns and influence in an organization, *Academy of Management Journal 28*, 327–43.

Brenner, O.C. 1982. Relationship of education to sex, managerial status, and the managerial stereotype. *Journal of Applied Psychology 67*, 380–3.

Brousseau, K.R. 1984. Job-person dynamics and career development. In K.M. Rowland & G.R. Ferris, eds., *Research in personnel and human resources management* (2: 125–54). Greenwich: JAI Press.

Butner, H., & B. Rosen. 1989. Funding new business ventures: Are decision makers biased against women entrepreneurs? *Journal of Business Venturing 4*, 249–61.

Cahoon, A.R., & J.I.A. Rowney. 1984, June. *Variables influencing job satisfaction and stress in female managers.* Paper presented at the meeting of the Canadian Psychological Association, Ottawa.

Calas, M., & L. Smirchich. 1989, August. Using the "F" word: *Feminist theories and the social consequences of organizational research*. Meeting of the Academy of Management, Washington, DC.

Caldwell, M.A., & L.A. Peplau. 1982. Sex differences in same-sex friendship. *Sex Roles 8*, 721–32.

Chaison, G.N., & P. Andrappan. 1982. Characteristics of female union officers in Canada. *Industrial Relations 37*, 765–78.

Colwill, N.L. 1990. Gender differences in management: The study of sex and circumstance. *Women in Management 1*(4), 8.

Colwill, N.L., & W.L. Josephson. 1983. Attitudes toward equal opportunity in employment: The case of one Canadian government department. *Business Quarterly 48*, 87–93.

Colwill, N.L., D. Perlman, & B. Spinner. 1982, June. *Effective power styles for women and men: A test of Johnson's model*. Paper presented at the meeting of the Canadian Psychological Association, Montreal.

Colwill, N.L., M. Pollock, & T.I. Sztaba. 1986. Power in home economics: An individual and professional issue. *Canadian Home Economics Journal 36*(2), 59–61.

Crosby, F. 1984. The denial of personal discrimination. *American Behavioral Scientist 27*, 371–86.

DeGeorge, C. 1987, 22 June. Where are they now? Business Week's leading corporate women of 1976. *Business Week*, 76–7.

Dipboye, R.L. 1987. Problems and progress of women in management. In K.S. Koziara, M.H. Moskow, & L.D. Tanner, eds., *Working women: Past, present, future* (pp. 118–53). Washington, DC: Industrial Relations Research Association Series, the Bureau of National Affairs.

Drazin, R., & E.R. Auster. 1987. Wage differences between men and women: Performance appraisal ratings vs. salary allocations as the locus of bias. *Human Resource Management 26*, 157–68.

Etzion, D. 1984. Moderating effect of social support on the stress-burnout relationship. *Journal of Applied Psychology 69*, 615–22.

Fagenson, E. 1988, April. *On women in management research methodology: Your theory is showing*. Proceedings, Women in Management Research Symposium, Mount Saint Vincent University, Halifax, NS.

Forisha, B.L., & B.H. Goldman. 1981. *Outsiders on the inside: Women and organizations*. Englewood Cliffs, NJ: Prentice-Hall.

Fraker, S. 1984, 16 April. Why women aren't getting to the top. *Fortune 109*, 40–5.

Friedman, D.E. 1988. The invisible barrier to women in business. *Inside Guide 2*(5), 75–9.

Gerdes, E.P., & D.M. Garber. 1983. Sex bins in hiring: Effects of job demands and applicant competence. *Sex Roles 9*, 307–19

Gomez-Mejia, L.R. 1983. Sex differences during occupational socialization. *Academy of Management Journal 26*, 492–9.

Gregory, A. 1988, April. *Where are we coming from and where are we going? Theoretical, research and methodological perspectives on women in management.* Proceedings, Women in Management Research Symposium, Mount Saint Vincent University, Halifax, NS.

Guimond, S., L. Dubé, & M. Abbondanza. 1984, June. *Représentations cognitives des inégalités entre les hommes et les femmes en France et au Québec: 1. Le domaine de l'education.* Paper presented at the meeting of the Canadian Psychological Association, Ottawa.

Hammer, T.H., & Y. Vardi. 1981. Locus of control and career self-management among nonsupervisory employees in industrial settings. *Journal of Vocational Behavior 18*, 13–29.

Harlan, A., & C.L. Weiss. 1982. Sex differences in factors affecting managerial career advancement. In P.A. Wallace, ed., *Women in the workplace* (pp. 59–100). Boston: Auburn House.

Hinrick, R., & M O'Brien. 1982. The woman entrepreneur as a reflection of the type of business. In K. Vesper, ed., *Frontiers of entrepreneurship research* (pp. 54–67). Wellesley, MA: Babson College.

Hodgins, D.C., & R. Kalin. 1985. Reducing sex bias in judgements of occupational suitability by the provision of sex-typed personality information. *Canadian Journal of Behavioural Science 17*, 346–58.

Hymowitz, C., & T.D. Schellhardt. 1986, 24 March. The glass ceiling. *Wall Street Journal*, pp. 1D, 4D–5D.

Izraeli, D.N. 1985. Sex differences in self-reported influence among union officers. *Journal of Applied Psychology 70*, 148–57.

Jabes, J. 1980. Causal attributions and sex-role stereotypes in the perceptions of female managers. *Canadian Journal of Behavioural Science 12*, 52–63.

Johnson, P. 1976. Women and power: Toward a theory of effectiveness. *Journal of Social Issues 32*(3), 99–110.

Johnson, A.L., F. Lathans, & H.W. Hennesey. 1984. The role of locus of control in leader influence behaviour. *Personnel Psychology 37*, 61–75.

Kanter, R.M. 1977. *Men and women of the corporation.* New York: Basic Books.

Kosinar, S. 1981. Socialization and self-esteem: Women in management. In B.L. Forisha & B.H. Goldman, eds., *Outsiders on the inside* (pp. 31–41). Englewood Cliffs, NJ: Prentice-Hall.

Larwood, L., E. Szwajkowski, & S. Rose. 1988. Sex and race discrimination resulting from manager-client relationships: Applying the rational bias theory of managerial discrimination. *Sex Roles 18*, 9–29.

Lefcourt, H.M. 1982. *Locus of control.* Hillsdale, NJ: Erlbaum.

– 1991. Locus of control. In J.P. Robinson, P.R. Shaver, & L.S. Wrightsman, eds., *Measures of personality and social psychological attitudes: Volume 1 of measures of social psychological attitudes* (pp. 413–99). New York: Academic Press.

Lips, H.M. 1981. *Women, men, and the psychology of power*. Englewood Cliffs, NJ: Prentice-Hall.

Mainiero, L.A. 1986. Coping with powerlessness: The relationship of gender and job dependency to empowerment-strategy usage. *Administrative Science Quarterly 31*, 633–53.

Major, B., & E. Konar. 1984. An investigation of sex differences in pay expectations and their possible causes. *Academy of Management Journal 27*(4), 777–92.

Mickalachki, D.M., & A. Mickalachki. 1984. MBA women: The new pioneers. *Business Quarterly 49*, 110–15.

Miner, J.B., & N.R. Smith. 1982. Decline and stabilization of managerial motivation over a twenty-year period. *Journal of Applied Psychology 67*, 297–305.

Mintzberg, H. 1983. *Power in and around organizations*. Englewood Cliffs, NJ: Prentice-Hall.

Moore, L.M., & A.V. Rickel. 1980. Characteristics of women in traditional and nontraditional managerial roles. *Personnel Psychology 33*, 317–33.

Morrison, A.M., R.P. White, & E. Van Velsor. 1987. *Breaking the glass ceiling*. Reading, MA: Addison-Wesley.

Nakamura, A., & M. Nakamura. 1989, July. *Children, work and women: A managerial perspective*. Working Paper Series No. NC 89-18, National Centre for Management Research and Development, University of Western Ontario.

Nelson, S., & K. Berney. 1987, 18–27 May. Women: The second wave. *Nation's Business*.

Nieva, V.F., & B.A. Gutek. 1981. *Women and work: A psychological perspective*. New York: Praeger.

Ragins, B.R., & E. Sundstrom. 1989. Gender and power in organizations: A longitudinal perspective. *Psychological Bulletin 105*, 51–88.

Rotter, J. 1966. Generalized expectancies for internal vs. external control of reinforcement. *Psychological Monographs 80*, 1–28.

Schilling, K.M., & A. Fuehrer. 1987, May. *Sex differences in social support in the workplace*. Paper presented at the meeting of the Midwestern Psychological Association, Chicago, IL.

Sekaran, U. 1988, April. *Methodological and theoretical issues in women in management research*. Proceedings, Women in Management Research Symposium, Mount Saint Vincent University, Halifax, NS.

Seligman, M.E.P. 1975. *Helplessness: On depression, development and death*. San Francisco: Freeman.

Sewell, W.H., R.M. Hauser, & W.C. Wolf. 1980. Sex, schooling, and occupational success. *American Journal of Sociology 86*, 551–83.

Spinner, B., & N.L. Colwill. 1982. Power. In N.L. Colwill, ed., *The new partnership: Women and men in organizations* (pp. 113–34). Palo Alto, CA: Mayfield.

Stang, D.J., & L.S. Wrightsman. 1981. *Dictionary of social behavior and social research methods.* Monterey, CA: Brooks/Cole.

Statistics Canada. 1988. *Business owners in Canada, 1981–1986.* Small Business and Special Surveys.

Steinberg, R., & S. Shapiro. 1982. Sex differences in personality traits of female and male Master of Business Administration students. *Journal of Applied Psychology 67,* 306–10.

Stewart, L., & W. Gudykunst. 1982. Differential factors influencing the hierarchial level and number of promotions of males and females within an organization. *Academy of Management Journal 97,* 586–97.

Stolte, J.F. 1983. Self-efficacy: Sources and consequences in negotiation networks. *Journal of Social Psychology 119,* 69–75.

Swift, C., & A. Riding. 1988. *Giving credit where it's due: Women business owners and Canadian financial institutions.* Paper presented at the International Council for Small Business Annual Meeting, Helsinki, Finland.

Sztaba, T.I., & N.L. Colwill. 1986. Genderlect and perceptions: Does it pay to be a lady? Unpublished manuscript, University of Manitoba.

Sztaba, T.I., & N.L. Colwill. 1988. Secretarial and management students: Attitudes, attributes, and career choice consideration. *Sex Roles 19,* 651–65.

Taylor, A. 1986, 18 Aug. Why women managers are bailing out. *Fortune 114,* 16–23.

Terborg, J.R., & P. Shingledecker. 1983. Employee reactions to supervision and work evaluation as a function of subordinate and manager sex. *Sex Roles 9,* 813–24.

Tsui, A.S., & B.A. Gutek. 1984. A role set analysis of gender differences in performance, affective relationships, and career success of industrial middle managers. *Academy of Management Journal 27,* 619–35.

Von Glinow, M.A., & A. Krzyczkowska-Mercer. 1988. Women in corporate America: A caste of thousands. *New Management 6,* Summer, 36–42.

Williams, J.E., & D.L. Best. 1982. *Measuring sex stereotypes: A thirty-nation study.* Beverly Hills, CA: Sage.

Yogev, S. 1981. Do professional women have egalitarian marital relationships? *Journal of Marriage and the Family 43,* 865–71.

5 Patterns of Cultural Awareness: Coping Strategies for Women Managers

JUDI MARSHALL

In this chapter I explore the contexts within which employed women interpret and cope with stress. Specifically, I look at issues of fit between women managers and the organizational cultures, and the consequences for individual women's coping behaviour. I paint a general picture, realizing as I do so that this is a world also of great variety. I am particularly interested in looking at how the subtle and powerful processes by which organizational cultures operate may affect the experiences of women.

I believe we cannot understand stress and coping fully unless we take a contextualized view. A specific instance makes limited sense if we do not appreciate the context of meaning in which it is interpreted. The analysis below shows how multilayered and contentious achieving interpretations of meaning is. This chapter therefore seeks to provide a general, theoretical complement to the more focused views taken elsewhere in the volume.

In looking at women's coping, I borrow a concept from social work, that of "failure to thrive." This is applied to children who, for no identifiable reason, are failing to show satisfactory development. I think many women managers are in similar positions. Their coping is directed more toward surviving than thriving, and may therefore be constraining in the longer term.

I look first at organizational cultures as they incorporate male and female values. This analysis identifies cultures as largely male-dominated and women as often symbols of difference. I then go on to look at how cultures and their underlying value patterns are maintained. From these bases, a model of forms of awareness as coping strategies is synthesized.

MALE AND FEMALE VALUES

To make sense of culture, I use a broad-brush distinction between male and female values that helps illuminate gendered aspects of organizational and individual life. The model is drawn from a range of sources that depict male and female values as two potentially complementary viewpoints on the world, reflecting an archetypal polarity (Bakan 1966; Marshall 1984), closely paralleling the Chinese concepts of yang and yin (Colegrave 1979, 1985; Singer 1976). Male values, or the male principle, can be characterized as self-assertion; separation; control; competition; focused perception; rationality; analysis; clarity; discrimination; and activity. Underlying themes are independence, focus, and control of the environment. Female values, or the female principle, can be characterized as interdependence; cooperation; receptivity; merging; acceptance; awareness of patterns, wholes, and contexts; emotional tone; being; intuition; and synthesizing. Underlying themes are interdependence and openness.

Despite the potential disadvantages of polarization, this framework has been a valuable vehicle through which notions of the socially muted female principle have recently taken shape.

In my use of this modelling, both male and female principles have both high or adaptive and low or degenerative forms. Control can be appropriate structure or reductive overcontrol; open responsiveness can be creative or the cause of flooding and losing one's own ground. We need to be aware of this in theory-making, lest either female or male becomes typed as positive or negative per se.

I see male and female values as qualities to which both sexes have access. Through biological and physical makeup, socialization and social role, women are more often grounded in the female pole and men in the male pole, although this may well be contradicted or unclear for women with a strong patriarchal education (Hennig & Jardim 1978; Perera 1981). Individual development involves integrating or balancing the capabilities of one's grounding with appropriate aspects of the other perspective.

Women and men are, then, both the same and different. Until recently many researchers have emphasized similarities to win women acceptance in employment. But this theme of equality for similarity has distorted many women's lives and left organizational cultures largely unchanged by the inclusion of women. As the literature on women in management increasingly argues (Schwartz 1989), differences now also need to be recognized. The male-female values model offers a view of what is dominant and valued in organizations, and in our theory-making about them, and of what is excluded, suppressed, and marginalized.

SOCIAL VALUES AND ORGANIZATIONAL CULTURES

The female and male principles depicted above can be seen as potential complements (as in androgyny theory, Sargent 1981), but this is currently an idealized picture. Through patriarchy, Western society has emphasized male values, and these have shaped its organizations, cultural norms, language, and so on. Female forms are relatively devalued, underdeveloped, and muted. This dominance affects all organizations, including the academic. It affects, for example, norms of behaviour, management styles, definitions of career and success, notions of truth, and acceptable research methods (e.g., Asplund 1988; Kanter 1977; Loden 1985; Marshall 1984; Sheppard 1989). Organizational cultures are therefore (white, heterosexual) male-dominated (Hearn, Sheppard, Tancred-Sheriff, & Burrell 1989). This is shown, for example, by emphasis on individualism, competition, clear boundaries, and control. Male-positive, female-negative is such a pervasive aspect of our Western public cultures that it is unusual to identify ways in which women differ from men without the assumption being made that women are somehow inferior. Female characteristics and values, such as emotions, intuition, and interdependence, are denied legitimacy and are covertly or actively suppressed.

Also, we have distorted the male principle by developing it in isolation. Many male writers are now calling for a reemergence of the feminine to create a more whole society (Bakan 1966; Berman 1989; Capra 1982; Robertson 1983). As social groups, therefore, men and women experience cultures differently (Bernard 1981; Gilligan 1982; Kanter 1977; Miller 1976, 1988).

There have recently been some surface changes in organizational life, with equal-opportunities legislation and initiatives. But women's acceptance in employment seems "stalled," as recent reviews of the situation in Canada (Burke 1991), the United Kingdom (Davidson 1991), and Australia (Vilkinas 1991) show. People are puzzled by this apparent lack of "progress" – Burke calls it "one of the greatest social paradoxes of our era" (Burke 1991, 16). I suggest, with other commentators, that change has seldom reached the deep structural levels that underpin organizational cultures. The male domination of cultures therefore goes largely unrecognized by organizational members and in mainstream organizational theory (Marshall 1985a; Pringle 1989; Sheppard 1989). For example, core texts on organizational culture such as Peters and Waterman (1982) and Frost, Moore, Louis, Lundberg, and Martin (1985), pay little attention to gender. As Sheppard (1989) concludes:

The notion of organizational structure as an objective, empirical and genderless reality is itself a gendered notion. In a structure where male dominance is taken for granted, the assumption of the invisibility of gender can be understood as an ideological position. It masks the extent to which organizational politics are premised on the dominance of one set of definitions and assumptions that are essentially gender based. (Sheppard 1989, 142)

This lack of appreciation has been fostered by the emphasis in much employment literature on women's similarities to men. People are realizing that this is only half the story. Women inhabit different worlds from men as well (Bernard 1981; Marshall 1984). In a separate realm of research, writers are exploring roots of women's identity that may currently be different from those of men. They take aspects of the feminine and seek to recover them from their muted, marginalized, and devalued places in patriarchal culture (Callaway 1981; Rich 1972). They reveal the female values depicted above as an important base on which women managers also draw. These values become translated, for example, into more intuitive cognitive styles (Keller 1980), relational identity (Gilligan 1982), affirmation of affiliation and connection (Miller 1976, 1988), and an interest in exercising power *with* rather than power *over* (Loden 1985; Marshall 1984).

It seems, then, that many women managers are operating, at least in part, from values, assumptions, and perspectives that reflect their female grounding, but which are not widely represented or accepted in organizational life. The research literature on women managers supports this suggestion (Asplund 1988; Marshall 1984, 1989; Sheppard 1989). This incompatibility creates conflicts and pressures. Many women feel "different," or "out of place" and describe themselves as working in "hostile environments." It is significant how repetitive the story of women managers as marginal is. For example, Sheppard (1989) gives a very familiar account from her work on women managers in Canada. We see the women coping with the incongruity they represent by monitoring their own behaviour, masking issues of gender, accommodating to dominant norms, and adopting subtle strategies to avoid overt discrimination. The women therefore try to avoid confronting the organization with its unresolved issues. It is in such contexts of meaning that many women appraise and cope with stress.

CULTURAL STABILITY IN THE FACE OF WOMEN AS DIFFERENCE

This is the context in which most women operate. Despite larger numbers of women, and despite equal-opportunities policies, fundamental patterns of values and behaviour seem highly resistant to change. Women are not defining, influencing, and changing cultures as significantly as many people had expected or hoped. We need, therefore, to pay theoretical attention to this repetitive message. I have chosen to do this next, by looking at the dynamics of maintaining order in organizational cultures.

Cultures are persistent and resilient. The persistence draws partly from being outside conscious awareness, and is facilitated by the amazing redundancy in cultural symbolism and messages. Expressions of cultural norms are overdetermined, to encourage stable interpretations of meaning in a potentially polysemic world. Language and imagery persistently mirror back to women a male-dominated, male-positive, female-excluding world. For example, in a recent edition of *Best of Business International* (1988–9), which offers "a quarterly selection of the world's best business articles," we find mainly pictures of men, and language that implies that all business people are men. An article on "Sacking the CEO," suggests "a dissatisfied board has to ask, 'What did we expect of this guy? Where did he fall short?'" (26). Another looks at "Renaissance man: A tough new breed of manager emerging from the trauma of the '70s" (8). An analysis of work-home conflicts is illustrated with a man carrying a brief-case being divided from a woman and child; examples in the text mostly support the image of the man being the one with a corporate identity. As a woman, I cannot find myself in this imagery and language; as an academic, I may be encouraged to shape my view of the world to give priority to men and their definitions of reality.

The encoding of male positive, female negative in organizational symbolism is often more subtle than in the above illustration. It may, for example, appear in a rhetoric of rationality or organizational commitment. But women experience such environments as antagonistic or disconfirming. Their, and the organization's, attempts at change are likely to be futile unless underpinning assumptions can be addressed.

LIVING IN HIGH-CONTEXT CULTURES[1]

E.T. Hall (1976), the anthropologist, offers a framework for exploring both the profound significance of culture as a backcloth of meaning and the reasons why Western, male-dominated cultures may be
so resistant to change. He distinguishes between *high-context* and *low-
context* cultures. "High context transactions feature preprogrammed
information that is in the receiver and in the setting, with only minimal information in the transmitted message" (Hall 1976, 101). Simple messages with deep meaning flow freely. Communicators have to
know a lot about what is going on at a covert level to function. Low-
context transactions are the reverse: "most of the information must
be in the transmitted message in order to make up for what is miss-
ing in the context" (Hall 1976, 101). Hall identifies Western cultures
such as the United States as largely low-context, in contrast to cultures such as Japan (although here he identifies dual tendencies).

I would like to transpose this theory. Hall (1976) saw from his own
gendered cultural assumptions; he saw Western cultures as restricted
in ways that many would now identify as male-dominated (e.g., rational, disconnected, relying on linear notions of time). He took
these features for granted. I suggest that women experience organizational cultures as high-context, preprogrammed with male values.
They do not share much of the contexting that makes communication understandable. Nor, because of their subordinate social position, do they have equal rights to engage in defining meaning within
the patterns of communication that are experienced by men as low-
context. This right is subverted by preprogrammed high-context
features, and undermined by institutional patterns of power. In her
history of women of ideas, Spender (1982) details how women's attempts to contribute their definitions of reality to the pool of socially
accepted knowledge have been repeatedly undermined: "All human
beings are constantly engaged in the process of describing and explaining, and ordering the social world, but only a few have been, or
are, in a position to have their version treated as serious, and accepted" (9). In male-dominated society these few are mainly men.
Women have not been, and are still generally not, accepted as legitimate meaning-makers if their interpretations of reality differ significantly from established, male-based, notions of truth. Their values
are unlikely to gain general validation and so are unlikely to transform the context of meaning in which they operate. For example, an
individual woman manager will find it difficult to influence basic at-

[1] The following section is reproduced with permission from Marshall (1993).

titudes about stress and acceptable coping behaviour in her organization. Rather she will be under pressure to adapt to existing norms, and will be judged accordingly. Women's abilities to interpret the world and have those interpretations validated by others, i.e., their abilities to make publicly accepted meanings, are severely restricted by living in high-context, male-dominated cultures. They are therefore cut off from a fundamental source of social power, one much used by those who shape organizational cultures.

So there is always tension, especially if we are trying to address issues of sexism, or issues on which a male view of the world is accepted and female equivalents devalued or repressed. Conversations become covert dialogues of power. To speak to men, women must approach such topics through low-context language, with the meaning mainly in the transmitted message. They are heard by most men from implicit value frameworks and so do not share a language for discussion or understanding. This helps me to appreciate how impenetrable these issues often are. It also shows how women's opportunities for coping may be restricted to indirect tactics, as the empirical literature suggests they are.

Hall (1976) sees high-context cultures as providing stability and handling information overload. They act as a unifying, cohesive force, and are rooted in the past, long-lived, and slow to change. In general, high-context cultures "have greater mass and are therefore more predictable, if, and only if, one is familiar with the system" (Hall 1976, 53).

Women have a long history of having to read the dominant culture in order to survive as members of the subordinate group (Miller 1976; Spender 1980). But if they are trying to operate as members of the dominant group, they can never be sure of knowing fully the culture in which they must function. Research shows that many women managers feel precarious, as if they are impostors, concerned that they may suddenly discover there are vital things they do not know (Clance & Imes 1978; Sheppard 1989). Women often translate these feelings into lack of self-confidence, as if their feelings are an individual phenomenon. Although they try to manage these tensions through conformity – for example, manipulating the image they present (Hall 1989; Marshall 1984; Sheppard 1989) – women are continually judged from contexts of meaning over which they have little influence. These contexts invoke male values as positive, encourage the assessment of women's behaviour against double standards, and so on.

As they create their individual lives in organizations, women therefore encounter deep-rooted aspects of culture that devalue the characteristics that they have come either to symbolize or to carry. Living in this potentially hostile world, women often describe themselves as struggling to survive rather than thriving. This makes women often vulnerable, on guard, their competence, credibility, and membership continually precarious.

COPING WITH STRESS:
A TWO-TIER MODEL

From the above analyses I take a picture of potential incongruity between women and organizational cultures, which will vary in its magnitude and manifestations depending on many other factors. There are some organizational environments in which women are "at home" and thriving. But in far more they are precarious and marginal. The root of this, for me, is because the context of meaning is not theirs, and their attempts to make meaning alongside men are repeatedly frustrated by the dynamics of social, institutional, and interpersonal power. These inequalities of power are the background context to women's coping behaviour.

Patriarchal value systems more often confer legitimacy to define the world on men than on women. In this culture women are disconfirmed (Laing 1961) or negated (Spender 1984). Laing sees disconfirmation as more damaging for the identity than rejection. The latter paradoxically affirms identity in its message of "you are wrong." Disconfirmation sends the message "you do not exist." Women managers experiencing this implicit, culture-based response are placed in a classic double bind. They hear a positive message – that of equal opportunities – undermined by a covert negative message – that of the repression of female values. The double bind is sealed by the injunction not to mention the incongruity; this is affirmed by the high-context culture, which takes its assumptions for granted and has no ready means of discussing and negotiating them.

Much of women's communication is therefore trying to assert their legitimacy and maintain membership. They are not guaranteed inclusion – a first step in many models of group process (e.g., Srivastva, Obert, & Neilsen 1977) and individual health (Bowlby 1969).

In this context, women know that they are vulnerable to others' definitions, that at any time they can be put in their place and told that they have gone too far. Miller (1988) talks about the low-profile, recursive denials of women's other voice that are part of everyday interaction. These create a persistent, and iteratively encoded, context of male dominance. In such situations, women may resist, and may argue assertively for their meanings, and for their right to make meanings. But the latter is always in doubt. Women are challenging and being resisted by the context. The processes involved have the appearance of coordinated action (but are probably largely unconscious), as if they are a sustained cultural initiative to contain and suppress women's meanings. For example, Hearn et al. (1989) contains numerous case examples of how men set or change agendas, trivialize women's contributions, and use sexual innuendo and activity as forms of organizational control of women.

There is much research reporting the range of coping strategies women have developed for interfacing with dominant cultures and with the latter's potentially punitive power. This research portrays how women, including women academics, often work on other people's ground (Marshall 1993; Rakow 1986), translate their experiences into male forms of speech (called "telling it slant" by Spender 1980), screen out potentially unacceptable material (Marshall 1985b; Pringle 1989; Sheppard 1989) and are silenced (Goldberger, Clinchy, Belenky, & Tarule 1987). These strategies tend to be adaptive.

Feeling unable to manipulate situations or define meaning in ways that will be accepted by the dominant culture, women tend to manipulate their own consciousness. Doing so is, in itself, a potential source of stress. Women are continually judging contexts and accommodating to them in processes of coping that address their own potential incompatibility with organizational cultures.

I suggest that we can therefore identify two levels of coping in which women engage. At a general level they develop an awareness of the organizational context and whether it is influenced by issues of gender. I believe that most organizational cultures are high-context in Hall's (1976) terms and male-dominated. The stance women take is a form of coping, largely preemptive and often unconscious. Simply being an organizational member requires coping behaviour from women managers. I develop below a four-stage model of awareness that maps key positions for women managers in their perceptions of the organization as male-dominated.

At a more specific level, women also appraise and respond to specific incidents of stress. Their general awareness will have a major shaping influence on how they see these incidents and the repertoire of coping at their disposal. The potential incongruities between female values and organizational cultures show what may be stressful. For example, women may pay more attention to contexts than men do and may find that their analyses of problems are therefore rejected as being confusing.

In the remainder of this chapter I concentrate on elaborating my model of general coping. At the more specific level of incidents, I shall merely illustrate some possibilities. The model refers only to women coping in high-context, male-dominated cultures, as I think such contexts are in the majority, and because they represent the frontier of progress toward equal opportunities.

AWARENESS PATTERNS AS COPING STRATEGIES

I have identified four broad choices for women managers, which reflect a development from little to more awareness of organizational cultures as male-dominated. These patterns of coping are depicted in figure 1. The figure offers the metaphor of perspective as a vehicle for exploring factors that profoundly influence an individual's perceptions of stress and repertoire of coping skills. As will emerge below, no position is inherently positive or negative. The model is tentative and in the process of development; there may well be other positions or broad possibilities. Between stages A and B and C and D are thresholds to developing further awareness, which I have depicted as venetian blinds. At stages A and C, the individual may glimpse the possibility of the next stage, but her view is obscured until internal or external processes force her through. The view through the blinds is only clear looking backwards from B and D. The stages are cumulative rather then sequential; that is, each stage incorporates the possibility of all those before it.

Stage A: Muted

The first choice, stage A, is to be unaware of contexting. The literature on women managers suggests this as the most common pattern (Freeman 1990; Marshall 1984). The individual does not see organizational cultures as male-dominated. These managers say that they want to be treated as people rather than as women, and that if they play down sexuality and gender these will not be salient characteristics for other people. Typically they will argue that being a woman has made no difference to their working life or career progress. They declare that they do not look for sexual discrimination and therefore do not find it. For some women this a "realistic" assessment of their organizational environment. But for the majority I believe it is largely a process of denial (Crosby 1984).

This awareness choice is adaptive to the current organizational culture, probably largely unconsciously. Potential disjunctions are repressed or muted. The manager, however, also probably somehow recognizes that the environment is potentially hostile, and may ex-

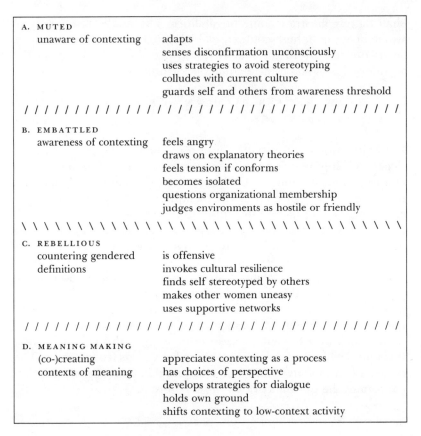

Figure 1
Patterns of cultural awareness as coping strategies for women managers

perience disconfirmation of her identity and competence in every-day interactions (Miller 1988).

Typically, although denying the salience of gender, the manager will also report consistent and elaborate strategies to avoid sex stereotyping (Marshall 1984; Sheppard 1989). For example, she will take care not to show emotions in public, will mask sexuality and gender via dress and speech, and will not mix with other women as this may be perceived as threatening by men. In this position women avoid potential stress by monitoring their own behaviour. They guard themselves and others from the recognition that they are women and potentially different. They act symbolically and cope on behalf of the system. They tend to be punished if the attempt goes wrong. They may also, paradoxically, help to make it difficult to discuss gender openly, because they have invested heavily in its suppression. This stage has much in common with the silence identified by Goldberger et al. (1987) as one of women's ways of knowing.

Despite its potential advantages of surface harmony, the muted coping pattern is also one of continual strain. It is fundamentally in-authentic, demanding masking and patrolled boundaries rather than the openness and interconnection sympathetic to female values. Discordant feelings and material must be denied. Membership is achieved by colluding with the current culture, which is therefore not challenged to change. Some women think that adaptation is a phase, and that later they will change things. But this is difficult to achieve. However senior they are, most women's organizational membership, and their power, remain in doubt.

This basic pattern will shape what potential episodes individuals define as stressful and will constrain their potential coping strategies. For example, situations where issues of gender and potential differ-ences may become apparent are likely to raise anxiety disproportion-ate to their other content. Emotion-based coping may be restricted for fear of matching the stereotype of the emotional woman. Task-based coping may also be limited if the manager has different, but unarticulated and unlegitimized, perceptions of task demands.

Between this position and the next there is a one-way blind; only if she deliberately approaches and peers can the manager see through it. Data suggest that women know intuitively that there is a danger-ous edge of awareness here (Marshall 1984). On the other side is the recognition of society as male-dominated and of men as the main holders of power to define social meaning. This is coping pattern B.

Stage B: Embattled

The first response to this recognition of basic inequality is often an-ger. The foundations of the individual's previous way of seeing the world are shaken. The manager may feel she has previously been "blind to what has truly been happening" (Marshall 1984, 152). This radical shift in world view is difficult to manage. Potentially trivial instances, such as having one's ideas dismissed at a meeting, are seen as symbolic of social inequality. At this stage, individuals run the con-tinual risk of becoming unable to cope, as they find their previous strategies ineffectual or reject them as collusive. They are learning a new view of the world in which they are discriminated against and "oppressed." Most relationships, especially those with men, will be thrown into doubt. Previously tolerated behaviour – for example, a male boss's arm round their shoulder – can become violently distasteful. The woman struggles to manage this awareness and survive without disrupting everything around her; she is embattled. Her highly reactive behaviour may well cause problems in relationships. When she conforms she feels the tension of this herself.

New-found explanations of the world, perhaps informed by feminist theory, may provide a sense-making framework. But they may also become protective distancing devices, a language and set of truths that cannot be shared. They can also fuel the manager's anger. She may become isolated. One choice will be whether to identify herself as "a feminist" – a label seldom welcomed in organizations.

The embattled manager may well feel her organizational membership in doubt as she struggles to reconcile her behaviour and newly formed beliefs. But she is unlikely, for various practical and psychological reasons, to be able to cope by leaving.

One survival tactic is to judge organizational environments as hostile or more potentially friendly to women, and adapt behaviour accordingly. Women have a history of self-preservation through such contextual sensitivity. In all situations, clarity about boundaries and competence in managing emotions will be heavily in demand as coping strategies.

This phase can also involve searching suspicion of one's own behaviour. Having realized that so much of the world she took for granted is ideologically flawed, the manager may become very aware of sexism in her own language and assumptions and feel guilty about this.

I can write with some feeling about this stage. It is one I reluctantly went through, having initially decided never to become involved with "women's studies" (as I report in Marshall 1984). It is also one I see a lot of postgraduate students engage with, when they decide to study gender and discover that it is an issue of direct personal relevance rather than a topic "out there." It is in student theses that I find the most evocative writing about stage B. Unfortunately, most have limited academic circulation. Otherwise this phase does not seem widely described, although much feminist writing comes from it.

Daly (1979) suggests that once this awareness is developed it is impossible not to know, that there is no going back through the blind to position A. I am no longer convinced of this. I think we can go back, and that sometimes it is necessary to do so as respite, as short-term coping.

I see stage B as inevitable in individual consciousness-raising. Its heat and passion can become a way of life, but are demanding to sustain. They make the individual continually vulnerable and volatile.

This is therefore an inherently unstable coping pattern. The manager is motivated to find a more viable public identity. One choice is to suppress awareness and live as before, if a little resentfully. Many people, however, want to do something with their perceptions of inequality, and take on the task of countering gendered definitions organizationally and socially. This, in the model, is stage c. The manager may, however, return to the embattled position in situations of stress. The boundary between stages b and c is therefore more permeable than others in the model.

Stage C: Rebellious

The rebellion of this stage may be more or less public. Some people choose to live out alternative models of management and power within their area of influence. Others take on the more public mission of confronting the dominant culture in its various expressions; for example, by challenging sexist language or speaking for women's experience. These people are "offensive" in at least two senses. They attack inequality. Also they cause offence because they challenge what others take for granted. Spender (1982) writes: "Openly questioning the way the world works and challenging the power of the powerful is not an activity customarily rewarded" (9). Cultural resistance is likely to be mobilized against them (Kanter 1977). Other women may become uneasy if their own coping patterns therefore come under implicit scrutiny.

To speak out in this way, individuals need a robust sense of self and of their values; they may need to live with conflict in close colleague relationships. They are likely to be stereotyped as feminist. This position is therefore demanding. Individuals may need the support of like-minded women and men to affirm their interpretations in a world that generally disconfirms or rejects them.

This position has many potential pitfalls that may result in limited coping behaviour in specific situations. One danger is isolation in the face of massive demands. Another is that the person can become an educator of others, particularly of men, doing the learning work about inequality for them (again coping on behalf of the wider system). Another possibility is that, to sustain her views in the face of disconfirmation, the individual may rigidify them, living by stereotypes rather then encountering situations fully and awarely. This form of coping therefore runs the risk of becoming perceptually blinkered or behaviourally stylized in order to sustain a positive sense of self.

Women at this stage are still largely constrained by male-dominated cultures. Men tend to be the main audience of women's efforts to speak, convince, and change, as men remain dominant power holders. The managers may set up alternative worlds in their own areas of influence, and network with other women as a strong reference group, but do so aware of the wider system and its values and potential power.

Despite the challenge people in this position offer the dominant culture, they are also constrained by what is acceptable. Much of their effort goes into trying to communicate in forms that will not be immediately rejected. What can be said, and how, in male-dominated discourse largely shapes these women's public speech. Breaking the rules completely is likely to make them marginal and ineffectual as potential agents for change. Conversation with other women is typically less guarded.

I see much feminist writing, including my own at times, as constrained by the dominant culture in this way. One indication is the adoption of traditional forms of rhetoric such as rational, depersonalized analysis and reliance on copious references to prove credibility. Rakow (1986) points out how often women academics are working on ground men have defined as relevant.

Paradoxically, then, in their *mode* of expression (although not its content), rebels are often conforming to dominant norms of behaviour, and so may well be colluding in maintaining established power relationships. Torbert (1987) describes such behaviour as typical of the developmental stage he calls *Diplomat*. The emphasis is on seeking membership; the individual conforms and suppresses her own desires. In Torbert's hierarchy this is an early, relatively immature, stage of development, and certainly not that of someone able to define meaning or shape organizational culture. This profile is not surprising, given women's marginality in the male-dominated world. Managers are probably operating differently in the parallel, but socially less powerful, world of women (Bernard 1981).

I think there is, then, another major threshold of awareness, one very difficult to see if the individual is constrained by, and vulnerable to, male-defined cultures. On the other side is a vision of possibility, a pattern of awareness from which few women so far operate.

Stage D: Meaning-making

Stage D is founded on the assumption that women have equal power to shape cultures. This individual appreciates contexting as a process and attributes herself rights to define meaning. She recognizes that perspectives, including feminism, are choices, and so has flexibility about what perspective to adopt. Her sense of self is not dependent on having a label for her beliefs. This individual has developed strategies for dialogue with others. Her sense of self is not eroded in this process, nor does it require massive defence to survive.

This pattern of coping requires high levels of personal and contextual awareness, akin to the principles of *action inquiry* outlined by Torbert (1991). By adopting a continual strategy of inquiring into purposes and assumptions, the individual will help shift contexting to a low-context activity, opening the possibility to negotiate new meaning collaboratively. Increasingly, women managers I meet are talking about processes of organizational change and looking for strategies with these subtle characteristics. The collaboration and mutual development potentially involved fit well with female values.

At any stage the individual has available all preceding patterns of coping. This is particularly relevant at stage D, because her choices of which pattern to adopt are made with awareness. Silence could, for example, be a choice with very different connotation from the silence of stage A. This manager is combining aspects of the female and male principles and using contextual sensitivity to shape as well as adapt.

Moving from stage C to D is no easy matter. C's view of the world as male-dominated is shaped by a largely patriarchal upbringing and reinforced by low-level symbols of culture encountered every day. Such basic frameworks are learned in early infancy and held unconsciously, and are essentially self-validating. They determine how we "punctuate" our perceptions of the world (Bateson 1973). Seeing beyond dominant frames and realizing that there are other choices is a higher level of learning than is substituting one viewpoint on the world for another (Bateson 1973). It is such learning that is required in the move from stage C to D. It seems highly significant how many theorists are reaching for frame-transcending models in our current times of multiple perspectives. (For example, Berman 1989, who suggests that we need to learn to live beyond paradigms; and Torbert 1987).

Despite their socialization, I see this shift of consciousness as possibly more available to women than to men. By being the subordinate social group, women have had to live complex cognitive and emotional lives, aware that there are different socially created worlds, different frameworks of meaning. Men take organizational culture more for granted because their behaviour and values are largely affirmed. Women have its incongruities continually thrust upon them. Living discordant realities is potentially stressful, but has the advantage of promoting awareness.

To be helpful at stage D, feminist perspectives may have to be transformed, to offer more choice and subtlety of interpretation. For example, in a given situation the manager may choose to cope with what she perceives as potential sexism not by challenging sexist language, but by acting clearly and assertively from an interpretation of issues that draws on and enacts female values. In a different situation, she might seek to raise awareness about someone persistently interrupting her, without labelling this as sexist, but questioning it as a pattern of behaviour with consequences.

I find it hard to imagine seeing the devaluation of women in male-dominated cultures as a "choice of framing," however. There are echoes here of stage A in which the individual mutes her awareness. The difference in stage D is that consciousness is maintained, but the manager has choice about how to act from this, and can look from other perspectives simultaneously.

Stage D could become a new, and potentially oppressive, model of Superwoman. This is not my intention. She should not be aiming to be right in all she does, rather to pursue these agendas with an intent of inquiry that has the potential to heighten awareness and collaboration generally.

Reaching stage D requires a leap of faith in many ways. It also involves withdrawing consent and collusion from processes that affirm men as dominant power-holders. This may include challenging the power politics of body language (Henley 1977). For example, women may not respond as often to others with a smile. This extent of unlearning will be phenomenally difficult.

The meaning-making pattern offers the individual a wide range of coping strategies and behaviours. This flexibility gives potential power, as long as the individual can maintain her sense of identity in the shifting processes involved. Living this position will require a continuing commitment to self-reflection and personal and professional growth. An essential characteristic of this stage is that the manager's coping pattern will create organizational turbulence which she, in turn, will have to handle. For example, some organizational environments may not welcome the diversity of self-presentation made available in this pattern. Others may fear, and so try to undermine, the robust and multifaceted power the manager gains by having choice about her perspective.

This coping strategy is, then, a continuous dance, seeking to maintain high-quality awareness of personal and environmental factors, and connection to both. Social isolation is a significant threat, as the manager may have few like-minded companions.

JUDGING COPING EFFECTIVENESS

Looking back over this model of coping patterns, we see a schema that is increasingly full of choice. No pattern is, however, inherently effective. Judgments of appropriateness will depend on the criteria applied. Resonance with female values is one possible yardstick. From this viewpoint, stages A to C are potentially stressful for their disconnection and lack of authenticity. Stage D offers more opportunities for expressions of difference.

Another viewpoint is whether coping is adaptive or transformational. Stage A is the most adaptive. The remaining stages put the individual under pressure to be an organizational member but remain marginal. Stages B and C may well offer individual satisfaction, but probably have limited chance of organizational transformation, especially if the manager is forced into the Diplomat role to maintain inclusion.

We could also ask which patterns are more stable to maintain as life strategies. Stage A is stable, but on probably shallow foundations, and therefore may demand considerable unconscious adjustments. This is the claim made by writers such as Hardesty and Jacobs (1986). Stage B is inherently volatile and highly demanding emotionally. Stage C affords more stability, but with limited opportunities for "success" if its objectives are organizational change. The individual may therefore suffer from fluctuations of morale as the dominant culture is repeatedly reaffirmed. Stage D offers more potential stability as it incorporates choices about strategies and about criteria for success.

IN CONCLUSION

The model of awareness patterns presented here represents tentative steps toward affirming three major themes in theorizing about women's coping. First, coping must be viewed in context. Second, at the moment, organizational contexts are inherently gendered. The picture I paint, somewhat reluctantly, is of major constraints on women managers' coping repertoire as long as the latter is the case. To what extent women do have the potential to act from awareness akin to that of stage D is open to doubt. But unless they do so their interpretation and acceptance of the world as male-defined will not be significantly transformed. Third, I have tried to show that coping is a complex, multilevel process, and that the use of notions such as "effectiveness" is intrinsically contentious.

REFERENCES

Asplund, G. 1988. *Women and organizational cultures*. Chichester, UK: Wiley.
Bakan, D. 1966. *The duality of human existence*. Boston, MA: Beacon Press.
Bateson, G. 1973. The logical categories of learning and communication. In *Steps to an ecology of mind* (pp. 250–79). London: Granada.
Berman, M. 1989. *Coming to our senses: Body and spirit in the hidden history of the west*. London: Unwin.
Bernard, J. 1981. *The female world*. New York: Free Press.
Best of Business International. 1988–9. Vol. 1.
Bowlby, J. 1969. *Attachment and loss Volume 1: Attachment*. Harmondsworth, UK: Penguin.
Burke, R.J. 1991. Women in management in Canada: Past, present and future prospects. *Women in Management Review and Abstracts 6*, 11–16.
Callaway, H. 1981. Women's perspectives: Research as revision. In P. Reason & J. Rowan, eds., *Human inquiry* (pp. 457–71). Chichester, UK: Wiley.
Capra, F. 1982. *The turning point: Science, society and the rising culture*. London: Wildwood House.
Clance, P.R., & S.S. Imes. 1978. The impostor phenomenon in high achieving women: Dynamics and therapeutic intervention. *Psychotherapy: Theory, Research and Practice 15*, 241–7.
Colegrave, S. 1979. *The spirit of the valley: Androgyny and Chinese thought*. London: Virago.
– 1985. Cosmic masculine and feminine. In J. Welwood, ed., *Challenge of the heart: Love, sex and intimacy in changing times* (pp. 90–9). Boston, MA: Shambhala.
Crosby, F. 1984. The denial of personal discrimination. *American Behavioral Scientist 27*, 371–86.
Daly, M. 1979. *Gyn/Ecology*. London: Women's Press.
Davidson, M.J. 1991. Women managers in Britain – issues for the 1990's. *Women in Management Review and Abstracts 6*, 5–10.
Gilligan, C. 1982. *In a different voice: Psychological theory and women's development*. Cambridge, MA: Harvard University Press.
Goldberger, N.R., B.McV. Clinchy, M.F. Belenky, & J.M. Tarule. 1987. Women's ways of knowing: On gaining a voice. In P. Shaver & C. Hendrick, eds., *Sex and gender* (pp. 201–28). Newbury Park, CA: Sage.
Freeman, S.J.M. 1990. *Managing lives: Corporate women and social change*. Amherst, MA: University of Massachusetts Press.
Frost, P.J., L.F. Moore, M.R. Louis, C.C. Lundberg, & J. Martin. 1985. *Organizational culture*. Beverly Hills, CA: Sage.
Hall, E.T. 1976. *Beyond culture*. Garden City, NY: Anchor Press.
Hall, M. 1989. Private experiences in the public domain: Lesbians in

organizations. In J. Hearn, D. L. Sheppard, P. Tancred-Sheriff, & G. Burrell, eds., *The sexuality of organization* (pp. 125–38). London: Sage.

Hardesty, S., & N. Jacobs. 1986. *Success and betrayal.* New York: Franklin Watts.

Hearn, J., D.L. Sheppard, P. Tancred-Sheriff, & G. Burrell, eds., 1989. *The sexuality of organization.* London: Sage.

Henley, N.M. 1977. *Body politics: Power, sex and nonverbal communication.* Englewood Cliffs, NJ: Prentice Hall.

Hennig, M., & A. Jardim. 1978. *The managerial woman.* London: Marion Boyars.

Kanter, R.M. 1977. *Men and women of the corporation.* New York: Basic Books.

Keller, E. 1980. Feminist critique of science: A forward or backward move? *Fundamenta Scientiae 1*, 341–9.

Laing, R.D. 1961. *The self and others: Studies in sanity and madness.* London: Tavistock.

Loden, M. 1985. *Feminine leadership, or how to succeed in business without being one of the boys.* London: Times Books.

Marshall, J. 1984. *Women managers: Travellers in a male world.* Chichester, UK: Wiley.

– 1985a. Feminism as a critique of knowledge. In M. Pedler & T. Boydell, eds., *A guide to materials on women and men in organisations* (pp. 1–28). Manpower Services Commission, UK.

– 1985b. Paths of personal and professional development for women managers. *Management Education and Development 16*, 169–79.

– 1989. Re-visioning career concepts: A feminist invitation. In M.B. Arthurs, D.T. Hall, & B.S. Lawrence, eds., *A handbook of career theory* (pp. 275–91). Cambridge: Cambridge University Press.

– 1993. Viewing organizational communication from a feminist perspective: A critique and some offerings. In S. Deetz, ed., *Communication Yearbook 16* (pp. 122–43). Newbury Park, CA: Sage.

Miller, J.B. 1976. *Toward a new psychology of women.* Boston: Beacon Press.

– 1988. *Connections, disconnections and violations.* (Working Paper No. 33). Wellesley, MA: Wellesley College.

Perera, S.B. 1981. *Descent to the Goddess: A way of initiation for women.* Toronto: Inner City Books.

Peters, T.J., & R.H. Waterman. 1982. *In search of excellence.* New York: Harper and Row.

Pringle, R. 1989. Bureaucracy, rationality and sexuality: The case of secretaries. In J. Hearn, D.L. Sheppard, P. Tancred-Sheriff, & G. Burrell, eds., *The sexuality of organization* (pp.158–77). London: Sage.

Rakow, L.F. 1986. Rethinking gender research in communication. *Journal of Communication 36*, 11–26.

Rich, A. 1972. When we dead awaken: Writing as re-vision. *College English*
34, 18–25.

Robertson, J. 1983. *The sane alternative: A choice of futures.* Ironbridge,
Shropshire, UK: James Robertson Press.

Sargent, A.G. 1981. *The androgynous manager: Blending male and female styles
for today's organization.* New York: AMACOM.

Schwartz, F.N. 1989. Management women and the new facts of life.
Harvard Business Review, January-February, 65–76.

Sheppard, D.L. 1989. Organizations, power and sexuality: The image and
self-image of women managers. In J. Hearn, D.L. Sheppard, P.
Tancred-Sheriff, & G. Burrell, eds., *The sexuality of organization* (pp.
139–57). London: Sage.

Singer, J. 1976. *Androgyny: Towards a new theory of sexuality.* Garden City,
NY: Doubleday.

Spender, D. 1980. *Man made language.* London: Routledge & Kegan Paul.

– 1982. *Women of ideas (and what men have done to them).* London: Ark
Paperbacks.

– 1984. Defining reality: A powerful tool. In C. Kramarae, M. Schulz, &
W.M. O'Barr, eds., *Language and power* (pp. 194–205). Beverly Hills, CA:
Sage.

Srivastva, S., S.L. Obert, & E.H. Neilsen. 1977. Organizational analysis
through group process: A theoretical perspective for organization
development. In C.L. Cooper, ed., *OD in the UK and USA* (pp. 83–111).
London: Macmillan.

Torbert, W.R. 1987. *Managing the corporate dream.* Homewood, IL: Dow
Jones–Irwin.

– 1991. *The power of balance.* Newbury Park, CA: Sage.

Vilkinas, T. 1991. Australian women in management. *Women in
Management Review and Abstracts 6*, 17–25.

6 Examining Gender in Organizational Relationships and Technological Change

ANNE STATHAM

In this chapter, I consider several findings from my own work relevant to women's employment stress. However, unlike most other chapters in this volume, I do not focus so much on the content of the findings (though they may be illuminative) as on the fact that they arise from the use of a particular methodology. Although much of the work in the area of women's employment stress – indeed, stress in general – has used a traditional quantitative approach, I argue for the use of qualitative approaches in order to uncover the hidden or unexpected situations of women as they wrestle with the strains of modifying typical family and gender roles, and enter the often unfamiliar and/or hostile world of paid work.

First, let me define what I mean by "qualitative approach," and indicate specifically why I think this tactic may prove so useful. A qualitative approach is not just a data-collection technique; I have seen many researchers collect open-ended data, then proceed to quantify it and use standard analysis techniques. The qualitative approach, as I define the term, refers to a broader epistemological stance on the entire enterprise of social science. Several themes or characteristics run through the various qualitative strategies that exist. It is an inductive approach that builds from the field, from data, moving to theory from observation. Grand theories do not guide the research, but a grounded theory is the hoped-for outcome. This aspect of the qualitative approach is probably still best articulated in Glaser and Strauss's classic work, *The Discovery of Grounded Theory* (1967). The positivistic notion that a definite structure exists apart from the observer and actors, which needs only to be discovered, is seriously challenged. Rather, the qualitative approach focuses on the perspectives of those involved in a given situation, arguing that many realities exist, depending upon which perspective one considers. The goal of the research is often to uncover those different realities. As a result, one more often hears the voices of those commonly deprived of voice in our society – the underclasses, the disadvantaged, the dispossessed. Further, the emphasis upon multiple realities leads to a redefinition of the relationship between researcher and respondents. Because the researcher's perspective is not seen as the "final" or "real" truth, the relationship becomes more egalitarian, more collaborative.

I am not putting these ideas forward to suggest that the qualitative approach is the only acceptable way to proceed. Rather, I believe we ought to choose the most appropriate technique from the wide array available to us. Indeed, I have been well trained in quantitative techniques and readily use them when the situation warrants. What I am suggesting here is that this whole issue of women's employment stress and coping lends itself particularly well to a qualitative approach. This is because of the large gaps in our understanding of this phenomenon and the often unexpected ways gender interacts with any social process. We have gained quite a bit of knowledge using the quantitative and experimental techniques that have helped to build the prevailing model of stress, with the focus on the genesis of stress, its implications, and coping strategies. Now, qualitative research might give fruitful impetus to future directions for understanding women's situation.

Looking beyond methodological concerns and considering the issue of women's employment stress and coping, one must look at the broad social context of gender as it affects the totality of our lives. The specific nature of the job alone cannot account for the stress employed women may experience, or for how they respond to or cope with stress. More encompassing gender factors contribute to the situation in several ways, and are discussed by other contributors in this volume more fully (see e.g., the chapters by Nina Colwill, Barbara Gutek, and Judi Marshall).

In this chapter, I focus on two of these three factors – the unique or special approaches women bring to employment and the dynamics of the jobs women tend to be concentrated in – as factors that may give rise to employment stress. In particular, I discuss my own research that looks at women's differential approaches to management and at pressures, including technological innovations, faced by clerical workers. Both factors can contribute significantly to the problems women experience in coping emotionally with their jobs. By focusing on these two factors, I do not mean to undercut the importance of the first factor I discussed, that of the need to fulfil a complex set of family and employment demands. As shown by other authors in this volume, fulfilling these multiple demands is an important source of additional stress for women in today's world.

REVIEW OF LITERATURE

For the most part, these two issues – women's possible different approaches to employment and women's enhanced susceptibility to such pressures as technological change by virtue of work-force placement – have not been thoroughly examined in the more general literature on stress. These are relatively new areas of research, lending themselves nicely to qualitative approaches that can uncover hidden and/or surprising factors in uncharted territory.

Relevant Literature on Stress and Employment among Women

It has long been known, in a general way, that gender is related to stress and distress. Mirowsky and Ross (1989) summarize the literature that shows women to be more distressed in a myriad of ways than men, particularly women who are housewives or who have husbands who do not share equally in household responsibilities. The early research on the topic of gender and stress focused on the impact of women's family roles. Now that the majority of women are in the labour force, a new focus on the impact of women's employment conditions has developed.

It is often posited that, because of women's increased labour market activity, women will "catch up" with men in such particular stress- or distress-related symptoms as coronaries (Cooper 1983; Hauston & Kelly 1989) and suicide (Alston 1986). Although some argue that women's employment stress levels may be no different from men's (Billings & Moos 1982; Cherry 1984; Crabbs, Black, & Morton 1986), others continue to find greater levels of overall stress and distress among women. (See Jick & Mitz 1985 for a summary of some of this research, also Lowe & Northcott 1988.)

In attempting to link this stress to employment experiences, some have argued that women experience the workplace differently. For example, Jick and Mitz (1985) have developed a model that takes into account both the socialization and the structural differences men and women experience, incorporating such factors as pay structure, opportunity for mobility, achievement motivation, and various coping strategies. Burke (1986) argues that men and women may simply be exposed to different stressors. If so, they may perceive the jobs they actually have as equally stressful, but still experience tremendous differences in the total gestalt of the workplace and in the managing of non-work roles.

Several studies have indicated that women respond differently to certain pressures. Nelson, Quick, and Hitt (1989) found that professional women reported more stress than men from organizational politics, and Bradley (1988) found women to be more troubled by contradictory job demands, irregular work pace, and lack of influence on scheduling. Richard and Krieshok (1989) found that women faculty continued to feel stress levels after being promoted to full professor, whereas men experienced a significant decline. Beyond these broad generalizations, however, not much research on stress has addressed how women experience employment differently and how this leads to stress, much less how they cope with stress.

Some researchers have considered the impact of labour-force segregation. Lowe and Northcott (1988) argue that perceived job characteristics contribute most to the difference in how men and women experience paid work, particularly the degree of variety and challenge in the job and the extent of competing demands. Billings and Moos (1982) had previously argued that several job characteristics contribute to the stress felt at work. These include (a) the heaviness of the work load with resulting time pressures, (b) role ambiguity or lack of clarity about job expectations and evaluation criteria, and (c) lack of control coupled with the little input into decisions and pacing of work load. Perhaps jobs more often occupied by women have these stress-producing characteristics.

The situation is quite complicated and, perhaps, can only begin to be entirely unravelled if we consider that women in various situations respond to some of these factors differently. For example, marital and parental status, and age, have been found to interact with certain predictors of stress. Arber, Gilbert, and Dole (1985) found that multiple role demands result in health problems for married women under the age of forty with children. For women without children – or women over forty with children – multiple roles actually enhanced overall health. Krausz and Freiback (1983) found that Israeli women reacted differently to flexible work schedules depending upon whether or not they were married or had children.

Professional or Managerial Women

Thus, to understand the situation in all its complexity, it seems important also to examine the situations of various employment groups separately. Hence, one focus in this chapter is on professional or managerial women and another is on clerical workers. Literature exists for both groups. King and Winnett (1986) found surprising similarities between "dual-career" and "dual-worker" women (faculty women and clerical workers) in terms of most frequently cited problems (time pressures) and supports (social supports such as advice, listening, etc.). To some extent, their situations are similar (as we shall see below), but a few critical differences also exist.

Several studies have identified particular job characteristics likely to affect professional women. Sex discrimination is a factor related to stress (Greenglass 1987; Nelson & Quick 1985), as is the social isolation professional women often experience by virtue of being in male-dominated work settings (Nelson & Quick 1985; Robinson & Skarie 1986). Other contributing factors include role ambiguity, overload, and strain (DiSalvo, Lubbers, & Rossi 1988; Robinson & Skarie 1986; Zappert & Weinstein 1985), as well as organizational politics (Nelson et al. 1989).

Several researchers have begun to explore these issues using quantitative analysis. Women's particular approaches to work, particularly their more people-intensive and nurturant style, may generate higher levels of stress for professional women. Greenglass (1987) suggests that some of these approaches may generate stress for only certain types of professional women – those who exhibit the Type A personality syndrome. Others suggest that individual traits or strategies, such as "hardiness," coping, or influence strategies, determine the amount of stress professional women actually experience (Levo & Biggs 1989; Long 1988; O'Neill & Zeichner 1985; Steffy & Ashbaugh 1986; Wallston, Hoover-Dempsey, Brissie, & Rozee-Koker 1989).

Clerical Workers

The situation of women clerical workers is somewhat different. They do not work in a male-dominated setting, at least so far as their peers are concerned. Hence, they do not experience the same pressures of tokenism that professional women must contend with. They are more likely to complain about their jobs being boring, about not being consulted about decisions that affect them, about the fast pace of work, or about not being part of the planning process (Bradley 1988; Kahn & Cooper 1986; Katz & Piotrkowski 1983; Lowe & Northcott 1988; Marek, Noworol, & Karwowski 1988). Kahn and Long (1988) found that for clerical workers, diminished self-efficacy and high work stress resulted in greater reported impairment of work performance.

Some of the problems clerical workers encounter in today's world involve the use or introduction of new technology. Factors contributing to these problems are thought to include loss of control and exclusion from the planning process (Alcalay & Pasick 1984; Alfredsson, Karasek, & Theorell 1982; Karasek 1979; Karmaus 1984; Morgall 1983; Spector 1986). One particular example of loss of control involves working with computers that are "counting" productivity (Feldberg & Glenn 1983; 9 to 5 1986; Smith, Cohen, Stemmerjohn, & Hopp 1981; Westin 1985). Specific problems include the feeling that workers are left with only the dullest portions of the work tasks (Morgall 1983), and specific physical problems for users of VDTs including eyestrain, musculoskeletal pain, and repetitive motion disorders (Marshall & Gregory 1983; Scalet 1987; Stellman & Henifin 1989). Smith et al. (1981) and Eason (1985) believe these problems result from increased job pressure and an unusual lack of control over the employment process.

This literature has concentrated a great deal on determinants of stress and much less on how women cope with this stress. In both areas, problems arise because researchers often use concepts derived from studies of mostly male respondents to examine behaviours of females. As a result, the special situations and approaches of women can easily be ignored. For example, most researchers tend to assume coping strategies similar to Goode's (1960) classic typology of role conflict reduction techniques or Lazarus and Folkman's (1984) instrumental/emotional classification scheme. Perhaps women, because of the types of conflicts they experience, see different sources of stress and use different methods for coping. These possibilities provide fertile ground for possible contributions of qualitative methods.

The Studies

Building upon the literature, I developed two related studies. The first one is a qualitative study of forty men and women managers and their secretaries conducted in the mid-1980s in southeastern Wisconsin. This study revealed several clear gender differences in approaches to management – and some interesting comparisons in the work situation of managers and secretaries. Open-ended interviews were conducted in three work settings: a medium-sized financial institution, a large manufacturing firm, and a technical (vocational education) institution. These interviews were tape-recorded, fully transcribed, and analysed using the constant comparison method explicated by Glaser and Strauss (1967). This method involves a meticulous content analysis, where information about certain topics is continuously read until concepts begin to emerge, often within categories, such as male and female or secretary and manager or high-level and lower-level manager. These respondents were asked very general questions about various aspects of their jobs, difficulties they encountered, conflict between work and family, and, last, their perceptions of men and women at work.

In the second study, as a follow-up, I did a mail survey of approximately 161 secretaries in the same geographic area as the original interview study, to explore further the issues of stress and technological innovation uncovered in the focused interviews. These respondents were asked about their experiences with new technology (a topic that had emerged spontaneously in the interviews), including stress reactions and planning difficulties. Surveys were distributed to secretaries in various work settings and, overall, I obtained a return rate of 64 per cent.

APPLICATIONS FROM QUALITATIVE APPROACHES

In this chapter I use data from my studies to illustrate several strengths of qualitative approaches. First, this approach can often illustrate the complexity of interactions among variables such as management expectations, hierarchical position, and gender more richly than traditional quantitative approaches, particularly in an exploratory situation. It is often simply impossible to anticipate accurately all the information one might need in a structured format. In my own study, the flexibility I had to explore nuances and unexpected directions proved to be invaluable.

The Stressor of Opposing Realities

The first point I wish to make about stress – and related coping strategies – concerns the existence of different realities in the workplace. One of the most striking findings from my studies – a factor with a tremendous potential for generating stress for employed women – was the existence of fairly distinct management models used by the men and women. Let me give you some idea of what I found. (Fuller details are available in Statham 1987a, and Statham 1987b.) In general, women tended to use a management style that I call *task-engrossed/person-invested*, whereas men used a management style that I call *image-engrossed/autonomy-invested*. This information comes not just from self-reports of the managers' own behaviour, but was corroborated by their secretaries. These differences directly contradict a popular belief that managers tend to be *either* people- or task-oriented. The women managers tended to be both. Many described themselves as "people-oriented," one calling herself a "teacher," another a "mother," and their secretaries agreed, saying things like "I think women are much more respectful of their secretaries, more sensitive to them, appreciate more the things they do."

At the same time, these women were equally task-oriented; they could easily recite long lists of all the things they needed to accomplish. Rather than seeing people- and task-orientation as mutually exclusive, they tended to believe that their people-orientation helped them accomplish the tasks. "I know my people and use a different management style with each [of them] because each one ... is different," one women said, and another said, "If my people are happy, they are going to do a better job for me – and they do."

The men, in contrast, when asked about their jobs, talked very little about how they went about doing the work, getting the task accomplished. Rather, they focused on the *importance* of their jobs – for the organization and for society. This I call *image-engrossment*. "This is where the rubber hits the pavement," one man said to me several times during his interview. Others expressed the same sentiment about their own jobs. "This is a big-buck project for the company. Its whole future may ride on it," another man said.

Another way the men and women differed involved delegation. Although most women described themselves as delegators (and their secretaries confirmed this), many also said they liked to "stay involved" in the projects they delegated. One woman said she liked "to have time lines," though her secretary insisted that she "follows up without making you feel that she's checking up on you ... She's an *excellent* delegator."

The men, by contrast, emphasized independence – both for themselves and for their subordinates. As opposed to the need for involvement with subordinates expressed by the women managers, these men believed it was necessary to "give people responsibility and let them be responsible for their actions." For the men, good management entailed not being involved in what their subordinates were doing. The basic strategy is illustrated by the following comment: "Hire people who take pride in their work ... and get out of their way ... back off and let them do it."

Implications of managerial style differences. These findings point to some potential stress-generating problems for women employed in the male-dominated world of management. Women managers are misunderstood in terms of their people-orientation and handling of delegation. The real difference, it seems, involves the salience of power positions (image engrossment) and the value placed on autonomy. Past research has shown that men value autonomy in their jobs (Miller 1980) and women value structure (Jurik & Halemba 1984).

These differences, however, were not discussed in value-neutral terms by the participants; instead each sex showed a strong preference for its own style and, at times, belittled the other's approach. The women often complained that men "got all the credit but women did all the work." They also felt that women were more effective workers. The men's secretaries sometimes complained about their lack of organization. "I have to haul him out of one meeting to get to another on time ... and be sure he has all the papers that he needs as he goes flying out the door," one secretary said.

Women expected bosses to invest time and energy in helping them develop, feeling angry and confused when they did not. One woman talked about a male manager who "set me in an office across the street ... gave me a stack of files, and said, 'This is your job. Do it'. I was totally frustrated; I had no guidance." This particular manager allowed that "eventually, it clicked," but it was a painful experience.

Even more significant, perhaps, for women attempting to function in a male-dominated, "foreign" world, was the disdain men often expressed for women's styles. One of the women I interviewed had supervised other respondents, both male and female; she was one of the strongest proponents of the person-invested strategy. One of the men she had supervised said, "She doesn't delegate enough ... stays too ... involved in the nitty gritty ... doesn't have confidence in the people working for her." He interpreted her behaviour as lack of confidence. Other male managers had also intimated that this particular supervisor was "doing too much of what ... [her] subordinates should be doing." A female subordinate of this manager, however, although recognizing that others may resent this style, felt it was "perfectly acceptable ... I learned a lot working for her."

Some of the men also expressed misgivings about the "people concern" evident in the approaches used by these women. One man complained that a subordinate "knew everybody's wife or husband's name ... the kids' names ... she would get on the phone and instead of spending one minute ... would spend two." He assumed this was problematic. "You can't go out to lunch with them and get chummy with them and then come back at 1:00 and say 'Okay, you've got to do this job,' and chew them out." Another man noted that differences in "how women relate to others ... [being] more sensitive ... which can affect their performance ... makes them less willing to confront the problem and solve it." This man eventually demoted a high-level woman who was reporting to him because of this very issue.

This illustrates a particularly stressful point for women. So long as women are evaluated primarily by men, this misunderstanding can only contribute to the stress women managers must cope with in their work situations. The question I am raising is about how these different realities affect employment behaviours, stress, and coping in unrecognized ways. Each sex was, in general, approaching the management enterprise very differently, with a great deal of misunderstanding resulting between the sexes. The subtleties described here would have been very difficult to uncover with a more structured, less qualitative approach. In recognizing the different expectations about management style as a source of stress, we find other questions. For example, one might begin to look for resulting coping strategies that attempt to reconcile situations that call for behaviours at odds with one's self-image. Will women press to convince others of the strengths of a new, unacknowledged approach, or conform to the men's expectations? And under what conditions? Their propensity to use combinations of people- and task-orientations in their managerial styles suggests they may also opt for blended coping strategies, a combination of emotional and instrumental, for example.

Stress and coping reactions. I asked these managers directly if they were ever troubled by feelings of anxiety or depression and, if so, how they coped. The women were more likely to admit to currently feeling stress or anxiety than the men. The men, however, often talked about times in the past when they had experienced a great deal of stress or anxiety, claiming that, now, they "did not let it get to me." A few men said their wives disagreed. "My wife tells me I worry a lot. I try not to let it bother me, but I guess it does," one male manager said, and another, "I started to realize that those kinds of pressures I can sometimes just shove aside. My wife claims that's not entirely true because she can feel me tensing up." None of the women reported other people telling them that they were feeling stressful, which suggests that women were more aware of the need to cope.

The men were more likely than the women to report a coping style that involved steeling oneself emotionally or mentally, to "rise above it," not to feel anxiety or stress in reaction to certain circumstances. Their asides about their wives, however, suggest that they were not entirely successful. Many other men talked about coping strategies that involved "getting away," "going up north," getting outside, or doing physical exercise. Several also reported a strategy of "doing the best work I can," so they felt at ease with themselves, no matter what the outcome; therefore, never feeling symptoms of stress.

Only one woman reported "doing the best I can" as a successful coping technique. Most of them reported coping strategies of doing physical exercise, visiting friends, socializing and entertaining, shopping, sleeping, and eating. Two women reported "not letting it get to me," "taking a deep breath" as successful coping mechanisms, and one woman claimed, "I really enjoy stress."

In summary, the managers were all functioning in very male-dominated settings. One result of this, immediately obvious from the interviews, is that women experienced a great deal more stress than men. They were also more in touch with the stress they felt, never reporting, as men did, having a spouse tell them they were acting stressful when they believed they were not. Further, none of the men who admitted to feeling stressful reported using instrumental coping strategies. Instead, they cited means of escape – going "up north," getting away, or exercise.

The women reported using a broader array of strategies. One recounted an instrumental strategy of doing her best work. However, most of them, like the men, reported escape mechanisms such as eating, sleeping, and shopping. They also discussed friendships as important sources of strength enabling them to cope. These results suggest that individuals subjected to relatively high levels of stress by virtue of structural features of the workplace, such as these women were, will rise to the occasion by employing various coping strategies. However, I found little evidence of these women acting to modify their work environment to accommodate their unique approaches. Neither the men nor the women reported much use of instrumental strategies.

These results are suggestive about the coping strategies used by the participants, since this study did not focus on stress and coping, but rather on management styles and strategies. However, a qualitative study that took stress and coping as its focus could probe more fully into these behaviours, and explore such issues as the use of instrumental coping strategies that include attempts to have one's unique management approach recognized and the blending of instrumental and emotional strategies.

Similar Stressors/Different Jobs

Another strength of the qualitative approach is to clarify the specifics of pressures/stressors operating for certain groups. In my study of secretaries and managers, for example, I was surprised to discover both groups of women describing similar types of time pressures, given the assumption in much of the literature that these are very different types of jobs. For example, in response to the general question "Tell me about your job," both groups of women gave me long (and exhausting) lists of all of the things they had to do. Demands on their time often seemed overwhelming. One manager complained about

getting time lines from four different people. That's difficult to cope with ... I can do one thing very well, but I can't do ten things very well ... and when I say, "If I do this, I can't do that," my boss just says, "You'll have to do it tomorrow." That's seventy-two hours of work!

Secretaries also found the time pressure very disconcerting.

There are times when it is very overwhelming. I find myself losing grasp of what I have to do and I just have to sit down and think, "Now, what it is I have to do? What is it I would like to do? What it is I want to do?" And then I constantly have to keep prioritizing the situation, otherwise I lose control of what I am doing and feel very uncomfortable, and I don't like that feeling of not being able to keep control.

For both groups of women, miscalculations could be devastating, and the overload is likely to cause stress reactions for both managers and secretaries. Again, the nuances of the situations that give rise to these problems are not readily apparent; hence the value of qualitative approaches that can probe more deeply beneath the surface reality. Certainly, past studies based upon more traditional quantitative approaches seem to assume that the work demands of such different jobs are really quite distinct. Many of the coping strategies discussed above were used in reaction to time pressures. As I stated before, these women generally felt unable to alter their work demands and, instead, emphasized means of reducing tension or "blowing off steam" outside their place of employment.

Unexpected Stressors

Qualitative techniques are also useful for uncovering unexpected sources of stress, in addition to exploring coping mechanisms. In this study, I unexpectedly came upon stress generated by the introduction of new technology in the three employment settings – financial institution, manufacturing firm, and technical institute – that I studied. (See a fuller description of this in Statham & Bravo 1990.) The problems that emerged in these interviews involved lack of worker input into the planning process, something that I then chose to explore further in a more structured follow-up study. The situation at the financial institution was the worst, with workers having serious physical symptoms, in part, they believed, because a *major* project of bringing "in-house" their computer services was done with what they perceived to be unreasonable deadlines. A feasibility study done by the implementors previously suggested one conversion date, but higher management had ignored this advice and opted instead for a date nearly a year earlier. Attempts to meet the deadline had required enormous amounts of overtime on the part of certain women managers and branch workers below the level of vice-president.

Similar problems existed in the other two work settings. In the manufacturing firm, a shortage of workers made the amount of work demanded unreasonable. For example, one massive conversion attempt in the parts-specification unit was undertaken with only one employee who could type. She did all of the work, entering a large amount of data, though some plans were being made to add more typists to that work force. The parts specifications, done by hand by several women before computerization, sat in large mounds waiting to be entered.

The situation with the technical institute also affected clerical workers. Here, the problem was a lack of new technology. However, a similar dynamic seemed to be operating; input from below was not acted upon, and the result – stress for the workers – was the same. Although a computer was on the main campus, very few of the internal operations were computerized. The computer staff would respond, "It's impossible" to all requests to begin computerizing various functions. No one seemed to be enough in charge to demand that the computer staff produce the needed work. Registration and financial aid were still handled manually, as was the bi-weekly pay process for part-time teaching staff and course-work preparation. In general, many time-consuming tasks were done manually, when the same work could have been done "so much more quickly" with a computer. "The administrators here just don't seem willing to move on this," one of them said. "They just don't seem to have the push."

When, during the analysis phase, I began to see the pervasiveness of these problems, I realized I did not have enough information in my interview transcripts to explore this issue thoroughly. I decided, instead, to distribute structured questionnaires to a larger group of individuals, testing hypotheses I had begun to formulate while doing the qualitative interviews. I believed certain planning deficiencies uncovered in the interviews would lead to stress reactions, generating certain types of health problems.

I collected survey data from secretaries in the same geographic area where the interviews had been done. The secretaries who responded to the survey were asked about the planning problems mentioned in the interviews: too many deadlines, unreasonable deadlines, too few workers, too little equipment/technology, overwork, insufficient training, unclear access to the equipment, unreasonable expectations concerning amount of output that can reasonably be expected from the technology. They were also asked about the existence of health problems similar to those reported in previous studies of ill health (cf. Gurin, Veroff, & Feld 1960; Johnson & Meile 1981). Eye strain and muscle strain, exhaustion, and "nerves" were the most common problems reported. Periods of instability or anger, depression, and skin rashes were somewhat less common, though consistently reported. Many of these symptoms have been associated with the physical demands of spending long hours before video display terminals. Psychological (nerves, anger, depression) and psychosomatic (skin rashes, exhaustion) symptoms have also been found to result from the physical demands and the psychological pressure to produce a certain amount of work under a certain type of work arrangement (see, for example, 9 to 5 1986).

I looked at the relationship between planning problems and symptoms. Each of the implementation problems was related to the incidence of health problems. However, some problems were more strongly correlated than others. When workers were not included in the setting of deadlines, when the output expected of the technology was unreasonable, when the time spent with the technology was excessive and other supervisors requested utilization of the technology, the workers tended to report nearly all of the health problems considered. The most commonly reported health problems – eye and muscle strain, headaches, exhaustion, skin rashes, "nerves," unstable feelings/anger – increased in frequency as the problems of implementation increased.

These particular results show the potential of combining both qualitative and quantitative data. Here, a qualitative approach suggested unexpected problems that could be explored more broadly using a quantitative approach. Without the former, I would not have known specific issues to explore. Without the latter, I would not have as much sense about how widespread the problems were – or what were their implications. In this way, qualitative techniques can be used to uncover issues that can be further delineated with the quantitative techniques traditionally used to explore the issues of stress and coping.

These results show one way that stress is generated for clerical workers, an occupation with one of the highest concentrations of women in the labour force. Although my study did not deal specifically with how these women *coped* with the stress, certainly understanding the process giving rise to stress may suggest where to look for coping strategies. The physically demanding nature of the technology leads one to suspect that women would be forced to act directly on their work environment in order to effectively reduce the stress they feel. The results from the qualitative interviews with clerical staff, however, suggest that this may be difficult for women to do.

DISCUSSION

These results show important ways that a qualitative approach can be useful in exploring the issues of stress and coping among women. Because women's roles are changing so rapidly, it may be impossible to adequately predict all the important parameters in this regard. Hence, the flexibilities involved in qualitative research become particularly useful. In this chapter I illustrated four contributions a qualitative approach can make, by (a) facilitating the exploration of the complex interactions among variables more fully and flexibly than is often possible with quantitative approaches; (b) enhancing the possibilities for uncovering misconceptions about specific jobs; (c) facilitating the discovery of unexpected stressors; and (d) serving as useful guides in the construction of appropriate quantitative measures.

Concerning the first point, the material on differences in managerial style illustrated how a complex interaction among expectations about management, hierarchal position, and gender may influence stress and coping reactions. Women managers, using a different managerial style from their male counterparts, are often judged harshly for their techniques by their male supervisors, and supported by their female secretaries. Few women attempted to act directly upon the situation; rather, most used strategies outside the situation, such as running or shopping. In general, using research strategies that allow women to tell their own stories allows for the possibility that unexpected processes and situations will be uncovered. For example, much previous research had assumed that women were more person- than task-oriented in their approaches to work. The findings presented here suggest that this may be a false dichotomy, as women described themselves (and were described by others) to be using both approaches in a complicated interplay designed to get the job done. Similarly, they may be using both emotional and instrumental coping strategies, rather than favouring one over the other. Qualitative research designed specifically to explore this issue of coping may uncover a myriad of unexpected findings.

Qualitative approaches have the potential to uncover previously unsuspected similarities in sources of stress across jobs: I found professional and clerical workers to be operating in a similar fashion, particularly with respect to time constraints. This finding sharply contradicts common assumptions that these two groups of workers face markedly different employment situations. Future research might well explore the importance of autonomy and power in framing the coping responses of both groups. Each may respond to time pressure for different reasons.

Since Kanter's (1977) ground-breaking look at managerial women, much evidence has been amassed showing that women in token situations of authority feel inordinate performance pressures (to be "twice as good" as male peers). So, women managers, still a minority in their occupations, may feel pressure to do both more work and better work. Clerical workers, on the other hand, may be those experiencing the "speed-up" described and predicted by writers such as Braverman (1974). This pressure comes not from the tokenism situation, but from the lack of power and control typical of the jobs that women are recruited into.

Qualitative approaches can also uncover whole new avenues for research by suggesting unexpected sources of stress. In my case, the problems arising from the introduction of new technology were illuminated. My focused interviews suggested that lack of worker control or input into the entire process of introducing new technology is a critical stressor for clerical and lower-level managerial workers. In exploring this issue, I showed how qualitative research can lead directly to the more effective construction of a quantitative study. In this case, I constructed mail questionnaires for a larger sample to follow up the hunches derived from my focused interviews.

By incorporating qualitative approaches into the literature on stress and coping, one can uncover and/or clarify many previously unsuspected facts and puzzling findings. For example, Staats and Staats (1982) found that professional and managerial women experienced significantly greater levels of many types of stress than professional and managerial men. However, they could find no work-related source of this difference, only outside sources, such as family pressures. Although these latter pressures are undoubtedly important, perhaps the researchers were not asking the right questions about employment. As I said at the beginning of this chapter, women's employment stress is a complicated issue. To unravel it, we must take a broad look at gender relations in the entire society, particularly as we look beyond sources of stress to coping strategies. How does gender constrain the ways women and men respond to stress?

REFERENCES

Alcalay, R., & R.J. Pasick. 1984. Psycho-social factors and the technologies of work. *Social Science and Medicine 17*, 1075–84.

Alfredsson, L., R. Karasek, & T. Theorell. 1982. Myocardial infarction risk and psychosocial work environment: An analysis of the male Swedish working Force. *Social Science and Medicine 16*, 463–7.

Alston, M. 1986. Occupation and suicide among women. *Issues in Mental Health Nursing 8*, 109–19.

Arber, S., N. Gilbert, & A. Dole. 1985. Paid employment and women's health: A benefit or a source of role strain. *Sociology of Health and Illness 7*, 375–400.

Billings, A., & R. Moos. 1982. Work stress and the stress-buffering roles of work and family resources. *Journal of Occupational Behavior 3*, 215–32.

Bradley, G. 1988. Women, work, and computers. *Women and Health 13*, 117–32.

Braverman, H. 1974. *Labor and monopoly capital: The degradation of work in the twentieth century*. New York: Monthly Review Press.

Burke, R. 1986. The present and future status of stress research. *Journal of Organizational Behavior and Management 8*, 249–67.

Cherry, N. 1984. Women and work stress: Evidence from the 1946 birth cohort. *Ergononics 27*, 519–26.

Cooper, C.L. 1983. Coping with the stress of being a woman executive. *Leadership and Organizational Development Journal 2*, 15–16.

Crabbs, M., K. Black, & S. Morton. 1986. Stress at work: A comparison of men and women. *Journal of Employment Counseling 23*, 2–8.

DiSalvo, V., C. Lubbers, & A. Rossi. 1988. The impact of gender on work-related stress. *Journal of Social Behavior and Personality 3*, 161–76.

Eason, K.D. 1985. Job design and VDU operation. In B. Pearce, ed., *Health Hazards of VDTs?* (pp. 217–30). New York: Wiley.

Feldberg, R., & E.N. Glenn. 1983. Technology and work degradation: Effects of office automation on women clerical workers. In J. Rothschild, ed., *Machine ex dea: Feminist perspectives on technology* (pp. 59–78). New York: Pergamon.

Glaser, B., & A. Strauss. 1967. *The discovery of grounded theory: Strategies for qualitative research*. New York: Aldine.

Goode, W.J. 1960. A theory of role strain. *American Sociological Review 25*, 483–96.

Greenglass, E. 1987. Anger in Type A women: Implications for coronary heart disease. *Personality and Individual Differences 8*, 639–50.

Gurin, G., J. Veroff, & S. Feld. 1960. *Americans view their mental health.* New York: Basic Books.

Hauston, K., & K. Kelly. 1989. Hostility in employed women: Relation to work and marital experiences, social support, stress, and anger expression. *Personality and Social Psychology Bulletin 15*, 175–82.

Jick, T., & L.F. Mitz. 1985. Sex differences in work stress. *Academy of Management Review, 10*, 408–20.

Johnson, D.R., & R.L. Meile. 1981. Does dimensionality bias in Langer's 22-item index affect the validity of social status comparisons? An empirical investigation. *Journal of Health and Social Behavior 22*, 415–32.

Jurik, N., & G. Halemba. 1984. Gender, working conditions, and job satisfaction of women in a non-traditional occupation: Female officers in men's prisons. *Sociology Quarterly 25*, 551–66.

Kahn, H., & C.L. Cooper. 1986. Computing stress. *Current Psychological Research and Reviews 5*, 148–62.

Kahn, S., & B. Long. 1988. Work-related stress, self-efficacy, and well-being of female clerical workers. *Counseling Psychology Quarterly 1*, 145–53.

Kanter, R.M. 1977. *Men and women of the corporation.* New York: Basic Books.

Karasek, R.A., Jr. 1979. Job demands, job decision latitude, and mental strain: Implications for job redesign. *Administrative Science Quarterly 24*, 285–308.

Karmaus, W. 1984. Working conditions and health: Social epidemiology patterns of stress and change. *Social Science and Medicine 19*, 359–72.

Katz, M., & C. Piotrkowski. 1983. Correlates of family role strain among employed black women. *Family Relations 32*, 331–9.

King, A., & R. Winnett. 1986. Tailoring stress-reduction strategies to populations at risk: Comparisons between women from dual-career and dual-worker families. *Family and Community Health 9*, 42–50.

Krausz, M., & N. Freiback. 1983. Effects of flexible work time for employed women upon satisfaction, strains, and absenteeism. *Journal of Occupational Psychology 56*, 155–9.

Lazarus, R.S., & S. Folkman. 1984. *Stress, appraisal and coping.* New York: Springer.

Levo, L., & D. Biggs. 1989. Cognitive factors in effectively coping with home/career stress. *Journal of Cognitive Psychotherapy 3*, 53–68.

Long, B. 1988. Work-related stress and coping strategies of professional women. *Journal of Employment Counseling 25*, 37–44.

Lowe, G., & H. Northcott. 1988. The impact of working conditions, social roles, and personal characteristics on gender differences in distress. *Work and Occupations 15*, 55–77.

Marek, T., C. Noworol, & W. Karwowski. 1988. Mental fatigue at work and pain perception. *Work and Stress* 2, 133–7.

Marshall, D., & J. Gregory, eds. 1983. *Office automation, Jekyll or Hyde? Highlights of the international conference on office work and new technology.* Cleveland: Working Women Education Fund.

Miller, J. 1980. Individual and occupational determinants of job satisfaction: A focus on gender differences. *Sociology of Work and Occupations* 7, 337–66.

Mirowsky, J., & C. Ross. 1989. *Social causes of psychological distress.* New York: Aldine.

Morgall, J. 1983. Typing our way to freedom: Is it true that new office technology can liberate women? *Behavior and Information Technology* 2, 215–26.

Nelson, D., & J. Quick. 1985. Professional women: Are distress and disease inevitable? *Academy of Management Review 10,* 206–18.

Nelson, D., J. Quick, & M. Hitt. 1989. Men and women of the personnel profession: Some differences and similarities in their stress. *Stress Medicine 5,* 145–152.

9 to 5, National Association of Working Women. 1986. *Computer monitoring and other dirty tricks.* Cleveland, OH: 9 to 5.

O'Neill, C.P., & A. Zeichner. 1985. Working women: A study of relationships between stress, coping and health. *Journal of Psychosomatic Obstetrics and Gynaecology 4,* 105–16.

Richard, G.V., & T.S. Krieshok. 1989. Occupational stress, strain, and coping in university faculty. *Journal of Vocational Behavior 34,* 117–32.

Robinson, S., & E. Skarie. 1986. Professional women: Job role stresses and psychosocial variables. *American Mental Health Counselors Association Journal 8,* 157–65.

Scalet, E.A. 1987. *VDT health and safety: Issues and solutions.* Lawrence, KS: Ergosyst.

Smith, M.J., B.G. Cohen, L.W. Stemmerjohn, & A. Hopp. 1981. An investigation of health complaints and job stress in video display operations. *Human Factors 233,* 387–400.

Spector, P.E. 1986. Perceived control by employees: A meta-analysis of studies concerning autonomy and participation at work. *Human Relations 39,* 1005–16.

Staats, T., & M. Staats. 1982. Sex differences in stress: Measurement of differential stress levels in managerial and professional males and females on the stress vector analysis – research edition. *Southern Psychologist 1,* 9–19.

Statham, A. 1987a. The gender model revisited: Differences in management styles of men and women. *Sex Roles 16,* 409–29.

– 1987b. Women working for women: The manager and her secretary. In A. Statham, E.M. Miller, & H.O. Mauksch, eds., *The worth of women's work: A qualitative synthesis* (pp. 225–43). Albany, NY: State University of New York Press.

Statham, A., & E. Bravo. 1990. The introduction of new technology: Health implications for workers. *Women and Health 16*, 105–29.

Steffy, B., & D. Ashbaugh. 1986. Dual-career planning, marital satisfaction and job stress among women in dual-career marriages. *Journal of Business and Psychology 1*, 114–23.

Stellman, J., & M.S. Henifin. 1989. *Office work can be dangerous to your health: A handbook of office health and safety hazards and what you can do about them.* New York: Pantheon.

Wallston, B., K. Hoover-Dempsey, J. Brissie, & P. Rozee-Koker. 1989. Gatekeeping transactions: Women's resource acquisition and mental health in the workplace. *Psychology of Women Quarterly 13*, 205–22.

Westin, A. 1985. *The changing workplace: A guide to managing the people, organizational and regulatory aspects of office technology.* White Plains, NY: Knowledge Industry.

Zappert, L.T., & H.M. Weinstein. 1985. Sex differences in the impact of work on physical and psychological health. *American Journal of Psychiatry 142*, 1174–8.

PART THREE

Coping Resources: Stress Moderators

7 Stress, Coping, and Social Support among Women Managers

KAREN KORABIK,
LISA M. McDONALD,
AND HAZEL M. ROSIN

The purpose of this chapter is to examine women managers' ways of coping with occupational stress. To this end, we review the literature on sex differences in job stressors and offer several explanations for the frequent finding that women managers do not suffer more negative stress-related consequences than their male counterparts despite their exposure to a greater number of job stressors. In particular, we examine women managers' coping abilities and the manner in which they utilize social support in an attempt to understand whether these factors serve to buffer the negative effects of the stressors that they encounter.

SOURCES AND CONSEQUENCES OF OCCUPATIONAL STRESS

Research has indicated that certain job characteristics such as a lack of autonomy, role conflict and ambiguity, and heavy demands are particularly important sources of occupational stress (Billings & Moos 1982; LaCroix & Haynes 1987; Spector, Dwyer, & Jex 1988). In addition, several other categories of job stressors have been identified, including one's role in the organization, interpersonal relationships, career development, the organizational climate, and career/family interface (Cooper & Marshall 1978).

We would like to thank M. Ellen Mitchell for her comments on an earlier version of this manuscript.

For the most part, these job characteristics have been cited as potential stressors based on studies finding an association between the characteristics and negative outcomes such as job tension. Job stressors have been found to result in a multitude of adverse consequences for the emotional and physical well-being of individuals, as well as for organizations, in the form of decreased productivity, turnover, low job involvement, and absenteeism (Kalimo & Mejman 1987; Levi 1987).

It has recently been recognized, however, that the relationship between occupational stress and detrimental outcomes is highly complex. Not all stressors have the same impact on all individuals. Characteristics of the job, the degree of perceived control, the presence or absence of other roles, and the amount of social support available all appear to be important in determining how well individuals cope with employment-related stressors (Frankenhaeuser et al. 1989). Furthermore, because cognitive appraisal is significant in mediating the stress-illness relationship, there has been an increasing emphasis on studying stress, coping, and social support in terms of the subjective perception of employment situations by individuals (Lazarus & Folkman 1984).

Sex Differences in Occupational Stressors

Many occupational stressors are especially applicable to those in managerial positions (Nelson & Quick 1985). Although the role of manager is similar for men and women, there are important differences in the contingencies that male and female managers experience in the workplace (Cahoon & Rowney 1984). It is surprising, therefore, particularly because increasing numbers of women have been entering managerial positions, that most studies of managerial job stress have either failed to include women at all, or have not examined sex differences (Haw 1982; Jick & Mitz 1985).

Studies of sex differences in occupational stress show contradictory results. Several comparisons of stress among employed men and women who are not managers suggest that women may experience more physical and emotional distress than do men (Jick & Mitz 1985; Nelson & Quick 1985; Zappert & Weinstein 1985). Yet, a recent meta-analysis revealed no sex differences in occupational stress (Martocchio & O'Leary 1989). However, the methodological weaknesses of prior research, which has been primarily cross-sectional and has neglected to consider important moderating variables (e.g., occupational level, the type of stress experienced, or the presence of other roles), may explain why such inconsistencies arise.

Research with managerial samples shows that men and women share several stressors, including time pressures and work overload (McDonald & Korabik 1991a; Nelson & Quick 1985). However, there is also reason to believe that women managers are subject to more employment-related stressors than are men in comparable positions (Jick & Mitz 1985; Nelson & Quick 1985; Powell 1988). Some problems that have been postulated to be especially applicable to women managers are prejudice and discrimination, stereotypes, social isolation, job strain, and career/family interface.

Prejudice and discrimination. Research demonstrates that even when male and female managers are similar in age, experience, and work status, the women are paid less than the men (LaCroix & Haynes 1987; Rosin & Korabik 1990). This inequity in pay is a significant source of stress for women managers (Davidson & Cooper 1983; Nelson, Quick, & Hitt 1989). Women are also more likely than men to report stress because of the prejudiced attitudes of others and because colleagues of the opposite sex are treated more favourably in their organizations (McDonald & Korabik 1991a). Likewise, women report stress as a result of failing to receive the same training opportunities as their male colleagues (Cahoon & Rowney 1984; Davidson & Cooper 1983) and being blocked from promotion because of prejudice and discrimination within their organizations (Davidson & Cooper 1983).

Because these data are based upon self-reports, they could result from a tendency by women to view themselves as victims of prejudice. However, considerable research confirms that prejudice and discrimination actually are significant problems for women managers (Korabik 1990; Powell 1988), that women managers face many real gender-based barriers to their advancement (Morrison, White, & Van Velsor 1987), and that women's deficits in salary and promotions are often due to systemic bias against them (Powell 1988).

Stereotypes. Female managers also report stress from having stereotyped roles imposed on them by others in the organization (Davidson & Cooper 1983; Nelson & Quick 1985; McDonald & Korabik 1991a). In addition, they experience role conflict because the executive role is perceived as more appropriate for men than for women (Davidson & Cooper 1983). Male managers tend to hold negative stereotypes of their female colleagues to a greater extent than the women themselves do, and the damaging consequences of such stereotypes have been well documented (Nieva & Gutek 1981).

Managerial women are also more likely than their male colleagues to report problems in the area of managing subordinates (McDonald & Korabik 1991a). This may be a consequence of the very real difficulties that women encounter with the authority aspects of leadership (Butler & Geis 1990). It has been suggested, for example, that women find it more difficult to be assertive in employment situations because such behaviour is inconsistent with societal stereotypes about appropriate behaviour for women (Davidson & Cooper 1983; Nieva & Gutek 1981). Such stereotypes also may make it more difficult for male subordinates to accept supervision by women (Nieva & Gutek 1981).

Social isolation. Women managers suffer from social isolation because they are much more likely than men to be in minority or token positions (Kanter 1977). Female managers often find being in such male-dominated environments and the resulting organizational politics stressful (Nelson & Quick 1985; Nelson et al. 1989). Moreover, these particular stressors have been linked to low organizational commitment, low job satisfaction, and a high propensity for turnover among managerial women (Rosin & Korabik 1991). Other stressful effects related to women managers' social isolation are role ambiguity, the lack of same-sex role models (McDonald & Korabik 1991a), the unavailability of mentors (Cahoon & Rowney 1984), exclusion from "old boy" networks (Cahoon & Rowney 1984; Nelson & Quick 1985), and men's lack of willingness to share job-related information with women (Nelson et al. 1989).

Job strain. Job strain is a function of a lack of autonomy coupled with heavy job demands. LaCroix and Haynes (1987) have found that women workers who are not managers have jobs with higher levels of strain than do men and that such jobs predispose women to illness. Although the findings in this area have been mixed, there is some evidence that women managers also may experience higher levels of job strain than their male counterparts.

Managerial women report stress because of jobs that are characterized by a lack of control (Frankenhaeuser et al. 1989; Zappert & Weinstein 1985) and a lack of access to power and resources (Davidson & Cooper 1983). Furthermore, low levels of job characteristics like leadership, responsibility, autonomy, time flexibility, and variety appear to result in low job satisfaction and organizational commitment and a high intention to leave among women managers (Rosin & Korabik 1991). Likewise, the more the jobs of women managers underutilize their skills, the lower their job satisfaction and the greater their anxiety, depression, psychosomatic symptoms, and propensity for turnover (Greenglass 1990a).

It has been suggested that women managers also may be susceptible to work overload in that they have to work harder than their male colleagues to "prove" themselves (Kanter 1977) and they are more likely than comparable men to report stress from feeling they have to perform better than their opposite-sex colleagues (McDonald & Korabik 1991a). However, research outcomes in this domain are contradictory: one study showed that women managers experienced more job pressure and worked longer hours than did men in similar positions (Cahoon & Rowney 1984), whereas another found no differences in job characteristics or number of hours worked when male and female managers were equated on age, experience, and work status (Rosin & Korabik 1990). Moreover, two recent studies reported that male managers found their jobs to be more demanding than did female managers in comparable positions (Long 1990; Rosin & Korabik 1990).

Obviously, more research is needed before this issue can be resolved. In particular, better measures of perceived work demands and clearer distinctions between role overload and other similar concepts like role conflict and role ambiguity are necessary (Haw 1982).

Career-family interface. The literature on employed women indicates that they, more often than men, also are expected to fulfil the majority of the demands associated with domestic roles (Nelson & Quick 1985; Zappert & Weinstein 1985). This is supported by Hochschild's (1989) research that documents the disproportionate responsibility of employed wives for household and child-raising tasks. Although women managers are less likely to be married or to have children than their male counterparts (McDonald & Korabik 1991a; Rosin & Korabik 1990), they are more likely to report that the combined demands of their professional and family roles are stressful (Frankenhaeuser et al. 1989; Greenglass 1990a; McDonald & Korabik 1991a; Tung 1980). For example, McDonald and Korabik (1991a) found that 45 per cent of the female managers in their study reported experiencing stress due to career-family conflict, whereas none of the male managers did so. Greenglass (1990a) also found that a substantial number of women managers experienced career-family conflict and that it resulted in job anxiety and depression.

There are some indications, however, that this pattern might be changing. Some recent research has revealed no sex differences in career-family conflict (Beutell & O'Hare 1987; Rosin & Korabik

1990). This may be because more and more men are becoming affected by the competing demands of career and family, so that the attitudes of managerial men are rapidly approaching those of women (Maier, Thompson, & Thomas 1991).

Perceptions and Consequences of Occupational Stress

The preceding discussion suggests that women managers currently are subject to many more stressors than are their male colleagues. Furthermore, although information about these stressors has been obtained primarily from women's self-reports, there is objective evidence that corroborates that many of these stressors do, in fact, exist and that they have a negative impact upon these women's lives. Consequently, we might expect female managers to perceive themselves to be under more stress and to suffer more detrimental stress-related outcomes than do comparable men. Yet this does not appear to be the case.

Several studies have found no differences between male and female managers in general self-reported occupational stress (Etzion 1984; McDonald & Korabik 1991a; Rosin & Korabik 1990). Although Parasuraman and Cleek (1984) found that female managers reported higher stress levels than males did, they claim that this was because the women in their sample were less experienced than the men, rather than because of their gender. Besides, Tung (1980) found that among school administrators women actually reported lower stress levels than men.

Moreover, despite steady increases in the number of women in high-status occupations, there have not been attendant increases in stress-related illnesses, physical or mental health problems, or mortality rates for women (Baruch, Biener, & Barnett 1987). In addition, there do not appear to be any sex differences in stress-linked outcomes like job satisfaction, organizational commitment, or propensity to leave, once sex differences in age, managerial experience, and work status are controlled (Rosin & Korabik 1990).

Why is it then that despite being subjected to more occupational stressors than their male counterparts, women managers do not appear to experience more stress or more negative stress-related consequences? We will discuss three possible explanations for this phenomenon.

Subjective perceptions. According to this viewpoint, it is one's subjective impression of the demands encountered in a situation rather than the objective characteristics of that situation that is important. The argument from this perspective is that situations will be appraised as stressful only if one's perceptions of their demands exceed what one expects.

Nicholson and West (1988) contend that women in male-dominated professions like management are strongly motivated "survivors" who set high standards for themselves (see also Jick & Mitz 1985) and fully expect their careers to be very demanding. Thus, if their jobs are consistent with these expectations, they may not be experienced as stressful. Yogev's (1982) study of subjective perceptions of overload among a sample of women faculty illustrates this. Those women reporting the highest number of hours worked weekly (i.e., married women with children) were also those who had the lowest subjective perceptions of overload.

Positive spillover. It is possible that the multiple roles held by women managers result in positive spillover from the nonoccupational to the occupational domain, thus mitigating the effects of the extra stressors that they encounter. Two opposing points of view with respect to the impact of holding multiple roles on mental and physical health have been advanced (see Baruch et al. 1987). According to the scarcity hypothesis, the greater the number of roles one assumes, the greater the potential for stress, overload, conflict, and negative consequences for well-being. Human energy is viewed as fixed and limited such that any additional roles serve to reduce available resources. According to the enhancement hypothesis, on the other hand, added roles may increase energy resources because of the increased potential for benefits related to self-esteem, stimulation, privileges, social status, and social identity. Also central to the enhancement hypothesis is the assumption that the greater the number of roles one has, the greater the possibility that the disliked aspects of these roles can be delegated to others.

Although the data relevant to this issue are limited, they seem to favour the enhancement hypothesis. The positive consequences of multiple role participation for employed women have been reported in several studies and the benefits of holding multiple roles appear to outweigh the disadvantages (Kirchmeyer 1992). Multiple roles, particularly family roles, appear to reduce women's job strain (Cooke & Rousseau 1984) and enhance their job satisfaction (Kirchmeyer 1992). Moreover, Baruch et al. (1987) found that employed women, particularly those at higher occupational levels, had better physical and mental health than unemployed women.

Nonetheless, multiple roles do not invariably result in beneficial effects. The type and quality of the roles and the amount of control available to the individual must be considered (Kirchmeyer 1992). Yet, for women, managerial roles may produce positive spillover because such roles may be perceived as higher in both quality and control than the other roles (e.g., domestic) that are available to them (Baruch et al. 1987). The high status associated with the managerial role also may serve to insulate women from the impact of various life stressors (Vaux 1985).

Coping and social support. It is possible that women managers can manage multiple stressors because they have better coping skills and/or can better utilize available social support networks than men. These superior skills may help to buffer the negative effects of the stressors that they experience. The following sections of the chapter address this possibility.

SEX DIFFERENCES IN COPING WITH STRESS

Jick and Mitz (1985) contend that sex differences might be present not only in the types of work stressors experienced but also in the cognitive appraisal of such stressors and in coping behaviour. Although there is widespread support for the idea that the manner in which people cope with stress affects their emotional and physical well-being (see Edwards 1988 for a review), very few studies have examined the ways that individuals deal with the actual occupational stressors that they encounter. Moreover, most of these studies have not included women as subjects (Haw 1982) and those that have investigated sex differences have ordinarily employed either nonmanagerial samples or samples where men and women are in noncomparable positions.

Coping Strategies

Some studies suggest that sex differences in coping may exist, with women utilizing more social-emotional coping strategies than do men. For example, research on general stress indicates that women are more likely than men to cope by seeking social support or by venting their emotions, whereas men are more likely to use behavioural, mental, or drug/alcohol disengagement (Carver, Scheier, & Weintraub 1989). Similarly, research with managerial samples shows that women are more likely than men to talk to others as a way of coping with stress, whereas men are more likely than women to change to an engrossing nonwork or play activity (Burke & Belcourt 1974; McDonald & Korabik 1991a; Nelson et al. 1989).

In addition, some authors contend that problem-focused coping is more characteristic of men, whereas emotion-focused strategies are more characteristic of women. Folkman and Lazarus (1980) found that men in stressful work situations used more problem-focused coping than women. Similarly, Ilfeld (1980) reported that women were more likely than men to adopt a rationalization/resignation coping strategy and less likely than men to take direct action. But, because women are more likely than men to be in lower-level jobs that restrict the use of problem-solving strategies, these differences may be attributable to differences in the characteristics of jobs held by men and women (e.g., differences in position power) rather than to sex differences in coping preference (Folkman & Lazarus 1980).

When males and females who are equivalent in education, occupation, and/or position are studied, few sex differences in coping emerge. For example, Zappert and Weinstein (1985) found no differences in the styles of coping with work stress of men and women holding MBA degrees. Similarly, Richard and Krieshok (1989) concluded that male and female university faculty did not use different coping strategies to deal with occupational stressors. Moreover, Greenglass (1990a) showed that male and female managers were similar in instrumental and preventive coping and internal control and that for both sexes these strategies resulted in reductions in job anxiety. Although Long (1990) found that women managers were more likely than men who were in equivalent occupational groups to use avoidance and problem-reappraisal coping, she reported no sex differences in active problem-solving coping.

Our research (McDonald & Korabik 1991a) also showed that comparable male and female managers were similar in the strategies they adopted to cope with employment-related stress, except that women talked to others more as a way of coping. Most male and female managers in our study reported coping with stressful job situations by taking direct action to solve the problem. This result is contrary to the finding of Pearlin and Schooler (1978) that strategies aimed at changing the situation were infrequently used to deal with occupational sources of stress. However, it supports Folkman and Lazarus's (1980) finding that problem-focused coping is used more often than emotion-focused coping to deal with stressful job situations, and also the contention of Menaghan and Merves (1984) that those in high-prestige occupations are more likely to use direct action to cope with occupational stressors.

It is therefore important, when studying sex differences in coping, to recognize the importance of situational context in influencing the form of coping utilized (Long 1990) and to use samples where the men and women are comparable in occupation, level, and experience (Jick & Mitz 1985). But there may be yet another explanation for why the sex differences in problem- versus emotion-focused coping found in nonmanagerial samples have not been replicated with managers. Sex-role orientation (i.e., the degree of instrumentality and expressiveness in the personality) may be acting as a moderator variable (Long 1990; Nezu & Nezu 1987).

Persons high in instrumentality have been found to prefer problem- to emotion-focused coping strategies (Nezu & Nezu 1987). Such high instrumentality is characteristic of both male and female managers. However, in nonmanagerial samples, men are significantly higher in instrumentality than women (Korabik 1990). This may explain why problem-focused strategies are typical of both male and female managers, but only of men and not women in the general population. Thus, the preference for a problem- or emotion-focused approach to coping may be less a function of an individual's biological sex than of that person's sex-role socialization.

Coping Effectiveness

Pearlin and Schooler (1978) claim that women traditionally have been socialized in a way that predisposes them to ineffective coping. For example, some researchers have suggested that women get sick as a way of coping with stress more often than men do (Zappert & Weinstein 1985). Other research, however, indicates that women do not have more inadequate coping repertoires than men (Menaghan & Merves 1984). Additionally, there is some evidence that women administrators can cope with job-related stress better than men (Tung 1980). For example, in their study of first-level managers, Parasuraman and Cleek (1984) controlled for management level and found that, when faced with stressful occupational situations, women more often than men engaged in "adaptive" coping behaviours, such as planning, organizing, prioritizing assignments, and requesting needed resources.

Clearly, more research on sex differences in coping with managerial stress needs to be done. Past research has suffered from a tendency to equate problem-focused coping with effectiveness and to view emotion-focused coping as invariably ineffective. Not only has this approach been demonstrated to be too simplistic (see Carver et al. 1989), it has been detrimental to women because they have long been stereotyped as more emotional than men. In fact, there is little evidence that problem-focused strategies are any more or less effective in bringing about real changes in work-related stressors than are emotion-focused coping strategies (Menaghan & Merves 1984), that emotionality is a sex-linked characteristic (Korabik 1990), or that comparable male and female managers differ significantly in their proclivity to adopt problem- versus emotion-focused coping strategies.

Research on sex differences in coping also has been hampered by the failure to consider important moderators like sex-role orientation and situational context. As Long (1990) points out, it is critical to study men and women in similar contexts. In our society, situationally determined resources and rewards are frequently sex-linked, as are the demands of one's social roles at particular life stages. These elements may interact to determine the level of problems an individual encounters and the degree of distress experienced may be less a function of sex or of individual differences in coping ability than of the severity of the problem (Menaghan & Merves 1984).

THE ROLE OF SOCIAL SUPPORT IN ALLEVIATING WORK STRESS

Although social support has long been presumed to play an important role in coping with work stress, much controversy exists about the exact nature of its influence (Greenglass, this volume, also reviews the nature of social support). Not surprisingly, somewhat inconsistent and contradictory findings have emerged, owing to the fact that social support has been measured in different ways, different indices of job strain have been used, and different job-stress variables examined (Beehr 1985). Measures of job satisfaction have often been used to operationalize the concept of social support (Beehr 1985), and the relationships between global measures of the supportiveness of those in families or in organizations and certain job-stress variables have been used to indicate that social support alleviates occupational stress. Such research shows that support has a positive impact upon physical and mental health, absenteeism, burnout, work stress, and performance (see Mitchell & Ayman 1991). For example, stress levels are lower for those who are satisfied with and involved in their jobs and for those who have supportive supervisors and cohesive relationships with their co-workers (Cooper & Marshall 1978). Likewise, social support from both organizational and family sources appears to result in decreased job stress and improved physical and mental health (Holahan & Moos 1981; LaRocco, House, &

French 1980). If, however, support is viewed as a resource in the environment that must be sought out and mobilized by the person experiencing a stressful work situation, then the actual support received by individuals may differ from their perception of the support available to them should they need it (Lazarus & Folkman 1984).

Sex Differences in Social Support

Support resources. We might expect sex differences to emerge with respect to social support in the business environment because women have more and different types of supportive ties and larger support networks than men (Vaux 1985). Studies show that employed women appear to value their relationships with co-workers to a greater extent than do men (Nieva & Gutek 1981) and that women managers have larger support networks than comparable men (McDonald & Korabik 1991b). However, although they view the organizational environment as more supportive than male managers do, women are more likely than men to perceive the interpersonal conflicts in these environments as stressful (Long 1990).

Sources of support. Research with nonmanagerial samples indicates that career-related sources of social support are more important for men, whereas family-related sources of support are more important for women. For example, Billings and Moos (1982) found that the relationship between occupational stress and job strain was buffered by both career and family sources of support for men, but only by family sources of support for women. Similarly, Holahan and Moos (1981) showed that employment was a more important source of support for men than for women and that interpersonal relationships within organizations were related to the psychological adjustment of men, but not women.

Leavy (1983) points out that such results may be due to the fact that women have traditionally been socialized to place a higher value on family than on employment. But this may not be true for career-oriented women, and such findings may not generalize to them. For example, Wetzel and Redmond (1980) found that, for those women who had high independence in their occupational roles, the relationship of social support at work to depression was more similar to the pattern typically found among men than that found among women. Likewise, after controlling for vocational variables that were confounded by gender, Fusilier, Ganster, and Mayes (1986) demonstrated that the effects of biological sex on physical health and on the amount of support received were minimal. They also found a reversal of the typical effects in regard to psychological problems – employment-based support was more important for women, whereas family-based support was more important for men.

Unfortunately, research on sex differences on sources of social support among managers is extremely sparse. Still, at first glance, the results of those studies that have been carried out appear to substantiate the conclusions drawn from research using nonmanagerial samples. Etzion (1984) found that, although occupational stress was moderated by social support from supervisor and co-workers for male managers, female managers tended to rely more on family and friends as sources of social support. Similarly, Schilling and Fuehrer (1987) found that most of the professional women in their study reported relying on extraorganizational sources of support, especially spouses, male intimates, and close same-sex friends. Few men in their sample reported relying on such sources in helping them deal with work stress, but more often cited people at the office. Burke and Weir (1975) also established that men chose those in the organizational environment (superiors, co-workers, and subordinates) as the most likely source of help with employment-related problems. Women, on the other hand, overwhelmingly reported that they would turn to their husbands.

In all these studies, however, there was a failure to control for differences in the positions held by men and women. When we (McDonald & Korabik 1991b) studied men and women managers at comparable job levels, we found that, contrary to previous research, male managers did not tend to talk with others within the organization about employment-related problems more often than female managers. When asked to indicate helpful persons they spoke with when they were experiencing stressful situations, male and female managers were equally likely to mention others in their place of business, especially their peers.

Our finding that comparable male and female managers were just as likely to turn to their bosses for support and to consider their bosses to be helpful in resolving employment-related issues contradicts the results of research showing that women managers report receiving less support from their superiors than their male colleagues do (Frankenhaeuser et al. 1989; Greenglass 1990a). But the fact that the women in previous studies were likely to be in lower-level positions than the men could have accounted for the sex differences that were found. Women in higher-level positions may benefit more from talking to others within their organizations, especially peers, about employment-related problems than would women in lower-level positions. That is, those in higher-level positions may be more likely to encounter problems that are best resolved through negotiation with, and the cooperation of, others within their organizations. High-level managers, for example, may be more likely to require the involvement of their bosses, or of other managers controlling different functions within the organization, to resolve employment-related issues.

Consistent with previous research findings, however, we found that female managers more often than male managers reported talking to their spouses and finding them supportive (McDonald & Korabik 1991b). This finding is surprising, considering that the female managers in our study were less likely to have spouses than were the male managers. It also contradicts results from the nonmanagerial literature on social support suggesting that wives are more important to their spouses' support systems than husbands are and that husbands are more likely to mention their wives as confidants than wives are to mention their husbands (Greenglass 1990b; Vaux 1985).

It may be that the employment status of the spouse is related to the amount of support the spouse can offer in buffering occupational stress. Though the women in our sample were less likely to be married than the men, those who were married were more likely to have spouses who were employed outside the home and who may thus have been able to understand their problems. Schilling and Fuehrer (1987) found that the reason that professional women turned to their spouses for support with job-related problems was because they saw them as knowledgeable and able to provide them with relevant information. This also may be true for men. When the male managers in our study (McDonald & Korabik 1991b) reported that they found talking to their wives helpful, their wives invariably held jobs outside the home. These men often said their wives could relate to the situations they described because of their understanding of the kinds of stressors associated with employment. Sometimes these women were employed by the same company as their husbands and so were even more likely to have an understanding of the kinds of stressful situations their spouses encountered.

Another difference between our study (McDonald & Korabik 1991b) and previous research on sex differences in social support is that most prior studies have been predicated on the assumption that all sources of support are helpful. In our study, female managers did report speaking with sources external to the business environment more often than did male managers. But these people were often not seen as helpful. In particular, women tended to find their mothers, mothers-in-law, and friends without careers to be ineffective in helping them deal with job-related sources of stress. This was often because these people made unrealistic suggestions (e.g., just quit), possibly owing to a lack of understanding about employment in general or the job situation in particular. Thus, although we found that female managers spoke with more people than did males, and more often spoke with others outside the organizational environment, these additional people did not necessarily provide help in dealing with occupational stress.

Functions of support. Some research indicates that men describe social support as beneficial because it helps them to realize that they are not the only ones in a certain situation and because it provides them with a different point of view about the situation (Schilling & Fuehrer 1987). Likewise, we (McDonald & Korabik 1991b) found that male managers were more likely than female managers to report that receiving information and advice about how a job-related problem might be solved was helpful, whereas behaviours that did not lead to problem resolution were characterized as not helpful. Furthermore, our results showed that male managers most often sought the involvement of those who could understand or provide information about the problem and those whose opinions the managers trusted because of job performance.

Women, on the other hand, are more likely than men to choose helpers because of the emotional support that they provide (e.g., their sympathy, sensitivity, and ability to listen) (Burke & Weir 1975; McDonald & Korabik 1991b; Schilling & Fuehrer 1987). Moreover, the behaviours of others considered not beneficial by female managers are most often those that involve a lack of consideration for how they are feeling (McDonald & Korabik 1991b). In addition, women are more likely than men to describe support in terms of receiving tangible assistance from specific people that helps them to deal with the demands of their career and family roles (Schilling & Fuehrer 1987). However, at least among attorneys, men appear to receive more support from their families for participation in social activities than women do (Mitchell & Ayman 1991).

Thus, male and female managers appear to differ both in the kinds of support they receive from others and in the kinds of support they find helpful in dealing with occupational stress. The fact that women report that having someone simply listen to their problems in an understanding way is helpful, whereas men say that those who can supply them with specific problem-focused information and advice are more helpful than those who just listen, may have important implications with respect to the working relationships of men and women in management. Although male managers may find emotional support helpful for dealing with occupational problems, the failure also to provide suggestions/advice conducive to problem resolution may reduce the perceived helpfulness of well-intentioned attempts at support. Similarly, female managers may find information and suggestions about how to deal with a problem much less helpful if such actions are not accompanied by emotionally supportive dimensions such as sincere concern and an attempt to understand how they are feeling.

Sex-role Orientation and Social Support

Ashton and Fuehrer (in press) caution that sex differences in social support may be attributable, at least to some extent, to the moderating effects of sex-role orientation. They found that women sought both emotional and instrumental support, but that men (especially those who were low in femininity) sought less emotional than instrumental support. Similarly, Burda, Vaux, and Schill (1984) found social support to be a function of expressiveness, with feminine and androgynous individuals having more support resources available to them than masculine and undifferentiated individuals. Both studies, however, employed nonmanagerial samples.

CONCLUSIONS AND SUGGESTIONS FOR FUTURE RESEARCH

Research on sex differences in coping and social support using managerial populations is very sparse. It does appear, though, that findings from nonmanagerial samples will not necessarily generalize to managers, nor will findings from men necessarily generalize to women. Overall, then, this review demonstrates that we know very little about how women managers cope with occupational stressors and even less about their utilization of social support networks to help them alleviate stress. There is clearly a need for more research in this area, particularly research that overcomes the problems that have been characteristic of the majority of previous studies.

Primary among these problems has been the failure to control for situational and individual difference variables that are often confounded with gender. As this review has demonstrated, apparent sex differences are often a function of various facets of women's current position in organizations (e.g., their education, experience, hierarchical level, or position characteristics) rather than of their biological sex. Thus, to avoid drawing the wrong conclusions, it is important to equate male and female managers on such situational characteristics.

The effects of individual difference variables, such as sex-role orientation, also may be mistakenly attributed to biological sex. Sex-role orientation appears to be an important moderator of both coping and social support and "future studies incorporating [the] distinction between sex and sex-role identity might clarify many of the inconsistencies identified in the existing research on sex differences in work stress" (Jick & Mitz 1985, 417).

The manner in which these personal and situational variables interact with one another and with biological sex should also be examined. As Nelson and Quick (1985) point out, the context in which stress occurs cannot be studied independently of the individual experiencing the situation. Sex is a salient characteristic of individuals that often influences others' perceptions, and, in our society, roles and status are often sex-linked (Nieva & Gutek 1981). Thus, even when male and female managers are in equivalent positions, they may not be equivalent in authority (LaCroix & Haynes 1987). Likewise, the presence or absence of other social roles (e.g., parent) may affect male and female managers differently. Women managers are also likely to be subject to special pressures, like discrimination, that men are not (Baruch et al. 1987). It is, therefore, essential to investigate these issues through research that compares women to men as well as research that concentrates solely on the issues most salient to women (Baruch et al. 1987).

Finally, a host of methodological problems has plagued this area of research. There has been a failure to use standardized operationalizations, assessment techniques, and methodologies. This has made cross-study comparisons difficult. Constructs have often been inadequately defined and insufficiently distinguished from one another. The measures that have been used frequently lack sufficient reliability or validity (Spector et al. 1988) and may not be applicable to women (Baruch et al. 1987). In addition, there has been an overreliance on retrospective and self-report methodologies, which may be subject to various types of bias (i.e., memory, social desirability) and to common method variance. Rapidly changing social, organizational, and historical conditions make more longitudinal research necessary. There is also a need for more research that specifies the links "between objective environment and subjective perception, and between perceptions and responses/outcomes" (Haw 1982, 141).

In this respect, there has been a general failure to recognize the complex interrelationships that exist among stress, coping, social support, and various outcomes, or to acknowledge the reciprocal causality that may underlie such processes. Stressors may lead to negative outcomes, but such outcomes also may cause individuals to perceive situations as stressful (Spector et al. 1988). Likewise, although coping may act as a strong elicitor of social support, social support also may exert an influence on the manner in which an individual copes (Dunkel-Schetter, Folkman, & Lazarus 1987).

REFERENCES

Ashton, W.A., & A. Fuehrer. In press. Effects of sex and sex-role identification of participant and type of social support resource on support seeking. *Sex Roles.*

Baruch, G.K., L. Biener, & R.C. Barnett. 1987. Women and gender in research on work and family stress. *American Psychologist 42*, 130–6.

Beehr, T.A. 1985. The role of social support in coping with organizational stress. In T.A. Beehr & R.S. Bhagat, eds., *Human stress and cognition in organizations: An integrated perspective* (pp. 375–98). New York: Wiley.

Billings, A.G., & R.H. Moos. 1982. Stressful life events and symptoms: A longitudinal model. *Health Psychology 1*, 99–117.

Beutell, N.J., & M.M. O'Hare. 1987. Work-nonwork conflict among MBAS: Sex differences in role stressors and life satisfaction. *Work and Stress 1*, 35–41.

Burda, P., Jr., A. Vaux, & T. Schill. 1984. Social support resources: Variations across sex and sex-role. *Personality and Social Psychology Bulletin 10*, 119–26.

Burke, R.J., & M.L. Belcourt. 1974. Managerial role stress and coping responses. *Journal of Business Administration 5*, 55–68.

Burke, R.J., & T. Weir. 1975. Receiving and giving help with work and non-work related problems. *Journal of Business Administration 6*, 59–78.

Butler, D., & F.L. Geis. 1990. Nonverbal affect responses to male and female leaders: Implications for leadership evaluations. *Journal of Personality and Social Psychology 58*, 48–59.

Cahoon, A., & J. Rowney. 1984. Sex differences in occupational stress among managers. In R.J. Burke, ed., *Current issues in occupational stress: Research and intervention* (pp. 79–113). Downsview, Ont.: Faculty of Administrative Studies, York University.

Carver, C.S., M.F. Scheier, & J.K. Weintraub. 1989. Assessing coping strategies: A theoretically based approach. *Journal of Personality and Social Psychology 56*, 267–83.

Cooke, R.A., & D.M. Rousseau. 1984. Stress and strain from family roles and work-role expectations. *Journal of Applied Psychology 69*, 252–60.

Cooper, C.L., & J. Marshall. 1978. Sources of managerial and white collar stress. In C.L. Cooper & R. Payne, eds., *Stress at work* (pp. 81–105). Chichester, UK: Wiley.

Davidson, M., & C. Cooper. 1983. *Stress and the woman manager.* New York: St Martin's Press.

Dunkel-Schetter, C., S. Folkman, & R.S. Lazarus. 1987. Correlates of social support receipt. *Journal of Personality and Social Psychology 53*, 71–80.

Edwards, J.R. 1988. The determinants and consequences of coping with stress. In C.L. Cooper & R. Payne, eds., *Causes, coping and consequences of stress at work* (pp. 223–63). Chichester, UK: Wiley.

Etzion, D. 1984. Moderating effect of social support on the stress-burnout relationship. *Journal of Applied Psychology 69*, 615–22.

Folkman, S., & R.S. Lazarus. 1980. An analysis of coping in a middle-aged community sample. *Journal of Health and Social Behavior 21*, 219–39.

Frankenhaeuser, M., U. Lundberg, M. Fredrikson, B. Melin, M. Tuomisto, A. Myrsten, M. Hedman, B. Bergman-Losman, & L. Wallin. 1989. Stress on and off the job as related to sex and occupational status in white-collar workers. *Journal of Organizational Behavior 10*, 321–46.

Fusilier, M.R., D.C. Ganster, & B.T. Mayes. 1986. The social support and health relationship: Is there a gender difference? *Journal of Occupational Psychology 59*, 145–53.

Greenglass, E.R. 1990a, July. *Stress and structural factors: Implications for women.* Paper presented at the meeting of the 22nd International Congress of Applied Psychology, Kyoto, Japan.

– 1990b, August. *Social support: Effective coping in women.* Paper presented at the annual meeting of the American Psychological Association, Boston, MA.

Haw, M.A. 1982. Women, work and stress: A review and agenda for the future. *Journal of Health and Social Behavior 23*, 132–44.

Hochschild, A. 1989. *The second shift: Working parents and the revolution at home.* New York: Viking Press.

Holahan, C.J., & R.H. Moos. 1981. Social support and psychological distress: A longitudinal analysis. *Journal of Abnormal Psychology 90*, 365–70.

Ilfeld, F.W. 1980. Coping styles of Chicago adults: Description. *Journal of Human Stress*, June, 2–10.

Jick, T.D., & L.F. Mitz. 1985. Sex differences in work stress. *Academy of Management Review 10*, 408–20.

Kalimo, R., & T. Mejman. 1987. Psychological and behavioural responses to stress at work. In R. Kalimo, M.A. El-Batawi, & C.L. Cooper, eds.,

Psychosocial factors at work and their relation to health (pp. 23–36). Geneva: World Health Organization.

Kanter, R. 1977. *Men and women of the corporation.* New York: Basic Books.

Kirchmeyer, C. 1992. Perceptions of nonwork to work spillover: Challenging the common view of conflict-ridden domain relationships. *Basic and Applied Social Psychology 13*, 231–50.

Korabik, K. 1990. Androgyny and leadership style. *Journal of Business Ethics 9*, 9–18.

LaCroix, A.Z., & S.G. Haynes. 1987. Gender differences in the health effects of workplace roles. In R.C. Barnett, L. Biener, & G.K. Baruch, eds., *Gender and stress* (pp. 96–121). New York: Free Press.

LaRocco, J.M., J.S. House, & J.R.P. French. 1980. Social support, occupational stress, and health. *Journal of Health and Social Behavior 21*, 202–18.

Lazarus, R.S., & S. Folkman. 1984. *Stress, appraisal and coping.* New York: Springer.

Leavy, R.L. 1983. Social support and psychological disorder: A review. *Journal of Community Psychology 11*, 3–20.

Levi, L. 1987. Psychosomatic disease as a consequence of occupational stress. In R. Kalimo, M.A. El-Batawi, & C.L. Cooper, eds., *Psychosocial factors at work and their relation to health* (pp. 78–91). Geneva: World Health Organization.

Long, B.C. 1990. Relation between coping strategies, sex-typed traits and environmental characteristics: A comparison of male and female managers. *Journal of Counseling Psychology 37*, 185–94.

Maier, M., C. Thompson, & C. Thomas. 1991. Corporate responsiveness (and resistance) to work-family interdependence in the United States. *Equal Opportunities International 10*, 25–32.

Martocchio, J.J., & A. O'Leary. 1989. Sex differences in occupational stress: A meta-analytic review. *Journal of Applied Psychology 74*, 495–501.

McDonald, L., & K. Korabik. 1991a. Sources of stress and ways of coping among male and female managers. *Journal of Social Behavior and Personality 6*, 185–98.

– 1991b. Work stress and social support among male and female managers. *Canadian Journal of Administrative Studies 8*, 231–8.

Menaghan, E.G., & E.S. Merves. 1984. Coping with occupational problems: The limits of individual efforts. *Journal of Health and Social Behavior 25*, 406–23.

Mitchell, M.E., & R. Ayman. 1991. Gender, occupation and social support: A comparison. *Equal Opportunities International 10*, 46–52.

Morrison, A.M., R.P. White, & E. Van Velsor. 1987. *Breaking the glass ceiling.* Reading, MA: Addison-Wesley.

Nelson, D.L., & J.C. Quick. 1985. Professional women: Are distress and disease inevitable? *Academy of Management Review 10*, 206–18.

Nelson, D.L., J.C. Quick, & M.A. Hitt. 1989. Men and women of the personnel profession: Some differences and similarities in their stress. *Stress Medicine 5*, 145–52.

Nezu, A.M., & C.M. Nezu, C.M. 1987. Psychological distress, problem solving, and coping reactions: Sex role differences. *Sex Roles 16*, 205–14.

Nicholson, N., & M. West. 1988. *Managerial job change: Men and women in transition*. New York: Cambridge University Press.

Nieva, V.F., & B.A. Gutek. 1981. *Women and work: A psychological perspective*. New York: Praeger.

Parasuraman, S., & M.A. Cleek. 1984. Coping behaviors and managers' affective reactions to role stressors. *Journal of Vocational Behavior 24*, 179–93.

Pearlin, L.I., & C. Schooler. 1978. The structure of coping. *Journal of Health and Social Behavior 19*, 2–21.

Powell, G.N. 1988. *Women and men in management*. Newbury Park, CA: Sage.

Richard, G.V., & T.S. Krieshok. 1989. Occupational stress, strain and coping in university faculty. *Journal of Vocational Behavior 34*, 117–32.

Rosin, H.M., & K. Korabik. 1991. Workplace factors and female managers' attrition from organizations. *Journal of Occupational Psychology 64*, 317–30.

– 1990, July. *Work experiences, dissatisfaction and stress: Are male and female managers different?* Paper presented at the meeting of the International Congress of Applied Psychology, Kyoto, Japan.

Schilling, K.M., & A. Fuehrer. 1987, May. *Sex differences in social support in the work place*. Paper presented at the meeting of the Midwestern Psychological Association, Chicago, IL.

Spector, P.E., D.J. Dwyer, & S.M. Jex. 1988. Relation of job stressors to affective, health and performance outcomes: A comparison of multiple data sources. *Journal of Applied Psychology 73*, 11–19.

Tung, R.L. 1980. Comparative analysis of occupational stress profiles of male versus female administrators. *Journal of Vocational Behavior 17*, 344–55.

Vaux, A. 1985. Variations in social support associated with gender, ethnicity and age. *Journal of Social Issues 41*, 89–110.

Wetzel, J.W., & F.C. Redmond. 1980. A person-environment study of depression. *Social Service Review 54*, 363–75.

Yogev, S. 1982. Are professional women overworked? Objective versus subjective perception of role loads. *Journal of Occupational Psychology 55*, 165–9.

Zappert, L.T., & H.M. Weinstein. 1985. Sex differences in the impact of work on physical and psychological health. *American Journal of Psychiatry 142*, 1174–8.

8 Social Support and Coping of Employed Women

ESTHER R. GREENGLASS

The study of work stress and coping, like so many other areas of psychology, has been dominated by an androcentric approach that conceptualizes stress and its effects from a male perspective. The same approach has traditionally regarded work and family spheres as separate and unrelated (Burke & Greenglass 1987), a compartmentalizing that permits men to concentrate on their work regardless of what is happening in the family sphere. Moreover, in the same vein, approaches to coping have tended to revere the individualistic, with its emphasis on direct problem-solving and instrumentality (Folkman & Lazarus 1980).

Taken together, this approach to the study of work stress and coping in women has been detrimental because it obscures some of the fundamental realities of women's lives. First, the traditional approach to work stress provides us with a very narrow and restrictive definition of work by excluding consideration of the work involved in maintaining a household and raising children. Second, traditional conceptions of work stressors, by compartmentalizing the work and family spheres, have not incorporated the strain that often results from attempting to balance the demands of each, strains most often experienced disproportionately by employed women. Finally, although there is ample evidence for the effectiveness of a cognitive approach to coping, this approach should not preclude the inclusion

Grateful acknowledgment is due to Imperial Oil Ltd for supporting this research in part.

of other kinds of coping, namely coping techniques involving interpersonal skills and the extensive utilization of social support networks.

SOCIAL SUPPORT AS COPING

The extent to which a woman experiences work stress and its deleterious effects depends not only on stressful events and work/family
conflict but also on the resources she may have to cope with these
stressors. To date, research has tended to focus on individual resources, particularly coping strategies used by the individual. Previous research has found individual problem-focused coping or the
managing of the source of stress to be negatively related to depression and physical symptoms and positively related to self-confidence
(Billings & Moos 1984). Moreover, O'Neill and Zeichner (1985) have
found problem-focused coping to be the most effective individual
coping strategy in a study of employed women. And Long (1988) reports that the more effective copers in her sample of twenty professional and managerial women seem to have used problem-focused
coping, such as seeking information or advice or taking problem-
solving action, whereas less effective copers seem to have used strategies such as resigned acceptance.

Increasingly, research is demonstrating the beneficial effects of social support on psychological and physical well-being. Moreover, research suggests that social resource factors either may serve as buffers in the coping process or may directly improve well-being (Cohen
& Wills 1985; Hobfoll 1988). The buffer argument suggests that
stress may affect some persons adversely, but that those who have social support resources are relatively resistant to the deleterious effects of stressful events. Direct effects of social support are found
when health (psychological and/or physical) is improved, independent of levels of stress. Although there are several different definitions of social support, there is no generally accepted measure for it
(Alloway & Bebbington 1987). In theory, several helpful functions
are provided by relationships that could contribute to adjustment.
Moreover, these functions can occur simultaneously or sequentially.
Taken together, research suggests at least three distinct types of functions provided by interpersonal relationships. First, interpersonal relationships may contribute to health because they are a source of acceptance and intimacy, i.e., emotional support. Second, there is
consensus that social support may provide useful information, advice, and guidance, i.e., informational support. Third, people may
assist with instrumental problems by providing financial assistance,

goods, or services, i.e., instrumental support. Often, research demonstrates high correlations among these measures. For the most part, research has tended to focus on self-report measures of social support. Although the issue of the relationship between perceived support and actually received support is beyond the scope of this chapter, some research has shown that the two are almost uncorrelated when both concepts have been measured (Dunkel-Schetter 1984; Dunkel-Schetter & Bennett 1990).

There are several important implications of conceptualizing social support as a coping mechanism. These include both empirical and theoretical facets. First, in viewing social support as a form of coping, one can theoretically link two areas that have previously been viewed as conceptually distinct. This allows for the elaboration of traditional constructs using theoretical developments in different areas. Second, the conceptualization of social support as coping broadens the concept of coping to include interpersonal and relational skills in behaviour. This is in direct contrast to the traditional view of coping as individual problem-solving. At the same time, it is not argued here that coping precludes individual problem-solving; rather, the concept of coping, as conceptualized here, is broadened to include social and interpersonal skills *as well*. Finally, it should be pointed out that the inclusion of interpersonal and relational behaviours as coping entails the positive valuation of behaviours, skills, and abilities that have been inculcated, rewarded, and expected in women. Relational behaviours and concern for the interpersonal arena have traditionally been relegated to the "dependency" field and thus have not been highly valued. However, according to the present reformulation, interpersonal strength and relational skills are conceptualized here as positive coping strengths that can be developed equally in both sexes.

Social coping is also used by persons experiencing stress where individuals draw on the resources of their social networks (Cohen & Wills 1985). Further data indicate that when social support is high, it may buffer the individual from the deleterious effects of work stress (LaRocco, House, & French 1980; Wilcox 1981). The importance of social support is seen in research that demonstrates that it is a major resource in combating the negative effects of strain (Dean & Linn 1977). Lack of support on the job has been associated with depression in women in concurrent analyses (Holahan & Moos 1981).

Several definitions of social support have been offered. For example, Cobb (1976), a leading researcher in the area, talks about social support as the exchange of information leading a person to believe she is cared for, valued, or part of a network having mutual obligations. Kahn and Antonucci (1980) see social support as an interpersonal transaction including one or more of the following key elements: affect, affirmation, and aid. Caplan, Cobb, French, Van Harrison, and Pinneau (1975) discuss two types of social support: tangible help and emotional help. And, according to House and Wells (1978), social support consists of frequent interactions, strong and positive feelings, and the availability of emotional and instrumental support when needed. There are, then, many different definitions of social support that vary in the dimensions on which they focus. Social support may differ as well in terms of the source of the support: for example, whether it comes from one's supervisor, coworkers and/or spouse, friends or family. One may focus as well on whether the support given tends to be primarily for work- or family-related activities.

GENDER-ROLE DIFFERENCES IN SOCIAL SUPPORT

Additional research indicates the function of the family as a buffer of stress. Families in general and spouses in particular serve as significant sources of social support for coping with minor daily hassles and major stressful life events (Barbarin, Hughes, & Chesler 1985; Cohen & Wills 1985). Additional data, however, show that the function of the family as a buffer of stress is also gender-related. Gutek and Stevens (1979) report that wives are better providers of both instrumental and emotional support than husbands. There is ample evidence to support the contention that husbands and children are sources of stress for employed women (Gutek, Repetti, & Silver 1988). Not only do women experience greater demands at home, both emotional and practical, they are also often expected to protect their spouses from family-related stress (Kessler, McLeod, & Wethington 1983).

Additional research, this time with successful professionals, shows that high-achieving men tend to be married whereas high-achieving women tend to be unmarried (Houseknecht, Vaughan, & Statham 1987). Further, the same researchers report that women who remain single in graduate school achieve greater occupational attainment than women who marry while they are still students. It appears, therefore, that domestic demands, disproportionately experienced by married women versus married men, not only result in greater role conflict and role strain for women, but can also hinder their occupational attainment.

There is some question whether the family does buffer work strain in women. Among managers and professionals, again, women are less likely to marry and to have children (Greenglass 1988, 1990; Greenglass & Burke 1988; Greenglass, Burke, & Ondrack 1990). Moreover, data support the view that wives function more often than husbands as an important part of their spouses' support system. For example, Lowenthal and Haven (1968) report that wives were mentioned most often by husbands as confidantes, and husbands were mentioned least often by their wives. Booth (1972) also reports that, among married couples, husbands most often mention their wives as confidantes and wives less frequently mention husbands. Burke and Weir (1975, 1977) report that wives recognize, more than husbands, the emotional state of their spouses and respond more readily as helpers to their spouses than husbands to their wives.

Not surprisingly, however, employed women, compared to housewives, are less likely to provide emotional support for their husbands. Burke and Weir (1976) found that husbands of employed women, when compared with men married to full-time housewives, had lower marital satisfaction, greater job pressure, and poorer mental and physical health. These data suggest, then, that because of their own pressures, employed wives may not be providing the same level of emotional support for their husbands as do full-time housewives.

WOMEN, SOCIAL SUPPORT, AND INTERPERSONAL DEMANDS

Women, by virtue of their social networks, generally appear to have more support demands placed on them than do men. For example, women, compared with their male counterparts, are more likely to cite the well-being of their spouses (Campbell, Converse, & Rodgers 1976), parents (Brody 1981), and children (Menaghan 1978) as important sources of concern. Among college students, women report having larger social networks than men (Burda, Vaux, & Schell 1984). Moreover, women become more involved in the lives of their friends and family and are more likely to experience the distress felt by others. Women appear to be more negatively affected by events that take place in the interpersonal domain – they take on the burdens and problems of family and friends. Women, compared with men, are more emotionally involved in others' lives and serve a nurturing role for a wider network of people. Kessler et al. (1983) report national survey data indicating that women are 30 per cent more likely than men to give support to a loved one. Kessler et al. add that, although the kinds of support women and men give to people in a crisis are very similar, women spend more time assisting others and therefore are more vulnerable than men to the life events occurring to loved ones. They suggest that men care about fewer people beyond their loved ones. Kessler et al. conclude that, although lack of distress was correlated with amount of time "doing things to help others," the costs of caring may outweigh the rewards.

On the basis of his qualitative research, Bell (1981) found that women have more close friends than do men and in fact emphasize intimacy and disclosure in their friendships. Women appear to value friendship more for its own sake and value the interdependence that is an integral part of a close friendship. In one Canadian study, for example, women and men school personnel were compared on a variety of stressors and distress symptoms (Greenglass et al. 1990). Although respondents tended to be primarily teachers, some were, as well, department heads, vice-principals, and principals. Approximately 40 to 45 per cent of the sample was employed at the elementary school level, one-third were from the junior high school level, and one-quarter were from secondary school. Greenglass et al. (1990) have shown that women were significantly higher than men on the "Investment in Friends" Scale. This scale is a subscale of a larger measure of "Quality of Life," an instrument that assesses, among other things, memories, enjoyment of nature, cultural activities, and investment in friends. The premise of the scale is that the more the individual employs strategies that maximize each of these activities, the greater the person's quality of life, which in turn should be associated with less stress, conflict, and burnout. A person scoring high on the "Investment in Friends" subscale is one who highly values her/his friendships. Items centre around the importance of friendship for its own sake. A sample item is "I invest a lot of myself in the lives of my friends and family members." Further data indicated that "Investment in Friends" is an effective coping strategy in reducing burnout.

INTERPERSONAL COMPETENCE AND COPING IN WOMEN

Results showing women's greater investment in, and valuation of, friendship are in line with previous findings by Norcross, DiClemente, and Prochaska (1986) that women, compared with men, employ more coping processes involving interpersonal relationships. The results are not surprising, given that women, more than men, are expected to be sensitive, comforting, and empathetic to other people and to their concerns. Also, it is seen as more acceptable for women to confide in others, something that may be interpreted as a sign of weakness in men. At the same time, the quality of daily life in the Greenglass et al. (1990) study was reported to be higher among women. It may be that women's ability to turn to and enjoy activities other than work (i.e., socializing, the arts) may enable them to resist becoming callous as a result of a stressful work situation. Data from the same study (Greenglass et al. 1990) showed that women were significantly lower on depersonalization, a subscale of the Maslach Burnout Inventory (Maslach & Jackson 1986) – a finding reported in the past by several other researchers (Anderson & Iwanicki 1984; Ogus, Greenglass, & Burke 1990).

Men may be higher on depersonalization as a result of gender-role prescriptions relating to the masculine role, particularly its emotional restrictiveness (Pleck 1980). Because interdependence and relating to others on an emotional basis entail a certain level of vulnerability and risk, men may be more likely to suppress these behaviours because they are not acceptable according to masculine gender norms (Miller 1976). As a result, men may be less likely than women to employ interpersonal processes as a way of coping with stressful events.

Other data show the beneficial effects of social support for women on the job. Self-reported depression levels were higher among women tellers in bank branches rated as nonsupportive by peers. Other data, this time obtained from women managers, demonstrate the importance of social support from one's boss for healthy psychological functioning. In one study, Greenglass (1985) examined the relationship between various indices of physical and mental well-being and occupational stressors in a sample of 113 women managers and administrators selected from an association for managerial women. They worked in a variety of spheres, including corporate, educational, and public service institutions. The majority (79 per cent) occupied middle or senior management positions. Included in the measures employed was an assessment of social support from the respondent's boss that covered the extent to which the boss was said to provide support by being a good listener and being reliable when assistance was needed. Anxiety was assessed using a state anxiety measure (Spielberger, Gorsuch, & Lushene 1970) that assesses feelings of tension, nervousness, worry, and apprehension. In addition, depression and irritation were assessed (Caplan et al. 1975), as were job satisfaction (Quinn & Shepard 1974), intention to turnover (Quinn & Shepard 1974), and drug-taking. Drugs included tranquillizers, sleeping pills, and pain medication.

Results of correlational analyses indicated that low support from one's boss was associated with higher anxiety, depression, psychosomatic symptoms, irritation, drug-taking, and greater intention to turnover. Low perceived support from one's boss was also associated with lowered job satisfaction. These data clearly underline the need for the boss's support and show the deleterious psychological effects in women managers when this support is low. While support from one's boss may be critical to the functioning of all workers, it may be important to the job functioning of women in nontraditional spheres, such as management, particularly when the boss's attitude takes the form of rejection or conveys the impression that these women should not be there in the first place.

Further research findings illustrate the positive benefits of social support, particularly in women. Francis and Greenglass (1991) examined the relationship between various types of social support, coping forms, and job anxiety in a matched sample of 114 female and male supervisors employed within government social service agencies. Men were matched with women on a number of variables, including number of people supervised, number of hours worked per week, number of years spent at the present job, and annual salary. Three-quarters of the men and 56 per cent of the women were married. Social support from the three sources was assessed, including support from one's boss, co-workers, and family (Caplan et al. 1975). Job anxiety was assessed using the STAI Anxiety Scale (Spielberger et al. 1970), and coping was measured using Wong and Reker's (1984) Coping Inventory, which assesses instrumental and palliative coping. Instrumental coping refers to coping strategies that are problem-focused and involve taking some action to solve the problem. This may include trying to change the situation, or one's behaviour, or both. Palliative coping refers to coping strategies that enable the person to feel better without actively changing the situation in any way. Palliative coping includes wishful thinking (fantasizing some kind of rescue) and self-blame (viewing the problem as the result of one's own unworthiness).

Results of correlations showed significant and negative relationships between boss support and job anxiety in both women ($r = -.42$, $df = 50$, $p < .01$) and in men ($r = -.31$, $df = 52$, $p < .05$); whereas in women *only*, family support was significantly and negatively related to job anxiety ($r = -.47$, $df = 48$, $p < .001$) (Francis & Greenglass 1991). This relationship was nonsignificant in men. Thus, the more support that the women managers received from their families, the lower their job anxiety. These findings follow from the observation that home and job spheres are more interrelated in women than in men (Burke & Greenglass 1987). It should be pointed out that the family support provided here was for work-related concerns. Thus, higher job anxiety would appear to occur when the woman manager's family does not support her work-related activities. Men's level of job anxiety appears to be independent of level of family support, thus suggesting that, in men, family and work spheres are more independent of each other.

In one study (Francis & Greenglass 1991), additional relationships were observed in women, but not in men, between various supports and palliative coping. For example, in women managers only, higher boss support and higher support from one's family were associated with lower palliative coping – in particular, self-blame and wishful thinking. And palliative coping, particularly self-blame, was significantly lower with greater co-worker support, only in women. Thus, the data suggest that women are able to employ their interpersonal skills to lower their use of dysfunctional coping strategies. (Palliative coping only modifies one's feelings about a situation and does not contribute effectively to the solution of a problem.) Thus, women may have utilized social support to seek information or advice approaching the source of their stress, lessening their reliance on palliative coping. These findings parallel results reported by Long (1988) on twenty professional and managerial women. More effective copers used strategies that relied on seeking information or advice from others. Data thus suggest that women are empowered by their interpersonal skills to cope more effectively with job stress. Data obtained from their male counterparts do not indicate a similar trend. On the contrary, the data reviewed here suggest that men tend to compartmentalize various aspects of their social/work lives such that less interdependence is observed between interpersonal involvement and work-related issues.

Further research reveals that social support lessens role conflict in women and not as much in men (Greenglass, Pantony, & Burke 1988). Moreover, research shows that role conflict is a significant contributor to distress in women. For example, Greenglass (1985) reports significant positive relationships between psychosomatic measures and various forms of interference between home and job. Interference between home and job was assessed by giving a sample of senior women administrators a list of nine ways in which job and family interfered with each other and asking them to check the ones that applied to them. A total of 35 per cent of the sample reported that their work schedule interfered with their family life. The next most frequently reported form of interference was that "work makes me too tired or irritable to participate or enjoy family life." This form of interference was endorsed by 32 per cent of respondents. The total number of interferences reported was computed for each respondent and correlated with various psychological distress measures. Results indicated significant positive relationships between the total number of interferences reported and measures of depression, irritation, and anxiety. These findings coincide with those of Greenglass et al. (1988) that suggest an association between higher role conflict, incidence of headaches, and depression – results also reported by Cortis (1973) and Price (1970).

Research with teachers suggests that women are better able than men to utilize support from others – particularly from their supervisors, families, and friends – to lessen role conflict between their work and family roles. In one study, Greenglass et al. (1988) assessed role conflict using Holahan and Gilbert's (1979) six role-conflict scales, which measure conflict between the roles of professional and those of parent and spouse. Respondents were 556 women and men employed within a school board in a large Canadian city. Respondents tended to be mainly teachers, although some were department heads, vice-principals, and principals. Ninety-three per cent of the men and 80 per cent of the women were married and living with their spouse. Respondents had an average of two children. Social support from one's supervisor, co-workers, and family was assessed using the scales designed by Caplan et al. (1975). Results indicated significant negative relationships between support from one's supervisor and family, and reports of role conflict, predominantly in women. Thus, in women teachers as in women managers, there is a significant and negative relationship between support from one's supervisor and family, and the experience of stressors, in this case, role conflict.

WOMEN'S INTERPERSONAL COMPETENCE AND SOCIAL SUPPORT

As mentioned earlier, employed women experience greater demands and stressors than their male counterparts, and many of these demands emanate from interpersonal relationships and multiple roles whose demands tend to conflict more with each other in women than in men. But considerable research was cited showing that, paradoxically, it is within interpersonal relationships that employed women find resources to cope with these demands. Further research suggests that women may utilize support from others through talking with one another. Traditionally, this attention to the interpersonal domain has tended to be interpreted as a sign of dependency (Wine, Moses, & Smye 1980), a "weakness" inherent in women that forces them to turn to others for "help." However, recent research suggests that the role women enact interpersonally is not a passive-dependent one but an active one that tends to utilize others' resources in a positive and constructive way. Etzion and Pines (1981) suggest that women are often able to make more effective use of their support network than men because they tend to talk with one another as a way of coping with stress. Likewise, Burke and Belcourt (1974) note that women are more likely than men to mention "talking with others" as a way of dealing with work stress. Thus, women's interpersonal competence empowers them to relate better to others, which may explain why women are better able to give and receive social support than men. Recent research on women suggests that interpersonal competence, and thus greater ability to relate to others, may also result in less reliance on dysfunctional coping forms. Because the receipt of social support likely contributes to constructive and functional strategies for change, the individual is less likely to feel frustrated and angry, and thus is less likely to engage in palliative coping that does not remedy or change a problematic situation. At the same time, women and girls are higher on interdependence, the ability to express interpersonal needs, particularly in emotional relationships, and to relate meaningfully to others in interpersonal relationships (Greenglass 1982).

Women's interpersonal strength is discussed by Wine et al. (1980), who, in their review of existing data relevant to sex differences and interpersonal interaction, reinterpret some original findings. For example, they cite differences found in the literature that were used as evidence of women's weakness and/or of men's strength – for example, that women are better listeners and that women's speech patterns, compared with men's, reflect emotional involvement. Their reinterpretation of the data suggests that women have greater interpersonal social competence than men, as seen, for example, in their being more responsive to variations in social input, and having language and speech patterns indicative of greater interpersonal sensitivity.

SOCIETAL VALUES AND INTERPERSONAL COMPETENCE: NEED FOR REDEFINITION

To summarize, women's interdependence and social competence are strengths, as demonstrated in recent research on women and how they cope (and help others to cope) with stressful conditions both on the job and at home. Moreover, it is argued that interpersonal competence in women is empowering, particularly in enabling them to cope effectively with a variety of work and home demands and the conflict between these. Future research could benefit from theoretical and empirical constructions that incorporate this growing body of knowledge into existing theories of coping, work stress, and organizational dynamics that affect both women and men. But the strengths involved in the processes through which women give and receive social support have generally been overlooked in psychological research. When the issue has been raised, women's interpersonal strengths in this area have been devalued by a patriarchal belief system that has tended to equate sensitivity with weakness. This belief system has been premised on the underlying assumption of a gender dichotomy of human nature that has been differentially valued. Men come to value self-assertion, separateness, and independence, whereas women value interdependence, cooperation, and receptivity. Moreover, it has been argued that the values structured into women's experiences, such as caretaking, nurturance, and empathy, differ greatly from those at the basis of the bureaucratic world. This world of anonymous social relations is dominated by norms of instrumental rationality, a cognitive style that is instrumental, functional, and purposive (Symons 1987).

Thus, through patriarchy and the enforcement of its value systems, society has emphasized and inculcated men's values, which in turn have been primarily responsible for shaping the organization, cultural, norms, and language of our society (Marshall, this volume). At the same time, behaviour that is not seen as rational, purposive, or functional tends to be devalued. Thus, values usually associated with women's behaviours tend to be rejected, devalued, and excluded.

The issue of coping for women cannot be separated from the interpersonal domain, where the values structured into women's experience are those of caretaking, nurturance, empathy, and connectedness. A growing body of research on employed women continues to demonstrate that interpersonal coping is effective. But bureaucratic structures need to expand their ideological and value systems in ways that see this kind of coping as important. Both men and women can engage in interpersonal coping with equal success. The task, then, is to expand our view of the true utilization of human potential to include interpersonal skills, affiliation, and connectedness, and to accord them the same value that is associated with functional rationalization.

REFERENCES

Alloway, R., & P. Bebbington. 1987. The buffer theory of social support – a review of the literature. *Psychological Medicine 17*, 91–108.

Anderson, M.B.G., & E.F. Iwanicki. 1984. Teacher motivation and its
    relationship to burnout. *Educational Administration Quarterly 20*, 109–32.
Barbarin, O.A., D. Hughes, & M.A. Chesler. 1985. Stress, coping and
    mental functioning among parents of children with cancer. *Journal of
    Marriage and Family 47*, 473–80.
Bell, R.R. 1981. *Worlds of friendship*. Beverly Hills, CA: Sage.
Billings, A.G., & R.H. Moos, 1984. Coping, stress and social resources
    among adults with unipolar depression. *Journal of Personality and Social
    Psychology 46*, 877–91.
Booth, A. 1972. Sex and social participation. *American Sociological Review
    37*, 183–92.
Brody, E.M. 1981. Women in the middle and family help to older people.
    Gerontologist 21, 471–80.
Burda, P.C., A. Vaux, & T. Schell. 1984. Social support resources:
    Variation across sex and sex role. *Personality and Social Psychology Bulletin
    10*, 119–26.
Burke, R.J., & M.L. Belcourt. 1974. Managerial role stress and coping
    responses. *Journal of Business Administration 5*, 55–68.
Burke, R.J., & E.R. Greenglass. 1987. Work and family. In C.L. Cooper &
    I.T. Robertson, eds., *International review of industrial and organizational
    psychology* (pp. 273–320). New York: Wiley.
Burke, R.J., & T. Weir. 1975. Receiving and giving help with work and
    non-work related problems. *Journal of Business Administration 6*, 59–78.
– 1976. Some personality differences between members of one-career
    and two-career families. *Journal of Marriage and the Family 38*, 453–9.
– 1977. Husband-wife helping-relationships: The "mental hygiene"
    function in marriage. *Psychological Reports 40*, 911–25.
Campbell, A., P.E. Converse, & W.L. Rodgers. 1976. *The quality of American
    life: Perceptions, evaluations and satisfactions*. New York: Russell Sage
    Foundation.
Caplan, R.D., S. Cobb, J.R.P. French, Jr, R. Van Harrison, & S.P. Pinneau.
    1975. *Job demands and worker health: Main effects and occupational
    differences*. Washington, DC: U.S. Government Printing Office.
Cobb, S. 1976. Social support as a moderator of life stress. *Psychosomatic
    Medicine 5*, 300–17.
Cohen, S., & T. Wills. 1985. Stress, social support, and the buffering
    hypothesis. *Psychological Bulletin 98*, 310–57.
Cortis, G.A. 1973. The assessment of a group of teachers in relation to
    earlier career experience. *Educational Review 25*, 112–23.
Dean, A., & N. Linn. 1977. The stress-buffering role of social support
    problems and prospects for systematic investigation. *Journal of Nervous
    Mental Disease 165*, 403–17.
Dunkel-Schetter, C. 1984. Social support and cancer: Findings based on

patient interviews and their implications. *Journal of Social Issues 40*, 77–98.

Dunkel-Schetter, C., & T.L. Bennett. 1990. The availability of social support and its activation in times of stress. In I.G. Sarason, B.R. Sarason, & G.R. Pierce, eds., *Social support: An interactional view*. New York: Wiley.

Etzion, D., & A. Pines. 1981. *Sex and culture as factors explaining reported coping behavior and burnout of human service professionals. A social psychological perspective*. Tel Aviv: Tel Aviv University. Israel Institute of Business Research.

Folkman, S., & R.S. Lazarus. 1980. An analysis of coping in a middle-aged community sample. *Journal of Health and Social Behavior 21*, 219–39.

Francis, J., & E.R. Greenglass. 1991. Processes of coping and social support: Gender differences. Unpublished manuscript. York University, Toronto, Canada.

Greenglass, E.R. 1982. *A world of difference: Gender roles in perspective*. Toronto: Wiley.

– 1985. Psychological implications of sex bias in the workplace. *Academic Psychology Bulletin 7*, 227–40.

– 1988. Type A behavior and coping strategies in female and male supervisors. *Applied Psychology: An International Review 37*, 271–88.

– 1990. Type A behavior, career aspirations, and role conflict in professional women. *Journal of Social Behavior and Personality 5*, 307–22.

Greenglass, E.R., & R.J. Burke. 1988. Work and family precursors of burnout in teachers: Sex differences. *Sex Roles 18*, 215–29.

Greenglass, E.R., R.J. Burke, & M. Ondrack. 1990. A gender-role perspective of coping and burnout. *Applied Psychology: An International Review 39*, 5–27.

Greenglass, E.R., K.L. Pantony, & R.J. Burke. 1988. A gender-role perspective on role conflict, work stress and social support. *Journal of Social Behavior and Personality 3*, 317–28.

Gutek, B.A., R. Repetti, & D. Silver. 1988. Nonwork roles and stress at work. In C.L. Cooper & R. Payne, eds., *Causes, coping and consequences of stress at work* (pp. 141–74). Chichester, UK: Wiley.

Gutek, B.A., & D.A. Stevens. 1979. Effects of sex of subject, sex of stimulus cue and androgyny level on evaluations in work situations which evoke sex role stereotypes. *Journal of Vocational Behavior 14*, 23–32.

Hobfoll, S.E. 1988. *The ecology of stress*. Washington, DC: Hemisphere.

Holahan, C.J., & L.A. Gilbert. 1979. Conflict between major life roles: Women and men in dual career couples. *Human Relations 32*, 451–67.

Holahan, C.J., & R.H. Moos. 1981. Social support and psychological distress: A longitudinal analysis. *Journal of Abnormal Psychology 90*, 365–70.

House, J.S., & J.A. Wells. 1978. Occupational stress, social support, and health. In A. McLean, G. Black, & M. Colligan, eds., *Reducing occupational stress* (pp. 8–29). U.S. Department of Health, Education and Welfare Publication No. 78-140.

Houseknecht, S.K., S. Vaughan, & A. Statham. 1987. The impact of singlehood on the career patterns of professional women. *Journal of Marriage and the Family 49*, 353–66.

Kahn, R.L., & T. Antonucci. 1980. Convoys over the life course: Attachment roles and social support. In P.B. Baltes & O. Brim, eds., *Life-span development and behavior* (3:253–80). Boston, MA: Lexington Press.

Kessler, R.C., J.D. McLeod, & E. Wethington. 1983. The costs of caring: A perspective on the relationship between sex and psychological distress. In I.G. Sarason & B.R. Sarason, eds., *Social support: Theory, research and application* (pp. 491–506). The Hague: Martinus Nijhof.

LaRocco, J.M., J.S. House, & J.R.P. French, Jr. 1980. Social support, occupational stress and health. *Journal of Health and Social Behavior 21*, 202–18.

Long, B.C. 1988. Work-related stress and coping strategies of professional women. *Journal of Employment Counseling 25*, 37–44.

Lowenthal, M.F., & C. Haven. 1968. Interaction and adaptation: Intimacy as a critical variable. *American Sociological Review 33*, 20–30.

Maslach, C., & S.E. Jackson. 1986. *Maslach Burnout Inventory Manual* (2nd ed.). Palo Alto, CA: Consulting Psychologists Press.

Menaghan, E.G. 1978. The effect of family transitions on marital experience. Unpublished doctoral dissertation, Department of Human Development, University of Chicago.

Miller, J.B. 1976. *Toward a new psychology of women*. Boston: Beacon Press.

Norcross, J.C., C.C. DiClemente, & J.O. Prochaska. 1986. Self-change of psychological distress: Laypersons' vs. psychologists' coping strategies. *Journal of Clinical Psychology 42*, 834–40.

Ogus, D., E. Greenglass, & R.J. Burke. 1990. Gender role differences, work stress and depersonalization. *Psychological Reports 5*, 387–98.

O'Neill, C.P., & A. Zeichner. 1985. Working women: A study of relationships between stress, coping and health. *Journal of Psychosomatic Obstetrics and Gynaecology 4*, 105–16.

Pleck, J.H. 1980. Male sex role identity: Fact or fiction? *Wellesley College Working Paper*. Boston, MA: Wellesley College.

– 1985. *Working wives/working husbands*. Beverly Hills, CA: Sage.

Price, L.W. 1970. Organizational stress and job satisfaction in public high school teachers. Doctoral dissertation, Stanford University. *Dissertation Abstracts International 31*(11-A), 5727–8.

Quinn, R.P., & L.J. Shepard. 1974. *The 1972–1973 Quality of Employment Survey: Descriptive statistics, with comparison data from the 1969–70 Survey of Working Conditions.* Ann Arbor: Institute for Social Research.

Repetti, R.L. 1987. Individual and common components of the social environment at work and psychological well-being. *Journal of Personality and Social Psychology 52*, 710–20.

Spielberger, C.D., R.L. Gorsuch, & R.E. Lushene. 1970. *The State-trait Anxiety Inventory.* Palo Alto, CA: Consulting Psychologists Press.

Symons, G. 1987, April. *Managerial women in the bureaucracy: A critical perspective.* Paper presented at the Fourth Annual Conference of Women Managers, Israeli Center for Management, Haifa, Israel.

Wilcox, B.L. 1981. Social support, life and psychological adjustment: A test of the buffering hypothesis. *American Journal of Community Psychology 9*, 371–86.

Wine, J.D., B. Moses, & M.D. Smye. 1980. Female superiority in sex difference competence comparisons: A review of the literature. In C. Stark-Adamec, ed., *Sex roles: Origins, influences, and implications for women* (pp. 148–63). Montreal: Eden Press Women's Publications.

Wong, P.T.P., & G.T. Reker. 1984, May. *Coping behaviors of successful agers.* Paper presented at the 30th Annual Meeting of the Canadian Psychological Association, Ottawa.

9 Marriage Matters: Young Women's Health

LOIS M. VERBRUGGE

In the last decades of the twentieth century, young women have increasingly engaged in multiple roles; namely, combining job, marital, and parent responsibilities. Popular thinking persists that women with multiple roles experience high stress and dissatisfaction, and that this leads to poor physical and mental health. By contrast, scientific research shows more optimistic results: women with multiple roles are happier and healthier than those who are less actively engaged (Baruch & Barnett 1986; Baruch, Biener, & Barnett 1987; Crosby 1987; Froberg, Gjerdingen, & Preston 1986; Hibbard & Pope 1985; Kotler & Wingard 1989; Moen, Williams, & Dempster-McClain 1989; Ross, Mirowsky, & Goldsteen 1990; Sorensen & Verbrugge 1987; Thoits 1983, 1986; Verbrugge 1983, 1986; Verbrugge & Madans 1985; Waldron & Jacobs 1989; Welch & Booth 1977; Woods & Hulka 1979). Research shows that employment is associated with good physical and mental health; so is marriage. But having children present (in the home) has variable effects – sometimes it is linked with better health for mothers than nonmothers, sometimes with worse (Ross, Mirowsky, & Goldsteen 1990; Sorensen & Verbrugge 1987; Verbrugge 1983). The importance of strong coping resources among highly involved persons has been noted (Baruch et al. 1987; Haw 1982; Kessler & McRae 1982; Pearlin & Johnson 1977; Radloff 1975; Wheaton 1983, 1985).

An earlier version of this chapter was presented at the American Psychological Association meetings, Anaheim, CA, 1983. Data collection for the Health in Detroit Study was funded by the National Institute of Mental Health (RO1 MH29478).

This article extends scientific research by concentrating on young women ages 18 to 34, an age group with many combinations of job, marriage, and motherhood. I studied the links of stress, satisfaction, and competence to physical health in the various role combinations. (a) I first asked which young women are most stressed, most dissatisfied, and least confident about their coping skills: Is it those with triple roles (married employed mothers) or with few (such as nonemployed nonmarried women)? Turning then to physical health, (b) I studied which role groups have the best physical health and (c) I determined which psychological features pose risks for poor health. (d) Finally, I asked if social involvement (job, marriage, parenthood) buffers negative impacts of stress on health, on the one hand, and enhances positive impacts of satisfaction and competence on health, on the other.

DATA AND VARIABLES

The data source is the Health in Detroit Study, a survey of white adults residing in the Detroit metropolitan area conducted in 1978. It is a probability sample of households, with one adult selected for interview in each sampled household (Verbrugge 1979, 1980). The survey included an initial interview with questions about physical health, health attitudes, and life stresses. After the interview, respondents kept daily health records for six weeks. Each day, they entered information about general health status, symptoms, and curative and preventive health actions. The interviews are retrospective and provide a picture of long-term health; the diaries are prospective and provide a picture of short-term health. A total of 714 persons (302 men, 412 women) completed the initial interview, and 589 (243 men, 346 women) kept daily health records for one week or longer. This chapter uses the subsample of women ages 18–34: 162 completed the initial interview and 144 kept health diaries for at least one week.

There are 31 dependent variables on physical health; they cover a broad spectrum of health-status, health-behaviour, and health-attitude items. From the initial interview, I used items on chronic conditions and ensuing limitations, subjective evaluations of health status, attitudes about pain and frequency of activity reduction for symptoms, and recent illness and injury. From the daily health records, I used counts of symptoms, restricted activities, medical care, and medical drug use over a six-week period. Table 1 shows the health variables and their mean values for the young women. All items are scored so that high scores indicate "poor health."

Table 1
Health, Roles and Psyche Variables (Young Women Ages 18–34 in Detroit)

Health – initial interview[a]	Mean
No. of chronic conditions in past year	3.73
Health in past year	2.76
(1 = very best health possible TO 10 = very serious health problems)	
Satisfaction with health	1.64
(1 = very satisfied TO 4 = very dissatisfied)	
Vulnerability to illness	2.41
(How often sick compared to age peers; 1 = a lot less often TO 5 = a lot more often)	
Work limitations due to health	0.14
(0 = no limitations, 1 = limited in kind or amount of work, 2 = unable to have a job)	
Nonwork limitations due to health	0.45
(index based on housework/chores, sport/hobbies, other mobility and physical activity; range 0–6)	
How feel physically each day	3.24
(1 = wonderful all the time TO 10 = terrible all the time)	
How much physical feelings vary from day to day	2.34
(1 = not at all TO 4 = a lot)	
Self-rated health status	1.75
(1 = excellent TO 4 = poor)	
Health status compared to age peers	2.59
(1 = better, 3 = same, 5 = worse)	
Can ignore pain or discomfort without taking medicine	2.47
(1 = always TO 5 = never)	
Propensity to reduce activities for illness	1.94
(helps you get better if you cut down usual activities; 1 = a lot TO 4 = not at all)	
How often worn out when finished with daily work or household tasks	2.93
(1 = never TO 5 = every day)	
How good a job in taking care of own health	2.30
(1 = excellent TO 4 = poor)	
In past two weeks, no. of days not felt well because of illness/injury	1.83
In past two weeks, any days not felt well for other reasons	0.20
(0 = no, 1 = yes)	

Health – daily health records	Mean
(All items refer to six-week diary period)[b]	
Average physical feeling	7.57
("How do you feel physically today?", 1 = wonderful TO 10 = terrible)	
No. of symptomatic days	16.2
Total no. of health problems[c]	23.6
No. of days cut down usual activities (#)[d,e]	3.30
No. of days cut down chores or errands (#)	2.77
No. of days missed work (#)	0.48

Table 1 (continued)

Health – daily health records		Mean
No. of days with curative medical care (#)[f]		0.68
No. of days talked with friends/family about symptoms (#)		8.26
No. of days with preventive medical care		1.90
No. of days took pills, medicines, or treatments (drugs) (#)		21.4
Total no. of drugs taken (#)[g]		40.1
No. of curative drugs (#)		12.8
No. of preventative drugs (#)		16.8
No. of nonprescription drugs (#)		19.1
No. of prescription drugs (#)		14.3

Roles		Percentage
EMPLOYMENT STATUS		
employed		59.3
MARITAL STATUS		
currently married		58.6
previously married		13.6
never married		27.8
PARENT STATUS		
parent (own child at home)		50.0
ROLE GROUPS		N
nonempl, nev married, no chd	At Home	6
nonempl, nev married, chd	At Home	2
nonempl, prev married, no chd	At Home	1
nonempl, prev married, chd	At Home	7
nonempl, married, no chd	Homemakers	14
nonempl, married, chd	Homemakers	36
empl, nev married, no chd	Career Women	33
empl, married, no chd	Career Women	22
empl, prev married, chd	Two Roles "Plus"	9
empl, married, chd	Triple Roles	23
empl, nev married, chd	–	4
empl, prev married, no chd	–	5

Psyche	Mean
STRESS	
Chronic stress	9.97
(index based on 3 items: work pace, worry about future, chance to do things you like to do; range 3–15)	
Acute stress	12.4
(index based on 4 items: nervousness, strain, relaxation, anxiety in past month; range 4–20)	
Any stressful events in past year	84.2%
(0 = no, 1 = yes)	
How often feel rushed	3.30
(1 = never TO 5 = always)	
SATISFACTION	
Liking for job[h]	3.63
(1 = unqualified dislike TO 5 = unqualified like)	

Table 1 (continued)

Psyche	Mean
Liking for housework	3.66
(1 = unqualified dislike TO 5 = unqualified like)	
Life in past year	7.44
(1 = worst life you could expect TO 10 = best life could expect)	
COMPETENCE	
Resistance resources	7.73
(index based on 2 attitude items: it is a weakness to admit problems, better off to look at positive side of life; range 2–10).	
Internal locus of control	11.7
(index based on 3 attitude items: feel helpless in dealing with problems of life, can do anything I set my mind to do, little I can do to change things; range 3–15)	
Self-esteem	10.7
(index based on 3 attitude items: feel useless at times, have a number of good qualities, wish I could have more respect for myself; range 3–15)	

Source: Health in Detroit Study, 1978
Note: N = 162 for initial interview, N = 144 for diary
[a]Most items are ordinal-scaled; minimum and maximum categories are stated.
[b]There is little selectivity among the young women who dropped out over the six-week diary period.
[c]The daily health record had a symptom chart for each day. Respondents entered details about health problems of that day. This variable is the number of health problems summed across 42 charts. If the same problem occurred on more than one day, it is counted several times.
[d]#: Regressions were estimated twice, with and without a morbidity control (no. of symptomatic days).
[e]Days spent in bed, cut down household chores/errands, missed work, or cut down other planned activities.
[f]Days made an appointment, telephoned an office/clinic, visited an office/clinic, was admitted to hospital, or had other curative medical care.
[g]The daily health record had a drug chart for each day. Respondents entered details about drugs taken on that day. This variable is the number of drugs summed across 42 drug charts. If the same drug was used on more than one day, it is counted several times. Drugs are categorized by purpose (curative, preventive) and by prescription status (nonprescription, prescription).
[h]Nonemployed women receive the middle score (=3). See note 1 for details.

Three *roles* were studied: employment, marriage, and parenthood. Employed women are defined as those with a paid job. Married women have a spouse or opposite-sex partner. Previously married women are separated, divorced, or widowed women. Never-married women are the third marital group. Parents (mothers) are women with an own child (one or more, by birth or adoption) at home. There are 12 possible role combinations of these statuses (2 × 3 × 2); sample sizes are shown in table 1.

The psychological variables were of three types: stress, satisfaction, and competence. Stress was measured by 4 items: chronic stress, acute stress, stressful life events in past year, and feeling rushed (time pressure). Satisfaction had 3 items: liking for job (employed women), liking for housework (all women), and rating of life in past year (all women). Competence had 3 items: resistance to stress, internal locus of control, and self esteem. Table 1 describes the variables in detail.

METHOD

Statistical procedures involve correlations, cross-tabulations, and multiple regressions. The sample size of 162 is modest, so statistical significance ($p<.05$) occurs only for pronounced effects. Given this situation, I look for consistency in effects across the 31 dependent variables, significant or not. This reveals patterns even if effects are weak on an item-by-item basis.

Question 1

Which young women feel most stressed, most dissatisfied, and least competent about life? This is answered by examining correlations of role × psyche variables, and cross-tabulations of same.

Question 2

Which role groups of young women are healthiest, and which are least healthy? This is studied in multiple regression models:

Model 1 $Y = f [E, M, P]$
Model 2 $Y = f [E, M, P; E \times M, E \times P, M \times P]$
Model 3 $Y = f [E, M, P; E \times M, E \times P, M \times P; E \times M \times P]$

Model 1 shows main (additive) effects of employment, marriage, and parenthood on health. These are abbreviated E, M, P. Model 2 shows if combining two roles has any special effect (two-way interactions). Model 3 shows if combining three roles has any effect (three-way interactions). Models 2 and 3 are suitable tests of hypotheses about multiple roles, since they indicate if putting two or three roles together is especially beneficial or problematic for health, beyond the general (additive) effect each role has.

How many predictors does each model contain? Predictors are all in dummy form. There are 4 main effects: E, M1, M2, and P. For employment, E = 1 for employed and 0 for nonemployed. Marital status is represented by 2 dummy variables, M1 for previously married women (= 1, else 0) and M2 for currently married women (= 1, else 0); never-married women score 0 on both of these. For parent status, P = 1 for parent and 0 for nonparent. There are 5 two-way interactions: E × M1, E × M2, E × P, M1 × P, M2 × P. E × M1 shows a special effect of being employed and previously married; etc. There are 2 three-way interactions: E × M1 × P, E × M2 × P. When together in a model, the 11 dummies fully represent observed differences in group means. Model 1 has 4 predictors, model 2 has 9, and model 3 has 11.

Models 1 to 3 are computed for each of the 31 dependent variables. For these models, I studied regression coefficients (size, sign, statistical significance, $p<.05$) to see how roles and role combinations affect health. I also tested increments in R^2 for statistical significance ($p<.05$) from model 1 to model 2, and from model 2 to model 3. The increments show if "combining two roles" or "combining three roles" has special effects on health; the regression coefficients must then be studied to see which specific combinations are important.

Question 3

Do stressed, dissatisfied, and nonconfident women have poorer health? This is studied by the model:

Model 4   Y = f [E, M, P; Psyche Variables]

It shows how psychological factors (stress, satisfaction, competence) influence health apart from role effects. I included the 4 main effects of roles (E, M1, M2, P) and all 10 psychological variables (interval-scaled). The psyche variables enter by a stepwise procedure, so the most important (statistically strongest) ones enter first. The entry criterion is a significant F increment ($p<.05$) from the prior model. Psyche variables failing to meet the criterion do not enter an equation. The role variables are viewed as controls and included in every equation.

To assess how psyche variables affect health, I examined regression coefficients and also how early and often those variables pass the F criterion. The R^2 increment from model 1 to model 4 is tested for significance to see if "psychological factors in general" affect health. The increment does not identify just which psyche variables matter.

Question 4

Do some role groups buffer stress and thereby enjoy better physical health? And do some exploit psychological resources (satisfaction and competence) with the same result? This is studied by the model:

Model 5 $Y = f$ [E, M, P; Two-Way Roles*; Top 3 Psyche;
E × Psyche, M × Psyche, P × Psyche]

The crucial variables here are the interactions E × Psyche, M × Psyche, and P × Psyche. They are role × psyche interactions, showing if women in different roles (employed, previously married, married, parent) react to pressures or satisfaction differently from women without those roles. The role × psyche interactions are created by multiplying each role dummy with each psyche variable. Each resulting variable is interval-scaled; women with the designated role take the score of their psyche variable, and those without the role score 0. Every equation has 12 such terms (4 role dummies × 3 psyche variables).

The other variables in model 5 serve as controls: role main effects (E, M1, M2, P), any two-way interactions that proved significant for the given health variable (from model 2, $p<.05$), and the 3 psyche variables that entered model 4 earliest for it. (Significant three-way interactions from model 2 are not included; to do so, we would have to include all component two-way interactions whether significant or not.) Including 3 psyche items is adequate; model 4 typically has just 2 or 3 significant coefficients for the set of 10 psyche variables.

When model 5 is estimated, the controls are always included. The role × psyche terms enter by a stepwise procedure ($p<.05$ for the F increment). A specific example of model 5 is:

Number of chronic conditions $= f$ [E, M1, M2, P; no 2-way role effects;
Self-esteem, Like job, Life in past year;
E × Self-esteem, E × Like job, E × Life in past year;
M × Self-esteem, M × Like job, M × Life in past year;
P × Self-csteem, P × Like job, P × Life in past year]

For testing R^2 increments due to the role × psyche items, I needed a suitable baseline model containing just the controls. So for each dependent variable, I estimated model 5':

Model 5' $Y = f$ [E, M, P; Two-Way Roles*; Top Three Psyche]

Two other operational matters are described in footnote 1.

RESULTS AND DISCUSSION

The results will show that marriage offers a supportive milieu in which women can add other roles and enjoy high rewards of happiness and good health. By contrast, previously married and never-married women are more stressed and dissatisfied about life, and having a job or children does not always enhance their health. Involved women (e.g., employed) learn to buffer stresses, thus reducing its health decrements. Noninvolved women (e.g., nonemployed) learn to exploit satisfaction, thus enhancing its health benefits.

Two points about interpretation need mention at the outset. (a) I discuss some results in a *causal* way, "how roles and psyche influence physical health." But care is taken to note any important alternative interpretations. Causal statements are sounder for the diaries, since predictors precede in time the health events. The fact that findings for the diaries and interviews are usually parallel lends support to our causal statements for the interviews. (b) The analysis provides *comparative* results: groups have "better" or "worse" health relative to others. For the sake of emphasis, I sometimes portray a role group as having "good health" or "bad health." But I caution readers to maintain a relative, rather than absolute, perspective on the results.

Which Young Women Feel Most Stressed, Most Dissatisfied, and Least Competent about Life?

Table 2 presents correlations between role and psyche variables. The top panel shows correlations for each separate role, and the bottom panel for common role combinations. Owing to the modest sample

---

[1] (a) Some diary variables are health actions taken on symptomatic days (see table 1). Their values are strongly affected by how often a woman experienced symptoms. For these items, all analyses were rerun with a morbidity control (number of symptomatic days) included among the predictors. Remarkably, this scarcely changes the regression coefficients or R^2 increment tests. Its only impact is to boost substantially the R^2 of each model. Thus, for our substantive results about roles, psyche, and role × psyche effects, it makes no difference whether morbidity is controlled or not for these diary variables. (b) One of the psyche variables, Liking for Job, poses a problem. Nonemployed women were not asked this question for obvious reasons. All analyses were run twice, first with this predictor included (nonemployed women were assigned the middle score of 3) and then without it. The substantive results are virtually unchanged. Only the R^2 levels differ, being higher when the job variable is included. Thus, whether liking for job is among the psyche variables or not makes no difference in our conclusions about other predictors.

Table 2
Correlations between Role and Psyche Variables (Young Women Ages 18–34)[a]

			Stress		
	N	Chronic stress	Acute stress	Stressful life events	Rushed
ROLE					
Employed	96	.089	.041	.061	.253*
Married	95	−.025	−.095	.090	−.170*
Prev married	22	.069	.107	.071	.067
Never married	45	−.025	.024	−.153*	.136
Parent	81	.172*	.002	.186*	.107
ROLE COMBINATION					
At Home	16	−.022	.005	−.030	−.007
Homemaker, no chd	14	−.113	−.009	−.233**	−.239**
Homemaker, w/chd	36	−.013	−.046	.107	−.131
Career Women never married	33	−.016	.034	−.122	.066
Career Women married	22	−.069	.009	.071	−.072
Two Roles "Plus"	9	.109	.137	.104	.144
Triple Roles	23	.140	−.080	.121	.180*

	Satisfaction		
	Liking for job[b]	Liking for housework	Life in past year
Employed	.445**	.069	.054
Married	–	.086	.328**
Prev married	–	−.019	−.415**
Never married	–	−.080	−.047
Parent	–	−.092	−.060
At home	–	−.148	−.304**
Homemaker, no chd	–	.090	.107
Homemaker, w/chd	–	−.036	.076
Career, never married	.105	−.024	.106
Career, married	.061	.108	.146
Two Roles "Plus"	.170*	.036	−.287**
Triple Roles	.251	−.014	.139

		Competence	
	Resistance resources	Locus of control	Self-esteem
Employed	.044	.132	.150
Married	.031	−.001	.146
Prev married	.079	−.068	−.037
Never married	−.093	.052	−.133
Parent	.148	−.025	.018

Table 2 (continued)

		Competence	
	Resistance resources	Locus of control	Self-esteem
At Home	−.043	−.161*	−.264**
Homemaker, no chd	−.054	.028	−.016
Homemaker, w/chd	.014	−.031	−.011
Career, never married	−.054	.133	−.036
Career, married	−.122	−.009	.132
Two Roles "Plus"	.132	.006	.092
Triple Roles	.188*	.057	.066

Note: *p<.05, **p<.01. No asterisk means p>.05.
[a]Each row is a dummy variable scored 1 for women with the role or role combination, 0 otherwise.
[b]Results are for employed groups only. A dash (−) means inapplicable.

size, many correlations are nonsignificant ($p \geq$.05). In the text and table, significant ones are noted by asterisks (*p<.05, **p<.01).

Separate roles. Employed women feel much more rushed than nonemployed ones (**), but they report only slightly more stress. Employment is associated with satisfactions (including liking for housework), higher self-esteem, and higher personal control, compared with nonemployed women. *Married* women are less rushed (*) and stressed than their nonmarried peers. They are much more pleased with life in the past year (**), like housework more, and have higher self-esteem. Circumstances are less propitious for nonmarried groups: *Previously married* women stand out for their dissatisfaction with life (**). Otherwise, they feel slightly more stressed and less competent (2 items) than other women. *Never-married* women are distinctive for feelings of low competence: lower self-esteem and lower resistance to stress than other marital groups. They have inconsistent results for other psyche items. Having children at home is associated with stress; *mothers* feel chronic stress (*), report stressful life events (*), and feel rushed more often than nonmothers. But mothers also tend to have more resistance to stress. They are more likely to be dissatisfied about life than nonmothers are.

Of the three roles, marriage offers the strongest unqualified rewards. Employment has offsetting features – more stress, but also more satisfaction and competence. Parenthood is most likely to prompt stress; this is not offset by satisfactions.

Role combinations. The role combinations were arranged into basic types: Women at Home, Homemakers, Career Women, Two Roles "Plus," and Triple Roles. (Ten role combinations go into these types;

two are too small to be analysed on their own and cannot be sensibly consolidated with others; see table 1.) I examined correlations and cross-tabulations of these role types with the psyche variables.

Distinct psychological profiles emerge: *Women at Home* (nonmarried without a job; $n = 16$; most are living with their parents) are dissatisfied with life (**) and report low competence (*,**). With few role commitments, they feel no special stress or time pressure. *Homemakers* (nonemployed married women; $n = 14$ without children, 36 with children) have a neutral psychological profile, neither troubled nor sanguine. They feel less stress and time pressure than other women, especially when there are no children to care for (**). They are not distinctive (about average) for satisfaction or competence. *Career Women* (employed childless women; $n = 33$ never married, $n = 22$ married) have a positive psychological profile – no consistent evidence of pressures, above-average satisfaction, and average or better personal control and self esteem. *Two Roles "Plus"* (employed previously married mothers; $n = 9$) are not numerous in the study; they have a distinctive profile of elevated stress, time pressure, and unhappiness in the past year (**). They have heavy responsibilities and shore up some psychological resources (resistance to stress). *Triple Roles* women (employed married mothers; $n = 23$) feel more stressed than others (* for rushed), but this is offset by satisfaction with life and job and by strong resistance resources (*). Note that Two Roles "Plus" and Triple Roles women differ only by marital status, but their psychological profiles are very different. Apparently, marriage offers a much happier setting for the mix of job and motherhood.

In sum, involved ("with roles") women feel more stress, but also more satisfaction and competence, than do noninvolved women. The principal exception is for previously married women who have both job and parent responsibilities.

Which Role Groups of Young Women Are Healthiest, and Which Are Least Healthy?

Models 1 to 3 show how roles and role combinations are related to physical health. Table 3 shows results for selected items (10 of the 31 dependent variables). The following discussion covers all 31.

Main effects of roles on health (Model 1). I hypothesized that young women with role responsibilities (job, or marriage, or motherhood) are healthier than women without them. Three reasons could account for this: (a) social causation – beneficial effects of roles on

Table 3

Effects of Job, Marital, and Parent Statuses and of Psyche Variables on Health (Young Women Ages 18–34)[a]

			Initial Interview		
	H_o	Health in past year	Vulnerable to illness	How feel physically each day	How often worn out end of day	Days ill, injured past 2 weeks
Grand mean $(\bar{Y})$		2.76	2.41	3.24	2.93	1.83
MAIN EFFECTS OF ROLES AND PSYCHE[b]						
Employed (E)	−	−.49	−.15	−.35	.21	−.91
Prev marr (M1)	+	.48	.01	.56	−.18	.60
Married (M2)	−	−.17	−.22	.04	.09	−1.25
Parent (P)	−	−.58	−.42*	−.60*	.22	−1.51*
Chronic stress	+	.05	.06	.08	.06	.05
Acute stress	+	.02	−	.05	−	.09
Life events	+	−.25	−.35	−.08	.31	−.40
Rushed	+	−.06	−.04	−.16	.22*	−
Liking for job	−	−.29*	−.17*	−.37*	−.10	−.88*
Liking housework	−	−	−.02	−	−	−.22
Life in past year	−	−.25**	−.02	−.18**	.02	−.20
Resistance	−	−.04	−.10	−.11	.04	−.06
Locus of control	−	−.03	−.10*	−.08	−.04	−.11
Self-esteem		−.03	.02	−.06	.04	−.19
INTERACTION EFFECTS OF ROLES[c]		EP: 1.49* EM1P: 5.25*	EM1: −1.42*	−	EP: .98**	EP: 2.87*
R^2 FOR MODEL						
1 [main effects]		.049	.056	.039	.024	.093**
2 [main effects, 2-way]		.108	.097	.062	.103	.162**
3 [main, 2-way, 3-way]		.160**	.116	.082	.116	.185**
4 [main, psyche]		.201**	.186**	.295**	.134**	.230**
SIGNIFICANCE OF R^2 INCREMENT[d]						
Model 1 → 2		NS	NS	NS	*	*
Model 2 → 3		*	NS	NS	NS	NS
Model 1 → 4		**	*	**	*	**

*$p<.05$, **$p<.01$. No asterisk or NS means $p \geqslant .05$.

[a]Results are shown for 10 of the 31 dependent variables. High scores on health variables mean poor health. High scores on psyche variables mean high stress, high satisfaction, high competence. The role variables are dummies scored 1 for women with the role, 0 otherwise.

Table 3 (continued)

	Daily health records				
	Average physical feeling	Symptom- atic days	Days cut down activity	Days consulted friends or family	Total no. of drugs
Grand mean ($\overline{Y}$)	7.57	16.2	3.30	8.26	40.1
MAIN EFFECTS OF ROLES AND PSYCHE[b]					
Employed (E)	−.48	−2.08	−1.74*	−2.22	−15.8
Prev marr (M1)	.62	−2.10	4.04**	2.12	8.2
Married (M2)	−.40	−1.56	1.00	1.50	−2.4
Parent (P)	−.19	−1.55	−2.00*	−3.07*	−21.2*
Chronic stress	.03	1.00*	.54**	.40	5.2*
Acute stress	.08**	.30	.06	.06	−
Life events	−.32	2.36	−1.64	.38	13.6
Rushed	−.09	.89	−0.91	1.29	−3.8
Liking for job	−.26*	−.38	−.65	−1.10*	−5.3
Liking housework	−	−2.37**	−.23	−1.14**	−4.3
Life in past year	−.18**	.54	−.22	.27	−
Resistance	−	.69	−	−	4.2
Locus of control	−.02	−.58	−.09	−.40	4.1*
Self-esteem	.05	.58	−	.27	−
INTERACTION EFFECTS OF ROLES[c]					
	EP: 1.33*		EM1: −10.64**	EP: 5.99*	EP: 45.0*
			EP: 4.07*		
			M1P: −8.36*		
			EM1P: 1.54**		
R^2 FOR MODEL					
1 [main effects]	.081*	.014	.107**c	.056c	.054c
2 [main, 2-way]	.153**	.096	.284**	.157**	.128*
3 [main, 2-way, 3-way]	.154*	.108	.360**	.175**	.143*
4 [main, psyche]	.272**	.173*	.243**	.224**	.142*
SIGNIFICANCE OF R_2 INCREMENT[d]					
Model 1 → 2	NS	NS	**	*	NS
Model 2 → 3	NS	NS	**	NS	NS
Model 1 → 4	**	*	**	**	NS

[b]For roles, regression coefficients from model 1 are shown. For psyche, coefficient are from the final stepwise equation of model 4. Psyche variables that do not appear in the final equation have dashes (−).

[c]Significant 2-way (model 2) and 3-way (model 3) effects are shown.

[d]F-tests are performed to determine if the increments are significant.

[e]With a morbidity control, the R^2s for Model 1 are .278, .554, and .278, respectively.

health owing to expanded social ties, use of personal skills, and access to resources; (b) social selection – ability of healthy women to take on roles; and (c) attitudes – tendencies to ignore symptoms and avoid curative actions because of role responsibilities.

The results show that employment and motherhood are clearly linked to good health (Employed: 27 of 31 regression coefficients are negative; 8 $p<.05$; Parent: 27 negative; 10 $p<.05$). Marriage is only weakly related to health for young women (16 coefficients; 0 $p<.05$). Instead, never-married women tend to have the best health (21 negative coefficients; N.A. $p<.05$). [The coefficients for never-married women are hand-computed from the married and previously married coefficients. Statistical significance is not assessed (N.A.)]. Previously married women have worst health (21 negative coefficients; 3 $p<.05$). Footnote 2 has detailed results.

Interaction effects of roles on health (Models 2 and 3). I hypothesized that women who combine roles are healthier than women with one role or "none." The reasons stated earlier for main effects apply here as well: social causation (direct health benefits from multiple involvements), social selection (healthy women are able to take on multiple roles), and attitudes (women with numerous responsibilities pay little attention to symptoms and shun curative actions).

Two- and three-way interactions are created to reveal special effects of role combinations after controlling for main effects of each role. I discuss consistent results across the 31 dependent variables, with special attention to the statistically significant interactions (some are shown in table 3).

What are effects of combining two roles (two-way interactions)? (a) Parallel results appear for *marriage with employment* and *marriage with children*: married women with a job, or with children, obtain no health benefit from having two roles (half of the coefficients are negative, half positive). For comparison, consider the other marital groups. Previously married women who have a job, or have children, do obtain a health

---

[2] The text summarizes results for the 31 dependent variables. Some specific effects are: Employed women have especially good self-rated health (*), few limitations due to health (**), little restricted activity (*), and low drug use (**). Mothers have few limitations due to health (**), feel less vulnerable to illness (*), avoid restricting activity for symptoms (*), feel they can ignore pain without medicine (*), and use fewer drugs during the diary period (*), compared to their nonmother peers. Never-married women feel good physically (interview and diary), have fewer chronic conditions, and do not restrict activities or take drugs for short-term symptoms (despite having more of them), compared to other women. Previously married women cut down activities readily for symptoms (**), cannot ignore pain easily (*), and take more drugs (nonsignificant) than other women.

benefit (27 of 31 coefficients negative for EM1; 24 for M1P). These effects appear for all kinds of health variables, not just health behaviours (in that case, we would argue the women are too burdened to take care of their symptoms). This suggests that some real health benefits come from adding on job *or* parent activities. By contrast, never-married women with a job, or with children, show small consistent decrements in health (24 positive coefficients for former, 20 for latter). (Coefficients for employed never-married women are computed from the EM1 and EM2 coefficients; those for never-married mothers are computed from M1P and M2P.) (b) Consider *employment and motherhood*: this pairing is clearly linked with health problems (EP: 26 of 31 coefficients positive). Women with both roles tend to be fatigued (**), feel bad physically (**), rate their health worse (*), cut down activities for symptoms (**), talk with people about their symptoms (*), and take substantially more prescription and nonprescription drugs (*,**).

What are the effects of combining three roles (three-way interactions)? *Triple Roles* women enjoy distinct health benefits from being so engaged (22 of 31 coefficients negative for EM2P). In particular, they have fewer chronic conditions and short-term symptoms than other women, rate their health better, and take notably fewer prescription drugs (none $p<.05$). For comparison, consider previously married women who combine job and parenthood (Two Roles "Plus"): their health suffers (22 of 31 signs positive for EM1P, all large). These women rate their health worse (*) than others do and report more chronic conditions and long-term limitations (**); in the six-week diary period, they have very high drug use (**) and restricted activities (**) despite fewer symptoms.

Briefly stating the two- and three-way interactions: when previously married women have *just one* other role (job or motherhood), they show health benefits; but those with *both* roles show health deficits. One reasonable interpretation is that some involvement enhances physical health of divorced/separated women, but high involvement jeopardizes health. It is married women who seem to flourish with two added roles (job and children). Thus, the two-way results for EP (employed mothers) really mask diverse outcomes: benefits for one subgroup (married women) and intensified deficits for another (previously married women).

In sum, singly or in combinations, roles are consistently associated with good health for young women. Roles indicate social ties and support, responsibilities and obligations, use of skills, and access to resources – factors that can enrich or tax women's lives. Marriage and employment appear to offer enrichment overall. Parenthood is different; its beneficial vs detrimental effect depends on a woman's marital status.

R^2 *levels and increments.* Roles account for a modest degree of variation in physical health: R^2s for model 1 range from .014 to .127 for the 31 dependent variables (8 of 31 $p<.05$). Including two-way and three-way interactions boosts R^2 a little: model 2 has values of .038 to .284 (12 $p<.05$) and model 3 values of .047 to .373 (14 $p<.05$).

The interactions in models 2 and 3 have modest prediction strength. R^2 increments from model 1 to model 2 are significant ($p<.05$) 10 of 31 times; and increments from model 1 to model 3, 9 of 31 times.

Do Stressed, Dissatisfied, and Nonconfident Women Have Poorer Health?

Model 4 shows how psyche variables are related to physical health. Table 3 has results for selected dependent variables; the following discussion covers all 31.

Main effects of psyche on health. I hypothesized that stresses are related to poor health (especially short-term symptoms and actions), but that satisfactions and competence are related to good health. Three reasons can account for this: (a) Satisfaction may enhance health, whereas stress harms it. (b) Alternatively, good health can increase satisfaction and feelings of competence, whereas poor health increases stress. (c) Lastly, attitudes also come into play; stressed women may focus on symptoms and seek relief in curative actions, whereas happy and competent women ignore symptoms and care.

Four of the 10 psyche variables are consistently related to health: (a) Women feeling *chronic stress* are less healthy, especially in the diaries. (b) Women who *like their jobs* enjoy better health than those dissatisfied with that activity. (c) To a lesser extent, the same holds for women who *like housework.* (d) Women who feel their *lives were fine in the past year* are healthier than others. (See footnote 3 for detailed results.) The other six psyche variables have weak, inconsistent effects on health.

---

[3] For the four variables, respectively: 26 of 31 coefficients are positive, 6 significant ($p<.05$); 26 negative, 9 significant; 26 negative, 4 significant; 21 negative, 6 significant. Some specific results: Women with chronic stress have notably more symptomatic days (diary,**) and associated restricted activity (**) and drug use (**). Women who like their job have better self-rated health (*), have fewer sick days in the past two weeks (**), feel better physically (**), and take fewer drugs (*). Women who like housework have fewer symptomatic days (**) and less drug use in the diary period (**). Women who rate their life as fine have better self-rated health (**), feel better physically (**), and say they can ignore pain (*).

The results are limited to the four variables noted above. Brief attention to the nonwinners is helpful: major life events, recent stress, and feeling rushed are not nearly so important as is persistent, unrelieved stress. Competence is not as important as stress and satisfaction.

In sum, women who are persistently stressed or dissatisfied with their roles or life are "at risk" of poor health. They experience more health problems and are more likely to take curative actions for symptoms (morbidity controlled; footnote 1).

R^2 *levels and increments.* The R^2s for model 4 range from .063 to .295; the majority are significant (20 of 31).

Although the psyche variables are allowed to contribute only after role main effects, they still add 10–15 per cent more explained variance. Over half the increments from model 1 to 4 are significant (18 of 31 $p<.05$). In fact, psyche variables contribute more than role combinations do. The R^2 increments from model 1 to 4 tend to be larger than the increments from model 1 to 3 (23 of 31 times). The increments (model 1 to 4) are biggest for subjectively toned items such as how women feel physically each day, self-rated health in past year, etc. Understandably, psychological factors are more implicated in subjective aspects of health than in objective ones.

Do Some Role Groups Buffer Stress or Exploit Psychological Resources, and Thereby Enjoy Better Physical Health?

Model 5 shows if stress, satisfaction, and competence affect health more strongly for certain role groups. Key findings for these role × psyche variables are in table 4; readers are encouraged to read the text before studying it.

I hypothesized that: (a) Married women are less sensitive to stress than others, and more benefited by satisfaction and competence. (b) Employment and parenthood should show these same effects. (c) By contrast, previously married women are especially sensitive to stress and unable to exploit their psychological resources.

For each dependent variable, a model with interactions of roles (E, M1, M2, P; respectively, employed, previously married, married, parent) with the top three psyche variables was estimated (details in Method, above). The psyche variables that appear most often in these interactions are chronic stress, job satisfaction, and life in past year. To support hypotheses 1 and 2, coefficients should be negative; this reduces the positive signs of stress on health items and increases the negative ones of satisfaction and competence. To support hypothesis 3, coefficients should be positive; this increases the positive

Table 4

Effects of Role × Psyche Interactions on Health of Young Women

STRESS

1. Employed women buffer stress, so its health-harming effects are reduced.
    E × Chronic Stress   71% (12/17) coefficients negative; 0 of them *
2. Mothers buffer stress, too.
    P × Chronic Stress   88% (14/16) coefficients negative; 6 *
3. Married women fail to buffer stress.
    M2 × Chronic Stress   69% (11/16) coefficients positive; 5 *

SATISFACTION

1. Nonemployed women derive health benefits from satisfaction with roles and life.
    E × Life in Past Year   83% (10/12) positive – thus *negative* for nonemployed; 0 *
    E × Liking Housework   75% (3/4) positive; 0 *
2. Nonmothers derive health benefits from satisfaction, too.
    P × Liking for Job   71% (12/17) positive – thus *negative* for nonmothers; 0 *
    P × Life in Past Year   82% (9/11) positive; 2 *
3. Never-married women also derive health benefits from satisfaction.
    Never-Married × Life in Past Yr.   85% (11/13) negative; NA *
4. Previously married and currently married women do *not* benefit from satisfaction.
    M1 × Life in Past Year   100% (12/12) positive but small; 4 *
    M2 × Life in Past Year   82% (9/11) positive but small; 0 *

COMPETENCE

1. Involved women (employed, married, parent) derive small health benefits from competence.

E × Locus of Control	83% (5/6) negative; 0 *
E × Self-Esteem	83% (5/6) negative; 0 *
M2 × Locus of Control	88% (7/8) negative; 3 *
M2 × Self-Esteem	80% (4/5) negative; 1 *
P × Resistance	100% (3/3) negative; 0 *

Note: This table is a prose summary of consistent results for specific role × psyche variables.
Negative coefficients mean that "stress is buffered" or "psychological resources are exploited" – both propitious for health.
Positive coefficients mean the opposite; that is, not propitious for health.
*means $p<.05$.
E = employed; M1 = previously married; M2 = currently married; P = parent

signs of stress on health items and reduces the negative ones of satisfaction and competence.

The results are: (a) Married women derive small health benefits from competence, but are not especially skilled in buffering stress or exploiting satisfaction. (b) Employed women buffer chronic stress better than their nonemployed peers and show health gains from competence, but they do not benefit from satisfaction. These results hold for mothers, too. (c) Previously married women do not gain from satisfaction (in fact, the data show health losses); no other consistent results appear for them. Overall, the evidence fits our hypothesis for employment best; employed women buffer stresses and gain from resources more clearly than other groups.

The statements above suggest that little has been found in the role × psyche interactions. If we organize the results by psyche, rather than role, we see otherwise (table 4): (a) *Stress*: employed women buffer chronic stress better than their nonemployed peers, and mothers do so better than nonmothers. Married women, however, fail to buffer stress. (b) *Satisfaction*: noninvolved women (nonemployed; nonmother; never married) benefit from satisfaction. Although they are less likely to feel satisfied than involved women, those who *are* satisfied get a health benefit. (An anomalous result for previously married women is noted above.) (c) *Competence*: the few competence variables that appear in model 5 show that involved women (job, married, parent) derive a small health benefit from that psychological resource.

In sum, involved women often learn to buffer stresses, and noninvolved women learn to exploit satisfaction. Specifically, women with jobs or with children buffer the increased pressures they sometimes confront; this was expected. But it is women "without roles" (nonemployed, no children, never married) who exploit satisfaction when fortunate enough to experience it; this was unexpected. Previously married women are an exception here; they derive no health benefits from satisfaction.

The role × psyche effects have modest, not tiny, statistical strength: they increase R^2 by 5 to 15 per cent from model 5′ to model 5. One third of the increments (10 of 31) are statistically significant.

CONCLUSION

The empirical results contain a story that is best told by focusing first on the psyche variables (stress, satisfaction, competence) and then on marital groups.

Stress

Chronic stress poses health risks for young women. By contrast, time pressures, recent stress, and even major upsetting events in the past year do not pose risks. Employed women and mothers (the second a role group that feels such stress often) find ways to buffer that impact. Role groups that seldom feel chronic stress do not buffer its effects on health; they seldom need to.

Satisfaction

Unhappiness about job, life in the past year, and housework are risk factors for poor health. Nonmothers, never-married women, and nonemployed women (a role group that often feels unhappy) exploit satisfaction when it exists. Groups that typically have high satisfaction do not capitalize on it; they do not need to.

Competence

Competence is not strongly related to physical health of young women. But involved women (job, married, parent) do capitalize on feelings of competence and show small health benefits. In sum, role groups who feel frequent stress or infrequent happiness develop coping strategies – buffering the former and exploiting the latter. This is where the needs for adequate coping are greatest. (Some other groups also buffer stresses and exploit resources, as the detailed text indicates. We are citing here the most striking interactions of role × psyche.)

Marital status proves to be central for psychological well-being and its impacts on health. (a) Women with three roles (employed married mothers) feel more stressed than others, but develop buffers to it in their job and parent roles, thus blunting the negative impacts of stress on health. These women feel more satisfaction and self-esteem than others, and enjoy health benefits therefrom. In short, women with triple roles enjoy many rewards from busy lives and blunt the troubles. Their physical health is the best of all role groups. The empirical link between marriage and solid coping is clear, but the exact causal tie is undetermined here: on the one hand, marriage may promote and nourish psychological strengths; on the other, such strengths may be formed early in individuals and enhance their chances of becoming married – as well as abilities to cope with multiple roles. (b) Previously married women have a far different experience. They have above-average stress and great dissatisfaction; they fail to buffer stress or exploit any satisfactions felt. Their health is enhanced by having one role responsibility (job or parent), but both roles prove too much and their health suffers. All in all, psychological factors and role responsibilities conspire to produce poor health among them. (c) Never-married women do not present a clear profile of health risks and outcomes; some aspects bode well for health, others do not.

Thus, young women's marital status proves critical for their health, especially for how they handle job plus parent responsibilities. Married women are able to have other roles without health penalty; in fact, having both a job and children appears propitious for them. Previously married women with job plus parent responsibilities have the opposite outcome of poorer health; this is partly due to low satisfaction about their lives.

REFERENCES

Baruch, G.K., & R.C. Barnett. 1986. Role quality, multiple role involvement, and psychological well-being in midlife women. *Journal of Personality and Social Psychology 51*, 578–85.

Baruch, G.K., L. Biener, & R.C. Barnett. 1987. Women and gender in research on work and family stress. *American Psychologist 42*, 130–6.

Crosby, F.J., ed. 1987. *Spouse, parent, worker: On gender and multiple roles*. New Haven, CT: Yale University Press.

Froberg, D.G., D. Gjerdingen, & M. Preston. 1986. Effects of multiple roles on women's mental and physical health: What have we learned? *Women and Health 11*, 79–96.

Haw, M.A. 1982. Women, work, and stress: A review and agenda for the future. *Journal of Health and Social Behavior 23*, 132–44.

Hibbard, J.H., & C.R. Pope. 1985. Employment status, employment characteristics, and women's health. *Women and Health 10*, 59–77.

Kessler, R., & J. McRae. 1982. The effect of wives' employment on the mental health of married men and women. *American Sociological Review 47*, 216–26.

Kotler, P., & D.L. Wingard. 1989. The effect of occupational, marital and parental roles on mortality: The Alameda County Study. *American Journal of Public Health 79*, 607–12.

Moen, P., D. Dempster-McClain, & R.M. Williams. 1989. Social integration and longevity: An event history analysis of women's roles and resilience. *American Sociological Review 54*, 635–47.

Pearlin, L., & J. Johnson. 1977. Marital status, life-strains, and depression. *American Sociological Review, 42*, 704–15.

Radloff, L. 1975. Sex differences in depression: The effects of occupation and marital status. *Sex Roles 1*, 249–66.

Ross, C.E., J. Mirowsky, & K. Goldsteen. 1990. The impact of the family on health: The decade in review. *Journal of Marriage and the Family 52*, 1059–78.

Sorensen, G., & L.M. Verbrugge. 1987. Women, work, and health. In L. Breslow, J.E. Fielding, & L.B. Lave, eds., *Annual Review of Public Health* (8: 235–51). Palo Alto, CA: Annual Reviews.

Thoits, P.A. 1983. Multiple identities and psychological well-being: A reformulation and test of the social isolation hypothesis. *American Sociological Review 48*, 174–87.

– 1986. Multiple identities: Examining gender and marital status differences in distress. *American Sociological Review 51*, 259–72.

Verbrugge, L.M. 1979. Female illness rates and illness behavior: Testing hypotheses about sex differences in health. *Women and Health 4*, 61–79.

– 1980. Health diaries. *Medical Care 18*, 73–95.

– 1983. Multiple roles and physical health of women and men. *Journal of Health and Social Behavior 24*, 16–30.

– 1986. Role burdens and physical health of women and men. *Women and Health 11*, 47–77.

Verbrugge, L.M., & J.H. Madans. 1985. Social roles and health trends of American women. *Milbank Memorial Fund Quarterly/Health and Society 63*, 691–735.

Waldron, I., & J.A. Jacobs. 1989. Effects of multiple roles on women's health – Evidence from a national longitudinal study. *Women and Health 15*, 3–19.

Welch, S., & A. Booth. 1977. Employment and health among married women with children. *Sex Roles 3*, 385–97.

Wheaton, B. 1983. Stress, personal coping resources, and psychiatric symptoms: An investigation of interactive models. *Journal of Health and Social Behavior 24*, 208–29.

– 1985. Models for the stress-buffering functions of coping resources. *Journal of Health and Social Behavior 26*, 352–64.

Woods, N.F, & B.S. Hulka. 1979. Symptom reports and illness behavior among employed women and homemakers. *Journal of Community Health 5*, 36–45.

10 Perceived Control and Employed Men and Women

CATHERINE A. HEANEY

Occupational stress research has, for the most part, embraced a transactional model. The term "stress" best describes a process by which objective physical and social conditions are appraised and responded to by individuals. An important aspect of this transactional model is its focus on the factors that influence the stress-appraisal process and the reactions of individuals to conditions perceived as stressful. These factors, which include characteristics of the individual and of the social environment, moderate the relationship between exposure to stressors and manifestations of strain.

One moderator that has received much attention is perceived control (Folkman 1984; Israel & Schurman 1990; Lewis 1987; Sutton & Kahn 1987). In this chapter I explore the role of perceived control in the experience of occupational stress by men and women. First, definitional issues are addressed. Second, a conceptual rationale for looking at sex differences in perceived control is provided. Third, the results of two studies of men and women in the paid labour force are presented and discussed. Finally, recommendations for future research and implications for practice are addressed.

This research was supported by a grant from the IFG/UAW/OSU Joint Research Project to the author and by NIMH grant #5P50MH38330 to the Michigan Prevention Research Center (Dr Richard Price, PI).

PERCEIVED CONTROL: DEFINITIONAL ISSUES

Perceived control can be defined as the "belief that one can influence the environment" (Ganster 1988, 88). Individuals have generalized beliefs about the extent to which they can control important events or outcomes. These beliefs have been labelled as locus of control (Rotter 1966), mastery (Pearlin & Schooler 1978), and personal competence (Husaini, Neff, Newbrough, & Moore 1982). For example, people with an internal locus of control believe that their behaviour can affect how their lives unfold. Those with an external locus of control believe that events and outcomes are determined either by others or by fate. People with high mastery and personal competence have the firm belief that they can be effective in bringing about desired outcomes in life.

Based partially on their generalized beliefs about control, people make specific appraisals of the possibilities for control in more narrowly defined domains or situations. Control appraisals may be specific to life pursuits, such as marriage, parenting, and work (Menaghan 1983). Within each of these pursuits, control appraisals may be specific to particular domains or facets of functioning. For example, employees may have beliefs about the controllability of work scheduling, work pace, and work tasks. At the most microanalytic level, beliefs about control can be specific to particular stressful situations (Folkman 1984). For the purposes of this paper, perceived control will refer to appraisals of specific work domains.

In order for individuals to feel that they have control over a work domain, they must (a) perceive that there are actions that can be taken that will be effective in modifying the situation (outcome expectancy), and (b) feel confident that they are able to perform those needed actions (efficacy expectancy), given their current abilities and worksite constraints (Bandura 1977). Thus, employees' perceptions of control are determined by their own skills and attitudes, as well as by organizational norms, structure, and policies. In some domains, employees' perceptions of control are clearly cued by the environment. For example, employees who work on a machine-paced assembly line that they cannot stop know that they have little control over work pace. As a second example, employees who are assigned to shifts according to seniority know that they have little control over their work schedule. However, other domains, such as the general domain of decision-making, are much more subjective. When employees consider how much say or influence they have in decisions that affect their jobs, they need to consider both the extent to which their employers allow participation in decision-making and their own predispositions toward and skills in exercising influence in it. Employees who are granted opportunities to influence decisions but who have not been articulate and persuasive in their attempts to do so would report less perceived control than employees who had been granted the same opportunities and managed them successfully.

Within the occupational-stress literature, perceived control has been conceptualized and operationalized in a number of different ways. Karasek and his colleagues (Karasek & Theorell 1990) have developed the concept of job-decision latitude, defined as control over the use of one's abilities and over the way in which work is accomplished. This concept has been widely used in epidemiological investigations of work stress. Unfortunately, the measurement of job-decision latitude has often confounded perceived control with the amount of skill and variety required by a job (Ganster 1988). Thus, studies using this measure may not be reflecting effects of perceived control, but rather of the amount of challenge or complexity inherent in a job.

Another concept that encompasses perceived control is autonomy or freedom from close supervision (Spector 1986). The beneficial effects of autonomy on employee performance and well-being have been attributed to employees having more control over how and when work tasks are accomplished (Spector 1986). However, autonomous jobs may also offer other benefits, such as less interpersonal conflict on the job. In studies of autonomous jobs, the effects of interpersonal benefits have not been separated from those of enhanced perceived control.

Other investigators have conceptualized control as the ability to gain accurate and clear information about job responsibilities (La-Croix & Haynes 1987). This conceptualization is more reflective of informational control or predictability (Sutton & Kahn 1987) than of behavioural control. Clearly, one must be able to predict the occurrence of aversive events or conditions in order to attempt to control or influence them. Equally clear is the fact that employees who have the reliable, accurate information necessary for prediction of stresses may still not have any behavioural control over those stresses.

Finally, participation and influence in decision-making have been used as indicators of perceived control. Participation is a necessary but not sufficient condition for having a say in or influence over decisions. Some studies have reported increases in perceived control when opportunities to participate were increased (e.g., Jackson 1983), but others have not (e.g., Neider 1980). Participation in processes that do not serve the needs or address the concerns of individual employees may not enhance perceptions of control. It should also be noted that influence in decision-making is not necessary for control over some specific domains of work. For example, an organization may enhance employee control over work scheduling by instituting a flextime policy, without allowing employees to participate in or influence the policy-making process. However, having a say in decision-making may be a powerful indicator of perceived control because influence over decisions can enhance perceived control in a multitude of work domains.

The constellation of concepts described above illustrates the complexity of the study of perceived control. Each concept captures a particular facet of perceived control. Little attention has been given to developing a more global conceptual framework and measurement strategy (Ganster 1988). The studies described herein use various measures of perceived control, with an emphasis on participation and influence in decision-making.

WOMEN, PERCEIVED CONTROL, AND COPING

Perceived control has been linked to decreased stress levels and improved worker health (Israel, House, Schurman, Heaney & Mero 1989; Jackson 1983; Spector 1986). The specific mechanism through which perceived control has these beneficial effects is not clear. Laboratory research indicates that control does not necessarily have to be exercised in order to be effective in enhancing well-being (Gatchel 1980). Perceived control may enhance self-esteem or it may simply reassure an individual that extremely aversive situations can be avoided (S.M. Miller 1979). Both of these hypothesized mechanisms could lead to a reduction in feelings of distress.

Perceived control also buffers the potentially deleterious effects of stress on mental and physical health. Karasek's epidemiological studies (Karasek 1979; Karasek, Baker, Marxer, Ahlbom, & Theorell 1981) have shown that workers with heavy job demands and little job-decision latitude will suffer the most adverse consequences. If workers have some control or influence over their work processes, job demands have less of an effect on well-being. Laboratory research also supports the buffering role of perceived control (Perrewe & Ganster 1989).

Perceived control may have these effects because of its influence on coping behaviour. Situational appraisals of control have been linked to performance of active problem-solving coping strategies (Folkman, Aldwin, & Lazarus 1981) and with persistence in coping (Bandura 1977). People who believe that they can have an effect on a stressful situation are more likely to try to deal with the situation and persist in these efforts even if they are not immediately successful. On the other hand, employees who believe that they have little control over particular work domains are less likely to engage in active problem-solving coping and more likely to perform emotion-focused strategies (Folkman 1984). For example, such employees might try to take a new perspective on the stressful situation, avoid the situation, or manage their distress symptoms. Some research suggests that psychological adjustment to stressful situations is enhanced when perceptions of control are matched with the use of appropriate coping behaviour (Compas & Orosan, this volume).

There are two important ways in which perceived control might contribute to differences in how men and women experience and respond to stress at work. First, women may experience less perceived control at work than men do. Second, perceived control may be differentially effective for men and women as an enhancer of well-being and as a stress-buffering agent. There is both a structural and a social psychological explanation for why women might experience less perceived control at the workplace. Karasek and Theorell (1990) have unequivocally documented that women are overrepresented in occupations with low job-decision latitude. In addition, they note that most of the high-demand occupations that employ women in large numbers have low decision latitude. In contrast, men's high-demand jobs typically have high decision latitude. This clustering of women in low-status jobs is the structural explanation for women experiencing less perceived control at work.

The social psychological explanation relies on gender-related differences in cognitions and behaviours. Within the same occupation, women and men may have differential access to control because of gender-differentiated treatment. Let us take the case of participation and influence in decision-making. It may be more difficult for a woman to gain the attention of decision-makers. Travis (1988) has observed a pattern that she has named the "invisible woman phenomenon." She claims that women are ignored much of the time even when they are taking the lead in an interaction or are making worthwhile contributions. She provides the following example: "Kathy participates in a meeting on how to improve safety at work. Kathy makes a suggestion; however, the discussion continues along other lines until Dave makes the same suggestion, which is greeted with enthusiasm and eventually adopted as Dave's idea" (Travis 1988, 43).

Supervisors may be more attentive when male employees offer suggestions. Male employees' advice may be solicited more often than that of female employees. Thus, women may have less say or control over important decisions than their male counterparts.

Finally, women, on average, may perceive the same objective conditions or events differently than men do. Bronfenbrenner's (1979) ecological theory of development describes how events and perceptions in one domain (e.g., work) are affected by socialization processes at the family, community, and cultural levels. Perhaps the socialization of women into a traditional gender role that does not clearly value autonomy and control results in women perceiving themselves as having less control. Some evidence suggests that women are less likely than men to have an internal locus of control or a strongly developed sense of mastery (Pearlin & Schooler 1978). Thus, in work situations that do not provide clear cues as to controllability, and hence where generalized beliefs about control may be strongly related to situational control appraisals (Folkman 1984), women may be less likely than men to perceive themselves to have high levels of personal control.

Over and above sex differences in mean levels of perceived control, control may play a different role in the stress processes of men and women. Theories of development have pointed out that females are encouraged in and rewarded for affiliative, nurturing, supportive behaviours, and males for autonomous, proactive, and assertive behaviours (Chodorow 1978; Erikson 1950; Gilligan 1982). Perceived control may be more important for the traditional male goals of successful accomplishment and achievement than the female goals of affiliation and nurturance. Thus, control may be more "identity-relevant" to men than women (Thoits 1987). If control is more important or central to the self-image or self-actualization of men, then it would perhaps be a more effective health enhancer and stress-buffering agent for men. In addition, one would expect that *not* having control would be more deleterious to men than to women.

The empirical evidence for sex differences in the effects of perceived control on well-being is fragmented and inconsistent. Most worksite studies of the buffering effect of perceived control have included only male employees, and the few studies that have included women have had mixed results (LaCroix & Haynes 1987). In the literature on generalized beliefs about control, a preponderance of evidence suggests that having an internal locus of control or believing that one can make a difference in how events unfold is more beneficial for men than women (Kobasa 1987). The research to date is not conclusive but does suggest that women experience and benefit from control differently than do men.

This chapter explores the role of perceived control in the experience of worksite stress among employed men and women. Specifi-

Table 1
Description of the Samples

| | Human service workers (N = 1309) | | Manufacturing workers (N = 859) | |
	Women (N = 999) %	Men (N = 310) %	Women (N = 171) %	Men (N = 688) %
Marital status				
Currently married	35	35	58	83
Never married	45	53	10	4
Separated, widowed, or divorced	20	12	32	13
Race				
White	84	76	74	88
Black	12	19	22	10
Other minority	4	5	4	2
Education				
Less than high school	3	3	12	5
High school graduate	43	36	64	58
Some post high school	39	42	12	20
College graduate	15	19	12	17
Average age (in years)	30.2	28.7	43.0	43.8
	(SD = 9.5)	(SD = 8.38)	(SD = 8.27)	(SD = 8.35)

cally, the following research questions are addressed: (a) Do levels of perceived control differ between men and women employed in similar occupations? (b) To what extent do men and women feel differently about their levels of perceived control? (c) Is perceived control more effective in enhancing health and buffering stress among men than women?

METHOD

These research questions are addressed in two very different work settings. Table 1 describes the men and women in each of the two samples. In the first study, workers were employed in a manufacturing setting where females constituted 20 per cent of the work force. Women who worked in this manufacturing plant were more likely to be black, separated or divorced, and less likely to be educated than their male counterparts. In contrast to the predominantly male manufacturing setting, 80 per cent of the workers in the human-services sample were female. The human-service workers, on the whole, were younger, more likely to be single, and more highly educated than the manufacturing workers. Female human-service workers were more likely to be white and separated or divorced than were male human-service workers.

Even though each of these samples is restricted to particular occupational settings, they are still somewhat heterogeneous in terms of
the jobs that people do. Sometimes subgroups are used in order to
look at sex differences within narrowly defined occupations. The
manufacturing workers included unionized production workers
(e.g., assemblers, machine operators, material handlers), unionized
skilled trades (e.g., electricians, pipefitters, carpenters), and non-
unionized salaried employees. Women were overrepresented in the
production group and underrepresented in the skilled trades group.
Seventy-seven per cent of the female employees were production
workers, as compared to 49 per cent of the men. Only 3 per cent of
the women were in the skilled trades, in contrast to 30 per cent of the
men. Twenty per cent of both male and female employees were salaried. Accountants, engineers, supervisors, and program administrators constituted the salaried group. It is a diverse group, including
several job categories that are nonmanagerial.

The human-service workers were direct-care staff and house managers in community residences for the mentally ill and the developmentally disabled. Direct-care staff, as their title indicates, provide
much of the care for the clients in the group home. Job responsibilities include helping clients with activities of daily living, carrying out
behavioural programming, and accompanying clients on community
experiences. House managers are the immediate supervisors of the
direct-care staff, and they spend most of their time in administrative
and supervisory capacities, rather than providing direct care. House
managers are supervised by agency directors who are usually based
outside of the group home. Nine per cent of the men and 11 per
cent of the women in the human-services sample were house managers. The house managers constitute the only group of supervisory
employees in these two studies.

The inclusion of both samples is instructive, even though direct
comparisons are inappropriate owing to differences in measurement. The study of perceived control in the workplace is in such
an early developmental stage that it is important to assess the extent
to which results generalize to various settings. Approximately 11
per cent of women currently in the work force are in manufacturing (U.S. Department of Labor, 1990). To a large extent, these
women are the "pioneers on the male frontier" (Walshok 1981),
occupying high-paying blue-collar jobs that have previously been
the exclusive domain of men. With a few exceptions (see e.g., Deaux
& Ullman 1983), blue-collar women have not been extensively
studied. In contrast to the male manufacturing setting, human services is a traditionally female occupation where men are a distinct
minority. The status-inconsistency literature (House & Harkins

1975) and studies of tokenism (Kanter 1977) suggest that the work experiences of women in different occupations may depend on the extent to which women have been integrated into the occupations (Hall 1990).

Data were collected from these workers through self-administered questionnaires. Approximately three-quarters of potential respondents in each setting returned a completed questionnaire. Measures of control, stress, and mental health differ between the two studies. Table 2 presents the measures and their descriptive statistics. In the manufacturing setting, there was a two-item index of control over work pace. These items tapped the extent to which the employee could take a desired break and could decide when to work fast and when to take it easy. Participation in decision-making and problem-solving was measured with an eight-item index. The items asked to what extent the employee participates in decision-making and problem-solving processes in various content areas, such as setting production standards, solving production problems, and determining work procedures. Single-item measures of say or influence over how one's job is done and over job-related procedures were used with the human-service workers. Although these items were moderately correlated ($r = .41$), they related to other variables differently and thus were treated as separate measures. Work stresses included role ambiguity, role conflict, and role overload (Caplan, Cobb, French, Van Harrison, & Pinneau 1980; Van Sell, Brief, & Schuler 1981). An additional stress measured among human-service workers was the receipt of ambiguous, impolite, and unconstructive feedback. Mental health measures included the Center for Epidemiological Studies of Depression (CES-D) index (Radloff 1977) and an adaptation of the Hopkins Symptom Checklist (Derogatis 1977). All multiple-item indices have acceptable internal consistency, with reliability coefficients of greater than .65.

Ordinary least squares regression models were used to explore effects of perceived control on mental health. Direct effects were investigated with the following hierarchical model-building procedure:

$Y = a + b_1(\text{Female})$

$Y = a + b_1(\text{Female}) + b_2(\text{Perceived Control})$

$Y = a + b_1(\text{Female}) + b_2(\text{Perceived Control}) + b_3(\text{Female} \times \text{Perceived Control})$

A significant interaction term indicated that perceived control was more strongly associated with mental health for one sex than the other. Buffering effects were explored with the moderated regression technique (LaRocco, House, & French 1980), following this procedure:

$$Y = a + b_1(\text{Stress})$$
$$Y = a + b_1(\text{Stress}) + b_2(\text{Perceived Control})$$
$$Y = a + b_1(\text{Stress}) + b_2(\text{Perceived Control}) + b_3(\text{Stress} \times \text{Perceived Control})$$

A significant interaction term in this model indicated that stress had a different effect on mental health depending on the level of perceived control. Buffering models were run separately for men and women. If buffering effects were found, a three-way interaction term (Sex × Stress × Perceived Control) was tested for significance.

Table 2
Measures and Descriptive Statistics

Concept	Variable	Range	Women Mean	SD	Men Mean	SD	t
Perceived control	Control over pace	1–5	2.80	1.13	3.04	1.02	−2.68**
	Participation in decision-making	1–5	2.94	.99	2.87	1.01	ns
Perceived stress	Role ambiguity	1–4	3.4	.65	3.47	.67	ns
	Role conflict	1–4	2.15	.84	2.16	.83	ns
Mental health	CESD depression index	0–60	12.30	10.09	9.69	9.13	3.26**
Perceived control	Say about how job done	1–7	4.28	1.80	4.32	1.81	ns
	Say in decisions about procedures	1–7	4.54	1.86	4.72	1.88	ns
Perceived stress	Role overload	1–7	3.66	1.23	3.32	1.13	−4.18**
	Poor feedback	1–7	2.61	1.10	2.52	1.07	ns
Mental health	HSCL overall Mental health	1–5	4.39	.73	4.50	.70	2.41*
	Depression	1–5	1.74	.80	1.62	.74	−2.30*
	Anxiety	1–5	1.57	.73	1.44	.66	−2.97**

*$p < .05$; **$p < .01$.

Analyses for this paper were done both with and without adjusting for demographic differences between men and women. Controlling for marital status, race, and education level did not substantially change any of the relationships between sex and perceived control, or between perceived control and mental health. For ease of presentation, estimates from unadjusted models are reported. However, all reported results remained significant even when adjusted for demographic differences.

LEVELS OF PERCEIVED CONTROL

Table 2 presents mean differences in perceived control, perceived stress, and mental health between men and women employed in both settings. Women in both settings reported worse mental health than men, even when marital status, race, and educational level were controlled. In general, there were no sex differences in perceived control. The one exception to this was that women in the manufacturing plant reported less control over their work pace. This was because women were overrepresented in the production assembly jobs that are machine-paced, and underrepresented in the more autonomous skilled trades jobs. When levels of control over work pace were compared between male and female production workers, there were no significant differences.

Thus, the structural hypothesis for gender differences in perceived control is supported by these findings. Women and men in similar jobs and similar organizational contexts reported the same level of perceived control. When aggregated across occupations, women in the manufacturing plant reported less control over work pace because they were concentrated in jobs that offered little opportunity for control. It is interesting to note that even though men and women in the manufacturing plant did not differ in their average age and length of time with the company, female production workers were significantly older and had longer tenure than male production workers. While men were moving up into the skilled trades or management, women were remaining in their production jobs.

FEELINGS ABOUT PERCEIVED CONTROL

Manufacturing workers were asked not only how much they currently participated in decision-making, but also how much participation they desired. Women desired slightly more participation than did men ($M_{FEMALE} = 3.84$ and $M_{MALE} = 3.74$, $p = .10$). Women were particularly more likely than men to desire participation in setting production goals, determining work procedures, and determining work schedules, rather than in solving problems. Among production workers, the sex difference was more pronounced ($M_{FEMALE} = 3.81$ and $M_{MALE} = 3.64$, $p = .04$). However, when current levels of participation were taken into account, there were no sex differences in how much participation was desired.

The human-service workers were asked to indicate, on a seven-point scale that ranged from terrible to delighted, how they felt about their current levels of control. Men felt slightly better about their levels of control than did women (e.g., influence over job procedures, $M_{MALE} = 4.72$ and $M_{FEMALE} = 4.54$, $p = .09$). When the employee's current level of control was included in the model, the effect

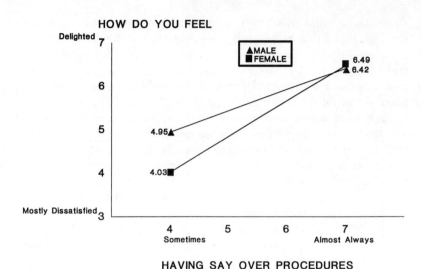

Figure 1
Primary appraisal of levels of perceived control among house managers

was strengthened (p = .02). Thus, at similar levels of control, women were less pleased than were men.

House managers, as one might expect, reported significantly more control than direct-care workers, but exhibited a similar sex difference (M_{MALE} = 5.83 and M_{FEMALE} = 5.33, p = .09). Interestingly, female house managers with high levels of control were as pleased as their male counterparts with their levels of say and influence. However, female house managers were markedly less pleased with low levels of control than were men. Figure 1 presents this relationship for influence over job procedures.

EFFECTS OF CONTROL ON MENTAL HEALTH

Direct Effects

Direct effects of perceived control on mental health were explored using regression models that included perceived control, sex, and an interaction of the two as independent variables. In the manufacturing setting, both control over work pace (b = −1.35, p < .001) and participation in decision-making (b = −1.30, p < .001) reduced depressive symptoms in men and women. There were no sex differences in the strength of the association between perceived control and depressive symptoms.

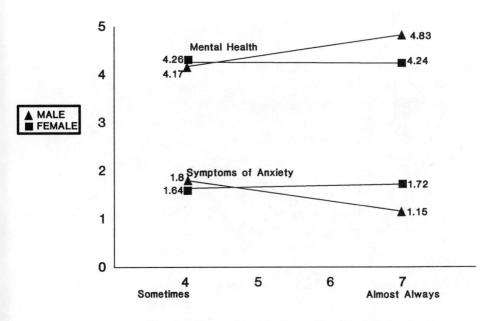

Figure 2
Direct effects of having say about how the job is done on mental health among male and female house managers

Among the human-service workers, having say about how to do one's work was only marginally linked to mental health ($b = .02, p = .06$), depression ($b = -.02, p = .10$), and anxiety ($b = -.02, p = .07$). Having say over procedures was more strongly associated with these outcomes ($p < .01$). For neither variable did sex differences in the strength of the relationship between perceived control and mental health appear. Perceived control did not reduce sex differences in mental health outcomes in any of the models in either occupational setting.

Once again, a different pattern of results was found among the house managers. Having say over procedures had a positive effect on mental health ($b = .09, p < .05$) for both men and women. However, having say about how the job was done enhanced mental health and reduced symptoms of anxiety for male house managers but not for females (see figure 2).

Buffering Effects

As indicated earlier, buffering effects were investigated using the moderated regression technique. Among manufacturing workers,

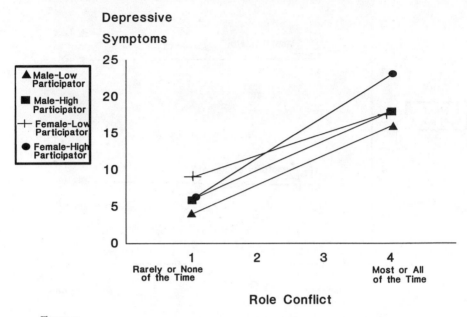

Figure 3
Moderating effects of participation in decision-making on role conflict among male and female manufacturing workers

control over work pace had no significant moderating effects for men or women. Participation in decision-making moderated the effects of role conflict for women, but the effect was in an unexpected direction. Figure 3 shows the interactive effects of participation with role conflict for both men and women. Participation had only a positive main effect for men. For women, participation was slightly beneficial at low levels of role conflict, but actually aggravated the effect at high levels. The three-way interaction between sex and participation and role conflict was not significant ($b = .30, p = .16$).

One explanation for this unusual finding is that levels of participation differed greatly between job categories in the plant. Thus, the effects of other factors that also varied significantly between job categories may have been confounded with the effects of participation. However, if one looks at buffering effects among production workers only, the same picture emerges. Women who participated in decision-making were protected from the adverse effects of stress at low levels, but were more susceptible to them at high levels. In this case, the three-way interaction between sex, participation, and role conflict approached statistical significance (b = .51, t (538) = 1.89, p = .06), indicating that the moderating role of participation differed for men and women.

Among the human-service workers, buffering effects were not pervasive. None of the buffering effects was significant for the men. For women, 3 of the 12 effects tested were significant. The effects for the women paralleled those of the manufacturing workers. Having say over job procedures was beneficial for women who rarely received poor feedback. However, for women who often received poor feedback, having say over job procedures was not a buffer and actually had deleterious effects on mental health, increasing symptoms of both depression and anxiety. As tested by a three-way interaction (i.e., sex × having say over the job × poor feedback), the sex difference in the moderating effects on depression was marginally significant (b = .02, t (1308) = 1.92, p = .06).

House managers again evidenced a different pattern of results. Say or influence did not buffer the effects of poor feedback or role overload in any of the models for females. In contrast, in 7 out of 12 tests, perceived-control variables effectively buffered male house managers from the adverse effects of poor feedback and role overload on mental health. Four of these effects are graphed in figure 4. Four of the three-way interactions were significant: having say over the job × sex × poor feedback on overall mental health (b = $-.05$, t (137) = -1.97, p = .04), and having say over the job × sex × role overload on anxiety (b = .04, t (137) = 2.33, p = .02), on depression (b = .04, t (137) = 1.92) and on overall mental health (b = $-.04$, t (137) = -2.75, p = .01).

SUMMARY AND DISCUSSION

To summarize, let me return to the research questions that were posed earlier.

1. Do levels of perceived control differ between men and women employed in similar occupations? Levels of perceived control, measured in three different ways and as expressed by two dissimilar groups of employees, did not differ by sex when comparisons were made within occupational settings and job types. This supports the structural hypothesis for differences in perceived control found between men and women in representative national samples or samples drawn from heterogeneous occupations. The social psychological hypotheses were not supported by these data. These findings are consistent with much of the research on sex differences in work experiences (Loscocco 1990; J. Miller 1980). When occupational status

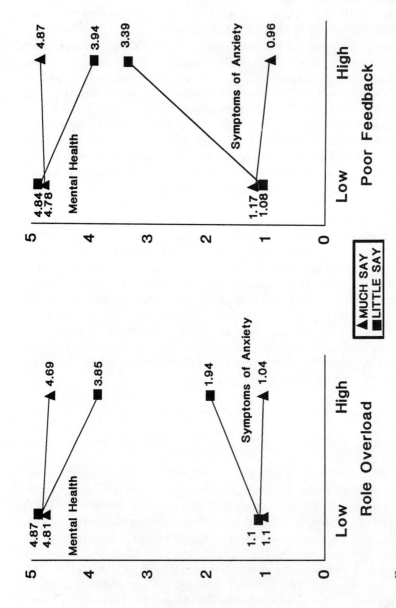

Figure 4
Buffering effects of having say over the job for male house managers

has not been taken into account, many differences have been found. However, they tend to disappear when men and women in similar occupations are compared.

2. To what extent do men and women appraise their levels of control differently? Perceived control was not seen as less important or less desirable by women. Among the manufacturing workers, there was a trend for women to desire more participation than men. In the human service field, women had more negative appraisals of their levels of control. Among house managers, women were more displeased with low levels of control than were men. There was no evidence that women, perhaps because of their socialization into a more docile or passive feminine gender role, wanted less control or were happy with less control than men.

3. Is perceived control more effective in enhancing health and buffering stress among men than women? The direct effects of perceived control on mental health were similar for both men and women. The lone exception was the stronger positive association of perceived control with mental health for male than for female house managers. The mechanism for this direct effect is not well understood. Nor is it clear whether the same mechanism is operating for men and women. Nevertheless, in general, having perceived control was associated with reduced distress for both sexes.

The results pertaining to the effectiveness of perceived control as a stress-buffering agent are least conclusive and most complex. In neither sample did perceived control buffer women against any of the role stresses. Perceived control did, however, heighten the effects of stress for women in both samples. For women in the human services, perceived control aggravated the adverse effects of receiving poor feedback. Participation in decision-making heightened the effects of high levels of role conflict for female manufacturing workers.

There is a reasonable post-hoc explanation for these unexpected "aggravation" effects of perceived control. As mentioned previously, employee coping behaviour is guided, in part, by perceptions of control. Those employees who believe they can modify a stressful situation are more likely to try to do so than employees who perceive themselves to have little control over the situation. Perhaps female employees' perceptions of control were *unrealistically* high. If this were the case, at low levels of stress, these perceptions of control would serve to enhance esteem and reduce anticipation of danger, thus reducing psychological symptoms. However, at high levels of stress, these same perceptions of control could have deleterious effects by causing employees to engage in problem-focused coping strategies that were doomed to be ineffective because the stressful situations were not truly within the employees' control. Thus, these employees may have exhibited increased distress because of the inefficacy of their actions and also because they did not fully engage in emotion-focused coping behaviour that could have alleviated some of their symptoms of distress. Also, some research indicates that finding out that one does not have the amount of control that one expected can be more stressful than not ever perceiving oneself to have control (Thompson, Cheek, & Graham 1988).

Let us take the example of the manufacturing workers. At low levels of stress, participation in decision-making may have been beneficial to well-being because affiliative needs were being met through dyadic and group interactions. However, at high levels of stress, affiliative goals were secondary to the goals of problem-solving and making changes in order to reduce stress. Participation in decision-making in this plant may not have provided effective avenues for making these changes, and may have taken up valuable employee time and energy that could have been expended on more effective coping strategies. Indeed, personal interviews with workers in the plant lent some credence to this hypothesis. Several work areas had instituted daily meetings for work groups to air concerns and work collectively to solve problems. Employees mentioned that the meetings were good opportunities to "shoot the breeze," but that thorny problems were not solved at these meetings, nor were employee suggestions and comments acted upon. The results of this study underscore the importance of *measuring* perceived control in decision-making, rather than assuming that control or influence will automatically result from increased forums for participation. The personal interviews did not shed light on why female employees were more adversely affected by the joint effects of high stress levels and high levels of participation than were men.

Strong and consistent buffering effects were found for male house managers, but not for females. The results for the house managers are the most alarming for those concerned about the well-being of working women. This study suggests that women in administrative and supervisory positions do not reap the benefits of perceived control that men do. Although female house managers did not report less perceived control than men, they were less pleased with low levels of control, experienced fewer direct benefits on well-being from perceived control, and were buffered from stress less effectively.

The explanation for the pattern of results indicating a lack of buffering effects and a presence of "aggravation" effects among female workers may lie in the cost-to-benefit ratio. Females may experience the same benefits of perceived control as their male counterparts, but the greater costs associated with exercising control could dampen positive effects or even create negative effects on well-being. Costs may be greater for women for several reasons. Research has shown that women often have less confidence in their ability to perform tasks, particularly tasks with which they are not familiar (Deaux 1976). If women have less confidence in their abilities to make good decisions, then responsibility may be a heavier burden for women than for men, and may undermine the benefits of perceived control. House managers compose the subgroup in this study that is called upon most often to exercise control in decision-making and to take responsibility for the consequences. Thus, the burden of responsibility may explain the lack of buffering effects among female house managers.

Another cost (or perceived cost) of exercising control may be negative effects on relationships with others. The traditional female gender role prescribes affiliation and, to a certain extent, dependence (Chodorow 1978). Having or taking control over situations may be counter-normative to this role and, hence, more likely to be sanctioned if performed by a woman. Exercising control, particularly in decision-making or problem-solving processes, may be perceived as threatening to important affiliative goals such as maintaining supportive relationships with one's co-workers or supervisor. For all of these reasons, the costs of exercising control may outweigh the benefits, resulting in perceived control being less effective as a stress buffer or even aggravating the effects of stress for women.

IMPLICATIONS FOR FUTURE RESEARCH

Research on perceived control *as it is experienced in the workplace* is in its infancy. Laboratory studies have indicated the importance of perceived control and suggested plausible hypotheses. It is time now to study perceived control in the real world. Only field studies will be able to identify the costs and benefits of having and exercising perceived control in a highly socialized, interactive environment. Contextual influences may be very important in understanding sex differences in perceived control. This study answers some basic questions about the role of perceived control in the worklives of men and women, and points to some future avenues of research.

First, the findings from this study need to be tested in other occupations. Given the uniqueness of the results for the house managers, it is particularly important to study other supervisory occupations. Second, the effects of perceived control on other outcomes should be explored. There is evidence that men and women tend to exhibit distress differently, men being more likely to turn to substance abuse and women to exhibit symptoms of depression (Biener 1987; Lennon 1987). Future research should investigate sex differences in the effects of perceived control using a variety of indicators of distress and other stress-related outcomes. Third, the use of longitudinal designs with multiple measurement points for stress, perceived control, and symptomatology would aid in sorting out causal processes and identifying spurious relationships.

Additional questions of interest await study. One set of questions addresses the relationships between control appraisals at varying levels of specificity. For example, to what extent and under what conditions do generalized beliefs about control influence appraisals of control over decision-making at work? To what extent do appraisals of control over decision-making affect control appraisals for specific worksite stressors? And do the answers to these questions differ for men and women? Another set of questions deals with the effects of control on other important moderators of the stress process, such as social support. Do women with low perceived control mobilize and use social support differently from those with high control? Does social support have different effects according to the recipient's level of perceived control? Johnson (1989) reported synergistic effects of perceived control and social support in protecting employees from the adverse consequences of stress. Husaini et al. (1982) suggested that people with low personal competence may interpret offers of social support as threats to their egos. Would a similar hypothesis be appropriate for employees with little control over decision-making? Lastly, there are the causal questions. If differences in the effects of perceived control on men and women are reliably replicated, what are their causes? Several possible mechanisms have been suggested in this chapter and need careful investigation.

At this point in our understanding of sex differences in perceived control, few clear-cut recommendations for practice can be made. The lack of significant differences in levels of control between men and women in similar occupations points toward the integration of women into higher-status jobs where they will have more opportunities for control as the preferred strategy for reducing inequities in levels of perceived control. Equal employment opportunities and affirmative-action programs are important elements in this strategy. The question of how to eliminate inequities in the experience of the benefits of control is more complex. Only through understanding *why* women do not benefit from perceived control as much as men do can we hope to design effective interventions for initiating appropriate organizational change and individual adaptation.

REFERENCES

Bandura, A. 1977. *Social learning theory*. Englewood Cliffs, NJ: Prentice-Hall.
Biener, L. 1987. Gender differences in the use of substances for coping. In R. Barnett, L. Biener, & G. Baruch, eds., *Gender and stress* (pp. 330–49). New York: Free Press.
Bronfenbrenner, U. 1979. *The ecology of human development: Experiments by nature and design*. Cambridge, MA: Harvard University Press.
Caplan, R., S. Cobb, J. French, R. Van Harrison, & S.R. Pinneau. 1980. Job demands and worker health: Main effects and occupational differences. *Research Report Series*. Ann Arbor, MI: Institute for Social Research.
Chodorow, N. 1978. *The reproduction of mothering*. Berkeley, CA: University of California Press.
Deaux, K. 1976. *The behavior of women and men*. Monterey, CA: Brooks/Cole.
Deaux, K., & J.C. Ullman. 1983. *Women of steel*. New York: Praeger.
Derogatis, L. 1977. The Hopkins Symptom Checklist (HSCL): A self-report system inventory. *Behavioral Science 19*, 1–5.
Erikson, E. 1950. *Childhood and society*. New York: W.W. Norton.
Folkman, S. 1984. Personal control and stress and coping processes: A theoretical analysis. *Journal of Personality and Social Psychology 46*, 839–52.
Folkman, S., C. Aldwin, & R. Lazarus. 1981, August. *The relationship between locus of control, cognitive appraisal, and coping*. Paper presented at the meeting of the American Psychological Association, Los Angeles, CA.
Ganster, D. 1988. Improving measures of worker control in occupational stress research. In J. Hurrell, L. Murphy, S. Sauter, & C. Cooper, eds., *Occupational stress: Issues and developments in research* (pp. 88–99). Philadelphia: Taylor & Francis.
Gatchel, R.J. 1980. Perceived control: A review and evaluation of therapeutic implications. In A. Baum & J. Singer, eds., *Advances in environmental psychology, Volume 2. Applications of personal control*. Hillsdale, NJ: Erlbaum.
Gilligan, C. 1982. *In a different voice: Psychological theory and women's development*. Cambridge, MA: Harvard University Press.
Hall, E.M. 1990. Gender, work control, and stress: A theoretical discussion and an empirical test. In J.V. Johnson & G. Johansson, eds., *The psychosocial work environment: Work organization, democratization, and health* (pp. 89–108). Amityville, NY: Baywood.
House, J., & E. Harkins. 1975. Why and when is status inconsistency stressful? *American Journal of Sociology 81*, 395–412.
Husaini, B., J. Neff, J. Newbrough, & M. Moore. 1982. The stress-

buffering role of social support and personal competence among the rural married. *Journal of Community Psychology 10*, 409–26.

Israel, B., J. House, S. Schurman, C. Heaney, & R. Mero. 1989. The relation of personal resources, participation, influence, interpersonal relationships and coping strategies to occupational stress, job strains, and health: A multivariate analysis. *Work and Stress 3*, 163–94.

Israel, B., & S. Schurman. 1990. Social support, control, and the stress process. In K. Glanz, F. Lewis, & B. Rimer, eds., *Health behavior and health education* (pp. 187–215). San Francisco: Jossey-Bass.

Jackson, S. 1983. Participation in decision-making as a strategy for reducing job-related strain. *Journal of Applied Psychology 68*, 3–19.

Johnson, J.V. 1989. Collective control: Strategies for survival in the workplace. *International Journal of Health Services 19*, 469–80.

Kanter, R. 1977. *Men and women of the corporation.* New York: Basic Books.

Karasek, R.A., Jr. 1979. Job demands, job decision latitude, and mental strain: Implications for job redesign. *Administrative Science Quarterly 24*, 285–307.

Karasek, R., D. Baker, F. Marxer, A. Ahlbom, & T. Theorell. 1981. Job decision latitude, job demands, and cardiovascular disease: A prospective study of Swedish men. *American Journal of Public Health 71*, 694–705.

Karasek, R., & T. Theorell. 1990. *Healthy work: Stress, productivity, and the reconstruction of working life.* New York: Basic Books.

Kobasa, S. 1987. Stress responses and personality. In R. Barnett, L. Biener, & G. Baruch, eds., *Gender and Stress* (pp. 308–29). New York: Free Press.

LaCroix, A., & S. Haynes. 1987. Gender differences in the health effects of workplace roles. In R.C. Barnett, L. Biener, & G.K. Baruch, eds., *Gender and stress* (pp. 96–121). New York: Free Press.

LaRocco, J.M., J.S. House, & J.R.P. French. 1980. Social support, occupational stress, and health. *Journal of Health and Social Behavior 21*, 202–18.

Lennon, M.C. 1987. Sex differences in distress: The impact of gender and work roles. *Journal of Health and Social Behavior 28*, 290–305.

Lewis, F.M. 1987. The concept of control: A typology and health-related variables. *Advances in Health Education and Promotion 2*, 277–309.

Loscocco, K.A. 1990. Reactions to blue collar work: A comparison of women and men. *Work and Occupations 17*, 152–77.

Menaghan, E. 1983. Individual coping efforts: Moderators of the relationship between life stress and mental health outcomes. In H. Kaplan, ed., *Psychosocial stress* (pp. 157–91) New York: Academic Press.

Miller, J. 1980. Individual and occupational determinants of job satisfaction. *Sociology of Work and Occupations 7*, 337–66.

Miller, S.M. 1979. Controllability and human stress: Method, evidence and therapy. *Behavior Research and Therapy 17*, 287–304.

Neider, L. 1980. An experimental field investigation utilizing an expectancy theory view of participation. *Organizational Behavior and Human Performance 26*, 425–42.

Pearlin, L.I., & C. Schooler. 1978. The structure of coping. *Journal of Health and Social Behavior 19*, 2–21.

Perrewe, P., & D. Ganster. 1989. The impact of job demands and behavioral control on experienced job stress. *Journal of Organizational Behavior 10*, 213–29.

Radloff, L. 1977. The CES-D Scale: A self-report depression scale for research in the general population. *Applied Psychological Measurement 1*, 385–401.

Rotter, J. 1966. Generalized expectancies for internal versus external control of reinforcement. *Psychological Monographs: General and Applied 80*, whole issue.

Spector, P.E. 1986. Perceived control by employees: A meta-analysis of studies concerning autonomy and participation at work. *Human Relations 39*, 1005–16.

Sutton, R., & R. Kahn. 1987. Prediction, understanding, and control as antidotes to organizational stress. In J. Lorsch, ed., *Handbook of organizational behavior* (pp. 272–85). Cambridge, MA: Harvard University Press.

Thoits, P. 1987. Gender and marital status differences in control and distress: Common stress versus unique stress explanations. *Journal of Health and Social Behavior 28*, 7–22.

Thompson, S.C., P.R. Cheek, & M.A. Graham. 1988. The other side of perceived control: Disadvantages and negative effects. In S. Spacapan & S. Oskamp, eds., *The social psychology of health* (pp. 69–93). Newbury Park, CA: Sage.

Travis, C. 1988. *Women and health psychology*. Hillsdale, NJ: Erlbaum.

U.S. Department of Labor. 1990. *Employment and earnings 37*. Washington: U.S. Government Printing Office.

Van Sell, M., A. Brief, & R. Schuler. 1981. Role conflict and role ambiguity: Integration of the literature and directions for future research. *Human Relations 34*, 43–71.

Walshok, M. 1981. *Blue-collar women: Pioneers on the male frontier*. New York: Anchor Books.

PART FOUR

Appraisals and Coping Strategies: Stress Mediators

11 Cognitive Appraisals and Coping with Stress

BRUCE E. COMPAS AND
PAMELA G. OROSAN

Work environments represent an essential context for understanding the role of stressful experiences in the adjustment and well-being of individuals. Adult men and women are exposed to a variety of circumstances related to employment that serve as sources of stress and adversity and contribute to somatic and psychological disorder. Because of the enormous changes that have occurred in the role of women in the labour force during this century, work settings form an especially interesting context for understanding women's stressful experiences, the ways that women cope with stress, and their adjustment to stressful circumstances. These changes have occurred at an increasingly rapid rate from 1970 to the present, and have enhanced the significance of studying employment-related stress for women (Matthews & Rodin 1989).

The rapid rate of social change in women's employment points to the importance of examining the broad social context in which women encounter stress in the workplace. Concerns have been raised regarding levels of stress and associated threats to somatic and psychological health that may increase for women as they assume different roles in the work force. Although changes in women's roles have certainly altered the frequency and nature of employment stress for women, analyses of the broader social changes in women's work roles do not suggest that women as a group are

Preparation of this manuscript and portions of the research described here were supported by National Institute of Mental Health Grant MH43819.

adversely affected by employment outside the home (Repetti, Matthews, & Waldron 1989). It appears instead that there are substantial individual differences in the effects of employment for women.

An important avenue for achieving an understanding of these individual differences involves analyses of individuals' appraisals of their circumstances, the meaning of those circumstances, and the ways in which individuals cope with employment stress. Analyses of this type can shed light on why some women are adversely affected by workplace stress while others may be unaffected or even benefit from similar circumstances. That is, analyses of individuals' appraisals and coping efforts may help in understanding why individual differences occur in women's responses to employment stress.

Processes of cognitive appraisal and coping have been shown to be essential for understanding sources of stress and adversity ranging from single traumatic events (e.g., life-threatening illness) to chronic daily hassles (e.g., financial strains, daily responsibilities), as well as for explaining differences between individuals in their levels of adjustment to these circumstances (e.g., Lazarus & Folkman 1984; Taylor 1983). From a cognitive-transactional perspective, appraisals and coping are seen as interacting in their influence on psychological and somatic adjustment (Folkman, Lazarus, Dunkel-Schetter, DeLongis, & Gruen 1986). Appraisals and coping mutually influence one another over the course of a stressful episode and play important roles in determining psychological and somatic outcomes (Folkman & Lazarus 1985; Folkman, Lazarus, Gruen, & DeLongis 1986). The ways in which individuals interpret their relationships with their environments and construct the meaning and significance of these relationships provide a basis for generating coping responses. Further, both appraisals and coping are influenced by broader contextual variables, including the social context in which stress is encountered and the developmental level of the individual.

Our purpose is to review some recent findings in research on cognitive appraisals and coping with stress, and to apply these findings to the study of women and employment stress. We first review recent research on the relation between cognitive appraisals and coping, emphasizing studies of appraisals of control and the use of problem-focused and emotion-focused coping. Next, we consider another important aspect of cognitive appraisals in relation to coping, specifically appraisals of the meaning or significance of a stressful encounter. Finally, we discuss the implications of appraisals and coping for understanding the ways that women perceive, cope with, and are affected by employment stress.

COGNITIVE APPRAISALS AND COPING: THE SPECIAL CASE OF PERCEIVED CONTROL

Cognitive appraisal is the process through which individuals understand themselves, their world, and their relationship with their world. Appraisal processes play a central role in a number of theories concerned with stressful experiences and the ways that people cope with them (e.g., Brown & Harris 1989; Hobfoll 1989; Lazarus & Folkman 1984; Taylor 1983). Among these, the cognitive transactional model of Lazarus, Folkman, and their colleagues (e.g., Folkman 1984; Lazarus & Folkman 1984; Smith & Lazarus 1990) has offered the most comprehensive description of appraisal processes and has had the most far-reaching influence on the field; this model will serve as the basis for the present description of appraisals and coping.

Appraisals are the vehicle through which individuals determine whether or not a given situation is stressful or benign, the meaning or significance of the situation, and the options that are available to cope with stressful circumstances (Lazarus & Folkman 1984). Briefly, primary appraisal encompasses the process of assessing the personal significance of the situation. The individual is asking the basic question, "Am I okay or am I in trouble?" More specifically, primary appraisals distinguish among relationships between the self and the environment that are perceived as threatening, challenging, or involving harm or loss on the one hand, and benign or positive circumstances on the other. Secondary appraisal involves the question, "What can I do about this stressful situation?" It includes an evaluation of one's personal and social coping resources and the relevance of these resources for resolving the particular stressful encounter.

Appraisals are thought to influence psychological and somatic outcomes of stressful encounters both directly and indirectly. Direct effects of appraisals are found in the relations between specific appraisals and emotions (e.g., Folkman & Lazarus 1988; Smith, this volume). For example, appraisals of threat are related to feelings of fear and anxiety, whereas appraisals of harm or loss are related to feelings of sadness, resignation, and depression. The second avenue through which appraisals affect psychological and somatic outcomes is an indirect path through their association with coping processes. Appraisals combine with objective aspects of the stressful situation

and personal characteristics of the individual to determine the selection and enactment of specific coping responses over the course of a
stressful encounter.

The dimension of cognitive appraisal that has received the most
attention in relation to coping is the perception of personal control
(Folkman 1984). Specifically, control beliefs are thought to be linked
to the function of coping responses as either problem-focused or
emotion-focused. Before describing the findings regarding control
and coping functions, it is important to define these two concepts
explicitly. Various conceptualizations have highlighted the importance of three aspects of control-related beliefs: (a) Judgments of
contingency (also labelled means-ends relations or response-
outcome expectancies) reflect expectations about the degree to
which outcomes are dependent on characteristics of people (e.g.,
effort or ability), external factors (e.g., luck or powerful others), or
unknown factors. (b) Judgments of personal competence (also labelled agency beliefs or self-efficacy expectations) refer to expectations that the self is capable of producing or executing the necessary
behaviours or other means to achieve a specific outcome. (c) Judgments of control, which are conceptualized as a function of contingency and competence beliefs, refer either to expectations about
one's own ability to produce a desired outcome (Skinner, Chapman,
& Baltes 1988) or to the accuracy of one's beliefs in relation to the
true controllability of the task (Weisz 1986b), and they are the result
of varying combinations of contingency and competence beliefs in
different situations or domains. Contingency and competence beliefs are both related to control beliefs, but they have been shown to
be independent of one another (e.g., Weisz 1986a). For example, a
woman may perceive herself as competent in relation to the demands of her job but recognize that, because of biases and other inequities, promotion and other rewards are not related to the characteristics and efforts of women in this setting, resulting in a low sense
of personal control.

The distinction between problem-focused and emotion-focused
functions of coping efforts is closely related to the concept of control
(Folkman 1984). Problem-focused coping efforts involve actions to
alter or change some aspect of the stressful person-environment relationship. As such, problem-focused coping acts are well matched to
stressful situations or aspects of situations that are appraised as amenable to personal control. In contrast, emotion-focused coping involves efforts to adjust or adapt aspects of oneself to stressful situations. This includes changing one's emotions, beliefs, goals, and

commitments in an effort to reduce personal distress associated with the stressful encounter.

A clear link has been established between perceptions of control and the use of problem- and emotion-focused coping (e.g., Folkman & Lazarus 1980). That is, perceptions of personal control over a stressful situation are associated with the use of relatively more problem-focused coping aimed at changing the nature of the stressor. The perception that one lacks control over a stressful situation is related to the use of relatively more emotion-focused coping to alter one's perceptions of the situation and to manage distressing emotions. Thus, individuals appear to attempt to match the function of their coping efforts with their appraisals of the controllability of the situation. Folkman (1984) summarized a complex set of relations among control beliefs, appraisals of threat and challenge, and the use of problem- and emotion-focused coping. Among these is the notion that problem-focused efforts are more adaptive when they are directed toward aspects of the person-environment relationship that are perceived as changeable, whereas emotion-focused efforts are more adaptive when a situation is recognized as unchangeable.

It appears that psychological and somatic adjustments to a stressful episode are related to the degree of congruence or the match between control beliefs and the relative use of problem- and emotion-focused coping (e.g., Compas, Malcarne, & Fondacaro 1988; Forsythe & Compas 1987). Psychological and somatic symptoms have been found to be lower when control appraisals and coping are matched (using relatively more problem-focused coping with events perceived as controllable and relatively more emotion-focused coping with events perceived as uncontrollable), and symptoms have been found to be higher when perceptions of control and coping are mismatched (using relatively more problem-focused coping with events perceived as uncontrollable and relatively more emotion-focused coping with events perceived as controllable). Elevated symptoms associated with a mismatch between control appraisals and coping are assumed to be the result of coping efforts that are experienced as ineffective in resolving or mastering the stressful situation. For example, repeated problem-focused efforts by a woman to change inequities in her place of employment, inequities that she perceives as ultimately beyond her control because of a lack of contingency between behaviours and outcome in this setting, would be likely to engender feelings of frustration, anger, and eventually helplessness.

This pattern of findings raises the question of why individuals would employ coping efforts that clearly contradict their perceptions of a stressful situation. This could occur for several reasons. First, individuals differ in their preferred ways of coping with stress. For example, they differ in their preference to seek out versus avoid information under stress (Miller 1980). Some individuals may pursue strategies that are consistent with their preferred ways of coping independent of their situational appraisals of control. In some situations, preferred ways of coping may be incongruent with the individual's perceived or actual degree of control, such as a woman who has been socialized to rely on emotion-focused coping methods in spite of opportunities to gain control in certain stressful encounters. Second, individuals also differ in their generalized beliefs about control, independent of their beliefs about the controllability of a specific stressful situation. Numerous studies have shown that individuals differ in their generalized locus of control, varying in the degree to which they believe that outcomes are contingent on their own behaviour as opposed to external forces (Rotter 1990). The coping efforts of some individuals may be guided more by these generalized beliefs than by their appraisals of control in the immediate situation. These possibilities warrant further research.

It is likely that control appraisals, coping, and psychological and somatic adjustment are related to one another in a reciprocal fashion. Coping is likely to be more effective when it is well suited to the perceived and actual degree of controllability in the situation. However, the use of problem-focused coping in successfully changing a situation and reducing the level of stress that is experienced is likely to contribute to the belief that one has control over the situation. Thus, control beliefs can guide coping efforts but coping can also change perceptions of control (Compas, Forsythe, & Wagner 1988).

More recent evidence indicates that problem-focused and emotion-focused coping are regulated by somewhat different cues. Specifically, it appears that problem-focused coping is closely related to perceived control while emotion-focused coping is linked more closely to emotional arousal and distress (Compas, Banez, Malcarne, & Worsham 1991). Individuals may adjust their use of problem-focused coping in accord with their control beliefs, whereas emotion-focused coping may be linked directly to internal cues of emotional distress. A preliminary model of control beliefs, coping, and emotional arousal is presented in figure 1. The relative importance of perceived control and emotional arousal and distress in regulating problem- and emotion-focused coping warrants continued attention in future research.

Primary Appraisal

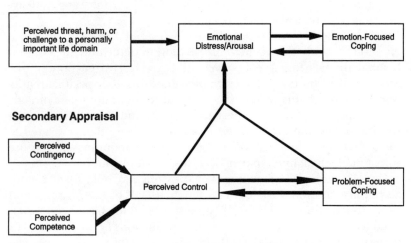

Figure 1
Model of contingency, competence and control beliefs, coping, and emotional distress

BEYOND PERCEIVED CONTROL:
APPRAISALS OF THE MEANING OF
STRESSFUL ENCOUNTERS

Perceptions of control in a specific stressful encounter are a part of the secondary appraisal process (Folkman 1984). That is, perceived control is related to the process of evaluating one's coping options, specifically the possibilities for problem-focused coping. However, analyses of control beliefs have often failed to address the question, "Control over what?" The focus of control appraisals may be contained in primary appraisals of the meaning of a stressful encounter. Perceptions of meaning or significance have been discussed by Lazarus and Folkman as what is at stake for the person in a stressful encounter, i.e., personal "stakes." Stakes involve those aspects of the person and his or her relationship with the environment that have been threatened, harmed, or challenged in a stressful episode. Understanding an individual's appraisals of meaning (or stakes) provides pertinent information for understanding why a particular situation is appraised as stressful by an individual and, therefore, is useful for examining differences between individuals in their responses to the same circumstances. Although perceptions of personal control contribute to the appraised meaning of stressful situations, control beliefs are not sufficient for understanding appraisals of personal meaning and significance. Previous research on perceived control and coping with stress, however, does provide some direction for research in the area of appraisals of meaning and significance in stressful encounters.

Smith, Lazarus, and colleagues have described the ways in which emotions provide the needed information to determine the core relational themes that are involved in any stressful encounter (see Smith, this volume). However, Smith notes that the specific identity or content of what is at stake in an encounter does not relate directly to the emotions that are experienced by the individual. Rather, the specific stakes that are involved in a stressful episode are related to the individual's personal values, goals, and commitments that are threatened, challenged, harmed, or lost in an encounter.

Understanding the meaning that stressors may hold for individuals requires a framework for describing patterns of values, goals, and commitments in people's lives. Numerous systems have been developed to this end, ranging from simple distinctions between two goals to more complex models with multiple categories. For example, stress researchers have distinguished between interpersonal/ affiliative concerns (sociotropy) and achievement/instrumental concerns (autonomy) (Hammen, Ellicott, Gitlin, & Jamison 1989; Hammen, Marks, Mayol, & deMayo 1985; Robins & Block 1988). Individual differences in the importance of these two domains have been found to relate to the level of perceived stress that is experienced in connection with major and minor events that occur in these domains and to the level of depressive symptoms associated with stress in these domains. A tripartite system has been proposed within cognitive evaluation theory, involving the domains of competence, autonomy, and relatedness (Connell 1990; Deci & Ryan 1987). Models including multiple commitment domains have been generated by numerous theorists and researchers (e.g., Emmons 1986; Murray 1938; Novacek & Lazarus 1988; Pervin 1983). In addition to the number and content of domains, these frameworks can be further distinguished based on whether the system was derived theoretically (e.g., Murray 1938) or empirically (e.g., Pervin 1983).

The central concern of researchers in this area has been to understand the patterns of commitments, values, and goals that are held by different individuals. The objective has been to determine what is most significant or important in a given individual's life. The application of these frameworks to the study of stress and coping processes shifts attention to the link between a specific stressful event and the goals, values, or commitments that are threatened in the stressful situation. Specifically, in our own research we are interested in understanding which of a person's values, goals, and commitments are at stake in a given stressful encounter in order to understand the meaning of the encounter for a given individual (Kottmeier & Compas 1991). We believe that this will provide us with a useful framework for understanding the focus of an individual's efforts at coping with this stressor; that is, for understanding what it is that he or she is trying to resolve in a stressful situation.

We are currently developing a framework to understand the meaning of the diagnosis and treatment of cancer for cancer patients and their family members (Kottmeier & Compas 1991). We are now evaluating the reliability and validity of a ten-category framework based on the work of Lazarus's cognitive transactional model of stress (Novacek & Lazarus 1988), Taylor's model of cognitive adaptation to threat (1983), and cognitive evaluation theory (Connell 1990; Deci & Ryan 1987). This framework includes the following categories: (a) affiliation (concern with interpersonal relationships, intimacy, love, and family); (b) achievement-power (concern with threats to job, financial security, career and leadership aspirations, as well as desire for recognition, popularity, dominance, and influence); (c) personal growth (concern with striving for personal development, self-understanding, a meaningful personal philosophy); (d) altruism-humanitarianism (concern with the need to help and be involved in organizations); (e) stress avoidance (concern with avoidance or nuisances, hassles, or uncertainty in the hope of having a stable, predictable, and easy life); (f) pleasure-seeking (concern with pursuing fun, excitement, novelty, and fun); (g) autonomy (concern with independence, personal control, and self-determination); (h) personal health (concern with physical health); (i) life and mortality (threats of loss of life); and (j) uncertainty.

The potential usefulness of this framework is best exemplified through a few examples of cancer patients' reports of the aspects of their illness or its treatment that have been the most stressful for them. One patient described her concerns about her family in the event she should die, with her most acute concerns centring on her youngest children. This response indicates that the cancer represented primarily a threat to her sense of affiliation with others, especially her family. A second patient discussed the effects of the cancer and its treatment on his ability to fulfil the demands of his job. He was a construction foreman and he reported that he had to get his crew started at work each morning before making the ninety-minute drive to the hospital to receive radiation therapy. This reflects a threat to achievement goals, especially his sense of competence at work. Thus, both of these cancer patients experienced their illness and its treatment as highly stressful, but for quite different reasons.

A framework of this type is based on the assumption that the meaning of a stressful event is not necessarily reflected in the context or situation in which the stressor is encountered. That is, in our research with cancer patients and their families we have quickly come to recognize that illnesses are not always stressful because they represent a threat to personal health. More pertinent to the present discussion, stressors that occur in the work environment are not necessarily stressful because they represent a threat to employment-related goals, values, or commitments.

The specifics of what is at stake in a stressful encounter may be important for understanding the coping process. That is, aspects of the individual's values, goals, or commitments that are involved are crucial to understanding what it is that the person is coping with. Much as the functions of coping efforts are matched to the perceived controllability of the stressful situation, coping efforts may be matched to the specific meaning of a stressor in an attempt to address the aspect of the person-environment relationship that has been threatened, harmed, or challenged. To provide some clarification by way of a brief example, a woman might be faced with demands from an employer to take on additional responsibilities and work extra hours. If the primary meaning of this encounter lies in the significance that it holds for her sense of competence and status on the job, she will be best served by focusing her coping efforts on working quickly and efficiently to meet the demands being made on her. On the other hand, if the primary meaning of this encounter lies in the disruption that it causes in her relationships with her spouse and children owing to increased time away from home, then at least some of her coping efforts will be best spent trying to manage and resolve the stress that this problem has created at home. We recognize that a single stressful episode may have several different meanings for an individual and therefore may require many different directions for coping, as is implied by this initial example. Thus, a single stressor may require a diverse set of coping strategies.

Individual differences in the perceived meaning of a stressful situation will vary as a function of a number of personal and environmental factors. We have been most concerned with the role of the individual's developmental level and gender as well as the values of others in the social context in influencing the construction of personal meaning in a situation. Consistent with developmentally oriented models of self-esteem and gender identity, we found that the frequency of different types of events that are encountered and the degree of stress associated with different life domains varied as a function of both gender and developmental level during adolescence (Wagner & Compas 1990). With regard to the frequency of stressful events, young adolescent females reported more stressful events involving family members, peers, intimate relationships, and others in their social network than did males; middle adolescent females reported more stressful events involving intimacy and social network events than males; and older adolescent females reported more stressful social network events than males. With regard to the perceived stressfulness of these events, older adolescent females perceived both social network and peer events as more stressful than did older adolescent males. No gender differences in perceived stressfulness were found in the young and middle adolescent samples. Thus, females appear to encounter more interpersonal stress and to perceive these events as more stressful than males even during early adolescence, indicating that there is an early onset of this pattern that has been well documented in adult samples. Further, the nature of gender differences in stress changes with development during adolescence. Changes in stress during the course of adult development have not been investigated.

The social context in which events are experienced is also likely to affect the degree to which they are stressful and the ways that individuals will cope with them. For example, we found that single and married mothers reported different levels of daily stress in certain life domains and utilized different types of coping responses (Compas & Williams 1990). Single mothers reported more daily hassles related to family, economic, and personal health problems. Further, in coping with stress, single mothers accepted more responsibility and relied more on positive reappraisal than did married mothers. These differences may be attributable to a variety of factors, including differential rates of exposure to stressful circumstances, availability of coping resources, and the differences in the perceived meaning of stressful circumstances. Clearly the life circumstances of women are important to consider in accounting for stress and coping processes.

In future research we will apply this classification system of perceived meaning to individuals' self-reports of coping. That is, we will classify the focus of the coping efforts as directed toward resolving stress related to one or more of the domains included in this system. It is noteworthy that the construction, or more accurately the reconstruction, of personal meaning has been identified as an important element in the coping process (e.g., Taylor 1983).

COGNITIVE APPRAISALS AND COPING:
IMPLICATIONS FOR UNDERSTANDING
WOMEN AND EMPLOYMENT STRESS

In their review of the association of employment and women's physical and mental health, Repetti et al. (1989) note that employment stress affects women in a variety of different ways and that continued research is needed to identify individual differences among women in their reactions to employment stress. That is, research is needed to determine which women in which types of jobs will experience employment as either health-promoting or health-damaging. We believe that the solution to this puzzle can be guided by examining differences in women's cognitive appraisals of employment stress and the ways that women cope with it. Information on women's appraisals and coping could then be integrated with the rich data already available on the social roles and constraints facing employed women. The research on appraisals of control, perceived meaning, and coping described above suggests several important directions for future research in this area.

Control Appraisals and Coping

The basic literature on control appraisals and coping has three important implications for the study of women and employment stress. First, control appraisals are composed of a complex set of beliefs, including contingency, competence, and control beliefs (Weisz 1986a). We know little about how women differ from one another and from men in the workplace on these beliefs. Further, no data are available on the association of these beliefs with coping and psychological adjustment among employed women.

Second, the study of control and coping among employed women would be well advised to include detailed assessments of women's levels of emotional distress, in order to determine the ways in which distress can guide as well as be affected by coping efforts. Previous research has suggested that the uses of problem-focused and emotion-focused coping are tied to different cues, with problem-directed coping related to control appraisals and emotion-directed coping related to emotional distress and arousal (e.g., Compas et al. 1991). In light of research indicating that women have different patterns of emotional reactivity to events in their environment than men (e.g., Diener, Sandvik, & Larson 1985), it will be important to examine gender differences in the cognitive and emotional cues that are related to coping for women and men.

Third, the process of control appraisals, coping, and emotional distress needs to be examined over the course of stressful encounters in the workplace as well as over the course of women's careers as their employment roles change and evolve. Process-oriented research on coping has shown that coping efforts are best characterized as an interaction of characteristics of the person and the setting, and that both person and environment typically change over the course of a single stressful encounter and across different encounters (e.g., Compas, Forsythe, & Wagner 1988; Folkman & Lazarus 1985).

Research on interactions between control appraisals and coping may prove useful in further understanding recent research findings concerning women and employment stress. For example, Heaney (this volume) found that personal control (as indicated by participation in decision-making) had a detrimental effect on the psychological well-being of some employed women under conditions of high stress (as reflected by high levels of role ambiguity, role conflict, and role overload). This effect was counter to the expected beneficial effects of control, as higher control was expected to serve as a source of protection from the adverse effects of stress. This suggests that the association between control and psychological well-being may be mediated by other factors. We suggest that the ways that women attempt to cope with employment-related stress are central for further understanding this unexpected association between high levels of personal control and poorer psychological well-being. A strong sense of personal control may lead to feelings of frustration and helplessness if women are blocked in their opportunities to use problem-focused strategies to cope with employment stress in some settings.

Further, as Heaney (this volume) points out, this unexpected finding may have been due to the meaning and significance of participation in decision-making, as participation may have arisen from pursuing affiliative goals rather than more instrumental goals related to achievement and productivity. Women may have directed their coping toward resolving the interpersonal and affiliative aspects of employment stress rather than the achievement aspects of this stress. As a result, time and energy for coping with the achievement-relevant aspects of employment stress may have been seriously curtailed for these women. This leads us to consider the importance of women's perceptions of the meaning of employment-related stress.

The Meaning of Employment-Related Stress for Women

A woman's way of coping with employment stress is likely to be affected by her understanding of what is at stake for her in a stressful encounter. Further, her appraisals of the stakes or meanings of stressful events are likely to be affected by her internal representations of herself, including her roles, competencies, and self-aspects. Linville (1987) suggests that individual differences in the meaning of stressful events may be due, in part, to differences in cognitive representations of the self.

Self-representation is organized through a set of cognitive structures that Linville refers to as self-aspects. These self-aspects are internal representations of one's roles, traits, relationships, and so forth. An employed woman, for example, may have self-aspects of manager, hard worker, friend, mother, and wife. The cognitive organization of self-knowledge is reflected in the individual's level of self-complexity, which is represented by the number of self-aspects and the degree of distinctiveness among these self-aspects (Linville 1987). Linville's research has supported the hypothesis that self-complexity serves a buffering function against the adverse aspects of stress; greater self-complexity acts as a cognitive buffer against stress-related illness in that it moderates the adverse effects of stress on mental and physical health. In contrast, for individuals who are low on self-complexity, stress in one self-aspect tends to spill over to other self-aspects if those self-aspects share features or cognitive elements and are not distinct.

The self-complexity model has clear implications for women faced with employment-related stress. Imagine, for example, a manager who feels she is ineffective in managing her staff. Further imagine she has a simple self-representation with two self-aspects, manager and mother, and that these self-aspects are not distinct because they share many features. To the extent that her two self-aspects share a goal of fostering affiliation with other people, the woman's negative feelings associated with her managerial ineffectiveness are likely to spill over to her thoughts and feelings about herself as a mother. Her sense of ineffectiveness in her interpersonal relationships with her staff may lead her to think, "I have a difficult time relating to people," thus colouring her thoughts and feelings about her ability to relate to her spouse and children as well. In contrast, for women with several distinct self-aspects, stress in any one aspect will tend to be confined to that aspect, and positive thoughts and feelings associated with the other self-aspects will act as buffers against the stress.

In light of recent social psychological research (Repetti et al. 1989; Verbrugge 1986) suggesting that commitment to multiple roles does not have a negative effect on women's health, it seems important to explore how women's multiple roles and self-aspects may be related in ways that are beneficial to women's health and well-being. It is noteworthy that research on the effects of women's multiple roles has not taken into account the internal self-representation of those roles. Comprehending how women internally represent their multiple roles may provide additional information about the ways that women appraise and cope with employment-related stress. The self-complexity hypothesis can be used to understand how stressors identified in the workplace may hold meaning for other domains of women's lives and, similarly, how stressors occurring outside the work environment may be meaningful because of their significance for employment.

Along this line, Verbrugge (1986) found that having numerous roles was associated with good health. Further, women were at higher risk for poor health than men because women were more likely to have few roles and to be dissatisfied with their primary role. Verbrugge concluded that the negative effects of role burdens may lie in the individual's subjective experience of the role rather than in objective characteristics. Verbrugge's conclusion is consistent with the self-complexity hypothesis; women with few and nondistinct self-aspects who are dissatisfied or experiencing stress in their main self-aspect would be expected to experience spillover of those negative feelings to other self-aspects. This spillover may colour their entire self-representation and thus their feelings about broader aspects of their lives. However, more information about how women in Verbrugge's study internally represented their roles is necessary to explore the self-complexity hypothesis fully.

An important step in determining the possible multiple meanings of employment stress for women will involve the development of a framework for classifying women's perceptions of the meanings (and relevant self-aspects) of employment stress. Long, Kahn, and Schutz (1992) have taken a step in this direction in their work by examining four "stakes" for employed women: self-esteem, losing respect for someone else, not achieving an important goal at work, and strains on financial resources. This type of detailed breakdown of the meaning of employment-related stress could be integrated with classification schemes such as those outlined earlier in this paper. That is, achievement and power goals could be further differentiated into the four categories described by Long et al. (1992) and used to make more fine-grained distinctions in the meaning of employment stress.

Further research is also needed to investigate many other factors that may influence women's appraisal of employment-related stressors. Three factors appear especially important for future research: (a) the personality traits of instrumentality and expressivity, (b) developmental level, and (c) the values and goals of significant others and the broader social environment in which a woman functions.

The gender-related personality traits of instrumentality and expressivity (Spence & Helmreich 1978, 1980) reflect the level of importance of interpersonal as opposed to instrumental goals for men and women. Women's greater expressivity reflects a greater commitment to and value for interpersonal relationships. This suggests that women may be more likely to perceive the meaning of stressful experiences in terms of their implications for relationships with others. Further, women with traditional versus egalitarian sex-role attitudes may differ in their commitment to achievement goals as opposed to affiliative goals. For example, Long et al. (1992) found that women with traditional sex-role attitudes had more positive appraisals of employment-related stressors (losing respect for someone else, not achieving an important goal at work) than did women who held more egalitarian sex-role beliefs. This suggests that traditional women may be less invested in and have less at stake in employment-related stressors that have meaning related to achievement goals.

In the study of stress and coping, concern with developmental processes unfortunately has been limited to studies of children and adolescents. However, life-span developmentalists have pointed to the importance of understanding developmental processes throughout adulthood as well. This may have important implications for understanding women and employment stress, as women at different points in adult and family development may encounter different types of employment stress, may perceive and cope with these stressors differently, and may be affected by stressful experiences in different ways. Further, it is unlikely that there is a universal pattern of adult development that would reflect the experiences of women from diverse ethnic and educational backgrounds. Women may encounter very different paths in terms of their careers and their involvement or lack of involvement with spouses and children. Thus, a variety of different developmental paths will need to be considered.

Finally, the significant values, goals, and commitments of employed women cannot be understood independent of the proximal and distal social contexts in which these factors are developed. Conflicts may arise when the pattern of goals, values, and commitments held by a woman are not supported or are even devalued by significant others in her life. A husband who does not value his wife's achievements and successes at work is unlikely to understand that the significance of employment-related stress for her may lie in implications for her feelings of accomplishment and competence. This may lead to a lack of support for her coping efforts or even direct interference with her efforts to focus on coping with achievement stress at work.

In summary, it is clear that employment holds both benefits and costs for the psychological well-being of women. Closer examination of the ways in which women appraise and cope with stressful events and circumstances at work will help to clarify who will gain and who will lose as a result of employment-related stress. We believe that appraisals of the controllability and the meaning of employment stress, as well as the ways that women cope with such stress, are prime targets for future research in this area. A closer understanding of appraisal and coping patterns could provide a needed foundation for efforts to improve the quality of work for women.

REFERENCES

Brown, G.W., & T.O. Harris, eds. 1989. *Life events and illness*. New York: Guilford.
Compas, B.E., G.A. Banez, V.L. Malcarne, & N. Worsham. 1991. Perceived control and coping with stress: A developmental perspective. *Journal of Social Issues 47*, 23–34.
Compas, B.E., C.J. Forsythe, & B.M. Wagner. 1988. Consistency and variability in causal attributions and coping with stress. *Cognitive Therapy and Research 12*, 305–20.
Compas, B.E., V.L. Malcarne, & K.M. Fondacaro. 1988. Coping with stressful events in older children and young adolescents. *Journal of Consulting and Clinical Psychology 56*, 405–11.
Compas, B.E., & R.A. Williams. 1990. Stress, coping, and adjustment in mothers and young adolescents in single-and two-parent families. *American Journal of Community Psychology 18*, 525–45.
Connell, J.P. 1990. Context, self, and action: A motivational analysis of self-system processes across the life-span. In D. Cicchetti & M. Beeghly, eds., *The self in transition: Infancy to childhood* (pp. 61–97). Chicago: University of Chicago Press.
Deci, E.L., & R.M. Ryan. 1987. The support of autonomy and the control of behavior. *Journal of Personality and Social Psychology 53*, 1024–37.
Diener, E., E. Sandvik, & R.J. Larson. 1985. Age and sex effects for emotional intensity. *Developmental Psychology 21*, 542–6.
Emmons, R.A. 1986. Personal strivings: An approach to personality and subjective well-being. *Journal of Personality and Social Psychology 51*, 1058–68.
Folkman, S. 1984. Personal control and stress and coping processes: A theoretical analysis. *Journal of Personality and Social Psychology 46*, 839–52.
Folkman, S., & R.S. Lazarus. 1980. An analysis of coping in a middle-aged community sample. *Journal of Health and Social Behavior 21*, 219–39.
– 1985. If it changes it must be a process: A study of emotion and coping

during three stages of a college examination. *Journal of Personality and Social Psychology 48*, 150–70.

– 1988. Coping as a mediator of emotion. *Journal of Personality and Social Psychology 54*, 466–75.

Folkman, S., R.S. Lazarus, C. Dunkel-Schetter, A. DeLongis, & R. Gruen. 1986. The dynamics of a stressful encounter: Cognitive appraisal, coping, and encounter outcomes. *Journal of Personality and Social Psychology 50*, 992–1003.

Folkman, S., R.S. Lazarus, R. Gruen, & A. DeLongis. 1986. Appraisal, coping, health status, and psychological symptoms. *Journal of Personality and Social Psychology 50*, 571–9.

Forsythe, C.J., & B.E. Compas. 1987. Interaction of stressful events and coping: Testing the goodness of fit hypothesis. *Cognitive Therapy and Research 11*, 473–85.

Hammen, C., A. Ellicott, M. Gitlin, & K.R. Jamison. 1989. Sociotropy/ autonomy and vulnerability to specific life events in patients with unipolar depression and bipolar disorders. *Journal of Abnormal Psychology 98*, 154–60.

Hammen, C.L., T. Marks, A. Mayol, & R. deMayo. 1985. Depressive self-schemas, life stress, and vulnerability to depression. *Journal of Abnormal Psychology 94*, 308–19.

Hobfoll, S.E. 1989. Conservation of resources: A new attempt at conceptualizing stress. *American Psychologist 44*, 513–24.

Kottmeier, C., & B.E. Compas. 1991. Cognitive appraisals of the meaning of stress: Cancer patients' perceptions of their illness. Unpublished raw data.

Lazarus, R.S., & S. Folkman. 1984. *Stress, appraisal and coping*. New York: Springer.

Linville, P.W. 1987. Self-complexity as a cognitive buffer against stress-related illness and depression. *Journal of Personality and Social Psychology 52*, 663–76.

Long, B.C., S.E. Kahn, & R.W. Schutz. 1992. A causal model of stress and coping: Women in management. *Journal of Counseling Psychology 39*, 227–39.

Matthews, K.A., & J. Rodin. 1989. Women's changing work roles: Impact on health, family, and public policy. *American Psychologist 44*, 1389–93.

Miller, S.M. 1980. When is a little information a dangerous thing? Coping with stressful life-events by monitoring vs. blunting. In S. Levine & H. Ursin, eds., *Coping and health* (pp. 145–69). New York: Plenum.

Murray, H.A. 1938. *Explorations in personality*. New York: Oxford University Press.

Novacek, J., & R.S. Lazarus. 1988. *The structure and measurement of personal commitments*. Tulsa, OK: Tulsa Institute of Behavioral Sciences.

Pervin, L.A. 1983. The stasis and flow of behavior: Toward a theory of goals. In M.M. Page, ed., *Nebraska symposium on motivation* (pp. 1–53). Lincoln, NE: University of Nebraska Press.

Repetti, R.L., K.A. Matthews, & I. Waldron. 1989. Employment and women's health: Effects of paid employment on women's mental and physical health. *American Psychologist 44*, 1394–1401.

Robins, C.J., & P. Block. 1988. Personal vulnerability, life events, and depressive symptoms: A test of a specific interactional model. *Journal of Personality and Social Psychology 54*, 847–52.

Rotter, J.B. 1990. Internal versus external control of reinforcement: A case history of a variable. *American Psychologist 45*, 489–93.

Skinner, E.A., M. Chapman, & P.B. Baltes. 1988. Control, means-ends, and agency beliefs: A new conceptualization and its measurement during childhood. *Journal of Personality and Social Psychology 54*, 117–33.

Smith, C.A., & R.S. Lazarus. 1990. Emotion and adaptation. In L.A. Pervin, ed., *Handbook of personality: Theory and research* (pp. 609–37). New York: Guilford.

Spence, J.T., & R.L. Helmreich. 1978. *Masculinity and femininity: Their psychological dimensions, correlates, and antecedents*. Austin: University of Texas Press.

– 1980. Masculine instrumentality and feminine expressivity: Their relationships with sex role attitudes and behavior. *Psychology of Women Quarterly 5*, 147–63.

Taylor, S.E. 1983. Adjustment to threatening events: A theory of cognitive adaptation. *American Psychologist 38*, 1161–74.

Verbrugge, L.M. 1986. Role burdens and physical health of women and men. *Women and Health 11*, 47–77.

Wagner, B.M., & B.E. Compas. 1990. Gender, instrumentality, and expressivity: Moderators of the relation-between stress and psychological symptoms during adolescence. *American Journal of Community Psychology 18*, 383–406.

Weisz, J.R. 1986a. Contingency and control beliefs as predictors of psychotherapy outcomes among children and adolescents. *Journal of Consulting and Clinical Psychology 54*, 789–95.

– 1986b. Understanding the developing understanding of control. In M. Perlmutter, ed., *Cognitive perspectives on children's social and behavioral development. Minnesota Symposium on Child Psychology* (18:219–75). Hillsdale, NJ: Erlbaum.

12 Evaluations of What's at Stake and What I Can Do

CRAIG A. SMITH

There can be little question that women face a number of employment-related stressors not fully shared by men. These stressors arise from a variety of sources and can present themselves in a multitude of forms. Without attempting to be exhaustive, global sources of employment-related stress that often affect women more than men include a hostile work environment, an unsupportive home environment, a disapproving social environment, and even conflicts within the individual's own self-concept.

Within each of these global categories there are a variety of distinct stressors that can affect any individual. For instance, within the work environment women may be explicitly or implicitly excluded from certain positions or career opportunities (e.g., Statham 1987); they may face gender-related hostility and prejudice from supervisors, co-workers, or supervisees (e.g., Korabik, McDonald, & Rosin, this volume); their values, working style, and job contributions may be trivialized and go unappreciated and unrewarded (e.g., Foschi 1991; Marshall, this volume; Statham, this volume); or they may be subjected to any of a number of types of sexual harassment.

Within the home environment women often bear the primary responsibility for maintaining a household and rearing any children (Scarr, Phillips, & McCartney 1989). If the woman is single, she will often bear the sole responsibility for meeting the often conflicting demands of career and family. If she has a spouse or partner, then the opportunity for significant mutual assistance on household matters exists but often remains unrealized (e.g., Hochschild 1989), which itself may serve as an additional source of stress (e.g., Belsky, Lang, & Huston 1986; Ruble, Fleming, Hackel, & Stangor 1988). In some cases, the spouse or partner may be threatened by and hostile to the woman's career aspirations. In others, the partner or spouse may offer emotional support and encouragement, but still fail to contribute substantially to the actual maintenance of the household. Even those who do contribute may often view their efforts as heroic sacrifices and not as equitable contributions to a cooperative task (Scarr et al. 1989).

Within the social environment, even the woman who has found a comfortable work environment, and who has achieved a personally satisfactory balance in meeting the demands of both her job and immediate family, may face stress-inducing disapproval from friends, neighbours, or parents if the solution she has achieved conflicts with the others' beliefs, norms, and attitudes. Such disapproval may arise when the household is maintained at a level of clutter rather than kept spotlessly clean, or when a young child is placed in day care rather than cared for full-time by the mother.

Finally, stress can arise from conflicts within the woman's own self-concept. If a woman is committed to fulfilling several roles, such as being a successful career woman, being a nurturant mother, and being feminine, and her conceptualizations of these roles include contradictory or mutually exclusive propositions, then there is the potential for considerable stress arising from within her belief system. For example, a woman who aspires to be both a "good mother" and a "successful executive" will be unable to fulfil both roles satisfactorily if she believes that a "good mother" should be a full-time caretaker of her preschool children and that a "successful executive" must be available to the company on nights and weekends in addition to the entire work week. As outlined by Higgins and colleagues (Higgins 1987; Strauman & Higgins 1987), such conflicts among one's "self-guides" may be inherently stress-inducing. Moreover, these conflicts virtually ensure that the woman's "actual self" will fall short of at least some of her self-guides, and when actively called to mind, such discrepancies can produce considerable dysphoria (e.g., Higgins 1987; Strauman & Higgins 1987).

Although it is probably true that at some point in her career virtually every employed woman faces at least some gender-specific stressors of the sort outlined above, and it is clearly the case that chronic stress is associated with poor mental and physical health (e.g., Selye 1976), the global conclusion that employment is inherently harmful to women is unwarranted. In a recent review, Repetti, Matthews, and Waldron (1989) found little evidence to support a global relationship between paid employment and either mental or physical health in women. Instead, they found that paid employment had clearly beneficial health effects on some women, and clearly detrimental effects on others. These effects were found to depend on both the characteristics of the individual woman and her family situation (e.g., the woman's marital status, her parental status, whether or not she wanted to work, whether or not her husband contributed significantly to the household labour), and the properties of her job (e.g., job classification, the presence of occupational hazards or stressors, the availability of social support at work).

Significantly, several studies have indicated that a woman's attitudes, beliefs, and expectations regarding her employment and the circumstances surrounding it are important in determining the effects of employment on her mental and physical health. Often these cognitive factors are at least as important as the objective circumstances (Baruch, Biener, & Barnett 1987; Verbrugge 1986). For example, it has often been hypothesized that the multiple, frequently conflicting roles of paid worker, wife, and mother can lead to stress-inducing *multiple role strain* or *overload* (Barnett & Baruch 1985; Verbrugge 1986, this volume), and in some studies the presence of multiple roles has been associated with increased psychological distress (e.g., Cleary & Mechanic 1983). However, across studies the evidence for the relationship between the existence of multiple roles and distress has been mixed (Repetti et al. 1989), and the relationship appears to be moderated by a number of subjective factors such as the perceived quality and meaningfulness of the roles for the person and the person's satisfaction with those roles. For those women who find their roles to be meaningful and of high quality, multiple roles have consistently been found to be associated with positive outcomes (e.g., Barnett & Baruch 1985; Baruch et al. 1987; Verbrugge 1986), and even to buffer the impact of negative life events on psychological adjustment (e.g., Brown & Harris 1978).

Similarly, the strategies a woman employs to cope with employment-related stress, as well as the resources available to her (e.g., social support), strongly influence her ability to alleviate or adapt to that stress (Compas & Orosan; Greenglass; and Korabik et al.; this volume). For example, in women managers and administrators a high level of support from one's boss was found to be associated with higher levels of job satisfaction, and lower levels of anxiety, depression, and psychological symptoms (Greenglass 1985).

Clearly, women's adjustment to employment-related stress is not a simple or monolithic phenomenon. Instead, to predict the effects of a particular set of employment-related circumstances on a particular woman or group of women, or to understand why, under similar conditions, some women thrive while others fare poorly, it is necessary to consider a host of factors concerning the properties of the women involved and their circumstances.

As reviewed by Repetti et al. (1989), the literature on employment and stress in women appears to be moving from the over-broad question of whether employment is harmful or beneficial to a consideration of the specific factors that determine the complex relationships among employment, stress, adjustment, and health. At present, however, the literature appears to lack an overarching theoretical framework for organizing and integrating these relationships (cf. McBride 1990). Although, as indicated above, a number of the factors influencing employment-related stress have been identified and some of their effects on adjustment and health have been examined (usually by considering one or two factors in isolation), there is currently little theoretical basis for identifying additional factors that influence the documented relationships, or for predicting how multiple factors will interact.

The purpose of this chapter is to describe a specific model of appraisal, stress, and emotion that might prove useful in developing an overarching theoretical framework to guide future research on employment-related stress in working women. The objective is neither to provide such a framework nor to analyse the sources of employment-related stress in depth, but to perform the prerequisite task of outlining the appraisal model and discussing its potential utility. First, the specific model and its theoretical context are reviewed. Then some potential applications of this model to the understanding of employment-related stress are considered. The focus throughout is on the relationship between appraisal and emotion, with the goal of illustrating the value of a more systematic consideration of emotion in the study of stress and coping than has characterized most previous research (cf. Smith 1991). The relationship between appraisal and coping is examined elsewhere in this volume (i.e., Compas & Orosan, this volume).

THEORETICAL OVERVIEW OF THE MODEL

The model to be described was developed within the framework of the general theory of appraisal, stress, and coping advanced by Lazarus and his colleagues (e.g., Lazarus & Folkman 1984). It is the product of an ongoing attempt (e.g., Smith & Lazarus 1990) to explicitly integrate recent theoretical and empirical work on specific emotions (e.g., Ellsworth & Smith 1988a, 1988b; Frijda 1986; Roseman 1984; Scherer 1984; Smith & Ellsworth 1985; Weiner 1985) into the more general theoretical framework.

The focus of the model is on the relationships between appraisals – cognitive evaluations of one's circumstances – and emotions. Emotions are examined, rather than stress, because whereas stress is essentially a unidimensional construct varying only in intensity, emotion is a richer, multidimensional construct, with clear qualitative distinctions among its individual variants. As detailed below, knowledge of a person's emotional state, combined with a theoretical understanding of the processes producing that state, allow one to make strong inferences about how the person is interpreting his or her circumstances, as well as how he or she is likely to respond behaviourally (Smith & Ellsworth 1985). Thus, knowledge of a person's emotional state – that the person is experiencing anger, guilt, anxiety, sadness, happiness, or hope – can provide a wealth of information about how he or she is interpreting and is likely to cope with his or her circumstances that is not available from knowledge that the person is experiencing "stress" (cf. Lazarus 1990; Smith 1991; Smith & Lazarus 1990).

Within the broader theoretical framework, emotions are viewed as largely adaptive responses to the perceived demands of a person's environment. They are hypothesized to serve the two general functions of physically preparing the person to cope with the environmental demands and communicating the person's emotional state and likely intentions and behaviours to others in the social environment (cf. Smith & Lazarus 1990). The emotions are produced based on the results of a *meaning analysis*, or appraisal, in which the implications of the person's circumstances for personal well-being are evaluated. The purpose of the appraisal process is, first, to indicate whether or not the circumstances have adaptational significance for the person's well-being – that is, whether they represent actual or potential harms or benefits to the person; and second, if they do, to classify the circumstances in terms of a relatively small number of categories of harm or benefit, each having different adaptational implications. Each distinct emotion is hypothesized to be the result of an appraisal of a distinct kind of harm or benefit. Each positive emotion is produced by a particular kind of appraised benefit, and each negative emotion is produced by a particular kind of appraised harm (Smith 1991; Smith & Lazarus 1990).

Several properties of emotion and appraisal, as conceptualized within this framework, deserve note. First, emotion is hypothesized to be a response to psychological meaning rather than objective stimulation. Second, the emotion-producing meanings, or appraisals, are relational in nature. That is, they are not simple reflections of either the stimulus situation or the person's dispositional characteristics. Instead, appraisals are an evaluation of the person-environment relationship that combines the environmental demands, constraints, and resources confronting the individual with the individual's own motivations, needs, beliefs, and abilities. The result is an evaluation of the adaptational significance of the circumstances for that particular person. In other words, the purpose of the evaluation is to determine what the circumstances imply for the person's well-being in light of his or her personal (and probably unique) configuration of wants, needs, abilities, beliefs, and expectations. Thus, two individuals confronted with essentially the same objective circumstances will often respond with quite different emotions, and, within the proper context, virtually any stimulus is capable of eliciting almost any emotion (cf. Smith & Lazarus 1990).

Finally, the range of evaluations that directly result in emotion appears to be quite constrained. Not all thoughts about the nature of one's circumstances have direct emotional consequences. Instead, it is only the appraisal of these circumstances with respect to their significance for personal well-being (whether they represent a personal harm or benefit, and if so, what kind) that is hypothesized to directly determine emotional state (cf. Lazarus & Folkman 1984; Smith & Lazarus 1990; Smith, Haynes, Lazarus, & Pope 1993). Within the present theoretical framework, appraisal is meant to encompass only those evaluations that directly result in emotion, and in describing the model below, only these evaluations are considered.

Appraisals – Evaluations of What Is at Stake? and What Can I Do?

Within the model, appraisal is described at two distinct levels of analysis. The first is molecular, describing the specific questions or issues evaluated to classify one's circumstances in terms of particular kinds of harm or benefit. The appraisal issues defined at this level are the individual *components* of appraisal. The second level of analysis is more molar, and it summarizes particular patterns of appraisal outcomes across the components as single categorical constructs, referred to as *relational themes*. These relational themes represent the significant answers to the appraisal questions that result in the experience of specific emotions. Each distinct type of appraised harm or benefit results in a different relational theme, and each emotion is hypothesized to be produced by its own distinct theme. For example, appraised *danger* or *threat* produces fear or anxiety, whereas appraised *irrevocable loss* or *helplessness about harm or loss* produces sadness, and so on. In sum, the components reflect the molecular questions evaluated in appraisal, the answers to which combine to produce the molar personal meanings – the relational themes – that directly result in specific emotions.

Each appraisal component is conceptualized as addressing one of the two global appraisal issues originally proposed by Lazarus and his colleagues in their theory of appraisal, stress, and coping (e.g., Lazarus & Folkman 1984). The first global issue, referred to as *primary appraisal*, concerns whether and how the encounter is relevant to the person's well-being, or in other words, asks the general question: "What is at stake?" The second global issue, referred to as *secondary appraisal*, concerns the person's resources and options for coping with the encounter, or in other words, asks the general question: "What can I do?" Both of these issues can be further subdivided, and the present model includes a total of six appraisal components, two related to primary appraisal, and four to secondary appraisal (cf. Smith & Lazarus 1990).

The two components of primary appraisal are motivational relevance and motivational congruence (or incongruence). *Motivational relevance* is an evaluation of the extent to which the encounter touches upon personal goals and concerns, or, in other words, issues the person cares about or has a stake in. *Motivational congruence* refers to the extent to which a transaction is consistent or inconsistent with what the person wants.

The two components of primary appraisal are involved in every emotional encounter. The evaluation of motivational relevance is necessary for strong emotion, since it indicates whether there is any personal stake in the encounter, and thus defines the person's level of affective involvement. In the absence of motivational relevance, the person's state is likely to be one of either apathy or quiet tranquillity (cf. Ellsworth & Smith 1988b). Assessments of motivational congruence combine with relevance to determine whether the encounter is *stressful* or *benign* (Lazarus, Kanner, & Folkman 1980). Benign encounters are ones that are appraised as both motivationally relevant and motivationally congruent (i.e., both important and desired), whereas stressful ones are appraised as both relevant and motivationally incongruent (i.e., important but, in some way, not as desired).

It should be noted that the primary appraisal – the evaluation of stakes – does not include the specific identity or content of the stakes involved in the encounter, or, in other words, which specific goal or need is implicated in the encounter. It is not the case that this information is irrelevant to appraisal and emotion. Indeed, evaluation of either motivational relevance or motivational congruence would be impossible without taking into account what, specifically, the person sees as being at stake in the encounter, what he or she desires with respect to that stake (i.e., what his or her goal is), and how strong or deep that desire is. Instead, this information contributes in highly systematic ways to the evaluations of motivational relevance and motivational congruence, but does not contribute directly to the production of the emotional response. Thus, emotions have considerable flexibility with regard to the range of stimuli that can evoke them (cf. Smith & Lazarus 1990). It is precisely the lack of goal-content specificity in primary appraisal that enables just about any objective stimulus, within the proper context, to elicit just about any emotion.

For example, the same simple event – being addressed by one's first name by a subordinate – could result in very different emotional reactions depending upon the person's concerns and the context in which it occurred. If the event occurred within a setting in which informal address was the norm (e.g., a typical academic setting), the event would most likely have little motivational relevance and result in little emotion of any kind. However, this event could be the occasion for considerable positive affect (i.e., be appraised as motivationally relevant and congruent) if the subordinate was a shy, over-formal graduate student with whom the person was attempting to establish a more collegial relationship. Conversely, if it occurred in a setting in which more formal address was expected (e.g., a typical medical setting), and the person was concerned about respect for his or her authority, this same event most likely would be appraised as motivationally relevant and incongruent, and would be the occasion for considerable negative affect.

Although sufficient to define the encounter as stressful or benign, the two components of primary appraisal are insufficient to define the relational themes associated with most emotions. Components of secondary appraisal must be added to determine the specific emotions that will be experienced. The four components of secondary appraisal are accountability, problem-focused coping potential, emotion-focused coping potential, and future expectancy.

The *accountability* evaluation provides direction and focus to the emotional response and the coping efforts motivated by it. The outcome of the accountability judgment determines who or what (oneself or someone or something else) is to receive the credit (if the encounter is motivationally congruent) or the blame (if it is motivationally incongruent) for the encounter, and thus provides the person with a specific target toward which to direct his or her subsequent coping efforts.

This accountability evaluation is related to, but not identical with, the attribution of locus of causality that Weiner (1985) and others have found to be related to emotion. The locus attribution contributes to the evaluation of accountability but does not fully determine it. As has been repeatedly demonstrated, the identified locus of causality will be held more or less accountable as a function of a number of additional attributions, including perceived intentionality, controllability, and justifiability. A person identified as the causal locus for an undesirable situation will be held less accountable, and hence will receive less blame, to the extent that his or her actions are further evaluated as uncontrollable, unintentional, and/or justifiable (e.g., McGraw 1987; Pastore 1952; Weiner, Amirkhan, Folkes, & Verette 1987). For instance, the same sexist remark is likely to result in less appraised accountability (and thus less anger) if, owing to the speaker's age and/or cultural background, the recipient believes the insult to have been unintentional than if the recipient believes it to have been deliberate.

The other three appraisal components all have to do with the evaluation of the potential for improvement of an undesirable situation or the maintenance of a desirable one. The two components of coping potential correspond to the person's evaluations of his or her abilities to engage in the two major types of coping identified by Folkman and Lazarus (1980, Lazarus & Folkman 1984).

Problem-focused coping potential reflects evaluations of the person's ability to act directly upon the situation either to bring it more in line with his or her desires if it is appraised as motivationally incongruent, or to maintain it if it is appraised as motivationally congruent. This evaluation is related to the evaluation of self-efficacy (Bandura 1986), but is not identical to it. As defined by Bandura (1986), efficacy judgments consist of two distinct components: (a) an evaluation of the consequences that will follow a particular course of action if performed effectively; and (b) the perceived ability of the person to effectively perform that course of action. These two evaluations combine to produce an outcome expectancy. The evaluation of problem-focused coping potential is more closely related to the outcome expectancy than it is to the contributing efficacy judgments. However, it is broader in scope than any single outcome expectancy, and it encompasses a more global assessment of the person's self-perceived ability to influence his or her circumstances in desired ways through any available course of action.

For instance, if a woman were distressed because she perceived herself as the target of verbal harassment from co-workers, the evaluation of problem-focused coping potential would reflect her overall evaluation of her ability to reduce or eliminate the harassment through any available means (e.g., by expressing her displeasure to the co-workers, by complaining to a supervisor, or by suing the company). In contrast, an efficacy judgment would combine the evaluation of the likely effects of pursuing any one course of action (e.g., of bringing suit) with the woman's self-perceived ability to perform that action.

Emotion-focused coping potential refers to the perceived prospects of psychologically adjusting to undesirable circumstances. It is important to note that emotion-focused coping does not simply involve "coping with one's emotions," nor does it exclusively involve attempts to distort reality through processes such as denial. Instead, whereas problem-focused coping encompasses one of the major routes to reducing discrepancies between one's circumstances and one's desires and motivations – namely altering the undesirable circumstances – emotion-focused coping encompasses the second major route – altering oneself and/or one's desires and beliefs (cf. Folkman & Lazarus 1988; Kimble 1990; Smith 1991; Smith & Lazarus 1990).

Many emotion-focused coping strategies overlap with those identified in a long tradition of research into cognitive dissonance (e.g., Festinger 1957; Wicklund & Brehm 1976). For example, one can reconstrue the nature of the situation, such as by deciding that a perceived offence was unintentional or unavoidable (e.g., that a sexist statement was somehow intended as a compliment), or that an inferred event did not actually occur. Or one can alter personal beliefs and attitudes relevant to the meaning of the encounter, and hence the encounter's appraised implications for well-being. For instance, one could decide that an impossibly boorish co-worker is potentially educable after all, and thus transform a hopeless situation into a more tractable one. In the face of a seemingly irresolvable unpleasant situation, one can also alter personal goals and values so that the encounter is no longer appraised as relevant to well-being, and no longer has the power to evoke strong emotion (cf. Klinger 1975). For instance, if a woman believes that her work is not getting the respect it deserves, she might decide that the true quality of her work is more important than attitudes of co-workers, and cease to care about the others' opinions. Or, she might cease to care about career advancement, and instead increase her commitment to family or community concerns.

Often emotion-focused coping techniques may operate outside of conscious awareness, and the person may remain relatively unaware of the processes through which adjustment is occurring, even though he or she may be acutely aware that it is happening. The appraisal of emotion-focused coping potential encompasses the person's evaluation of his or her ability to internally adjust to undesirable circumstances whether or not he or she is cognizant of the exact means through which the adjustment may occur.

Future expectancy refers to the perceived possibilities, for any reason (i.e., independent of whether the individual plays a role), for changes in the actual or psychological situation that could make the encounter more or less motivationally congruent. For instance, a woman might believe that a new change in evaluation procedures will result in greater recognition of her accomplishments, even though she personally may have had little to do with bringing about the new procedures. As will be discussed below, this appraisal component may be especially important for maintaining hope even under dire circumstances in which the person feels personally unable to change the situation and unable to accept or adjust to it if it does not change.

Specific Appraisals in Specific Emotions

As indicated above, the two components of primary appraisal are jointly sufficient to define one's circumstances as stressful or benign, but they need to be combined with components of secondary appraisal to define the specific relational themes associated with distinct emotions such as sadness, anger, and fear. Thus, examination of the appraisal components and relational themes associated with specific emotions vividly illustrates how "emotion" is a much richer, more informative construct than "stress."

Moreover, examination of the appraisal-emotion relationships described below reveals the existence of a highly logical, even "rational" structure to the proposed emotion system. In fact, the model was derived through rational analysis. This analysis started with the premise that the purpose of appraisal is to evoke functionally appropriate emotions under adaptationally relevant conditions, and then posited the functions served by individual emotions based on the proposals of a number of theorists (e.g., Izard 1977; Plutchik 1980; Tomkins 1963). Once these assumptions were in place, the primary task in deriving the model was to specify the information a person would logically require to determine whether this or that adaptational function (served by particular emotions) would be needed under a variety of circumstances. The results of this analysis are generally consistent with the findings of previous studies that have examined the relationships between cognitive activities and emotions (e.g., Ellsworth & Smith 1988a, 1988b; Frijda, Kuipers, & ter Schure 1989; Roseman 1984; Smith & Ellsworth 1985), and the model has received direct support in two recent studies explicitly designed to test it (Smith & Lazarus 1993; Smith et al. 1993).

Table 1 depicts the specific appraisals theoretically associated with six illustrative emotions. For each emotion the table first lists the emotion's proposed adaptive function, then the relational theme corresponding to the particular relationship with the environment in which that function is likely to be useful, and finally the major appraisal components that combine to define the relational theme. The first four entries depict "negative" or "harm-related" emotions that are often equated with "stress" in many theories (cf. Lazarus et al. 1980; Smith & Lazarus 1990). The fifth entry describes a cluster of more positive, or "benefit-related," emotions that are nonetheless associated with the stress-related primary appraisals of combined motivational relevance and motivational incongruence. The final entry describes a benefit-related emotion associated with appraised benign circumstances (i.e., motivational relevance and motivational congruence).

Starting with the first entry, the proposed function of anger is to motivate the person to remove a source of harm from the environment, and to undo the harm, if possible (cf. Ellsworth & Smith 1988a; Izard 1977; Plutchik 1980; Tomkins 1963). The relational theme that defines the circumstances under which this motivation is likely to be useful is "other-blame," which is defined by the components of motivational relevance, motivational incongruence, and other-accountability. In other words, anger arises when someone or something else is being blamed for a stressful situation, and it motivates the person to do something to remove the source of harm. It is important to note that the assignment of accountability provides a target for these coping efforts. For instance, a woman who has been passed over for a desired promotion because of a poor evaluation from her supervisor, whom she believes to be biased against the advancement of women, is likely to become angry and to experience a strong motivation to do something to prevent the supervisor from continuing to impede her advancement, and, if possible, to discredit the supervisor's damaging evaluation.

In an analogous fashion, guilt has been proposed to contribute to the development of one's conscience and the maintenance of social order. It motivates the individual to make reparations for harm he or she has caused to others, and generally to engage in socially responsible behaviour (cf. Ellsworth & Smith 1988a; Izard 1977). Consistent with these functions, the relational theme producing guilt is "self-blame." This theme is defined by holding oneself accountable

Table 1
Appraisals Associated with Six Emotions

Emotion	Proposed adaptive function	Relational theme	Important appraisal components
Anger	Remove source of harm from environment and undo harm	Other-blame	1 Motivationally relevant 2 Motivationally incongruent 3 Other-accountability
Guilt	Reparation for harm to others/motivate socially responsible behaviour	Self-blame	1 Motivationally relevant 2 Motivationally incongruent 3 Self-accountability
Fear/ Anxiety	Avoid potential harm	Danger/threat	1 Motivationally relevant 2 Motivationally incongruent 3 Low/uncertain (emotion-focused) coping potential
Sadness	Get help and support in the face of harm/ disengage from a lost commitment	Irrevocable loss/ helplessness about harm or loss	1 Motivationally relevant 2 Motivationally incongruent 3 Low (problem-focused) coping potential 4 Low future-expectancy
Hope/ challenge/ determination	Sustain coping/ motivate mastery	Effortful optimism/ potential for success	1 Motivationally relevant 2 Motivationally incongruent 3 High (problem-focused) coping potential 4 High future-expectancy
Happiness	Reward success	Success	1 Motivationally relevant 2 Motivationally congruent

for a stressful (important, motivationally incongruent) situation. Like anger, guilt is hypothesized to motivate the person to do something to remove the source of harm from the environment, but, because the focus in guilt is on oneself, this motivation takes the form of a desire to make reparations for any harm the self has caused (e.g., Carlsmith & Gross 1969). In addition, this motivation tends to be quite punishing (Wallington 1973), and therefore reduces the probability that the person will continue to engage in the harmful behaviour in the future. For instance, a woman who is concerned that her employment obligations are leading her to neglect her children, and who holds herself accountable for not spending enough time with them, will experience guilt that is likely to be accompanied by a strong motivation to somehow find ways to spend more time with her children.

Whereas the accountability component differentiates the relational themes responsible for anger and guilt, the three components addressing the potential for improving the stressful situation differentiate the themes for fear/anxiety and sadness. Both emotions are associated with stressful situations in which the prospects for improvement are uncertain or poor. However, they have distinct motivational functions, and their relational themes, as well as the secondary appraisal components that define them, reflect these differences.

The proposed function of fear/anxiety is to motivate the person to avoid potential harm (cf. Izard 1977; Plutchik 1980, Tomkins 1963), and the associated relational theme is an appraisal of "danger" or "threat." The secondary appraisal component that defines this sense of danger is uncertain or low coping potential. Although uncertainty about either problem- or emotion-focused coping potential can contribute to the appraisal of danger, emotion-focused coping potential is hypothesized to be particularly relevant. This component reflects the person's appraised ability to accept and psychologically adjust to a bad situation should things not work out as desired. Holding other factors constant, one's sense of danger, and hence fear/anxiety, should be particularly acute when, beyond seeing potential or actual harm in the situation, the person also believes that he or she will be unable to accept or adjust to this harm in the event it occurs. For instance, a woman facing a promotion review is likely to be especially anxious if she is uncertain about the review's likely outcome, and further believes that she will be unable to adjust to the situation if the promotion does not come through.

In contrast, the function of sadness is to motivate the person to get help and support in the face of harm or loss, and to disengage from lost commitments (cf. Izard 1977; Klinger 1975; Plutchik 1980). The theme for this emotion is an appraisal of "irrevocable loss" or "helplessness about harm or loss" (Abramson, Seligman, & Teasdale 1978). The secondary appraisal components hypothesized to produce this theme are a combination of low future expectancy and low coping potential. Low coping potential in sadness differs from that in fear/anxiety in two ways. First, it is more pessimistic. In threat there is considerable doubt about whether one can cope, but in loss/helplessness one is fairly certain that one cannot. Second, although emotion-focused coping potential is especially relevant for threat, and hence fear/anxiety, problem-focused coping potential is more relevant for loss/helplessness, and hence sadness. In a condition of irrevocable loss the focus is on the inability to undo the harm, and there is less focus on whether or not the person will ultimately be able to accept or adjust to the harm. Indeed, disengagement from the lost commitment, one of the proposed motivational functions of sadness, promotes such adjustment.

For instance, after failing to receive a much-desired promotion and coming to believe that further advancement within the company is impossible, an ambitious woman who is committed to her job is likely to feel considerable sadness and resignation. This reaction might then lead her to disengage from her current job and seek more promising employment elsewhere, or internally adjust to and accept her status within the company by altering her career goals and ambitions.

"Negative" harm-related emotions, such as those described above, all arise under conditions of appraised threat or harm, and they motivate the person to act in ways that will eliminate or reduce the harm, or to adapt to the harm if it cannot be avoided or undone. However, "stress" is not limited to the avoidance or amelioration of actual and potential harm. There is also a more positive side to stress, involving sustained striving toward mastery, and gain (Ellsworth & Smith 1988b; Lazarus et al. 1980; Selye 1974; Smith 1991; Smith & Lazarus 1990). Motivational incongruence can involve the perceived absence of potential benefits in addition to the presence of actual or potential harms.

Corresponding to this positive side of stress, there is a cluster of emotions, including hope and challenge/determination, that serve to sustain coping efforts to improve one's situation, and motivate striving toward mastery or gain. These emotions are described in the fifth entry of table 1. In general, the relational theme associated with these emotions is one of "effortful optimism" or "potential for success" – the belief that if the person tries hard enough, there is a good chance he or she will be able to improve matters. This theme includes the combined appraisals of motivational relevance and motivational incongruence associated with stress, but in direct contrast to the relational theme for sadness, there is also a high degree of problem-focused coping potential and high future expectancy.

Although, empirically, hope and challenge/determination have been found to co-vary strongly and to be associated with similar appraisals (e.g., Ellsworth & Smith 1988b), there may be important distinctions between these two emotions. In particular, a high degree of problem-focused coping potential, required to produce challenge/determination and its associated active striving for mastery and gain, may not be required to sustain hope. All that may be required for hope is a high degree of future expectancy – the belief that somehow conditions might improve even though the person may be unable to do anything to bring about the improvement. Thus, hope may serve the very important function of motivating the person to maintain commitments, even under dire circumstances, so long as some chance for improvement is perceived (Lazarus et al. 1980).

For instance, the slighted woman in the above anger example is especially likely to experience strong determination to act against her supervisor if she believes there is a potentially effective course of action available to her. However, even if she feels personally powerless to affect things, she may remain hopeful and forestall sadness and resignation about the situation so long as she believes that things might be rectified through other means.

Finally, as reflected in the last entry in table 1, some emotions do not involve stress-related appraisals at all, but are evoked under benign conditions. For instance, the proposed function of happiness is to reward "success," that is, a change in an important situation that increases its motivational congruence. The experience of happiness is highly rewarding, and by reinforcing successful coping efforts increases the probability they will be repeated. Happiness appears to be a general response to success, and all that seems necessary for it are the combined components of motivational relevance and motivational congruence (cf. Ellsworth & Smith 1988b; Weiner 1985).

The above descriptions of specific emotions and their associated appraisals are not meant to be exhaustive, and they in no way represent the full range of human emotions. Nonetheless, these particular examples were selected to represent the most important general categories of adaptational significance relevant to stress and adaptation, and they provide a firm foundation for examining the utility of the model for understanding stress-related processes in particular populations, such as working women.

It should be noted that the appraisal-emotion relationships outlined above are hypothesized to be universal to the human species. Given that a person is appraising his or her circumstances in a particular manner, the emotions corresponding to that appraisal are hypothesized to follow as an invariant and inevitable response to that appraisal (Smith & Lazarus 1990). Thus, the model is intended to be gender- and culture-fair. There is, however, considerable individual and cultural variability in how a particular set of circumstances is likely to be appraised, and thus responded to emotionally. Therefore, the utility of the model for understanding individual or cultural differences in emotion, or for understanding emotional processes within a particular population, depends upon an understanding of the determinants of appraisal. The nature of these determinants is considered next.

Dispositional and Situational Determinants of Appraisal

As presented thus far, the appraisal model specifies the appraisal outcomes associated with particular emotions but remains relatively silent with regard to the factors influencing these outcomes. This is partially a function of the existing research literature. Most research examining the relationships between appraisal and emotion has started with the person appraising his or her circumstances in a particular way and has asked which emotion(s) resulted (e.g., Ellsworth & Smith 1988a, 1988b; Roseman 1984), or has begun with a particular emotion and asked what appraisals were associated with that emotion (e.g., Smith & Ellsworth 1985). Relatively little research has directly examined the interactional factors hypothesized to influence appraisal.

Nonetheless, specification of the interactional factors is crucial for applying the model to significant problems and phenomena. Often it is not enough to know that if a person were to appraise his or her circumstances in such and such a way then he or she would experience this or that emotion, or that if the person were to experience such and such emotion then he or she would be appraising his or her circumstances in this or that way. Instead, there is often considerable interest in the situational and dispositional factors that contribute to appraisal, as well as the processes by which they are combined to produce particular appraisals. Knowledge of such factors and their relevance to appraisal provides considerable inferential power beyond that provided by knowledge of appraisal-emotion relationships alone. For instance, as discussed below, such knowledge gives one the potential not only to predict how a particular person or type of person is likely to respond to a certain set of circumstances, but also to diagnose why a particular individual or group is reacting to a certain set of circumstances in a specific way.

Fortunately, the model has been developed to the point where some of the global dispositional and situational factors relevant to appraisal have been identified, and the way these factors are likely to combine to produce particular appraisal outcomes has been described. As with the derivation of the appraisal-emotion relationships described above, these predictions were derived through a rational analysis. This analysis began with a consideration of the hypothesized appraisal components and the questions they represent, and asked about the types of information about both the person and the situation that would be most relevant to answering these questions.

Two general classes of personality variables, one motivational and one knowledge-based, have been identified as especially relevant to appraisal and emotion, and consideration of these variables suggests situational variables that are likely to be relevant as well. The motivational factors relevant to appraisal include the values, goals, and commitments the person brings into every encounter. These factors are closely related to motivational constructs such as "current concerns" (Klinger 1975), "personal projects" (Little 1983), and "personal strivings" (Emmons 1986). These factors are indispensable to the appraisal process. As previously discussed, the very construct of primary appraisal makes sense only when the person's circumstances are considered in relation to what the person wants, needs, or otherwise cares about.

Knowledge of the motivational factors – motivations, goals, and concerns – should make it possible to identify both the individuals who will react to certain situations with strong emotion and the particular kinds of situations to which a given individual is likely to react strongly. The basic principles guiding such predictions are straightforward: (a) The more an individual is invested in whatever is at stake in a particular situation, the more intense his or her emotional reaction to that situation will be; and (b) the more strongly or clearly a particular concern or commitment is implicated in a particular situation, the more intense will be the emotional reaction of a person who is committed to that concern (cf. Smith & Lazarus, 1990). Thus, a person who is highly committed to a particular goal or value (e.g., being treated equitably by superiors and co-workers) will react with strong emotion to situations in which he or she perceives that goal or value as being at stake (e.g., a situation in which he or she believes a prejudicial bias is operating). Similarly, if a person is observed responding to a particular situation with strong emotion, it can be inferred that the situation touches upon something about which the person strongly cares.

A number of studies illustrate the promise of these propositions. For example, Vogel, Raymond, and Lazarus (1959) found that people with strong achievement goals and weak affiliation goals reacted to achievement-related threats with more psychophysiological arousal than they did to affiliation-related threats, whereas the reverse pattern was found for people with strong affiliation and weak achievement goals. Similarly, Hammen, Marks, Mayol, and deMayo (1985) found that students who consider interpersonal goals to be central to their self-concepts were more likely to experience depression in relation to negative events involving interpersonal relationships than to stressful events involving achievement concerns, and the reverse tended to be true for students who identified with strong achievement goals.

The second type of personality factor relevant to appraisal is the person's knowledge-base, which consists of beliefs, both concrete and abstract, about the way things are, how they work, the nature of the world, and the person's place in it (Smith & Lazarus 1990). Whereas the motivational factors are proposed to be most relevant to primary appraisal, these knowledge-based factors are proposed to contribute principally to secondary appraisal.

For example, as previously discussed, beliefs about what is normatively appropriate, avoidable, legitimate, or excusable in a given situation influence whether, to what extent, and toward whom an appraisal of accountability for a stressful encounter will be made (cf. Pastore 1952; Weiner et al. 1987), and therefore, whether the encounter will result in any guilt or anger.

In addition, one's beliefs and expectations about the probable effectiveness of various courses of action and one's ability to perform those actions contribute to judgments of self-efficacy (Bandura 1986) and, therefore, to appraisals of coping potential. Thus, they partially determine whether a stressful situation will be appraised as a loss, a threat, or a potential gain, and hence, reacted to with sadness, fear/anxiety, or challenge/determination. More general beliefs about one's competencies can also affect appraisals of coping potential and related emotions in similar ways. All else being equal, when facing difficulty within a particular domain, individuals confident of their abilities should appraise their coping potential as relatively high and thus experience more challenge/determination and less sadness/resignation and anxiety than less confident individuals. For instance, when faced with a promotion evaluation, a person confident of his or her abilities and performance should appraise less threat and thus be less anxious than someone who is unsure of his or her abilities and performance.

Characteristics of the situation likely to affect the probability of success, such as the availability of potential courses of action, task difficulty, and the availability of social support and other forms of assistance, also contribute to appraisals of coping potential in systematic ways. For example, appraisals of coping potential should be relatively high, regardless of the individual's confidence level, when the person is confronted with a very easy task. Conversely, conditions of extreme difficulty should generally depress appraisals of coping potential. In a similar manner, the availability of social support should bolster appraisals of coping potential, whereas the absence of social support could undermine them.

Smith, Ellsworth, and Pope (1990) have recently provided data that lend support to these hypotheses. They presented individuals, selected to be either highly confident or unconfident of their math abilities, with a sequence of easy or difficult math word problems. The easy problems were within all participants' abilities, whereas the difficult ones were virtually unsolvable. In line with the present theorizing, when presented with easy problems both confident and unconfident individuals appraised their coping potential as high, and none reported feelings of sadness/resignation. When faced with the difficult problems the appraised coping potential was depressed and the reported sadness/resignation was elevated in both groups, but these changes were significantly more dramatic for the low-confidence individuals than for the high-confidence ones. Thus, rather than being direct functions of either the person's perceived abilities or the objective task demands, the appraisals of coping potential combined these two factors interactively, and reflected an assessment of the task difficulty in light of the person's perceived abilities.

The highly logical structure of this model deserves comment. In many respects this structure is a central feature of the model, and it provides the model with considerable generative power. For instance, using a logical analysis it should be relatively easy for investigators who so desire to go beyond the few illustrative examples presented here and to propose additional situational and dispositional factors relevant to appraisal as well as the ways in which these variables interact to produce specific appraisals. Nonetheless, the logical structure of the formal model does not imply that a person's emotional reactions will always look rational to an observer, nor does it imply that these responses will always be adaptive. The model contains plenty of room for error: circumstances can be misperceived, knowledge and beliefs can be incorrect, and motivations and commitments can be misguided (cf. Smith & Ellsworth 1985). Instead, the major claim inherent in the logical theoretical structure is that even maladaptive and seemingly "irrational" responses are the product of an organized system following orderly procedures, and that if the observer were to assume the responder's perspective – to perceive the circumstance as the responder does, and to share his or her motivations and beliefs – then even these responses would make considerable sense.

Taken together, the logical theoretical structure of the model, combined with its specification of a number of appraisal-emotion relationships, provides a powerful analytic tool for understanding the stress process in particular populations. Two of the main ways in which this tool can be used to advance our understanding of employment-related stress in women – as a predictive device, and as a diagnostic device – will now be considered.

UTILITY OF THE MODEL FOR UNDERSTANDING EMPLOYMENT-RELATED STRESS

Predictive Utility

Perhaps the most standard use of the model is to guide future research. The model can be used to derive theoretical predictions regarding how different individuals or groups are likely to respond to various sorts of circumstances, and can additionally be used to suggest a number of the important variables to assess in such research. More specifically, the model can be used to derive predictions regarding how a particular set of circumstances is likely to affect various individuals, or it can be used to derive predictions regarding how particular individuals are likely to respond to a variety of circumstances.

In general, the key situational variables to assess would include the potential stakes inherent in the circumstances, the potential of the situation to be altered in various ways (e.g., task difficulty), and the routes by which these changes could be effected. The key dispositional variables would include the nature of the person's goals and concerns relevant to the circumstances, the strength of the person's commitment to those goals, the person's beliefs about the appropriateness or justifiability of important aspects of the situations (e.g., of various potential courses of action, of the perceived causes of important situational properties), and the person's beliefs and expectations regarding his or her abilities to perform relevant courses of action within the situation.

For instance, in a study of individual differences in women's responses to the multiple demands of family and paid employment, situational variables to assess might include the nature of task demands imposed upon the women by both their families and their jobs, the degree to which the women are successfully meeting those demands, and the potential for them to alter the nature of the demands within either domain. Dispositional variables might include the women's degree of commitment to or concern about successfully meeting the demands within both domains and their beliefs about the justifiability or appropriateness of the demands, as well as their self-perceived abilities either to meet the demands or alter them if necessary.

Some general predictions that flow from the model are that individuals for whom the perceived situation was discrepant with their desires (e.g., women who were committed to meeting the demands of both job and family, but who were not succeeding) would experience stress, and that the degree of stress would vary as a function of the strength of their desires. Further, those who believed that the reasons for the discrepancy were externally caused and unjustifiable would likely feel anger, whereas those who felt they had largely brought the situation on themselves would likely feel guilt. Those who believed they possessed the means to reduce the discrepancy would likely feel challenged/determined to do so, whereas those who believed the circumstances to be unchangeable would likely feel sadness and resignation, perhaps tinged with anxiety if they also believed they would be unable to adapt to and accept the undesirable circumstances.

More specifically, consider the potential responses of various women experiencing stress because of the time pressures associated with attempting to simultaneously manage a household and hold a full-time job, and whose husbands do not contribute substantially to the household duties (cf. Hochschild 1989). Those women who hold traditional sex roles and believe housework to be the province of women would likely feel guilt about their inability to fulfil their perceived household obligations, and might well be more likely than others to quit their jobs if the opportunity arose. In contrast, women who view household duties as something that should be a cooperative venture with their husbands would likely experience considerable resentment toward their husbands' lack of contribution. To the extent that these latter women felt it was within their means to alter their husbands' behaviour, their anger would likely be tinged with determination to do so. Conversely, if they felt that their husbands would never change, their anger would likely be combined with feelings of sadness and resignation, and, to the extent that the stressful circumstances proved intractable and they considered the issue of fairness to be sufficiently important, these women might be especially likely to attempt to resolve the situation by ending the marriage.

Diagnostic Utility

A second and perhaps less obvious use of the model is as a diagnostic tool. The inferential power of the model is bidirectional – a fact that has not yet been fully exploited. Not only can the model be used to predict emotional responses based on information about situational and dispositional characteristics, but also it can be used to infer situational and dispositional characteristics on the basis of observed emotional reactions (cf. Lazarus 1990; Smith & Ellsworth 1985; Smith & Lazarus 1990). The model can be used diagnostically to identify the situational and dispositional factors that led a particular individual to react to a particular set of circumstances with a given emotional reaction.

The most straightforward and strongest inferences that can be made involve the appraisals, conceptualized at both the level of components and relational themes, underlying the observed emotions, because these relationships are hypothesized to be universal and invariant (Smith & Lazarus 1990). Thus, when a person reacts to a particular situation with strong emotion, one can infer that something in that situation touches upon one of the person's important concerns. Similarly, if the person responds with anger, one can infer that the person is blaming someone or something else for something unwanted in the situation, and if the person responds with sadness, one can infer that the person views the source of stress as intractable to change, and so on.

The next level of inference, regarding the dispositional and situational factors contributing to the appraisals (e.g., which particular stake(s) in the situation the person cares about, or which beliefs and situational factors have led the person to interpret the stressful situation as intractable), is more indirect, and can require considerable detective work. However, when armed with knowledge of (a) the questions asked in appraisal; (b) the types of situational and dispositional factors that typically contribute to appraisal; (c) shared cultural knowledge; and (d) (through the observed emotions) the answers to the appraisal questions arrived at by a particular individual under a particular set of circumstances, such inferences can often be made with considerable confidence. Once the source(s) of the person's stress have been identified, these variables can be used to evaluate and guide the person's attempts to cope with the stress-inducing conflict (cf. Compas & Orosan, this volume).

For instance, drawing upon the example used above, if a working woman were observed to frequently become angry at her husband while performing household chores – perhaps occasionally muttering something about "never getting any help around here" – it probably would not be difficult to infer that she was dissatisfied with the amount of housework she was having to do, and that she was blaming her husband's lack of assistance for her dissatisfaction.

This diagnostic potential has at least two uses. First, as clinicians and counsellors have known for years, emotions and their associated appraisals are invaluable aids in pinpointing the underlying difficulties for clients who seek assistance in coping with troubling life situations, and the present model provides considerable guidance as to the information conveyed by the emotions and how this information might be effectively utilized. For instance, once the problem has been clearly diagnosed as the woman being overburdened with housework and being resentful toward an uncooperative husband, the counsellor is in a stronger position to work with the woman (and perhaps her husband) to find a satisfactory resolution to the conflict. At the group or population level, the same sort of inferences can be applied to the emotional reactions common to women sharing similar work environments or job descriptions in order to identify sources of stress or inequity facing those women, and to guide policy decisions designed to improve matters.

Second, within a particular research domain, using the model to make the same types of diagnostic inferences about the circumstances and/or populations one wishes to study can be useful for identifying the important situational and dispositional variables to be assessed. Given the complexity of human affairs, it is often extremely difficult to determine which of the many potential variables it is most important to assess without considerable theoretical guidance. The present model is intended to provide some such guidance.

To summarize, the model presented above specifies a number of relationships between how a person appraises the adaptational significance of his or her circumstances and his or her emotional state. In addition it offers considerable guidance regarding the factors underlying those appraisals. This information has the potential to contribute much to the study of employment-related stress in women. When accompanied by the assessment of the relevant dispositional and situational variables, the model has the potential to predict and explain the frequently observed large individual differences in wo-

262   Craig A. Smith

men's responses to common stressors (cf. Repetti et al. 1989). Working in the other direction, given an individual's emotional response to a stressor, the model can be applied to assist in the identification of the situational and dispositional factors that contributed to that response. Once identified, these factors can then be assessed and utilized to understand and predict future responses in other individuals and other settings. Thus, the various uses to which the model can be put are highly complementary, which increases its potential contributions. It is hoped that these contributions will be realized – that the model will prove useful in advancing our understanding of the gender-specific stressors faced by women engaged in paid employment – and that through these contributions the model will help to alleviate some of the negative consequences associated with women's paid employment.

Abramson, L.Y., M.E.P. Seligman, & J.D. Teasdale. 1978. Learned helplessness in humans: Critique and reformulation. *Journal of Abnormal Psychology 87*, 49–74.

Bandura, A. 1986. *Social foundations of thought and action: A social-cognitive theory*. Englewood Cliffs, NJ: Prentice-Hall.

Barnett, R.C., & G.K. Baruch. 1985. Women's involvement in multiple roles and psychological distress. *Journal of Personality and Social Psychology 49*, 135–45.

Baruch, G.K., L. Biener, & R.C. Barnett. 1987. Women and gender in research on work and family stress. *American Psychologist 42*, 130–6.

Belsky, J., M. Lang, & T.L. Huston. 1986. Sex-typing and division of labor as determinants of marital change across the transition to parenthood. *Journal of Personality and Social Psychology 50*, 517–22.

Brown, G.W., & T. Harris. 1978. *Social origins of depression*. New York: Free Press.

Carlsmith, J.M., & A.E. Gross. 1969. Some effects of guilt on compliance. *Journal of Personality and Social Psychology 11*, 232–9.

Cleary, P.D., & D. Mechanic. 1983. Sex differences in psychological distress among married people. *Journal of Health and Social Behavior 24*, 111–21.

Ellsworth, P.C., & C.A. Smith. 1988a. From appraisal to emotion: Differences among unpleasant feelings. *Motivation and Emotion 12*, 271–302.

– 1988b. Shades of joy: Patterns of appraisal differentiating pleasant emotions. *Cognition and Emotion 2*, 301–31.

Emmons, R.A. 1986. Personal strivings: An approach to personality and subjective well-being. *Journal of Personality and Social Psychology 51*, 1058–68.

Festinger, L. 1957. *A theory of cognitive dissonance.* Stanford, CA: Stanford University Press.

Folkman, S., & R.S. Lazarus. 1980. An analysis of coping in a middle-aged community sample. *Journal of Health and Social Behavior 21,* 219–39.

– 1988. The relationship between coping and emotion: Implications for theory and research. *Social Science in Medicine 26,* 309–17.

Foschi, M. 1991, January. *Gender-based double standards in task groups.* Paper presented at the conference on "Coping and Working Women: An Integrative Approach," University of British Columbia, Vancouver, BC.

Frijda, N.H. 1986. *The emotions.* New York: Cambridge University Press.

Frijda, N.H., P. Kuipers, & E. ter Schure. 1989. Relations among emotion, appraisal, and emotional action readiness. *Journal of Personality and Social Psychology 57,* 212–28.

Greenglass, E.R. 1985. Psychological implications of sex bias in the workplace. *Academic Psychology Bulletin 7,* 227–40.

Hammen, C.L., T. Marks, A. Mayol, & R. deMayo. 1985. Depressive self-schemas, life stress, and vulnerability to depression. *Journal of Abnormal Psychology 94,* 308–19.

Higgins, E.T. 1987. Self-discrepancy: A theory relating self and affect. *Psychological Review 94,* 319–40.

Hochschild, A. 1989. *The second shift: Working parents and the revolution at home.* New York: Viking Press.

Izard, C.E. 1977. *Human emotions.* New York: Plenum.

Kimble, G.A. 1990. Mother nature's bag of tricks is small. *Psychological Science 1,* 36–41.

Klinger, E. 1975. Consequences of commitment to and disengagement from incentives. *Psychological Review 82,* 1–25.

Lazarus, R.S. 1990. Theory-based stress measurement. *Psychological Inquiry 3,* 3–13.

Lazarus, R.S., & S. Folkman. 1984. *Stress, appraisal and coping.* New York: Springer.

Lazarus, R.S., A.D. Kanner, & S. Folkman. 1980. Emotions: A cognitive-phenomenological analysis. In R. Plutchik & H. Kellerman, eds., *Emotion: Theory, research, and experience: Vol. 1. Theories of emotion* (pp. 189–217). New York: Academic Press.

Little, B.R. 1983. Personal projects: A rationale and method for investigation. *Environment and Behavior 15,* 273–309.

McBride, A.B. 1990. Mental health effects of women's multiple roles. *American Psychologist 45,* 381–4.

McGraw, K.M. 1987. Guilt following transgression: An attribution of responsibility approach. *Journal of Personality and Social Psychology 53,* 247–56.

Pastore, N. 1952. The role of arbitrariness in the frustration-aggression hypothesis. *Journal of Abnormal and Social Psychology 47,* 728–31.

Plutchik, R. 1980. *Emotion: A psychoevolutionary synthesis.* New York: Harper & Row.

Repetti, R.L., K.A. Matthews, & I. Waldron. 1989. Employment and women's health: Effects of paid employment on women's mental and physical health. *American Psychologist 44*, 1394–1401.

Roseman, I.J. 1984. Cognitive determinants of emotion: A structural theory. In P. Shaver, ed., *Review of personality and social psychology: Vol. 5. Emotions, relationships, and health* (pp. 11–36). Beverly Hills, CA: Sage.

Ruble, D.N., A.S. Fleming, L.S. Hackel, & C. Stangor. 1988. Changes in the marital relationship during the transition to first time motherhood: Effects of violated expectations concerning division of household labor. *Journal of Personality and Social Psychology 55*, 78–87.

Scarr, S., D. Phillips, & K. McCartney. 1989. Working mothers and their families. *American Psychologist 44*, 1402–9.

Scherer, K.R. 1984. Emotion as a multicomponent process: A model with some cross-cultural data. In P. Shaver, ed., *Review of personality and social psychology: Vol. 5. Emotions, relationships, and health* (pp. 37–63). Beverly Hills, CA: Sage.

Selye, H. 1974. *Stress without distress.* Philadelphia: J.B. Lippincott.

– 1976. *The stress of life* (rev. ed.). New York: McGraw-Hill.

Smith, C.A. 1991. The self, appraisal, and coping. In C.R. Snyder & D.R. Forsyth, eds., *Handbook of social and clinical psychology: The health perspective* (pp. 116–37). New York: Pergamon Press.

Smith, C.A., & P.C. Ellsworth. 1985. Patterns of cognitive appraisal in emotion. *Journal of Personality and Social Psychology 48*, 813–38.

Smith, C.A., P.C. Ellsworth, & L.K. Pope. 1990, Abstract. Contributions of ability and task difficulty to appraisal, emotion, and autonomic activity. *Psychophysiology 27*, s64.

Smith, C.A., & R.S. Lazarus. 1990. Emotion and adaptation. In L.A. Pervin, ed., *Handbook of personality: Theory and research* (pp. 609–37). New York: Guilford.

– 1993. Appraisal components, core relational themes, and the emotions. *Cognition and Emotion 7*, 233–69.

Smith, C.A., K.A. Haynes, R.S. Lazarus, & L.K. Pope. 1992. *In search of the "hot" cognitions: Attributions, appraisals, and their relation to emotion.* Manuscript submitted for publication. Vanderbilt University.

Statham, A. 1987. The gender model revisited: Differences in the management styles of men and women. *Sex Roles 16*, 409–29.

Strauman, T.J., & E.T. Higgins. 1987. Automatic activation of self-discrepancies and emotional syndromes: When cognitive structures influence affect. *Journal of Personality and Social Psychology 53*, 1004–14.

Tomkins, S.S. 1963. *Affect, imagery, consciousness: Vol. 2. The negative affects.* New York: Springer.

Verbrugge, L.M. 1986. Role burdens and physical health of women and men. *Women and Health 11*, 47–77.

Vogel, W., S. Raymond, & R.S. Lazarus. 1959. Intrinsic motivation and psychological stress. *Journal of Abnormal and Social Psychology 58*, 225–33.

Wallington, S.A. 1973. Consequences of transgression: Self-punishment and depression. *Journal of Personality and Social Psychology 28*, 1–7.

Weiner, B. 1985. An attributional theory of achievement motivation and emotion. *Psychological Review 92*, 548–73.

Weiner, B., J. Amirkhan, V.S. Folkes, & J.A. Verette. 1987. An attributional analysis of excuse giving: Studies of a naive theory of emotion. *Journal of Personality and Social Psychology 52*, 316–24.

Wicklund, R.A., & J.W. Brehm. 1976. *Perspectives on cognitive dissonance.* Hillsdale, NJ: Erlbaum.

PART FIVE

Women's Ways of Coping: Research and Theoretical Implications

13 Neglected Methodological Issues in Employment Stress

ELAINE WETHINGTON AND
RONALD C. KESSLER

A considerable body of research has been published on the relationship between work stress, coping, and psychological adjustment and health among women (see Repetti, Waldron, & Matthews 1989; or Rodin & Ickovics 1990 for reviews). This research provides important descriptive information that can be used to support the claim that women workers are coping with formidable job-related stresses arising from their working conditions and the simultaneous management of work and family demands. We know, for example, that the job conditions of women workers are generally worse than those of men (Lennon 1987; Miller 1980). We know that women workers report more work overload and conflict between the demands of home and work than men (e.g., Duxbury & Higgins 1991; Voydanoff & Donnelly 1989). We also know that the emotional correlates of these work stresses and work-family conflicts are comparable for men and women (Voydanoff 1988; Wethington 1987).

Nonetheless, even after a decade of intense research, we do not have a firm grasp of some very fundamental issues. A strong belief in this research area is that individual coping efforts are associated with

This research was sponsored by grants T32 MH16806, RO1 MH40136, MO1 MH16896 from the National Institutes of Mental Health to Ronald C. Kessler and by USDA Hatch grant 321–7419 to Elaine Wethington. We would like to thank Sharon Kahn, Bonita Long, Phyllis Moen, Karl Pillemer, and the participants in the University of British Columbia workshop, "Coping and Working Women: An Integrative Approach," for their comments on earlier drafts of this paper.

emotional adjustment to work stress and work-family conflict. It is not at all clear, though, whether *individual* coping is strongly associated with better adjustment, what types of coping are more efficacious, or how one might construct interventions to make individual coping efforts more effective.

Most important, the available evidence on women coping with work stress and work-family conflict does not provide clear directions for interventions. In our view, research designs currently used in this area have contributed to this situation. Two areas are particularly problematic: evaluating the real impact of work and work-family stress on women's psychological adjustment, and evaluating the efficacy of strategies used by women to cope with these stresses. In this chapter, we focus primarily on the methodological issues that have emerged in regard to the second issue. Kessler (1987) provides a detailed consideration of methodological difficulties that arise in evaluating the impact of stress on adjustment.

In this chapter we address three methodological issues, which were suggested by Kasl (1987) in a thoughtful analysis of current research dilemmas in stress and coping research. First, we consider the adequacy of the theoretical formulations used for predicting the efficacy of individual coping efforts among women workers. Second, we review the state of coping measurement. Third, we examine whether the most frequently used data-analytic strategies and research designs can resolve important questions about cause and effect, answers to which are critical for mounting successful interventions to help women workers. We conclude with some suggestions for improving analytic and research design strategies in this area.

EVALUATING THE IMPACT OF COPING ON PSYCHOLOGICAL ADJUSTMENT

Adequacy of the Theoretical Formulations

There are two general positions used to evaluate the impact of work stresses and coping on women's psychological adjustment. These two positions have their origins in research on multiple roles and health among women, rather than in the study of work stress and coping *per se*, although the latter research is gaining influence (see, for example, the other chapters in this volume).

The first position is based on the role-stress (or conflict) perspective, which argues that the combination of family and employment demands creates role overloads (more demands that one can handle) and role conflicts (the perception that role demands in one area affect the adequacy of one's role performance in another area). This increased exposure to stress is thought to create higher psychological distress among women workers (Coser & Rokoff 1971). This distress is presumed to come about because the buildup of competing demands on time and energy overwhelms most women's individual *coping* capacities at work and at home.

The second position is based on the role-expansion perspective, which argues that multiple roles have positive effects on health and well-being and consequently that the combination of family and work roles should be associated with improved mental health (Marks 1977; Sieber 1974; Thoits 1983; Verbrugge 1983). Although acknowledging that multiple roles increase exposure to role-related overloads and conflicts, role-expansion theorists argue that the alternative resources provided by multiple roles outweigh these stressors and help dampen their negative emotional effects (Kibria, Barnett, Baruch, & Marshall 1990; Thoits 1986). One of the most important resources thought to derive from maintaining multiple roles is increased exposure to social and personal situations that enhance successful *coping*, such as social support, personal validation, and opportunities to develop self-efficacy (Pearlin & Schooler 1978; Thoits 1983).

Adherents to these two theoretical positions have provided primarily descriptive and indirect, rather than etiological and behavioural, evidence to support them. The data utilized are typically cross-sectional, and only a small minority of the studies directly measure either the multiplicity of stresses or coping directly (for exceptions, see Barnett, Marshall, & Singer 1992; Wortman, Biernat, & Lang 1991; and the chapters in this volume). As a result, it is difficult, if not impossible, to conclude whether overall there is more empirical support for one position or the other. (Most likely, both positions have validity, depending on situational and personal factors; see Bolger, DeLongis, Kessler, & Wethington 1990 and Tiedje, Wortman, Downey, Emmons, Biernat, & Lang 1990). It is important to note that the research designs typically used make it impossible to rule out explanations other than those arising from these two positions.

Foremost among the possible alternative explanations is *selection* (Kessler & McRae 1984). The essence of the selection argument is that the relationship between multiple roles and emotional functioning is due to prior emotional characteristics of the individual. Since this position is generally regarded as "atheoretical" or as a "nuisance" (Kasl 1987) and is less developed in the literature as an alternative explanatory perspective, we spend some time describing it here.

There are three important variants of selection explanations that are relevant to the study of coping with work stress among women. The first is that prior emotional functioning plays a part in determining level and consistency of participation in the labour force across time, with women in poor mental health less likely to undertake additional role demands (Kandel & Davies 1986; Kessler & McRae 1984). The second is self-selection, which is that other emotional and attitudinal characteristics, such as socialized commitment to less traditional gender roles, make it more likely for some women to combine work and family roles than others (e.g., Wortman et al. 1991), and (presumably) to cope successfully with work and work-family stressors (cf. Hochschild 1983, 1989). A third variant of the selection perspective is that prior emotional and attitudinal characteristics affect how people *typically cope* with demands from work roles. This can mean that women's experience and perception of role stressors are partly determined by "failed" or inadequate coping related to an underlying emotional disturbance (Silver & Wortman 1980). It can also mean that some women engage in preventive coping to avoid stresses arising from combining work and family demands by reducing work hours at points in their lives when family demands are high (Moen & Dempster-McClain 1987). Unfortunately, many researchers are apt to dismiss selection explanations such as these as unimportant rather than to consider them alternative, testable explanations for their findings (Kasl 1987; Kessler & McRae 1984).

In our view, researchers must now turn to research designs that enable them to acquire a much better understanding of selection processes and their impact on stress exposure, coping, and adjustment. As we describe below, several sources of selection effects deserve attention when specifically evaluating the impact of coping. The existence of these selection effects complicates the measurement, typical analytic strategies, and research designs used in the study of coping itself.

CONCEPTUALIZATION AND MEASUREMENT
OF COPING

In evaluating the impact of coping on adjustment, researchers typically ask the following question: Do people who evolve a particular set of coping skills in handling stressors of work or managing competing work and family demands do better than those who do not develop those skills? The research goals arising from this question are to identify groups of women who have coping skills that "match" the demands of their situations, to map their efficacious coping skills, and then to use this information to design interventions that will help other women cope with work stress and work-family conflict.

Given this question, stress and coping researchers have turned their attention to identifying the processes of coping and the variations between situations that evoke different coping responses (the better, of course, to understand how situations and coping skills match). There arise, however, some serious complications. The first complication involves *measurement* of coping strategies. There remains a great deal of controversy about how coping should be evaluated and measured (see Cohen 1987; Kessler, Price, & Wortman 1985; Stone, Greenberg, Kennedy-Moore, & Newman 1991). These controversies revolve around the generation of comprehensive typologies of coping strategies, the relative impact of disposition and situation on choice of coping, the accuracy of recalling coping strategies retrospectively, and the measurement of coping strategies that research subjects are unlikely to recognize as coping.

The second complicating factor is the *selection process* that goes into the particular combination of work and family stress to which the woman exposes herself. Selection into occupations is known to be nonrandom (e.g., Kohn & Schooler 1982), and may depend on the coping skills that a person has acquired through education and family modelling (Pearlin & Schooler 1978). Among women, the situation may be somewhat more complicated. The acquisition of workplace coping skills may be dependent on an entire life history of attitudes toward labour force participation (Bielby & Bielby 1989; Wethington 1990), socialized commitment to giving either work or family priority (Gerson 1985), and selection of a marital partner who supports one's styles of coping (Bielby & Bielby 1989). Such life-history factors may also affect primary appraisal of work and work-family stressors, as well as coping (Long, Kahn, & Schutz 1992).

The third complicating factor is *chronicity*. The appraisal of an event as stressful may indicate previous failures with similar situations or underlying poor emotional functioning (Silver & Wortman 1980). In addition, exposure to some stressful situations may be diagnostic of prior failure to keep small problems from growing into bigger ones: that is, bad coping (Pearlin & Schooler 1978).

Important descriptive findings can emerge from research examining coping specific to different stressful situations (e.g., Lazarus & Folkman 1984; Mattlin, Wethington, & Kessler 1990; Pearlin & Schooler 1978). It is essential to note, however, that the evaluation of coping efficacy remains clouded by measurement, selection, and chronicity issues. Specifically, problems remain in regard to identifying relevant coping responses; improving accuracy in the recall of coping strategies after the fact; the confounding of coping with the chronicity or severity of the stressor; accounting for coping processes that respondents are not aware of using; and choosing the proper outcomes for evaluating the efficacy of coping.

Relevant coping responses. The identification of relevant coping responses is a fundamental ambiguity in the study of coping. One important issue involves measuring the strategies that people use to *prevent* or minimize chronic stress. At this stage, we know less about the roles that people play in creating or avoiding the stressful experiences that confront them in work and family than we know about what happens in coping after the fact. In typical coping research, people are asked to report how they coped with stress after it happened, rather than how they may have been successful in avoiding stress of that type. Yet it is plausible that some of the most successful copers are those who are so good at avoiding excessive stress that they report no problems at all in response to conventional measures of stressors (Pearlin & Schooler 1978).

Accuracy of recall. Another unresolved issue arises from the fact that cross-sectional research relies on retrospective recall of stressors and coping. Respondents are asked to report an "aggregate" frequency of experiencing stressors of a particular type over a period of time, and then are asked to report how they coped with them. Individual recall of stressors, however, is prone to biases arising from recency and lack of specificity in the question stimulus (Kessler & Wethington 1991). There is, moreover, some controversy over whether these same sorts of biases affect respondents' ability to report their coping efforts accurately (Kessler et al. 1985). These biases may be at their most intractable in situations involving the recall of chronic stress and how one has coped with it (Cohen 1987).

Confounding of coping with chronicity and severity of stress. Yet another methodological difficulty is the confounding of "coping" with severity of the chronic stress. Most people engage in a variety of strategies to cope with chronic stressors (Pearlin & Schooler 1978). This suggests the possibility that the absolute number and types of coping strategies reported may be confounded with the severity of situation (Cohen 1987). If this is the case, the reported frequency of using a particular coping strategy may be associated with worse adjustment, although overall it may not be a maladaptive strategy.

A telling illustration of this problem originates in research on social support and psychological adjustment. Although it is well established that perceptions of social support and its availability are associated with good psychological adjustment to stress (Cohen & Wills 1985; House, Landis, & Umberson 1988; Kessler & McLeod 1985), many naturalistic studies of the support process to date have found that actual support transactions as reported by respondents are not associated with good psychological adjustment to stress (Barrera 1986; Sandler & Barerra 1984; Sarason, Shearin, Pierce, & Sarason 1987; Wethington & Kessler 1986).

The failure to find a consistent "buffering" effect for received support is not well understood, but some possible explanations have important implications for research on coping efficacy. One possibility relevant to our major point is that people who receive support or who seek it out under stress have experienced a more severe stress than those who do not receive or seek support. Consistent with this explanation, Barrera (1986) has shown that the "maladaptive" effect of receiving support is reduced when situational differences in stress severity are controlled. The implication of this for research on coping is that evaluations of coping efficacy should account for severity of the stressor, as well as for its objective situational aspects.

A complicating factor, which further suggests that the aforementioned findings regarding social support should be taken seriously by coping researchers, is that most quantitative studies of coping have failed to find strong and consistent associations between coping with work stress and psychological adjustment. For example, Mattlin et al. (1990) found that controlling for use of coping strategies accounted for only about 7 per cent of the variance in psychological adjustment among respondents who reported coping with serious practical difficulties like work problems in the previous year; in addition, their analyses indicated that the use of some widely regarded and recommended individual coping strategies, such as positive reappraisal of the stressor and "versatile" coping, were significantly associated with worse, rather than better, adjustment.

Awareness of coping processes. Evidence has emerged, moreover, that even in very detailed, focused studies of coping, some important aspects of coping may not be accurately measured, given present interviewing and questionnaire technology that relies on respondent self-report (Stone, Helder, & Schneider 1988; Stone, Greenberg, Kennedy-Moore, & Newman 1991). For example, Haan (1982) has asserted that coping efforts are not always deliberate or consciously acknowledged. If this is true, measurement complications would arise in the instance when the coping strategies most effective in promoting adjustment to stress are not necessarily visible to the respondents themselves. In regard to one sort of coping strategy – seeking help and social support – Lieberman (1986) has suggested precisely this possibility. In a discussion of Brown's (1978) community study of support and psychological adjustment, which showed that the respondents who reported the most ready *access* to support apparently adjusted to stress without seeking help or reporting support from their networks, Lieberman proposed that people who are embedded in very effective support networks might get help so smoothly that they fail to recognize it (see also Cohen 1987). Lieberman went on to argue that this type of unnoticed support might actually be more effective than the "help" a person reports seeking, because receiving help without asking is not so much a threat to self-esteem as needing to ask for help (Fisher, Nadler, & Whitcher-Alagna 1982). In an instance of this sort, a respondent may not be able to report what actually happened, let alone report what may have been the most effective (see also Kessler 1990).

Evaluation of coping efficacy. Another issue that plagues coping research is the question of how to evaluate the efficacy of coping. It is standard in coping research to evaluate the efficacy of coping based on the level of psychological distress reported by the coper sometime after an event or in the midst of a chronic stress situation (e.g., Folkman & Lazarus 1988). This strategy, however, ignores a variety of difficult problems. The first of these is that, in a cross-sectional design, it may be impossible to determine that the chronic stressor is causally prior to the reported distress (Kasl 1987). This problem is well known. A less acknowledged problem, though, arises from the fact that coping with chronic stress is a dynamic, multifaceted process that may unfold over a long period of time. Coping associated with good short-time adjustment (this week) may not be associated with better long-term adjustment (next year) (Kessler et al. 1985).

Finally, there is the problem of selection and its effects on the investigator's ability to evaluate the efficacy of coping. Those who are observed engaging in the most efficacious strategies may be those who possess the most resilient personalities and the most favourable situational and personal resources. It cannot be determined whether it is their coping making the difference, or the unmeasured background factors that have given them more emotional resilience or social and personal resources to help them withstand stress.

Summary. Given the problems with measurement, selection, and chronicity, how do we go about understanding coping phenomena among employed women and evaluating the efficacy of these strategies? Five sorts of studies have been done to address these two questions. These are: (a) multivariate, quantitative surveys, generally cross-sectional; (b) longitudinal studies that use the same quantitative methods; (c) microanalytic process-oriented studies that consider day-to-day work stress and how one copes with it; (d) descriptive, qualitative surveys that generate very detailed information about the stresses that women experience and the way that they cope with them; and (e) experimental and quasi-experimental interventions among women facing an increase in work stress or work-family conflict. We have learned a great deal from each method, but each has its limitations, most particularly in regard to addressing methodological issues arising from measurement, selection, and chronicity.

CURRENT DATA-ANALYTIC STRATEGIES AND RESEARCH DESIGNS

Multivariate Quantitative Surveys

Large, representative multivariate quantitative surveys are particularly helpful in identifying groups at high risk for distress. In the area of work stress and work-family conflict, such large surveys have identified occupations that pose severer than usual stressors on employed women, and job conditions that seem to be strongly correlated with work-family conflict (e.g., Voydanoff 1988). Cross-sectional data collection, however, can be problematic as a design for assessing the impact of coping with such *chronic* stress on adjustment and for ruling out selection factors.

In cross-sectional studies of coping, the relationships between the stressors, coping, and psychological adjustment are generally examined in the following way. Researchers ask subjects to respond to a series of questions tapping work difficulties and work-family conflict as well as the respondents' characteristic coping responses to situations of this kind. Psychological outcomes are also measured. (Pearlin & Schooler 1978 provide a model for this sort of design.)

In studies of this sort it is possible to compare respondents who report similar difficulties but cope with them differently. It is also possible to see whether there is intra-individual consistency of coping responses across situations and whether the effectiveness of a particular coping response depends on the situation in which a person employs it.

Typically, researchers use a multivariate control approach when analysing the data generated in these surveys. Unfortunately, this approach is usually inadequate for ruling out selection interpretations. The inadequacy of the multivariate control approach is demonstrated clearly by considering work on the relationship between job demands and worker health (for a review, see Kahn 1981). A common research design used here is to conduct a general population survey of employed people in which each respondent is asked to describe the conditions of her work. A multivariate approach is then used to assess relationships between work stresses and the health of these respondents.

These analyses almost always introduce controls for selection factors that are preconditions for certain sorts of jobs, such as education, or factors that make some job conditions less likely, such as number of preschool children in the household. Yet even if one grants that controls of this sort might be adequate, it is still problematic whether the results of such analyses would yield valid information about the negative emotional effects of job conditions.

The problem with this approach can be understood if we begin with a consideration of the experimental analogue this strategy attempts to reproduce. Control variables are used in multivariate analysis to adjust for nonrandom exposure to job stresses so that the relationship between these stresses and health outcomes can be interpreted as if jobs are randomly assigned. But this is unrealistic, particularly in the case of women. Suppose we carried out an experiment in which we randomly assigned women within each educational (or parenting) category to a full array of jobs that exist in the general population. People with a grade-school education would be proportionately assigned to jobs that require complex technical skills, while those with technical training would be proportionately assigned to jobs that require physical labour and lack decision latitude. Mothers with infants would be assigned to split shifts, while college-educated women with nearly grown children would be working at minimum wage. The misfit between people and jobs would be enormous and would almost certainly result in rates of stress-related psychological distress in the experimental sample that would far exceed those in the normal population (Kasl 1981; Kessler 1987).

This hypothetical experiment would not provide useful information about the influence of job stress or coping on worker health because it would lack external validity. It would assign people with diverse backgrounds, experiences, and expectations across a range of job conditions that is considerably greater than the actual distribution of mismatches in the general population. Yet researchers who work with general population samples that include such a diverse array of people engage in an enterprise with the same validity problems as this experiment (see also Lieberson 1983).

Multivariate control approaches *can* result in unbiased estimates of associations and even causal impact if some restrictive conditions are met. Researchers probably overestimate the frequency, though, with which this happens. Kessler (1987) discusses the restrictive assumptions that must be made to use these techniques in studies of stress.

Another difficulty with the multivariate control approach is that the causes of chronic stress are seldom sufficiently well understood to construct the ideal model to "control" for confounding factors. Considering that some people may select themselves into jobs that have the potential for more chronic stress further complicates the picture. Personality determinants of job selection have been documented (Kohn & Schooler 1982). In most cases that we can think of, the requisite information about such processes does not exist in the area of chronic work stress, work-family conflict, and coping.[1]

Moreover, when a relevant "control" variable is not specified, no statement can be made about the *direction* of the bias introduced into the estimate of the chronic stressor effect. Duncan (1975) has pointed out that there is no reason to believe that the estimate of the effect yielded from a model with incomplete controls is any more accurate than an estimate yielded from a model with no controls at all.

It is important to note, though, that multivariate control analyses can provide useful *descriptive* information about the types of job settings and types of work-family conflicts that are associated with high rates of particular health problems and coping strategies that may be useful in managing the effects of stress (see also Stone, Kennedy-Moore, Newman, Greenberg, & Neale 1991). Once high-risk jobs and coping strategies are isolated, stronger research designs can be employed in order to justify making causal inferences about the effects of particular job settings and coping strategies on adjustment.

Longitudinal Research

As an acknowledgment of the known limitations of studying a dynamic process such as coping in a cross-sectional design, researchers studying women coping with work stress and work-family conflict have turned to longitudinal studies. In order to minimize the confounding from cross-situational inconsistency, most of these studies

[1] Heckman (1979) has recommended that researchers correct for selection effects of this sort by treating them as special cases of specification bias. The procedure here is to estimate for each case the probability of experiencing a particular sort of stressor based upon the known factors that produced exposure. The technical problems, however, that arise in attempting to develop explicit models of these selection procedures may be overwhelming, not the least of which will involve "complete" specification of conditions of which we know very little. Despite such difficulties, though, the use of Heckman's techniques could be extremely helpful in future research.

have focused on occupational groups of women predicted to be at higher risk for experiencing stress (e.g., Barnett et al. 1992).

Over the past five years, researchers in this area have attempted to design studies that observe coping as a process. Such dynamic studies are necessary to conceptualize the process of appraisal-coping-adjustment proposed by Lazarus and Folkman (1984). Long et al. (1992), Wortman et al. (1991), and Barnett et al. (1992) typify the current approach, by conducting studies that involve data collection over several years. These data collections utilize conventional questionnaire or interview technology.

Thus far, longitudinal surveys such as these have been very useful for refining our understanding about particular subgroups at higher risk for work stress and work-family conflict. Data collections by Wortman and her associates among professional women (1991) and by Barnett and her associates among women in traditional "service" occupations (1992) have uncovered rich patterns regarding the experience of such stressors, moderators of stress, and typical coping patterns.

In addition to the detailed information base generated by such studies, another factor that accounts for the popularity of this design is that researchers believe that they can better take account of selection factors when assessing the impact of a particular stressor on health. The usual justification for this strategy is that by obtaining data at multiple time points, one can study the process of adjustment to the stressor.

Using this approach, researchers typically assume that by controlling for an earlier value of the psychological outcome they can adjust for initial differences between subjects who subsequently were exposed to a stressor and those who were not, thus obtaining an unbiased estimate of the impact of the stressor (Wethington & Kessler 1989).

Unfortunately, such a procedure does not guarantee that selection bias is reduced or eliminated (Kasl 1987). It only eliminates bias under very restrictive conditions, which are rarely achieved in practice. In particular, these conditions are not achieved when examining situations like work stress and work-family conflict, which typically are *chronic* difficulties. The essence of the problem that chronicity poses to researchers is that one can seldom assume that exposure to chronic stress happened independently of prior emotional functioning. In other words, exposure to work stress is not random with respect to the health outcome under investigation, or random in respect to prior coping. For further information about this methodological problem, see Kessler (1987).

Microanalytic Process-oriented Research

As we have detailed elsewhere in this chapter, capturing the coping process itself is a difficult challenge with which to cope. We believe that longitudinal studies undertaken by the groups mentioned above are an important step, and they already have resulted in fascinating descriptive data about what family situations and aspects of life history contribute to more negative appraisals of work and work-family stressors (see especially Long et al. 1992; Wortman et al. 1991).

A more dynamic study of the coping *process*, however, may require much more frequent monitoring of coping behaviour than has been attempted by these investigators. The studies mentioned above conduct several interviews or administer several questionnaires over a period of a year or years. The major difficulty is that the lags between the interviews are often quite long, requiring respondents to report about stress and coping over a fairly long period. This sort of longitudinal data-collection strategy, therefore, does not minimize recall bias. It also cannot reproduce accurately the complexity of the coping processes that the stress-appraisal-coping model describes.

Such measurement problems are very difficult to overcome, and almost certainly require innovative data-collection technologies. One alternative technology, used by our research group, involves the use of daily diaries (Stone & Neale 1984). In these studies, we have collected daily information for a period of six weeks among a sample of 166 married couples. The daily questionnaires include questions about work and family stress, appraisal, coping, and mood (Bolger, DeLongis, Kessler, & Schilling 1989; Bolger, DeLongis, Kessler, & Wethington 1989; Bolger et al. 1990).

We consider the findings of our studies using these data, however, to be primarily descriptive, because serious methodological flaws still remain. Foremost among these problems, our studies were designed primarily to study coping with conflicts rather than the full range of work and work-family stress (McGonagle, Kessler, & Schilling 1991), and therefore we lack some critical information about daily coping with work stress.

In addition, even studies as detailed as daily-administered studies of coping have serious deficiencies. Since a diary study consists of a series of daily cross-sections of experience, cause and effect cannot be determined any more concretely than in a more conventional cross-sectional study. These data are self-reported as well, so retrospective recall biases that plague more conventional coping research are not eliminated, such as the bias due to differences between individuals in interpreting the questions and response categories (Stone,

Greenberg, Kennedy-Moore, & Newman, in press). We can assess whether the use of a particular coping strategy is associated with better mood, but since we measure coping and mood after the fact, it is still quite plausible that mood determines coping, rather than vice versa (Bolger, DeLongis, Kessler, & Schilling 1989). Stone and colleagues, moreover, have raised the possibility of another confounding between mood and the recall of coping. Subjects may calibrate their reports of how much they used a particular coping strategy to how well they thought the strategy worked for them (Stone, Greenberg, Kennedy-Moore, & Newman 1991). In addition, although we can follow the onset and resolution of a stressor over a series of days, we cannot necessarily assess its long-term, cumulative impact.

Another deficiency of our diary approach – a problem it shares with all research on coping – is that it focuses on problems that have *occurred*, rather than on all of the problems that potentially threatened, of which some were successfully avoided. Thus we have no direct information about the possible impact of "preventive" coping.

Qualitative Longitudinal Studies

Qualitative studies have provided some of the most creative ideas about measuring women's work stress and work-family conflict and describing the ways that women cope with it (e.g., Gerson 1985; Hochschild 1989). In contrast to the quantitative studies, qualitative studies like that of Hochschild (1989) report discoveries of coping strategies used by working women that appear to be highly effective in maintaining their long-term psychological equilibrium, despite intense career demands.

In several respects, these qualitative studies are superior to quantitative studies in providing useful and "valid" information in regard to coping with work stress and work-family conflict. The standards of proof for assessing efficacy are probably superior, because qualitative researchers are closer to the actual experiences of their subjects and typically assess "efficacy" multidimensionally.

For example, Hochschild (1989) identifies myriad individual coping strategies that were not described previously. She also assesses the relative efficacy of strategies across a variety of psychological, physical, and relational outcomes, thus allowing for the possibility that individual women differ in their typical expression of underlying psychological distress. She has taken the important step of identifying strategies that have short-term positive impacts, but long-term negative impacts on psychological adjustment among working women. She has also identified strategies that have positive psychological outcomes for the women themselves, but which may have negative impacts on family members. Questions such as these have been all but ignored in most of the quantitative studies, including our own.

Yet in other respects, there are serious limitations to qualitative research of this sort. Bias is a nagging concern in participant observation work. The conclusion that a strategy appears to be effective may be affected by after-the-fact rationalization of subject or observer rather than based on systematic monitoring of the research subjects' actual emotional states over time.

Qualitative work, moreover, is almost always done in very small samples, targeted in relatively homogeneous occupational groups, and carried out in small geographical areas. Generalizing from such samples is empirically suspect. These problems could be overcome by carrying out simultaneous qualitative studies in many areas of the country, and recruiting women from a wide range of occupations (Glasser & Strauss 1973).

A qualitative study of this sort, however, has never been done and would be a complicated task, certainly beyond the limits of most single investigators. The intense nature of the data collection might seriously limit the number and types of women who participate in the studies, excluding the less educated and the more "overloaded." In particular, recruitment difficulties may result in serious *selection* bias in the sample.

Experimental and Quasi-experimental Interventions

Experimental and quasi-experimental interventions to improve individual coping (e.g., Martelli, Auerbach, Alexander, & Mercuri 1987) have been used for about a decade. Most are based on the Lazarus and Folkman (1984) model of the stress and coping process.

One such "coping-enhancement" intervention is assisting first-time mothers with managing work stress and work-family conflict (Collins & Tiedje 1988). Although a significant and important first step, the sample size (less than thirty, including controls) and sample homogeneity necessitate replication and extension. It is very likely that additional interventions of this sort are under way, some of them sponsored by employers rather than research organizations. The existence of the business-based programs suggests that many data-gathering opportunities exist for researchers who are interested in monitoring naturally occurring coping strategies.

SUGGESTIONS FOR FUTURE RESEARCH STRATEGIES

In our view, the most fruitful path for furthering research on coping is to combine the insights of qualitative research with empirically rigorous quantitative designs and analytic strategies. The four possibilities we discuss in this section hold some promise for helping us overcome the problems brought about by selection and chronicity. We discuss the relative merits and shortcomings of (a) collecting life-history data about women and their work and family careers; (b) the use of more powerful statistical techniques, such as instrumental-variables estimation; (c) quasi-experimental research that takes maximum advantage of matched comparisons between women who have differential access to specific sorts of coping strategies (and which should build on descriptive information about choices and circumstances that emerge from the life-history research); and (d) experimental interventions to assist coping in work settings (which could grow out of the quasi-experimental research).

Retrospective Life-History Data

One opportunity for furthering our knowledge of coping with work and work-family stress is to adapt some of the qualitative approaches to design innovative methods and measures for quantitative studies. The techniques of gathering life-history data, described below, might be particularly helpful for gaining additional information about the complex selection processes that cause women to reduce or increase their hours of and commitment to participation in the labour force.

The *life-history calendar* has been one of the most intriguing innovations in stress and family-transition research in recent years. The calendar, typically filled out simultaneously by respondent and interviewer, aids the respondent in remembering and reconstructing events and role transitions over a period of years. These calendars are generally thought to produce more accurate reconstruction of events than standard interviewing techniques (Kessler & Wethington 1991). Such calendars have been used to provide a chronology of work and family role transitions over a number of years (Thornton & Freedman 1985).

The study most relevant to our proposed strategy has been conducted by Moen, Dempster-McClain, and Williams (1989). One aim of Moen and her associates was to extend the qualitative research of Gerson (1985), who collected detailed retrospective data on the role of childhood socialization, life history of labour-force participation, and marital and child-bearing history in affecting women's role choices and emotional adjustment. Moen and associates made several important innovations when designing their own, more quantitatively oriented study.

One key innovation was the collection of life-history data from a sample of respondents who had already provided direct information about these aspects of their lives some distance in the past. They conducted their study in a sample of women who had been interviewed thirty years before about social role status, economic, social, and health status of family of origin, family relationships, and mental health. Over 85 per cent of the women not known to be dead in 1986 were reinterviewed by the investigators. This technique represents an improvement over Gerson's qualitative study, where all information about past history was based on retrospective recall.

In addition, Moen and associates designed a life-history calendar to aid in the reconstruction of marital, parenting, work, and social participation transitions over the thirty-year period since the first study. During the interviewing process, explicit links between closely timed transitions were recorded (e.g., which was a "cause" and which was an "effect"). Moreover, in all cases where it was possible, a daughter was interviewed in order to provide additional information about family-role transitions during her lifetime (Moen et al. 1989). Such techniques as these could be adapted and extended to improve our current knowledge about the role of selection in determining which coping strategies are used to reduce the emotional adjustment problems brought on by increases in work and family-role demands.

More important, life-history techniques could be used to gather new information about coping strategies. Using information about coping resources (having the money, education, or status resources to escape a particularly bad situation) can provide the researcher some additional bases for examining why some women make use of a particular type of coping and other women do not. Researchers could also ask women who do not use seemingly effective strategies in managing particular work situations why they did not, and then ask a series of follow-up questions regarding (a) whether they would ever have thought of using the alternative strategies in that situation; (b) if they had used those strategies before, and if so, why they had decided to stop; (c) if they felt that they were unable to use them even though they thought such strategies might be effective (e.g., because co-workers or husband were not supportive of the strategies, they saw someone else use them and get into trouble, or they decided the strategy was not appropriate for the situation). Information such as this, which would be unique in coping research, could be used to design an appropriate monitoring apparatus for measuring coping in a follow-up prospective study of working women. It is interesting to note that one of the pioneer studies of coping with chronic role strain (Pearlin & Schooler 1978) utilized qualitative interviewing techniques such as these in a preliminary study. The open-ended material was used to write the standardized coping questions used in the interview.

Of course, none of these data would constitute "proof" that demonstrates the efficacy of particular coping strategies. This information about structural correlates, facilitators, and impediments to "effective coping," however, could be used to design studies in which cause and effect could be more plausibly inferred.

Instrumental-Variables Estimation

An underexploited method for studying the effects of work stress and coping on health is instrumental-variables estimation. As we explain below, this method has great potential.

An important problem that occurs in studies of chronic work and work-family stress involves the use of self-reported stress measures. These are popular because chronic stress is very difficult to measure objectively. Such self-reported measures, however, are problematic. The researcher can never be sure what the questions are measuring, because influences other than actual exposure to a chronic stressor can play a part in shaping the perception of stress. The association between reported exposure to a chronic stressor and psychological distress might reflect the influence of pre-existing psychological distress on the perception of stress as much as the influence of an objectively stressful situation on psychological distress.

Instrumental-variables analysis is a strategy that can help separate reciprocal causal influences such as these. This technique was developed by econometricians, where problems of reciprocal influence are frequently encountered (Fisher 1965). An instrumental variable is a variable that is assumed to affect one and only one of the two variables in a reciprocally related pair. The instrumental variable can "stand in" for the variable it is assumed to cause.

As it happens, instrumental-variables procedures are well suited to the cases discussed in this paper, where subjective appraisals of the stress situation and coping strategies are theorized to mediate the relationships between the stress-inducing situation and the health outcome, the process suggested by Lazarus and Folkman's model of the stress process (1984). An unbiased estimate of the influence of appraisal or coping on the outcome requires the researcher to adjust for the reverse influence of the outcome on self-reported stress and coping (Dohrenwend, Dohrenwend, Dodson, & Shrout 1984; Dohrenwend & Shrout 1985; Stone, Greenberg, Kennedy-Moore, & Newman 1991).

Such adjustments can be made when there is an indicator of the objective stress situation available that is independent of the respondent's perception of stress. A limiting condition is that the objective indicator of stress needs to have a meaningful association with the outcome variable. This kind of condition can easily be met in studies of work stress, where objective measures of the job environment are available from independent ratings. Measures based on the Dictionary of Occupational Titles job condition ratings (Roos & Treiman 1980), for example, meet these conditions, and have been used by some researchers (e.g., Lennon 1987; Wethington 1987) as indicators of job stress.

The critical assumption for using this technique appropriately is that the objective stress condition affects health only through the intervening mechanisms of *subjective stress appraisal* or *coping*. This assumption is most plausible when the health outcome is some measure of emotional functioning. This assumption reduces to the expectation that the regression on health on the objective stress measure is zero once the subjective measure of stress appraisal and/or coping is controlled.

These estimation techniques can be used to estimate the reciprocal influence of work stress on health if there is an instrumental variable available for the stressor and a second instrumental variable available for the health outcome. A discussion of these estimation procedures, which involve simultaneous equations, is available in Duncan (1975).

Quasi-experimental Designs

Although use of the life-history or instrumental-variable approaches is likely to result in gathering much useful qualitative and quantitative naturalistic data on how women cope with work stress over time, these approaches may still be inadequate in several important respects. The major problem is that, to make strong arguments in favour of one coping strategy being more effective than another in promoting adjustment, researchers need to have tighter control over the observations.

The trouble derives from the standard selection problem that we have been describing throughout this paper. Working women who report doing the better coping – things which are more original, clever, and seemingly effective – could be very different people from those who do not think of such strategies in the course of their problem-solving. The better copers could be more intelligent or emotionally stable than the less effective copers. How do we demonstrate that the strategies work, rather than simply being expressions of the woman's overall resiliency?

Matched comparisons, or studying naturally occurring conditions that mimic "experimental" stress exposure, should be carefully considered by researchers as a way to overcome this challenge (Cook & Campbell 1979). The use of these designs, though, is limited by the requirement that exposure to work stress be random.

There are many cases where the assumption of random stress exposure is plausible within some range of comparison. Indeed, Kessler (1987) has pointed out that this is true in most cases in regard to assessing the impact of work stress on psychological adjustment if the researcher is willing to consider a sufficiently *narrow* range of comparison. However, are matching strategies feasible to assess the impact and efficacy of coping with stress? Cook and Campbell (1979) have argued that attempts to randomize "exposure" may be impossible. The evaluation of coping efficacy may be a question that falls into this category.

For example, if a researcher were to use matching procedures to evaluate coping efficacy, the usual mechanical matching procedures, such as making sure that age, sex, and other demographic distributions of cases and controls are comparable, would be inadequate. The real power of matching would come in finding a subpopulation within which one can plausibly assume that use of a particular coping strategy was random.

The limiting condition in finding a comparison group is that the range within which exposure to the event can be considered random is often very narrow. Given our concerns about the role of selection factors in determining some portion of chronic stress exposure and choice of coping, what types of comparisons between the "stressed" and "controls" would be legitimate?

One possibility is to study the use of workplace day-care arrangements as a means of coping with work and child-care conflicts. If a worksite could be identified in advance where a day-care arrangement is being introduced, researchers could go into the company beforehand and assess the prior mental health, preferred coping strategies, and attitudes toward child care of the mothers within the company who might reasonably benefit from the introduction of the service. Assessments could be repeated after the service is introduced, in order to see who uses it, why or why not, and whether or not the users objectively benefit from the use of the day-care facility.

A second, more "qualitative" research approach would be to study women who are going to be exposed to the same work stressor. For example, a work group of women in a company that will experience a takeover by a different owner or management team could be monitored over a period of time as the consequences of the situation unfold. These women will probably display a variety of different ways in which to cope with the upcoming or ongoing stresses of adjustment. It is also predictable that the women will share with one another the ways they have of "coping" with the changes; the researcher could, as part of the study design, arrange for a meeting among all participants to discuss possible strategies and to "trade" what they think are the most effective ones. In subsequent interviews, the researcher could examine two important issues: (a) whether the discussed strategies had "diffused" among women other than the originator; (b) and whether the strategies seemed to be as efficacious in managing psychological distress for others as they had been for the originators.

Experimental Interventions in Work Settings

Another design strategy is to conduct the coping strategy-sharing manipulation suggested in the previous section as an experiment. Researchers could survey the naturally occurring strategies that a group of working women report using, and take these strategies to other work settings where women are undergoing work stressors of the same sort or level of severity. Standard evaluation techniques could then be used to monitor the use of the coping strategies, and both their short- and long-term effectiveness, in managing work stress. Presuming that the education in the use of the strategies could be randomized, and the consequences of use adequately monitored, a project like this could demonstrate that (a) a particular coping strategy is efficacious for a wider variety of women and settings than the person or place where it originated; and (b) such strategies could be taught in an intervention.

We can foresee some problems that would remain even in experimental interventions of this type. It is easy to imagine that stress can be randomly assigned. Plant closings, hostile takeovers, and switches in management style are independent of prior mental health or coping strategies of the individual workers that we study. It is also possible to randomize education about strategies and access to resources for coping, by mounting interventions in a number of different settings at the same time. It is a lot more difficult, though, to imagine that *coping* could ever be randomly used. If the sorts of coping strategies we are interested in involve making use of available *external* resources for coping (such as day care, family leave, and formal support), then our task becomes one of monitoring the benefits for individual women who have access to these strategies. But how do we do the same thing for more "micro" or "internal" coping strategies like redefining the situation, avoidance of ruminative thoughts, and use of relaxation techniques outside the work setting? Perhaps for evaluating the efficacy of such non-observable techniques, researchers and policy-makers will have to settle for a lower standard of proof when evaluating their efficacy.

CONCLUSION

Despite the enthusiasm shown for the construct of coping and the interest shown in providing information for evaluations, researchers have just barely begun to do the sort of research that is reliable and solid enough to provide truly useful data for informing interventions. Although it is widely assumed that individual choice of coping strategies can moderate the impact of stressful experiences, there is surprisingly little direct research that bears on this. Our aim has been to suggest ways in which subsequent research can augment current knowledge about the situational determinants of coping strategies, underlying personality characteristics that channel appraisals and coping efforts, conditions under which some coping efforts are more likely to be effective than others, how coping strategies are learned, and how maladaptive strategies can be changed.

Toward this end, we have described the relative merits and difficulties of various non-experimental research designs that are and could be used to assess the potentially negative emotional effects of work stress and work-family conflict on women and the role of individual coping in moderating them. These approaches were evaluated on the basis of their ability to account for "selection" in creating the association between work stress, coping, and psychological adjustment. The conclusion is that it is more difficult to provide unbiased estimates of the effects of work stress and coping than researchers typically think. The most popularly utilized research designs are likely to yield biased estimates.

Several broad implications may also be drawn. It is more difficult to make a causal interpretation involving the effects of chronic stress than acute stress, particularly when the stressor may be self-selected (Kessler 1987). Clear causal imputations can be made when exposure to a stressor is random. Work stress and work-family conflict usually do not meet this condition. The best ways to generate a data set in which one can plausibly assume random exposure are to use matching procedures or to mount experimental interventions. When these techniques are not possible, there are alternatives, but it is important to appreciate that their appropriateness varies depending on a number of conditions. If the data do not meet these conditions, the estimates will be biased.

It is a serious limitation of current research on work stress and work-family conflict that the implications of violations of such assumptions are not widely recognized. Progress in this area, though, is dependent on precise estimates of stress and coping effects.

REFERENCES

Barnett, R., N. Marshall, & J. Singer. 1992. Job experiences over time, multiple roles, and women's mental health: A longitudinal study. *Journal of Personality and Social Psychology 62*, 634–44.

Barrera, M. 1986. Distinctions between social support concepts, measures, and models. *American Journal of Community Psychology 14*, 413–45.

Bielby, W., & D. Bielby. 1989. Family ties: Balancing commitments to work and family in dual earner households. *American Sociological Review 54*, 776–89.

Bolger, N., A. DeLongis, R.C. Kessler, & E. Schilling. 1989. Effects of daily stress on negative mood. *Journal of Personality and Social Psychology 5*, 808–18.

Bolger, N., A. DeLongis, R.C. Kessler, & E. Wethington. 1989. The contagion of stress across multiple roles. *Journal of Marriage and the Family 51*, 175–83.

– 1990. The microstructure of daily role-related stress in married couples. In J. Eckenrode & S. Gore, eds., *Stress between work and family* (pp. 95–115). New York: Plenum.

Brown, B.B. 1978. Social and psychological correlates of help-seeking behavior among urban adults. *American Journal of Community Psychology 6*, 425–39.

Cohen, F. 1987. Measurement of coping. In S.V. Kasl & C.L. Cooper, eds., *Stress and health: Issues in research methodology* (pp. 283–305). New York: Wiley.

Cohen, S., & T.A. Wills. 1985. Stress, social support, and the buffering hypothesis. *Psychological Bulletin 98*, 310–57.

Collins, C., & L.B. Tiedje. 1988. A program for women returning to employment following childbirth. *Journal of Obstetrics and Gynecological Nursing 17*, 246–53.

Cook, T.D., & D.T. Campbell. 1979. *Quasi-experimentation: Design and analysis issues for field settings*. Chicago: Rand-McNally.

Coser, R.L., & G. Rokoff. 1971. Women in the occupational world: Social disruption and conflict. *Social Problems 18*, 535–54.

Dohrenwend, B.S., B.P. Dohrenwend, M. Dodson, & P. Shrout. 1984. Symptoms, hassles, social supports and life events: The problem of confounding measures. *Journal of Abnormal Psychology 93*, 780–5.

Dohrenwend, B.P., & P. Shrout. 1985. "Hassles" in the conceptualization and measurement of life stress variables. *American Psychologist 40*, 780–5.

Duncan, O.D. 1975. *Introduction to structural equation models*. New York: Academic.

Duxbury, L.E., & C.A. Higgins. 1991. Gender differences in work-family conflict. *Journal of Applied Psychology 76*, 60–74.

Fisher, F.M. 1965. The choice of instrumental variables in the estimation of economy-wide econometric models. *International Economic Review 6*, 245–74.

Fisher, J.D., A. Nadler, & S. Whitcher-Alagna. 1982. Recipient reactions to aid. *Psychological Bulletin 91*, 17–54.

Folkman, S., & R.S. Lazarus. 1988. Coping as a mediator of emotion. *Journal of Personality and Social Psychology 54*, 466–75.

Gerson, K. 1985. *Hard choices*. Berkeley, CA: University of California Press.

Glasser, B.G., & A. Strauss. 1973. *The discovery of grounded theory: Strategies for qualitative research*. Chicago: Aldine.

Haan, N. 1982. The measurement of coping, defense, and stress. In L. Goldberger & S. Breznitz, eds., *Handbook of stress: Theoretical and clinical aspects* (pp. 254–69). New York: Free Press.

Heckman, J. 1979. Sample selection bias as specification error. *Econometrics 47*, 153–61.

Hochschild, A. 1983. *The managed heart: The commercialization of human feeling*. Berkeley, CA: University of California Press.

– 1989. *The second shift: Working parents and the revolution at home*. New York: Viking Press.

House, J.S., K. Landis, & D. Umberson. 1988. Social relationships and health. *Science 241*, 540–5.

Kahn, R.L. 1981. *Work and health*. New York: Wiley.

Kandel, D., & M. Davies. 1986. Adult sequelae of adolescent depressive symptoms. *Archives of General Psychiatry 43*, 255–62.

Kasl, S.V. 1981. The challenges of studying the disease effects of stressful work conditions. *American Journal of Public Health 71*, 682–4.

– 1987. Methodologies in stress and health: Past difficulties, present dilemmas, future directions. In S.V. Kasl & C.L. Cooper, eds., *Stress and health: Issues in research methodology* (pp. 307–18). New York: Wiley.

Kessler, R.C. 1987. The interplay of research design strategies and data analysis procedures in evaluating the effects of stress on health. In S.V.

Kasl & C.L. Cooper, eds., *Stress and health: Issues in research methodology* (pp. 113–29). New York: Wiley.

— 1990. Perceived support and adjustment to stress: Some neglected considerations. Unpublished paper, Survey Research Center, University of Michigan, Ann Arbor.

Kessler, R.C., & J. McLeod. 1985. Social support and mental health in community samples. In S. Cohen & S.L. Syme, eds., *Social support and health* (pp. 219–40). New York: Academic.

Kessler, R.C., & J.A. McRae. 1984. A note on the relationship of sex and marital status to psychological distress. In J. Greenley, ed., *Research in community and mental health* (4:109–30). New York: JAI Press.

Kessler, R.C., R.H. Price, & C.B. Wortman. 1985. Social factors in psychopathology: Stress, social support, and coping. In M.R. Rosenzweig & L.W. Porter, ed., *Annual Review of Psychology* (36:531–72). Palo Alto, CA: Annual Reviews.

Kessler, R.C., & E. Wethington. 1991. The reliability of life event reports in a community sample. *Psychological Medicine 21*, 723–38.

Kibria, N., R.C. Barnett, G.K. Baruch, N.L. Marshall, & J.H. Pleck. 1990. Homemaking-role quality and the psychological well-being and distress of employed women. *Sex Roles 22*, 327–47.

Kohn, M.L., & C. Schooler. 1982. Job conditions and personality: A longitudinal assessment of their reciprocal effects. *American Journal of Sociology 87*, 1257–83.

Lazarus, R., & S. Folkman. 1984. *Stress, appraisal and coping.* New York: Springer.

Lennon, M.C. 1987. Sex differences in distress: The impact of gender and work roles. *Journal of Health and Social Behavior 28*, 290–305.

Lieberman, M.A. 1986. Social supports–the consequence of psychologizing: A commentary. *Journal of Consulting and Clinical Psychology 24*, 461–5.

Lieberson, S. 1983. *Making it count: The improvement of social research and theory.* Berkeley: University of California.

Long, B.C., S.E. Kahn, & R.W. Schutz. 1992. A causal model of stress and coping: Women in management. *Journal of Counseling Psychology 39*, 227–39.

Marks, S. 1977. Multiple roles and role strain: Some notes on human energy, time, and commitment. *American Sociological Review 42*, 921–36.

Martelli, M.F., S.M. Auerbach, J. Alexander, & L.G. Mercuri. 1987. Stress management in the health care setting: Matching interventions with patient coping styles. *Journal of Consulting and Clinical Psychology 55*, 201–7.

Mattlin, J.A., E. Wethington, & R.C. Kessler. 1990. Situational determinants of coping and coping effectiveness. *Journal of Health and Social Behavior 31*, 104–22.

McGonagle, K.A., R.C. Kessler, & E.A. Schilling. 1991. Determinants of marital arguments in a community sample. Unpublished paper. Ann Arbor, MI: University of Michigan.

Miller, J. 1980. Individual and occupational determinants of job satisfaction: A focus on gender differences. *Sociology of Work and Occupations* 7, 337–66.

Moen, P., & D. Dempster-McClain. 1987. Employed parents: Role strain, work time, and preference for working less. *Journal of Marriage and the Family* 49, 579–90.

Moen, P., D. Dempster-McClain, & R. Williams. 1989. Social integration and longevity: An event history analysis of women's roles and resilience. *American Sociological Review* 54, 635–47.

Pearlin, L.I., & C. Schooler. 1978. The structure of coping. *Journal of Health and Social Behavior* 19, 2–21.

Repetti, R., K. Matthews, & I. Waldron. 1989. Employment and women's health: The effects of paid employment on women's mental and physical health. *American Psychologist* 44, 1394–1401.

Rodin, J., & J.R. Ickovics. 1990. Women's health: Review and research agenda as we approach the 21st century. *American Psychologist* 45, 1018–34.

Roos, P.A., & D.J. Treiman. 1980. DOT scales for the 1970 census classification. In A.R. Miller, D.J. Treiman, P.S. Cain, & P.A. Roos, eds., *Work, jobs, and occupations: A critical review of the Dictionary of Occupational Titles* (pp. 336–89). Washington: National Academy Press.

Sandler, I.N., & M. Barrera. 1984. Toward a multimethod approach to assessing the effects of social support. *American Journal of Community Psychology* 12, 37–52.

Sarason, B.R., E.N. Shearin, G.R. Pierce, & I.G. Sarason. 1987. Interrelationships among social support measures: Theoretical and practical implications. *Journal of Personality and Social Psychology* 52, 813–32.

Sieber, S.D. 1974. Toward a theory of role accumulation. *American Sociological Review* 39, 567–78.

Silver, R.L., & C.B. Wortman. 1980. Coping with undesirable life events. In J. Garber & M.E.P. Seligman, eds., *Human helplessness* (pp. 279–375). New York: Academic.

Stone, A.A., & J.M. Neale. 1984. New measures of daily coping: Development and preliminary results. *Journal of Personality and Social Psychology* 46, 892–906.

Stone, A.A., M.A. Greenberg, E. Kennedy-Moore, & M.G. Newman. 1991. Self-report, situation-specific coping questionnaires: What are they measuring? *Journal of Personality and Social Psychology* 61, 648–58.

Stone, A.A., L. Helder, & M.S. Schneider. 1988. Coping with stressful events: Coping dimensions and issues. In L.H. Cohen, ed., *Life events and psychological functioning: Theoretical and methodological issues* (pp. 182–210). Beverly Hills, CA: Sage.

Stone, A.A., E. Kennedy-Moore, M.G. Newman, M. Greenberg, & J.M. Neale. 1992. Conceptual and methodological issues in current coping assessments. In B.N. Carpenter, ed., *Personal coping: Theory, research, and application* (pp. 15–29). Westport, CT: Praeger.

Thoits, P.A. 1983. Multiple identities and psychological well-being: A reformulation and test of the social isolation hypothesis. *American Sociological Review 48*, 174–87.

– 1986. Multiple identities: Examining gender and marital status differences in distress. *American Sociological Review 51*, 259–72.

Tiedje, L.B., C.B. Wortman, G. Downey, C. Emmons, M. Biernat, & E. Lang. 1990. Women with multiple roles: Role-compatibility perceptions, satisfaction, and mental health. *Journal of Marriage and the Family 52*, 63–72.

Thornton, A., & D. Freedman. 1985. *Study of American families – 1985.* Ann Arbor, MI: Survey Research Center, University of Michigan.

Verbrugge, L. 1983. Multiple roles and the physical health of men and women. *Journal of Health and Social Behavior 24*, 16–30.

Voydanoff, P. 1988. Work role characteristics, family structure demands, and work/family conflict. *Journal of Marriage and the Family 50*, 749–61.

Voydanoff, P., & B. Donnelly. 1989. Work and family roles and psychological distress. *Journal of Marriage and the Family 51*, 923–32.

Wethington, E. 1987. *Employment, family, and psychological distress: A study of married couples.* Doctoral dissertation, the University of Michigan. Ann Arbor, MI: University Microfilms.

– 1990, August. *Employment and family role characteristics and health: A longitudinal study of married women.* Paper presented at the annual meeting of the Society for the Study of Social Problems, Washington, DC.

Wethington, E., & R.C. Kessler. 1986. Perceived support, received support, and adjustment to stressful life events. *Journal of Health and Social Behavior 27*, 78–89.

– 1989. Employment, parental responsibility, and psychological distress. *Journal of Family Issues 10*, 527–46.

Wortman, C., M. Biernat, & E. Lang. 1991. Coping with role overload. In M. Frankenhaeuser, U. Lundberg, & M. Chesney, eds., *Women, work, and stress* (pp. 85–110). New York: Plenum.

14 A Theoretical Integration of Women, Work, and Coping

BONITA C. LONG AND
SHARON E. KAHN

The researchers who wrote chapters for this volume demonstrate the potential richness of a multidisciplinary approach to the study of women's ways of coping with workplace stress. Whether reviewing constructs long associated with women (such as social support), exploring the particular relevance of individual differences (such as control), or applying transactional models of stress and coping to employed women, these authors expand our knowledge of employed women's ways of coping.

Several important themes emerged from these chapters: (a) an appreciation for women's realities, including the duality of women's roles in the family and in the workplace, as well as the heterogeneity among women of different ethnic backgrounds, ages, and lifestyles; (b) an acknowledgment of the dynamic interplay between context, either structural or cultural contexts of the organization, and the individual, in addition to the invariant or gender- and culture-free stress and coping processes; (c) an awareness that personal resources may be both assets and liabilities depending on future stressors and coping strategies, and that personal meanings are central to the identification of stressor events; (d) an interest in those individuals who are able to act in ways that prevent stress; and finally, (e) a desire for process studies of stress and coping that examine change over time.

In this chapter, we place the important themes raised in this book

This paper has been supported by grants from the Social Sciences and Humanities Research Council of Canada.

into the theoretical context of Lazarus's (Lazarus & Folkman 1984) transactional stress model. In so doing, we provide an integration for the field that is relevant to a multidisciplinary audience who employs a variety of research techniques. Thus, we link "metatheoretical principles" (Lazarus 1991, 3) to the contributions in this volume and the several themes that recur in the chapters. In addition, we illustrate the utility of Lazarus's model by describing our test of his model with causal modelling techniques (Long, Kahn, & Schutz 1992).

TRANSACTIONAL MODEL OF STRESS AND COPING

Bruce Compas and Pamela Orosan, as well as Craig Smith, in their respective chapters, review aspects of one of the most extensive and cited transactional theories of stress, a cognitive phenomenological theory developed by Richard Lazarus (1991; Lazarus & Folkman 1984, 1987). Lazarus's approach to stress is "transactional, process, contextual, and meaning-centered" (Lazarus 1991, 1). Within Lazarus's theory, researchers may study context, personal meanings, and other psychosocial variables that capture the experiences of employed women. Moreover, this comprehensive model of stress provides an opportunity to integrate both individual and structural perspectives relevant to women's ways of coping.

Lazarus's model is useful because it reflects the multidimensional, dynamic, and complex nature of stress, including the interactions between individuals and the structures or contexts in which they operate. Stimulus models of stress, which focus on precipitating factors, or response models, which emphasize physiological reactivity, have been criticized for their limitations (e.g., Mason 1975; Perkins 1982). Lazarus and Folkman (1984) define psychological stress as a transactional relationship "between person and environment that is appraised by the person as taxing or exceeding his or her resources and endangering his or her well-being" (19). A transactional process means that relationships are not linear but reciprocal, continuously unfolding over time.

The theory "identifies two processes, cognitive appraisal and coping, as critical mediators of stressful person-environment relationships and their immediate and long-term outcomes" (Folkman, Lazarus, Gruen, & DeLongis 1986, 572). Thus, appraisals (or personal meanings) of the event itself and the choice and effectiveness of one's coping actions are crucial to the stress process. Appraisals are, in effect, an integration of the individual's personal agenda and perceptions of the environmental context. Several key components of this complex transaction have been identified and "include a stressor situation, cognitions about the situation and possible ways of dealing with it, stress reactions, coping strategies, duration over time, and a range of environmental factors (e.g., social supports) and individual characteristics (e.g., Type A personality, self-esteem) that can influence the stress coping process" (Latack 1989, 254).

To better understand the stress process, Folkman and Lazarus (1988) make an important distinction between mediating and moderating processes. They suggest that antecedent conditions, such as motivations (e.g., values, commitments, and goals), beliefs about oneself, and recognition of personal resources for coping, moderate the stress process because they interact with other conditions to produce an outcome. Moderators affect the perceptions of the situation and how it is appraised. Mediating processes, however, are generated in the stressful encounter and are hypothesized to change the relationship between the antecedent and the outcome variable (see also Baron & Kenny 1986). Because coping efforts determine which of the various short- and long-term effects occur (e.g., morale, health, psychological functioning), they are considered mediators of the stress-outcome relationship.

Cognitive appraisal is of central importance in this transactional model of stress and is defined as an evaluative or judgmental process through which the individual judges the significance of a transaction with the environment. Primary appraisal follows from the recognition that the situation is important and potentially taxing (i.e., appraisals of challenge, threat, or harm-loss). Secondary appraisal is a judgment about the options for coping, including the extent to which the outcome is amenable to change and appropriate coping resources are available. Secondary appraisal may cause revisions of the primary appraisal. The product of this appraisal process is the event's implicit meaning for that individual. For example, the loss of a business contract might mean, to one woman, a threat that can be handled, to a second a threat with which she cannot cope, and to a third a chance to demonstrate her worth. This process of appraisal of the stressor and resources available to deal with it are considered to be only partly conscious and intentional (Leventhal & Nerenz 1983).

Coping is defined as the efforts made by an individual when the demands of a given situation tax adaptive resources, and coping strategies are actions taken in a specific situation to reduce stress. It follows that coping does not carry negative connotations for the person; all forms may be effective means of reducing stress, depending on the demands and the context, and failure to reduce stress means that the demands exceed resources. Coping efforts therefore can be conceptually distinguished from the success of these efforts. In contrast, coping resources are antecedent moderators and may be physical, material, social, psychological, or intellectual in nature. Thus, the nature of the coping efforts generated by the individual will be determined by the coping resources in the person's environment. Although their list is not necessarily all-inclusive, Folkman, Schaefer, and Lazarus (1979) identify five important categories of coping resource: (a) utilitarian (e.g., socioeconomic status, money, services); (b) health, energy, morale; (c) social networks; (d) general and specific beliefs; and (e) problem-solving skills.

The extent to which an employed woman is stressed by events (real or imagined) varies and includes complex interactions among her appraisals of the event, the coping efforts she undertakes, and the personal and coping resources that she perceives to be available to deal with the event. In summary, a transactional process model of stress and coping can provide a comprehensive framework for research on the ways women cope with employment stress.

APPLICATIONS OF THE MODEL

In this section we link the chapters as well as the themes that recur throughout the book to Lazarus's framework, especially focusing on moderators and mediators of the stress-outcome relationship.

Coping Resources: Stress Moderators

Studies of moderators (i.e., the effects of personal or coping resources) have typically focused on variables such as the effects of sex segregation in the workplace, multiple roles, social support, and personality characteristics. In addition, the chapters in this book identify several other important moderators (e.g., organizational culture, power, interpersonal competence).

Although tremendous social/cultural changes have occurred and continue to occur, these changes are slow to address women's needs, and this slow pace of change continues to threaten women's coping resources. For example, Barbara Gutek details the effect women's segregation in the workplace has on coping resources, especially utilitarian resources such as money and services. Moreover, the fact that most women work a "second shift" (Hochschild 1989) in the home/family context takes a tremendous toll on coping resources such as relationships, health, energy, and morale. Furthermore, Lois Verbrugge reports that for women who are single parents the toll is much higher.

Verbrugge's study of multiple roles shows that women with particular roles and combinations of roles (e.g., married vs nonmarried) experience differential benefits from the paid work role (cf. Baruch, Biener, & Barnett 1987). Her study of young women also reveals that women in different roles use different coping resources – either they exploit satisfactions or they learn to buffer stress. From these chapters, it can be seen that social and institutional arrangements determine the types of, and access to, coping resources that employed women use.

Although the study of multiple roles reveals important moderating relationships, one could argue that roles are abstract constructs that do not reflect the lived experience of women. Therefore, an examination of the social and cultural context of women's experience of workplace stress and coping adds to our understanding of moderators of the stress-outcome relationship. Bowles (1989) suggests that organizations often provide meaning for symbols, images, and events for their members. In this vein, Judi Marshall suggests that, in male-dominated organizations, gender-role stereotypes as well as patriarchal work cultures adversely affect workplace norms and foster sex discrimination. Many women do not share the dominant "world view" of white, middle-class men.

Power is another moderator that affects women's ways of coping with work demands. Nina Colwill reviews the extent to which women have real or perceived power, and distinguishes between three types: personal, interpersonal, and organizational. Lack of power often means that women may have more difficulty than their male colleagues in accomplishing tasks or influencing important persons. Thus, how women experience stress and subsequently cope is linked to both real and perceived power in the workplace, and different sources of power are important moderators of the stress-coping relationship.

Individual characteristics have been the most frequently studied moderators of the stress-outcome relation. Karen Korabik, Lisa McDonald, and Hazel Rosin summarize what is known about managerial women's stress and coping, with particular attention to social support. They review their own research and that of others on the effects and types of social support, with particular attention to gender differences. There is some evidence that men and women find different types of social support to be differentially useful. Although both men and women find instrumental support helpful in dealing with work stress, women find empathy to be an important form of support. Perceived social support is usually considered to be a positive coping resource for women, but research also has documented the high cost of caring; this cost suggests that social networks can become sources of stress for women (Kaufmann & Beehr 1986). Esther Greenglass contends that women's interpersonal competence is an important coping resource, and that women's ability to seek and receive interpersonal support is more highly developed than men's.

Much has been written about the importance of a particular personal characteristic – one's sense of control – and its relationship to coping and health outcomes. Control has a long history in organizational and health research (Sauter, Hurrell, & Cooper 1989). Catherine Heaney finds that perceptions of control exacerbate work stress for women supervisors, whereas perceived control buffers stress for other workers.

Appraisals and Coping Strategies: Stress Mediators

An examination of stress and coping at a more micro level shifts the focus to mediators – appraisals and coping efforts that occur when a woman is confronted by a work-related stressor. We know little about women's specific appraisals in response to work stress, yet the nature of the appraisal process is central to determining coping efficacy. Bruce Compas and Pamela Orosan point out that, when individuals are stressed, personally meaningful goals and commitments are experienced as being threatened. For instance, one woman may find that staying late to finish a report is stressful because she also holds an expectation that she should be home with her family during the dinner hour; working late may threaten another woman's sense of competence because she believes that she should have accomplished the task without having to put in overtime. By knowing what is behind the appraisals of threat, harm/loss, or challenge – that is, by understanding what beliefs, values, or commitments are being threatened – one can better understand what the individual is trying to cope with and how to assess coping effectiveness. Furthermore, Craig Smith describes a recent elaboration of Lazarus's model of stress, coping, and emotions, and focuses on basic processes considered invariant (gender- and culture-free). This work highlights the importance of understanding the motivational relevance of stressors, as well as a woman's perceptions of accountability and emotional reactions, in determining not only what is stressful but how she copes.

In their review of managerial women's coping strategies, Karen Korabik and her colleagues ask the question: Do men and women cope differently with work-related stress? The belief that women do not cope with stress as well as men do – that is, that they respond passively and/or more emotionally to stressful situations – remains a strongly held gender-role stereotype. Although early studies (Billings & Moos 1981; Folkman & Lazarus 1980; Pearlin & Schooler 1978) tended to find that men used more problem-solving coping, compared with women, these studies were flawed because men and women were not matched on occupational level (or, for that matter, on organizational power). However, few or no gender differences are found on problem-solving forms of coping when occupation, education, and job level are generally equivalent.

Nevertheless, in studies of sex differences in coping some differences do consistently turn up. Women managers tend to talk through their work-related problems and turn to others more than men do, whereas men engage in nonwork activity (e.g., sports, exercise) more often than women. Long (1990) found no differences between men and women managers on problem-solving coping, but women used more problem-reappraisal coping and more avoidance coping. Moreover, when coping effectiveness was studied, women managers were more likely than men to use adaptive coping behaviours, or superior coping (Parasuraman & Cleek 1984; Tung 1980). These confusing gender differences may be attributable to at least three causes. First, women experience more and different work stressors than men (e.g., sex discrimination and harassment). Second, culturally shared beliefs (e.g., gender-role stereotypes) affect men's and women's perceptions of appropriate ways to cope with stress, such as disclosing to friends. Third, women are disadvantaged with regard to coping if they lack workplace coping resources (e.g., power, perceived competence), or other personal resources (e.g., child care, finances).

Judi Marshall also argues that a consequence of male-dominated organizational cultures is that managerial women, in order to survive, tend to manipulate their own consciousness. She describes how women's coping strategies and emotional reactions to work demands are strongly influenced by their awareness or consciousness that the organizational context is gendered. She proposes an interesting stage model of coping, describing responses that progress from denial and anger to the ability to be flexible in responding to a complex work milieu. She suggests that it is important to be able to choose one's battles and one's responses in order to "thrive" rather than just "survive" in the workplace.

An important caveat must be mentioned in understanding moderating and mediating processes. Although moderators and mediators have been discussed as though they are distinctly different processes, at times this distinction blurs. A coping resource becomes a mediator of the stress-outcome relation if it is used as a coping response to a specific stressor event. For example, if a woman turns to her friends to talk about a work stressor, either for the purpose of seeking advice or simply to ventilate emotions, the coping resource – social support – becomes, in this case, a coping mediator (cf. Harris 1991).

Research Strategies

Many feminist researchers have argued that traditional research methodologies fail to capture the complex and holistic nature of women's experiences. To illustrate this point, Allison Tom makes a strong case that dichotomies limit the questions researchers ask, and that traditional dichotomies (e.g., paid work vs unpaid work) do not accurately reflect women's experiences.

Research that focuses on the experience and meaning of women's ways of coping with work stress begins to challenge the inaccuracies of earlier assumptions about women and work. For example, Anne Statham's qualitative study illuminates the experiences of male and female managers and their secretaries. She is able to capture the subtle differential expectations men and women hold with regard to leadership styles, and describes the effects of these expectations on interactions between employees. Her work provides us with important clues as to how men and women cope differently in light of their appraisals and suggests that future research needs to focus on the interactions between individuals, and on their unique expectancies (cf. Deaux & Major 1987). Thus, qualitative research can enrich Lazarus's theory by providing a greater understanding of the meaning of employment stress and coping for women, and also by ensuring that women's realities are not dichotomized or decontextualized (see Grossman & Chester 1990).

Elaine Wethington and Ronald Kessler express concern for the lack of clear direction for work-stress interventions. They review the prevalent theoretical underpinnings for predicting coping efficacy and the state of coping measurement. In addition, they identify strengths and weaknesses in five major research designs that are commonly used to study women's ways of coping with workplace stress (e.g., multivariate quantitative surveys, longitudinal studies, microanalytic process-oriented studies, descriptive qualitative studies, experimental and quasi-experimental interventions). Critical issues in the study of women's ways of coping include the measurement of coping, subject selection, and chronicity. Wethington and Kessler also point out a much-neglected area of research, the importance of studying how stressful events are prevented.

WOMEN IN MANAGEMENT: AN INTEGRATION

To organize the large quantity of research on predictors of stress and coping, researchers need a comprehensive theory that can guide the research, and they need an appropriate methodology. Conducting research that is integrative is important because it allows a researcher to describe and test relationships among variables, and to determine the relative strength of multiple predictors.

In order to illustrate the integrative utility of Lazarus's stress model for the study of workplace stress, we tested his model with multivariate causal modelling techniques (Long et al. 1992). The purpose of our study was to test directly, and modify if necessary, the theoretical framework of psychological stress and coping first proposed by Richard Lazarus. We focused on cognitive appraisal and coping as critical mediators of stressful person-environment relationships (Folkman, Lazarus, Gruen, & DeLongis 1986), and we examined stress as a chain of manifestations of how a person perceives, appraises, reacts, and interacts with the environment, thereby providing a comprehensive explanation of the stress-coping process. The causal modelling analytic technique forces researchers to elaborate complicated causal chains; thus, the model is integrative, in that it unifies many variables into a causal ordering framework.

We collected data from women who were full-time managers employed in nontraditional occupations ($n = 249$). The mean age of the respondents was 38.8 years, 57 per cent were married, and 56 per cent had no children. The women averaged 16.1 years in the work force. Managerial women in male-dominated occupations were of particular interest to us because, although they hold a minority status in the workplace, they have achieved some measure of power within the organization. This combination of circumstances provided a unique opportunity to examine the relative impact of personal resources and the work environment on the ways women cope with work stress.

The model, presented in figure 1, contains three causal antecedent constructs or coping resources (Demographics, Sex-Role Attitudes, Agentic Traits), four mediating constructs (Environment, Appraisals, Engagement Coping, and Disengagement Coping), and three outcomes (Work Performance, Satisfaction, and Distress). The double-headed arrows reflect the correlations among the exogenous factors, and the single-headed arrows indicate the direction of the predicted relations among the latent variables. (In some cases there are reciprocal relations, thus the two arrows.) An important point is that we assessed the antecedent coping resources one month prior to

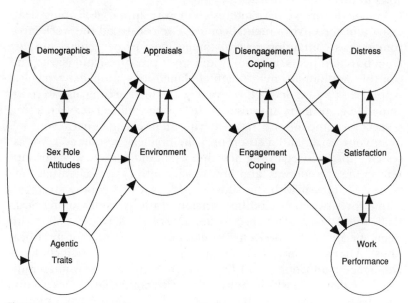

EXOGENOUS
Time 1

ENDOGENOUS
Time 2

Time 3

Figure 1
A structural equation model with moderators and mediators of stress-outcome
relations for managerial women – assessed at three time periods, one month apart

assessing stress appraisals, coping, and environment variables,
which, in turn, were assessed one month prior to the outcome variables. We tested the moderating constructs as exogenous variables,
coping and appraisals as mediating variables, and outcomes such as
satisfaction, work performance, and distress as the ultimate dependent variables.

Our choice of manifest (i.e., observed) variables and latent variables (i.e., constructs) was based on the stress/coping literature, in-
depth interviews with professional women (Long 1988), and variables relevant to women's nontraditional careers (e.g., Latack 1989;
Long 1989). For example, as antecedent moderators, we included
marital and parental status, income, job level, and years in the organization among other manifest demographic variables. Sex-role attitudes were also included as a coping resource because they have
been shown to play an important part in determining women's career orientation and choice (Betz & Fitzgerald 1987). With regard to
personality characteristics, we choose the construct agency because it

has been found to be important to both career theory and the stress process (Bandura 1986; Betz & Hackett 1987). We included optimism, self-efficacy, and instrumentality among the manifest variables in this latent construct.

The mediators we were interested in were appraisals, coping strategies, and the environmental context. We construed the work environment as containing several dimensions; in particular, support from boss and peers, autonomy and work pressures, and clarity and control. Additional environmental dimensions were daily hassles. Appraisals that we deemed relevant to the work setting also were included (e.g., primary appraisals were "losing your self-respect, losing respect for someone else, not achieving an important goal at your job or in your work, and a strain on your financial resources"). We assessed appraisals regarding how important the episode was, how upsetting the episode was, and how much control the women felt they possessed to deal with the situation. We assessed coping strategies with a forty-two-item modified version of the Ways of Coping Scale (Folkman, Lazarus, Dunkel-Schetter, DeLongis, & Gruen 1986) with items specific to the work environment (see Long 1990 for modifications). After preliminary factor analysis, two factors were included – Disengagement Coping and Engagement Coping. The women indicated the degree to which they used specific coping strategies to cope with a stressful event that had occurred during the previous month. Finally, we were interested in outcomes that were specific to work (e.g., work performance) as well as to the women's general psychosomatic health, and life satisfaction.

We analysed the data with the computer programs PRELIS (Jöreskog & Sörbom 1988) and LISREL 7 (Jöreskog & Sörbom 1989). The two-step approach recommended by Anderson and Gerbing (1988) was followed – first the measurement model was confirmed, then the structural model was tested. Modifications to the model were made at both steps, based on theory or empirical support. Hypothesized structural models are supported if the overall fit of the model to the observed data is adequate and if the relevant structural coefficients between latent variables are statistically significant and in the predicted directions. However, several alternative models can be generated, with each providing an adequate fit to the model. Thus, a plausible model depends more on theoretical soundness than on statistical significance. Furthermore, the data never confirm a model, but only fail to disconfirm it (Cliff 1983).

The final model, found to be most plausible in the sample population, accounted for 56 per cent of the total variance among the constructs. Lazarus's theory of psychological stress that postulates a central role for cognitive appraisals and coping was supported. In particular, we found that women managers who maintain traditional lifestyles (married with children) and who hold traditional sex-role beliefs appraise occupational stressors as less threatening. These women may have less at stake in workplace events when the stressors are related to occupational goals or achievements. The relationship between sex-role beliefs and appraisals can be interpreted as putting egalitarian managers at a disadvantage with regard to employment stress. For example, egalitarian managers appraised the stressor events as being less under their control, and they experienced greater negative emotional reactions to the stressors, than women who held traditional beliefs.

With regard to the mediators, positive appraisals related to less frequent use of disengagement coping, which, in turn, influenced engagement coping. Thus, finding ways to disengage (e.g., through emotional self-control) may be as important as task accomplishment for managerial women coping with job stress. Although appraisals and coping strategies were related (either directly or indirectly) to psychosomatic distress and satisfaction assessed a month later, egalitarian sex-role attitudes, perceptions of a demanding but nonsupportive work environment, and less agency were also associated with greater general dissatisfaction.

We have highlighted some of the findings from our study in order to illustrate the opportunities that Lazarus's model provides as a framework to study ways women cope with employment stress. Guided by the model, we were able to simultaneously examine several moderators and mediators of the stress-outcome relationship, test reciprocal relations, and include many of the coping resources and processes that are important in our understanding of women's experience of work stress. Lazarus's model of stress and coping emphasizes the extent to which appraisals and coping are multifaceted. In addition, the model moves toward a complete picture of important factors in the stress-coping process, as well as examining presumed invariant stress-coping processes. The results of our study lead us to a continued consideration of non-occupational roles, internal psychological factors, and structural components of the work environment, as well as the social forces that stem from gender-role stereotypes and discrimination. Furthermore, some promising leads for counselling interventions also flowed from our results (see for example, Long et al. 1992). Our research now examines whether the model is stable over time and whether the relationships are stable over time, so that we can explore such questions as whether or not women have a preferred coping pattern across time within a particular stressor domain.

CONCLUSION

In this chapter, we have used a theoretical perspective on stress and coping to review and integrate the various contributions in this volume on women, work, and coping. Women who are employed outside the home are confronted with many gender-related stressors that combine the burden of family responsibilities with workplace problems of discrimination and harassment. In this book, researchers have examined the sources of stress for employed women, the structural and psychosocial moderators of workplace stress, and the coping strategies and appraisals that mediate the stress-outcome relationship.

In an attempt to provide direction for future research, we argue that the themes from the various contributions in this volume, regardless of the discipline or research method they represent, can be studied from the perspective of Lazarus's transactional model of stress and coping. First, the study of stress and coping processes requires an awareness of the invariant context of gender and culture, as well as the dynamic interaction between individuals and their differing structural contexts. Second, the study of stress and coping processes benefits from methods that examine the personal meanings of stressors and measure change over time, as well as methods that identify resources that enhance one's ability to cope or eliminate one's need to cope. Third, the study of women's ways of coping with workplace stress must take account of the realities of women's experience, including gender-role stereotyping and discrimination, as well as the burdens and benefits of home and family responsibilities. We propose that Lazarus's theory provides a framework for organizing and integrating the multiple factors that influence the relationships among employment, stress, and coping. Thus, in our research we have been able to test the interaction of multiple factors: contextual and psychosocial factors, coping resources and strategies, stress moderators and mediators.

Future studies must continue to test empirically the fit between the model and the wide range of women's realities. Clearly, not all employed women work in similar jobs or at similar levels. Although Lazarus's model generally focuses on the individual, rather than the commonalities among members of a work group or universal effects of work environments (Brief & George 1991), these commonalities can be identified because of their importance to the development of interventions and policies (see Mawson, this volume). In addition to differences in the cultures of the organizations in which women work, future research must take into account individual differences among women, including their marital, parental, and other family roles. Moreover, studies that use a transactional framework can investigate the ways in which particular resources, such as social support, can moderate women's experience of stress. In addition to viewing women holistically within social, cultural, and work roles, researchers can use a transactional model to understand individual women's subjective, personal meanings of workplace stressors. Finally, researchers who use a transactional model can examine women as active participants in preventing and eliminating stress. Thus, another important contribution will be studies of women's strengths and coping skills to inform stress-management interventions and workplace policy.

REFERENCES

Anderson, J.C., & D.W. Gerbing. 1988. Structural equation modeling in practice: A review and recommended two-step approach. *Psychological Bulletin 103*, 411–23.

Bandura, A. 1986. *Social foundation of thought and action: A social cognition theory*. Englewood Cliffs, NJ: Prentice-Hall.

Baruch, G.K., L. Biener, & R.C. Barnett. 1987. Women and gender in research on work and family stress. *American Psychologist 42*, 130–6.

Baron, R.M., & D.A. Kenny. 1986. The moderator-mediator variable distinction in social psychological research: Conceptual, strategic, and statistical considerations. *Journal of Personality and Social Psychology 51*, 1173–82.

Betz, N.E., & L.F. Fitzgerald. 1987. *The career psychology of women*. San Diego, CA: Academic Press.

Betz, N.E., & G. Hackett. 1987. Concept of agency in educational and career development. *Journal of Counseling Psychology 34*, 299–308.

Billings, A.G., & R.H. Moos. 1981. The role of coping responses and social resources in attenuating the stress of life events. *Journal of Behavioral Medicine 4*, 149–57.

Brief, A.P., & J.M. George. 1991. Psychological stress and the workplace: A brief comment on Lazarus' outlook. *Journal of Behavior and Personality 6*(7), 15–20.

Bowles, M. 1989. Mismeaning and work organizations. *Organizational Studies 14*, 405–21.

Cliff, N. 1983. Some cautions concerning the applications of causal methods. *Multivariate Behavioral Research 18*, 115–26.

Deaux, K., & B. Major. 1987. Putting gender into context: An interactive model of gender-related behavior. *Psychological Review 94*, 369–89.

Folkman, S., & R.S. Lazarus. 1980. An analysis of coping in a middle-aged community sample. *Journal of Health and Social Behavior 21*, 219–39.

– 1988. Coping as a mediator of emotion. *Journal of Personality and Social Psychology 54*, 466–75.

Folkman, S., R.S. Lazarus, C. Dunkel-Schetter, A. DeLongis, & R. Gruen. 1986. The dynamics of a stressful encounter: Cognitive appraisal, coping, and encounter outcomes. *Journal of Personality and Social Psychology 50*, 992–1003.

Folkman, S., R.S. Lazarus, R. Gruen, & A. DeLongis. 1986. Appraisal, coping, health status, and psychological symptoms. *Journal of Personality and Social Psychology 50*, 571–9.

Folkman, S., C. Schaefer, & R.S. Lazarus. 1979. Cognitive processes as mediators of stress and coping. In V. Hamilton & D. Warburton, eds., *Human stress and cognition: An information processing approach* (pp. 265–98). London: Wiley.

Grossman, H.Y., & N.L. Chester. 1990. *The experience and meaning of work in women's lives*. Hillsdale, NJ: Erlbaum.

Harris, J.R. 1991. The utility of the transaction approach for occupational stress research. *Journal of Social Behavior and Personality 6*(7), 21–9.

Hochschild, A. 1989. *The Second shift: Working parents and the revolution at home*. New York: Viking.

Jöreskog, K.G., & D. Sörbom. 1988. *PRELIS: A preprocessor for LISREL* (2nd ed.), Mooresville, IN: Scientific Software.

– 1989. *LISREL 7: User's reference guide*. Mooresville, IN: Scientific Software.

Kaufmann, G.M., & T.A. Beehr. 1986. Interaction between job stressors and social support: Some counterintuitive results. *Journal of Applied Psychology 71*, 522–6.

Latack, J.C. 1989. Work, stress, and careers: A preventive approach to maintaining organizational health. In M.B. Arthurs, D.T. Hall, & B.S. Lawrence, eds., *A handbook of career theory* (pp. 252–75). Cambridge, UK: Cambridge University Press.

Lazarus, R.S. 1991. Psychological stress in the workplace. *Journal of Social Behavior and Personality 6*(7), 1–13.

Lazarus, R.S., & S. Folkman. 1984. *Stress, appraisal and coping*. New York: Springer.

– 1987. Transactional theory and research on emotions and coping. *European Journal of Personality 1*, 141–69.

Leventhal, H., & D.R. Nerenz. 1983. A model of stress research with some implications for the control of stress disorders. In D. Meichenbaum &

M.E. Jaremko, eds., *Stress reduction and prevention* (pp. 5–38). New York: Plenum.

Long, B.C. 1988. Work-related stress and coping strategies of professional women. *Journal of Employment Counseling 25*, 37–44.

– 1989. Sex role orientation, coping strategies, and self-efficacy of women in traditional and nontraditional occupations. *Psychology of Women Quarterly 13*, 307–24.

– 1990. Relation between coping strategies, sex-typed traits and environmental characteristics: A comparison of male and female managers. *Journal of Counseling Psychology 37*, 185–94.

Long, B.C., S.E. Kahn, & R.W. Schutz. 1992. A causal model of stress and coping: Women in management. *Journal of Counseling Psychology 39*, 227–39.

Mason, J.W. 1975. A historical view of the stress field, part 1. *Journal of Human Stress 1*, 22–6.

Parasuraman, S., & M.A. Cleek. 1984. Coping behaviors and manager's affective reactions to role stressors. *Journal of Vocational Behavior 24*, 179–93.

Pearlin, L.I., & C. Schooler. 1978. The structure of coping. *Journal of Health and Social Behavior 19*, 2–21.

Perkins, D.V. 1982. The assessment of stress using life events scales. In L. Goldberger & S. Breznitz, eds., *Handbook of stress: Theoretical and clinical aspects* (pp. 320–31). New York: Free Press.

Sauter, S.L., J.J. Hurrell, & C.L. Cooper, eds. 1989. *Job control and worker health.* New York: Wiley.

Tung, R.L. 1980. Comparative analysis of occupational stress profiles of male versus female administrators. *Journal of Vocational Behavior 17*, 344–55.

Author Index

Subject Index

CRITICAL PERSPECTIVES ON PUBLIC AFFAIRS
Series Editors: Duncan Cameron and Daniel Drache

This series, sponsored by the Canadian Centre for Policy Alternatives and co-published by McGill-Queen's University Press, is intended to present important research on Canadian policy and public affairs. Books are by leading economic and social critics in the Canadian academic community and will be useful for classroom texts and the informed reader as well as for the academic specialist.

The Canadian Centre for Policy Alternatives promotes research on economic and social issues facing Canada. Through its research reports, studies, conferences, and briefing sessions, the CCPA provides thoughtful alternatives to the proposals of business research institutes and many government agencies. Founded in 1980, the CCPA holds that economic and social research should contribute to building a better society. The centre is committed to publishing research that reflects the concerns of women as well as men; labour as well as business; churches, cooperatives, and voluntary agencies as well as governments; disadvantaged individuals as well as those more fortunate. Critical Perspectives on Public Affairs will reflect this tradition through the publication of scholarly monographs and collections.

Getting on Track
Social Democratic Strategies for Ontario
Daniel Drache, Editor

The Political Economy of North American Free Trade
Ricardo Grinspun and Maxwell A. Cameron, Editors

Poverty Reform in Canada, 1958-1978
State and Class Influences on Policy Making
Rodney S. Haddow

Women, Work, and Coping
A Multidisciplinary Approach to Workplace Stress
Bonita C. Long and Sharon E. Kahn, Editors